HOW MANY QUESTIONS?

Essays in Honor
of
SIDNEY MORGENBESSER

HOW MANY QUESTIONS?

Essays in Honor

of

SIDNEY MORGENBESSER

Edited by
Leigh S. Cauman
Isaac Levi
Charles Parsons
Robert Schwartz

HACKETT PUBLISHING COMPANY

Cover design by Richard L. Listenberger
Interior design by James N. Rogers

For further information, please address
Hackett Publishing Company, Inc.
P.O. Box 44937
Indianapolis, Indiana 46204

Library of Congress Cataloging in Publication Data
Main entry under title:

How many questions?

Bibliography: p.
1. Philosophy — Addresses, essays, lectures.
2. Morgenbesser, Sidney, 1921–   . I. Morgenbesser,
Sidney, 1921–   . II. Cauman, Leigh S.
B29.H653   1983   100   83– 10728
ISBN 0– 915145– 59– 6
ISBN 0– 915145– 58– 8 (pbk.)

Contents

CONTENTS

Preface

The idea of collecting essays in honor of Sidney
Morgenbesser in time for his sixtieth birthday
was proposed in the spring of 1979. Prior commitments dispersed the editors over different parts
of the globe during the period immediately following, and this caused a delay. Even so, two
years late, we are pleased to be able to offer
this volume as an expression of respect and
affection for Sidney from his colleagues,
students, and friends.

Had we sought contributions from everyone whose
life has been touched by Sidney's mind and sensibility we would have had material for several
more volumes, ranging not only over topics in
philosophy but in the social and natural sciences,
politics and public policy, and Jewish affairs.
The editors were not up to the task and had to
restrict the scope of their project more narrowly.
They are mindful of the inequities this selectivi-
ty may have produced.

We wish to thank the contributors to this volume
for their participation, their patience, and the
help of many in defraying expenses. Thanks are
also due to the philosophy department of Barnard
College, the philosophy department of Columbia
University, and the office staff of the *Journal
of Philosophy* for both moral and financial
support. The Bibliography of Sidney Morgenbesser's
works was prepared by Jonathan Lieberson with the
assistance of Israel Scheffler and Ernest Alleva.
We give special thanks to Nancy Roberts for over-
seeing the preparation of the typescripts. William
Hackett and Hackett Publishing Company have given
us invaluable help and encouragement.

We offer Sidney these essays as a very partial
indication of the admiration and love we all feel
for him.

Leigh S. Cauman

Isaac Levi

Charles Parsons

Robert Schwartz

Introduction

I have been told that Sidney Morgenbesser once fell into a conversation with a literary critic, greatly respected in his time and now dead, a man who, unlike Morgenbesser, was uneasy about his Jewishness, and who hinted that he preferred not to write or talk much about Jewish matters. After he heard yet another expression of this attitude from the critic at an academic meeting, Morgenbesser paused for a moment, searching for a pungent phrase that would sum up his view of the man, and then said to him, "I see that your motto is 'Incognito ergo sum'!".

The tale reminds one of the analytic cast, the impulse to disembowel bombast, the tendency to disclose serious opinions in indirect, usually jocose, ways, which characterize Morgenbesser's mind. It is perhaps less well known than other stories about him, such as the one about his listening to a linguistic philosopher propound the thesis that double affirmatives are not used as negatives in any known language and piping up from the back of the lecture hall, "Yeah, yeah". It is certainly less well known than Morgenbesser's question to a psychiatrist who had argued for an hour at an academic conference that mental disease is a myth: "Doctor, since you don't think there is any mental illness, do you think it's all in the mind?"

When I first encountered Morgenbesser in the late 'sixties, I knew only somewhat forbidding facts about him, for example, that Bertrand Russell had denominated him one of the cleverest young men he had met on one of his trips to the United States. Then there were rumors that Morgenbesser had undergone the arduous training necessary to become a rabbi, but, upon passing

1

these tests, had abruptly given up the rabbinate
to study philosophy. It was, therefore, a relief
to find that there was little intimidating about
him when we would occasionally meet in a *Lokal*
he found congenial to high philosophical discourse, the fetid center counter of the Chock
Full O'Nuts on Broadway at 116th Street, a place
he treated in those days as a kind of village
cafe - much as he called the stationer's down
the block "the candy store" - and where one could
often find him lolling in front of a ziggurat of
textbooks, discussing economics, politics, philosophy, and baseball history by turns.

To many philosophy students, I am sure, his
humor provided a release from the pompousities
and stiffness of much of philosophy. At times,
his humor seemed almost a way of doing philosophy, as when in those apocalyptic days, he
responded to the sharp demand of a student radical whether he believed Mao's Law of Contradiction with the terse "I do and I do not". At all
times, Morgenbesser's humor encouraged one to
suppose that it was possible to be a philosopher
and not become a stuffed shirt or a disembodied
idea. For example, I learned early on that Morgenbesser had his own extended family of philosophers. "Hermeneutics", he told me, was his
uncle from New Jersey; "Sui Generis" was a celebrated Chinese philosopher with a great and pro-
lific school. Everyone knew that Gilbert Ryle,
in his *Concept of Mind*, had described the Cartesian view of the mind as that of a "ghost in the
machine"; for Morgenbesser, a brilliant but dry,
hyper-precise logician from Princeton was "the
machine in the ghost". Then there was the man
whom Morgenbesser called "the quantum philosopher": "you can't figure out him and his position
simultaneously".

There were other remarks that endeared Morgenbesser to one. Thanks for a gift from its reci-

pient, W.V. Quine, were politely rebuffed: "Don't
mention it - use it". When he learned that a
student, completing her doctoral dissertation
under Albert Hofstadter, had complained of writer's
block and was advised by Hofstadter to do as he
did, "let the material take over" and "do the job
for you", Morgenbesser shouted to Hofstadter down
a crowded hall, "Albert! I hear you're being
written by a book!". I had occasion to probe him
for details of a trip he had recently made to
Israel, a trip I sensed had been emotionally trying: "déjà jew" was the cryptic reply. And who
else would have parodied the vogue of interdis-
ciplinary courses by asking what one could learn
from a course in torts and concerti - or by urging
that a joint course in philosophy and engineering
be offered, entitled "The Abstract and the Concrete"? Writers often feel, to invert and trans-
pose a celebrated remark of Cyril Connolly's,
that inside every thin article is a fat one wild-
ly signaling to be let out. It might be argued
that inside every bit of effective philosophical
humor is a thesis that could be expressed in an
orderly sequence of paragraphs complemented by
footnotes and references. In a reversal of Wittgenstein's proposal to write a book of philosophy
consisting entirely of jokes, a different type
of talent could have, no doubt, written many of
Morgenbesser's jokes as elaborate articles in
philosophical journals.

Morgenbesser's humor does not compete, but co-
exists, with a profound seriousness about philosophy; indeed, perhaps neither of these two traits
could have been refined to the high degree they
possess in Morgenbesser without the influence of
the other. His seriousness has made him an intellectual conscience and moral animateur among his
students and friends. It is wonderfully displayed
in his teaching. Morgenbesser will sit at the end
of a seminar table, his glasses posed on the

middle of his nose, his hair awry, his hands
clutching the sides of his chair, his demeanor
alert and restless. A traditional philosophical
question will be stated, but, he will ask, is it
really a problem in the first place? Why? For
whom? At Morgenbesser's hands, philosophical
problems rapidly cease to resemble the boxed-off,
tidy textbook quandaries familiar to the novice.
Rather, they are shown to be open, perhaps perm-
anently so, and bound up with each other in intricate ways. Answers to them are shown to be limited
and constrained by exceptions, counterexamples,
complexities. Indeed, to many the general effect
of a Morgenbesser class is that of witnessing the
building of an elaborate structure of doubts and
complications. A question concerning the nature
of physical objects will be introduced with the
aid of common sense illustrations; he will then
bring to bear a number of traditional views:
realist, idealist, subjectivist, Critical Realist,
and so on, comparing and contrasting all the while.
The discussion, though fascinating, can become
complicated: a Lockean doctrine of substance, let
us say, will be criticized as *seeming* to conflict
with some finding of modern science, but then
Morgenbesser will argue that it *might* be interpreted so that it does not. A Kantian, he will
show, would argue thesis *A* in response to the
classical doctrine, and a Jamesian or Bergsonian
thesis *B*; these two views are incompatible, but
some pragmatists have a modest thesis *C* - which
may or may not conflict with *A* - but which is
certainly incompatible with the view *D*, which
Professor *E*, in the current *Journal of Philosophy*,
does not see is only *one* interpretation that can
be assigned to *A*. After a couple of hours of this,
one may no longer know what one believes or believe what one knows. Knots are untied by Morgenbesser, to be sure, but frequently the remaining
bits of rope are retied into a new knot before

the class is over. No one generates uncertainty
about what one believes more skillfully than
Morgenbesser: he is a toxic for the intellectually arrogant, a godsend for the constitutionally
skeptical.

But Morgenbesser is not the Socratic teacher
multiplying criticisms and doubts beyond necessity; nor what Sidney Hook once described as Morris
R. Cohen's teaching ideal, a "sanitation engineer
sent into the world to free students' minds of
intellectual rubbish". Though he does not impose
upon his students a fixed body of doctrine, he
does aim to teach them how to argue; he does
convey a body of attitudes, or rather attitudes
about attitudes and beliefs, attitudes about how
to form - or discard - attitudes and beliefs. He
is generally a patient and avuncular teacher,
and he will often sacrifice his time for student
inquiries and pleas for exegesis. But, like any
good teacher, he can drive a point home so that
one will not forget it again. He can eviscerate
a pupil with a comment like "Your thesis has form
but no content". When I first took courses with
him, I was warned by well-intentioned seniors to
beware certain tell-tale signs of impending dis-
aster, to watch in particular for phrases like
"Let me see if I understand your thesis". These,
I was given to understand, were invariably augurs
of a public exhibition, conducted by Morgenbesser,
of some poor unfortunate's intellectual powers at
their weakest. Was there not some kind of legal
redress, I would wonder as I underwent this very
trial, to insulate a student from this kind of
humiliation? In short, there are several kinds
of teacher, and Morgenbesser is among the very
few who have compelled many to think for the
first time; he has even succeeded at times in
bruising what Veblen called the "trained in-
capacity" of scholars in the academy.

In and out of class, Morgenbesser is the most

distinguishing of men, in the Lovejoy-Broad
tradition. He will never be content with a dualism if a septet of distinctions is around, and
if one is not around, he can invent it. I do not
know how long this has been so, but 7 seems to be
his favorite number for enumerating the senses of
a term: "There are at least seven things meant by
the term 'theory'", he will say; "May I draw your
attention to at least 7 senses of the word 'privacy'?". His attachment to the number 7 rivals that
of Hegel or Pierce or Vico to the number 3. At a
claustrophobic seminar at Columbia - a guest
mandarin was present to dissect a trayful of con-
undra - I watched Morgenbesser furiously scribble
down the cardinal numbers from 1 to 7 on his
commentator's scratch pad; small matter that the
speaker had not yet opened his mouth.

This preoccupation with the collection and cross-
fertilization of distinctions may have a sevenfold
cause. The other six have momentarily escaped me,
but one might be a suspicion that if enough distinctions are drawn, most of the traditional problems of philosophy that once tormented us can be
shown to be confused and may therefore subsequently vanish like punctured balloons. But if, as he
would say, Morgenbesser ever did believe something
like this, I do not think he does so today. Certainly the problems that have exercised him the
most - the nature of choice, the freedom of the
will, the nature of scientific explanation, and
in particular the philosophical problems arising
from reflection on the theories and methods of
the social sciences - instead of disappearing
have been rejuvenated or at any rate kept alive
by his scrupulous reformulations of them. If he
were to write down his mature reflections on
these problems, together with the flotilla of
distinctions he has created over the years to
express them, I feel sure that those in the world
of philosophy who herald the imminent death of
philosophy would be chastened.

What are Morgenbesser's positive philosophical
beliefs and concerns? He will ask you rhetorical-
ly, "Do you know how many revolutions in philosophy I have seen?", and then enumerate them like
a hotel manager ticking off available rooms in
off-season. It is difficult to believe that he
has ever been taken in by any specific creed,
philosophical or other. He is too incredulous -
although he is also skeptical of his skepticism.
But he is strongly committed to certain values:
he is deeply concerned with social justice, and
with questions of identity and ideology; he
strongly believes that philosophy can be an instrument of assistance in clarifying these subjects and practical problems involving them; he
frequently comments on political questions and
their resolution, and refuses to rule out in
principle a dose of "radical", structural, political and economic change as a solution to per-
sistent social ailments in our country. Perhaps
he has had since his youth a fascination with
Marxism, but his discussions of this subject
today are so full of rococo criticism that no
once blames him when he says he has recently
had "a declining rate of interest in Marxism".
This reminds me, incidentally, of his excellent
idea of a lecture devoted to Marx and Spencer.
One must imagine a prestigious British university on the first day of term: the musty classroom
would gradually fill up, the bell would ring, the
idealistic youths would dutifully extract from
their satchels their bibliographies on the two
world-convulsing thinkers. Then the lecturer,
clad in stiff academic gown, would mount the
podium and gravely declaim in measured periods:
"The store was founded in 1871, when capital
was made available to the Marks family through
the intercession of a justly renowned financier
..."

Morgenbesser is not a systematic philosopher.
No one is more aware than he that philosophy is

frequently fantasy, supremely indifferent to
prosaic fact and intoxicated by the desire to
install some one-sided principle as the governing
law of the universe. He is not against system in
principle, but he has devoted much time to pro-
testing against theorizing and systematizing
where it is not necessary. "To explain why a man
slipped on a banana peel", he once wrote, "we do
not need a general theory of slipping";[1] in another place he said that "no one thinks that acci-
dents are explained by accidental laws".[2] Furthermore, he thinks that the universe rarely conforms
to the sort of simplified theory that philosophers
have traditionally constructed; many of our best
efforts, he believes, lie in clarifying what we
are looking for and why and in patiently reminding ourselves of the things that may have slipped
through the nets of our theories, the exceptions,
the multiple "ways" the world can be. We need, he
thinks, to respect the conclusions and methods
of the special sciences, to develop careful
habits of inference and inquiry - and habits for
breaking and remaking these habits should new
evidence lead us to question the old ones. Pure
reason, the toy of philosophers of centuries
past, is likely to get us nowhere.

  Morgenbesser is skeptical about many things,
but he does not subscribe to what he regards as
just as objectionable as a crude rationalism,
namely, the skeptic's quest for uncertainty. Although he does not employ a primitive razor like
that of the logical positivists, he does ask us
to eschew certain old-fashioned skeptical problems. This is especially true of efforts to
provide global justifications of our beliefs and
opinions: reminding us of common sense and ordinary life, he argues that many propositions do
not require justification in a great variety of
contexts. We are certain that there is an Atlantic
Ocean; we are certain that we have mothers.

Speaking of mothers, Morgenbesser typically refers to members of his family when reminding us
of what we would say and do in ordinary life. I
have heard that when he visited Oxford some years
ago, his mother became such a familiar hypothetical figure that local philosophers acquired the
habit of asking, when interpreting some especially intransigent formulation, "But what would Sidney's mother say?", much as, generations before,
Cook Wilson and H.A. Prichard would appeal to the
judgment of their postmen and bakers.
    It is rewarding to read Morgenbesser's various
essays in philosophy, baroque, even forbidding,
as they may seem. A first reading seems to leave
one with the impression that one has passed
through a jungle of distinctions interspersed
with apothegmatic sayings. But a second or third
reading reveals a structure and an argument one
had not noticed before. In these essays, there
can be found an approach that is deflationary of
many traditional problems and answers: in nearly
every case, some spurious dualism or problem is
exposed, unmasked, discredited. But their author
conceives his work not just as clearing away
dead wood, or "explaining away," but also as elu-
cidating genuine problems that might be confronted by scientists and others in thei˙ ongoing inquiries; it is a process of analysis which might
just as well be entitled "explaining toward" a
more adequate view of the issues. For example, in
his article, "The Realist-Instrumentalist Controversy",[3] he attempts to make sense of a conflict
which has bedeviled philosophers since the birth
of modern science and perhaps before. Is this a
genuine conflict? Apart from criticizing paradoxical or silly interpretations of realist and in-
strumentalist theses, Morgenbesser's answer is
that the conflict is not between two opposing
dictrines, but between approaches which are mutually reinforcing, and it is not unfair to say that

the method he employs in reaching this conclusion is one akin to that of the Scholastics, of
drawing distinctions and assigning everything its
proper realm. Along the way he draws many illumin-
ating discriminations, especially concerning the
notions of "theory". Developing points he articu-
lated long before the current vogue for "paradigms" and "research programs", he argues that a
central sense of the term 'theory' in science
refers to "sentences or semi-sentences which indicate the type of laws that [a] given discipline
might develop", "sentences which though lawlike
do not function as principles from which the
relevant laws are to be derived", but with which
they are "in accord". These higher-level theories
he calls "theories for" a discipline, not theories "in a discipline" (p. 208), and he provides
a penetrating discussion of their role and
function in scientific inquiry, a discussion that
is still useful as a corrective to some current
debates on the subject. Again, in his "Imperialism: Some Preliminary Distinctions"[4] a paper
which originated as a talk before the Society
for Philosophy and Public Affairs (of which he
was a founding member), he sought to clarify this
central concept in political science and economics
to the end of removing some of the "moral confusion" that envelops contemporary discussion in
international affairs. Characteristically, he
notes that there is no perfectly general theory
of imperialism, and no need for one, that the
term may have beneficial as well as malignant
senses, and that we must distinguish these if we
are to use the term responsibly. As in the paper
on realism and instrumentalism, Morgenbesser
employs the analytic apparatus and terminology
of much contemporary philosophy. But his distinctions are designed not to clear up puzzles, or as
exercises in cleverness, or as semantic rules in
a "language" of science or politics, but rather,

to provide guidance to current investigations
and debates among scientists and among politi-
cians and policy-makers. In other papers, he has
written extensively on such questions as whether
the concepts and methods of the social sciences
resemble, or ought to resemble, those of the
natural sciences, whether the aim of the social
sciences is to discover laws, whether the central
social sciences are reducible to natural ones; he
has discussed such topics as the deductive-nomological model of scientific explanation, the role
of lawlike, lawful, and law statements in the
sciences, and the debate among methodological
individualists, proponents of psychologism, and
methodological holists in the social sciences; in
several papers he has written about ethical objectivity and the justification of not only
beliefs but attitudes. Behind much of this work
lies his conviction that philosophical analysis
and theory can speak to human questions and that
social science might have a role to play in improving our practices and institutions. For
Morgenbesser, science is a model community from
which all of us have much to learn about conduct-
ing our lives and solving disputes; it is a
problem-solving community whose members "share
higher-order attitudes about beliefs and attitudes to revise them in light of the objections
to them brought by others";[5] it is "distinguished
by cooperative and shared work or at least by
institutionalized methods of communication of
results and criticism, methods which have resulted not in chaos, but in the miracle of modern
science".[6] For him, "it is by using as paradigmatic the techniques that the scientist has
institutionalized for the justification of belief
that we can suggest techniques for the justification of attitude. And it is by firmly entrench-
ing liberal and democratic habits that we facilitate the functioning of a free society in which
science best flourishes".[7]

When questioned on the matter of influences on
his thought, Morgenbesser will tell you that the
great influences on him have been John Dewey,
the prophet Jeremiah, and Joe DiMaggio. As the
remark is no doubt intended to suggest, there are
tensions in Morgenbesser. One of these is that on
the one hand, he does indeed seek to discuss
problems and issues that have sprung up in actual
inquiries that demand clarification; he does indeed strive to illuminate current problems, for
he thinks that philosophy should be an instrument
assisting us in criticizing, articulating, clarifying, and supplying fresh alternatives to, our
current identities, ideologies, social and political and economic institutions. But on the other
hand, there is in him as well a fascination with
questions and issues for their own sake, with
searching for the truth for itself, uninhibited
and undisturbed by questions of relevance and
application. In the latter mood, he has devoted
himself to problems, such as Hempel's paradox of
confirmation, which, it can be argued, philosophers like Dewey would not have pursued for five
minutes. It is not accidental that the critical
influences on Morgenbesser included not only
such thinkers as Dewey and Ernest Nagel, but
also G.E. Moore and Nelson Goodman.

Morgenbesser may not publish as often as some
other philosophers, but he certainly does talk
a good deal, and he attends numerous academic
conferences - even though, as he will tell you,
he is a follower of Heraclitus and will not step
into the same conference twice. It is in his
talk that Morgenbesser's influence has been felt
most - an influence that is never adequately
conveyed in lists of academic degrees and honors.
His metier is the disciplined conversation, disciplined especially, since it must be onerous for
this most spontaneously amusing of men to resist
painting the dull truth in exciting but mislead-

ing pigments. But there is a stabilizing sobriety
that lies behind his mercurial surface: a hard-
won patience, a seriousness, a caution that is
sometimes mistaken for procrastination, define
his intellectual tone as much as do his puns and
flights of fantasy.

There are some facts about Sidney I shall claim
to know in the common sense fashion celebrated by
G.E. Moore. He is suffused with a love of philosophy; it is not merely a game or a profession
for him. He is a man of decency and sweetness. He
has an extraordinary and Protean capacity for
imaginative sympathetic understanding and identification, and is drawn to people and ideas of
every variety. He has helped many students,
friends, and colleagues by offering them his
ideas, his books, his advice, and his professional and moral guidance. He is not self-dramatizing
or eccentric and does not yearn for agony and
transfiguration. One might be tempted to recall
Spinoza, the saintly Jewish bachelor, but this
would be pitifully unjust to Morgenbesser's
contumacious sportiveness, which allows him to
do what Spinoza never did, philosophize and yet
also join a *klatsch*, consume a categorical aperi-
tif or two with the rest of the gang, and above
all avoid the usual transmogrification of the
philosopher into a walking theorem. Sidney Morgenbesser I must own, somehow reminds me of a combination of Spinoza and the late Groucho Marx. The
metaphysician or psychologist may judge for himself the liklihood of such a combination. Lacking
the powers of a Gaunilo, I can only assert that
it has been embodied for over three score years
in a certain party who haunts the candy stores
and cafés of Morningside Heights.

Footnotes:

1. "Scientific Explanation," in David Sills, ed., *International Encyclopedia of the Social Sciences* (New York: Macmillan, 1968), vol. XIV, p.122.
2. "Is It a Science?" *Social Research*, XXXIII, 2 (Summer 1966).
3. In Morgenbesser, Patrick Suppes, and Morton White, eds., *Philosophy, Science, and Method* (New York: St. Martin's, 1969).
4. In Virginia Held, Morgenbesser, and Thomas Nagel, eds., *Philosophy, Morality, and International Affairs* (New York: Oxford, 1974), pp. 201-245.
5. "The Realist-Instrumentalist Controversy," *op. cit.*, p. 212.
6. "Is It a Science?" *op. cit.*
7. "Social Inquiry and Moral Judgment," in Israel Scheffler, ed., *Philosophy and Education* (Boston: Allyn & Bacon, 1958), p. 198.

Gary
Feinberg

THE SCIENTIST AND
THE PHILOSOPHER

The following remarks are not meant to be a formal contribution either to philosophy or to
science. Rather they should be taken as
thoughts about a comparison between what scientists and philosophers do in their work. Also,
they contain some speculations about what would
happen if the future of philosophy is substantially different from its past. While I have
worked at science and interacted with many other
scientists, I have never worked at philosophy
and have interacted closely with only a few
philosophers. Therefore, much of what I say
about philosophy is based on conversations
with these philosophers and on reading philosophy. This last comment is offered not as an
excuse, but as a suggestion to those readers
who like historical explanations.

The thing that strikes me most strongly about
scientists compared to philosophers is the different attitude that the two have toward progress
in their respective fields. Scientists typically
believe that they will eventually solve the
intellectual problems that confront them at a
given time. On the other hand, philosophers
tend to think that the questions of philosophy,
many of which were raised millennia ago, will
resist permanent answers, although answers have
been given which satisfy some philosophers for
a time. Aphoristically, I would say that scientists act as if they had no permanent questions,
whereas philosophers act as if they had no
permanent answers. This attitude among scientists is relatively recent, perhaps three
centuries old in physics, less than one century
in biology. But read almost anything written

currently by scientists about their subject, and
you will usually find references only to problems
that are a few years, or at most decades old. The
corresponding writings of philosophers often, although not always, are grappling with problems
first raised by Plato or Hume.   Schools of philosophy have flourished for a time, confident in
the belief that they have a coherent set of views
that provide answers to many of philosophy's perennial questions.   But this confidence tends not
to outlive the founder of the school, and a
century later little of the confidence remains.
Perhaps it is as a result of having been "burned"
by such false hopes that philosophers have developed a deep skepticism about finding permanent
solutions to their problems.

This picture is overdrawn, but only slightly.
Science does have its perennial problems, such as
the origin of irreversibility, in physics, or the
origin of life, in biology.   A few questions in
philosophy do have accepted answers that are
unlikely to change significantly. Also, some of
the problems that originally belonged to philosophy, such as that of infinite quantity, have
been transferred to other fields, especially
after their solution, and so do not count as
philosophical problems any longer.   Much of what
we now consider to be science had its beginnings
as an aspect of philosophy.   But there have also
been broad topics, such as ethics and epistemology, which have been recognized as central to
philosophy from its beginnings, and it is in
these central areas that the absence of permanent
answers is most striking.

One might speculate on the reasons for this
difference between science and philosophy. Some
possible explanations that come to mind include
the following: greater intrinsic difficulty
of the problems of philosophy; greater ability

on the part of scientists as opposed to philosophers; self-selection into each field of people
temperamentally suited to one or another style of
thought.   None of these strikes me as providing a
convincing explanation of the phenomenon.   I
think it more likely that the explanation lies in
different modes of organization of the two fields,
which modes reflect themselves both in the type
of problem selected in each one and in the attitude taken toward the solutions of the problems.

There is in science, at least as it is now
practiced, a strong pressure toward producing
agreement.   Scientists tend to be uncomfortable
about situations in which there is open dispute
about questions within the framework of science.
This does not mean that scientists do not express
disagreements with generally accepted views or
that these views do not sometimes change with
time.   What it does mean is that such disagreements, if they involve reputable scientists,
are a source of disquiet in the scientific
community and an indication that there is a
problem to be resolved, with some speed if
possible.   Of course, this kind of situation
becomes especially acute if experimental evidence is put forward on each side of the issue
in dispute.   However, even when it is theoretical
matters that are involved, scientists do not
rest easily when open disputes break out in
their field.

In contrast, my impression is that philosophers
are hardly disturbed by disagreements within
philosophy or within its subdivisions, such as
ethics.   It appears as if each philosopher is
more concerned with defining his position so that
it is clearly differentiated from that of other
philosophers, rather than with searching out the
areas of common agreement.   Another aspect of
this is that philosophy is much less a group

activity than science is now, although it is
more similar to the way science once was. Each
major philosopher feels the need to think through
the depths of his own position, à la Descartes,
rather than use the insights of his predecessors
and fellows as a springboard to future progress.
It is not clear to me whether philosophers consciously choose this approach or whether it is
forced on them by a kind of social pressure
within the discipline. Probably some interplay
between both factors is involved.

   This attitude of philosophers is not so different from that of many social scientists, in
whose fields there also appear to be many more
perennial questions than permanent answers. In
some ways, this situation in social science is
more understandable than the parallel one in
philosophy. In social science, many of the problems are perceived to have large normative components, and some social scientists are pleased
to allow the normative tail to wave the cognitive
dog in their search for answers. Whatever the
merits of this attitude, which I think are few,
it is not one which tends to produce permanent
agreement about answers. In philosophy, on the
other hand, as in natural science, there are
large areas of investigation where the normative
element is absent, or very small, so that normative disagreements should not play a significant
role. In spite of this I do not see any greater
extent of consensus in such fields of philosophy
as epistemology than in political philosophy,
where the normative element is much greater.

   Recognizing that a situation exists is one
thing, deciding whether something should be done
about it is quite another, and figuring out what
should be done yet a third. I do not propose to
act as an outside coach to philosophers, advising
them how to carry out their investigations, even

if I thought they would listen to me. But I
think it is interesting to speculate about
whether it would be better if philosophers did
find permanent answers to their questions. This
question is inextricably linked to another one,
viz., what is the purpose of doing philosophy?
The latter question has at least two aspects:
the purposes philosophers have in their activities, and the concern of nonphilosophers about
what philosophers are doing.

  To the extent that a major purpose of philosophers is to define and express their personal
views about philosophical questions, one cannot
fault the discipline of philosophy for enabling
them to carry out this purpose. Philosophical
systems are usually more personal expressions of
the views of their creators than are scientific
systems. To the extent that this is responsible
for the absence of progress in philosophy, the
situation is akin to the reason that there is no
"progress" in painting or music. Of course,
some, following Thomas Kuhn, would say that there
is no progress in science either, but this view
has been received with much greater enthusiasm
by social scientists, for whom it may be true,
than by natural scientists, for whom it is
demonstrably false.

  But this cannot be the entire reason for the
difference between natural science and philosophy. Few if any philosophers would agree that
their purpose in doing philosophy is similar to
the purposes of painters or musicians in their
work. It is perhaps impossible to do philosophy
at all unless one is convinced that one is
grappling with questions that originate outside
oneself and is formulating answers that are relevant to others as well as oneself. So the question should occur to each philosopher who is in
the process of devising a philosophical system,

of greater or lesser scope, of how his system
will escape the fate of previous philosophical
systems, and be eventually regarded as more than
a historical curiosity.

One response to this would be to accept the
situation and attempt not to provide answers, but
to pose new questions. Since a good question
will remain of interest even though a specific
answer may not, there is some social reinforcement to those philosophers who concentrate on
the questions rather than on the answers. There
is substantial difference here also between
science and philosophy. Scientists get very
little credit from their contemporaries or from
posterity for posing good questions, as opposed
to providing answers either to their own or
to other scientists' questions. Philosophy is
closer to mathematics in this respect, where
there are also problems that have remained for
centuries or even for millennia. I am not
sufficiently familiar with the original writings
of philosophers to know the extent to which they
are explicitly content with posing questions,
rather than trying to answer them, but my impression is that this practice is fairly common.

Let me turn to the attitude of nonphilosophers
to the lack of permanent answers to philosophical
questions. One effect is probably that many who
would otherwise be inclined to think about philosophical questions are put off from doing so by
the failure of their predecessors. This attitude
probably results more in the impoverishment of
those so dissuaded than in a loss to philosophy.

There is a more general question about the
effect of philosophy on those who are not professional philosophers. Would any aspect of
human life be very different if philosophers did
agree on answers to their perennial problems?
There have certainly been many examples in which

specific philosophical views have profoundly
influenced human affairs. Would such examples
multiply, or deepen, if philosophical agreement
became the rule? I would guess that there would
be some such effect, but it is hard to be sure.
The general agreement among natural scientists
on many of the ideas in their fields has led only
to limited direct influence of science on human
life. There is, of course, the application of
science through technology, but I do not see any
possible analogue to technology arising from
agreement among philosophers. Perhaps a better
analogy for what might be expected for human life
as a result of agreement among philosophers is
the influence of religious systems on social
institutions, in those cases where the religion
has been generally accepted. I must confess that
this analogy does not make me very enthusiastic
about having philosophers find answers to their
questions.

For example, suppose that philosophers were
able to reach agreement on the answer to a perennial question in ethics, such as, What is the
Good? Could one expect that such agreement would
be reflected in different behavior of society at
large, or even among ethical philosophers themselves? This would probably depend on the form
the answer took, but I would expect that a profound effect on social behavior would occur only
if there was some charismatic, quasi-religious
leader to spread the message in a form that could
catch the ears of the world. The fact of agreement among ethical philosophers would not in
itself have much effect on society at large, in
my perhaps overly pessimistic view.

Next consider what might happen if philosophers
came to agreement about questions in epistemology, such as whether an how inductive reasoning can be justified. Would such agreement affect

the activities of the natural scientists whose
reasoning patterns are presumably at issue? In
thinking about this it is important to distin-
quish between what scientists say they believe
and what they actually do in their work. Many
natural scientists are exposed at some time in
their lives to philosophical views about science.
Many scientists adopt some version of these
views, to the extent that if asked what they
believe, they will express these views. However,
I think that the adoption of one or another
philosophical stance usually has little direct
effect on how scientists actually do their work,
although exceptions certainly exist. For example,
the lip service to Popperism that is extant among
many prominent British scientists does not seem
to have resulted in much change in the ways these
scientists work compared to those scientists of
earlier times who didn't have the benefit of
Popper's ideas.
   Of course, Popper's views, though influential,
are not universally accepted. For some indication of the effects of universally accepted philosophical views on the work habits of scientists,
one can turn to the influence of dialectical
materalism on science in the Soviet Union. In
this instance also, it is hard to detect any
considerable effect on what scientists do, at
least in physics. What has influenced the development of Soviet science more than dialectial
materialism is the coercive power of the state.
However, it may well be that Soviet physicists
as a group are not really convinced of the validity of dialectical materialism, whatever they may
say in public, so that their behavior is not
a true test of the possible influence of a philosophical consensus on science. At least one
should conclude that this example lends no

support to the view that the effect would be profound.

I am inclined to think that agreement among philosophers about the answers to some of their perennial problems would nevertheless have some important effects outside philosophy and that these effects could be relatively independent of the specific matters of agreement. In some sense, the thing about science that impresses many nonscientists is that, by and large, scientists do agree about the answers to many of their questions. It is this fact of agreement that comes through most strongly, rather than any details of the answers. Certainly the ideal that many social scientists have had of achieving real knowledge in their fields has been based on the existence of agreement in the natural sciences, rather than on its content.

By analogy, if philosophers could find some generally accepted answers to their problems, this new situation would in itself make a strong impression on nonphilosophers, whatever the content of the agreement. In retrospect, it appears that one of the strong attractions that the views of the Vienna Circle had for nonphilosophers (including myself) was that these were views agreed upon by a group, rather than those of a single individual, however talented and persuasive. Perhaps it was the contrast with the previous history of philosophy, perhaps it was some perceived similarity with the situation in the natural sciences, but the very name 'Vienna Circle' gave the views of the logical positivists a greater cachet than they might have had as the writing of several isolated individuals.

Though the occurrence of some strong influence on people outside philosophy seems to me to be a plausible eventual consequence of agreement among philosophers, I do not have any clear idea of what the specific influence would be. To know that, we will have to await the event itself.

These remarks have been written in honor of Sidney Morgenbesser, who for twenty-five years, as friend and colleague, has stimulated my thoughts, helped shape my ideas, listened sympathetically but critically to my wilder flights of fancy, and provoked me to consider questions and answers that would otherwise never had occurred to me. It is with great joy that I join in this effort to express the deep gratitude that so many of us feel toward Sidney. If, as I believe, it is true that a measure of a man's worth is how he has influenced his friends, then the name of Sidney Morgenbesser should be inscribed at the head cf the role of honor. We are all immeasurably the better for knowing him.

Isaac
Levi

DOUBT, CONTEXT, AND INQUIRY

John Dewey insisted that "inquiry begins in doubt and seeks the institution of conditions which remove the need for doubt."[1] When such conditions obtain, settled belief, knowledge, or, as Dewey often preferred to say, "warranted assertibility" is achieved.

Dewey denied that inquiry seeks the elimination of doubt understood as a state of mind. The goal of inquiry is to remove the *need* for doubt. Men sometimes doubt unnecessarily. At other times, they are credulous when they should be skeptical. According to Dewey, whether there is a need for doubt or not depends on the situation or context in which the agent finds himself. Through inquiry one seeks to transform a doubt-provoking situation to a more determinate one.

What is transformed through inquiry? If the modifications concern the inquirer's beliefs, goals, and practices without necessarily leading to changes in his environment of any relevant kind, it may appear to some that Dewey's view lapses into a kind of psychologism or subjectivism according to which inquiry is, after all, concerned with changes in states of mind.

Dewey himself insisted that through inquiry not only are beliefs, goals, and practices modified but so is the external environment itself. His views on this score have often been the object of criticism.[2]

In my view, the ontology of contextualism is not a pressing issue. We may leave to inquiry itself the determination of the extent to which inquirers need to modify their environments in order to solve problems and find answers to questions. What is clear at the outset, and trivially

25

so, is that removing the need for doubt will entail a modification of beliefs, values, and practices. Whether removing the need for doubt requires modification of the external environment as well should not affect the charge of psychologism one way or the other.

The allegation of psychologism would be fair if Dewey's view allowed us to entertain the taking of a drug known for its doxogenic potency as a legitimate means for removing doubt. The charge is unfair. Reaching conclusions through deliberate and controlled inquiries requires justifying the conclusions reached--i.e., showing that the adoption of those conclusions does remove the need for doubt. Such justification requires appeal to the agent's beliefs, values, and goals in the situation immediately preceding the reaching of the conclusion. It is entirely entertainable that these beliefs, values, and goals would sometimes contain judgments that the external environment has been modified in some way or other-perhaps through experiment. But there is no need to insist that such judgments be made in order to avoid an illicit psychologism.

Fending off the charge of psychologism requires an account of the conditions under which revisions of judgment can be justified relative to the system of beliefs, values, and goals to which the investigator is committed prior to changing his opinion.

Such an account of the revision of beliefs should show how not only the beliefs to which the investigator is committed prior to making revisions are relevant to such justification but how other features of his situation as he appreciates it-in particular, his goals, values and practices-are or are not relevant.

Another feature of Dewey's characterization

of settled belief, knowledge, or warranted assertion threatens his efforts to ward off psychologism more seriously than do the ontological issues raised above. According to Dewey, every
special case of knowledge "is constituted as the
outcome of some special inquiry. Hence, knowledge as an abstract term is a name for the product of competent inquiries" (p.8).

Dewey argued that, if knowledge is not understood in this manner, it is understood as having
a "meaning of its own apart from connection with
and reference to inquiry" (p.8). The danger is
that the claim that knowledge is the appropriate
close of inquiry ceases to be the truism it ought
to be. It also implies that inquiry is subordi-
nated to some fixed end. Dewey, rightly I think,
wished to avoid thinking of inquiry as so sub-
ordinated.

In my view, Dewey overlooked an important feature of his own discussion of knowledge or settled
belief. Sometimes Dewey characterized settled
belief or knowledge not as the outcome of competent inquiry but as a resource for use in competent inquiries:

> The "settlement" of a particular situation
> by a particular inquiry is no guarantee
> that that settled conclusion will always
> remain settled. The attainment of settled
> beliefs is a progressive matter; there is
> no belief so settled as not to be exposed
> to further inquiry. It is the convergent
> and cumulative effect of continued inquiry
> that defines knowledge in its general mean-
> ing. In scientific inquiry, the criterion
> of what is taken to be settled or to be
> knowledge, is being so settled that it is
> available as a resource in further inquiry;
> not being settled in such a way as not to

be subject to revision in further inquiry
(pp.8/9).

At the beginning of this passage, "knowledge
in its general meaning" is "the convergent and
cumulative effect of continued inquiry." But
then there is a shift, and knowledge is characterized as a "resource in inquiry." Knowledge
is analyzed not in terms of its mode of acquisition but in terms of its function in inquiry.
Construing knowledge as a resource in inquiry
still preserves the link between knowledge and
inquiry. Knowledge is not given a meaning a-
part from connection with and reference to inquiry. But its meaning does not characterize
it as the outcome of inquiry. Dewey sometimes
writes as if this is the only characterization
that can connect knowledge with inquiry. His
own practice points to the existence of another
alternative.
Perhaps Dewey overlooked this alternative
because he thought knowledge characterized as
the outcome of competent and controlled inquiry coincides with knowledge characterized
as a resource in inquiry. Whatever his intent might have been, Dewey could not have
claimed this consistently.
When inquiry begins with an indeterminate
doubt-provoking situation, the agent can recognize it as such because of background assumptions, practices, and aims to which he is committed. Something must be settled if something
else is unsettled and if there is to be any
prospect of settling the unsettled.
On the other hand, what is settled at the onset of inquiry need not be settled as the outcome
of some prior inquiry. Perhaps the investigator
is committed to certain assumptions because of
tradition, education, or authority.

Even so, someone might insist that no item ought to be free from serious doubt at the beginning of inquiry unless its adoption as settled is justified as the close of some prior competent and controlled inquiry (where presumably the settled assumptions at the onset of such inquiries meet the same requirement). Such a view suggests that the chain of previous inquiries ought to extend indefinitely into the past or, at least, provide for infinitely many predecessor inquiries to any given inquiry. Otherwise skepticism or resort to other foundationalist or pedigree-theoretic strategems will be required. None of this should have been palatable to Dewey.

To be consistent, therefore, Dewey should have abandoned the assumption that knowledge as a resource in inquiry coincides with knowledge as the outcome of inquiry. Nor should he have suggested that it is even ideally desirable that every settled assumption that has not hithertofore been subject to critical scrutiny should become so in the future; for to make this suggestion is to imply that such settled assumptions are doubtworthy after all.

It ought to have been possible on Dewey's view that some settled assumptions never become doubtworthy. To use one of Sidney Morgenbesser's old examples, how many of us have acquired the conviction that we have mothers through inquiry? How many of us ever had good reason to doubt that assumption and engage in inquiry concerning its merits?

These considerations suggest that it is not enough to focus attention, as Dewey did, on the kind of inquiry that begins with an indeterminate situation where some issues are open to doubt and others are settled and where efforts are made to settle the doubts. Such a process

concerns the elimination of doubt and how such
elimination may be justified. On a pragmatist's
view, there should also have been an inverse
process whereby an erstwhile settled assumption becomes unsettled. Moreover, such unsettling of the settled should be subject to critical scrutiny so that we may ask whether it is
justified or not.

Dewey himself undoubtedly thought that indeterminate situations are objectively doubt-
provoking in some sense or other. And when the
investigator confronted with such a doubt-provoking indeterminate situation seeks to articulate the difficulty confronting him in a more
explicit manner, he can get the problem wrong.
For Dewey, the mere circumstance that the inquirer has personal feelings of doubt concerning
some matter is insufficient to warrant his en-
gaging in inquiry.

Even so, in the absence of some account of
the considerations relevant to justifying an
investigator who begins by taking some doctrine
for granted in coming to doubt it and without
some contrast and comparison between this sort
of occasion in which doubt arises and other
cases where inquiry seeks to fill in gaps in
knowledge without bringing into question antecedently settled assumptions, it is easy to be
left with the suspicion that whether a situation is doubt-provoking in the sense that there
is a need to remove doubt through inquiry is
not subject to critical control but is a matter
of psychological and social determination entirely. As Rudolf Carnap put it, Dewey's *Logic*
is not logic properly so called, but is concerned with "the art of thinking, that is, the
theory and technology of procedures for overcoming problematic situations."[3]

In Carnap's eyes, Dewey was absolved from the

sin of psychologism because his investigations
did not, for the most part, discuss questions of
objectivistic logic of the sort addressed by
Frege and Russell. He was not guilty, therefore, of confusing topics in objectivistic logic
with questions of psychology. Dewey's logic
does, indeed, consider psychological questions
properly so called. His calling them "logical"
is a merely terminological issue.

Carnap did not mean to suggest that Dewey's
investigations were simply matters for descriptive psychology. The "art" of thinking does
have a normative and technological aspect. As
Carnap understood Dewey, the art of thinking
focuses on how to remove the indeterminacy from
indeterminate situations. I suspect that, as
far as Carnap was concerned, if a pill for removing doubt could be invented, that would be
an important contribution to this art.

To be sure, Carnap did believe that how we
think ought to be subject to some sort of critical control. Insofar as we are certain of
anything, the set of assumptions concerning
which we are certain ought to be deductively
closed, and insofar as we are not certain our
judgments of uncertainty ought to conform to the
requirements of the calculus of probabilities.
These norms and others do, according to Carnap,
constitute norms for thought. But they are
grounded on an appeal to objectivist deductive
and inductive logic, respectively, and even
though they do make reference to the way one
ought to think, they are objective themselves
in the sense that they are applicable, like
categorical imperatives, to all rational agents
regardless of circumstance.

Norms of the sort relevant to Dewey's art are
not objective in this sense. The question of
their applicability is relative to the kind of

situation provoking inquiry and takes into account not only the currently settled doctrine
but also the gaps in doctrine to be settled,
the research programs of the investigator as
well as other values. They are relative to contextual parameters.

For Carnap, the study of contextual norms is
a task for psycho- or socio- therapy. We can
study the conditions under which settled beliefs
become unsettled and unsettled beliefs become
settled in order to promote conditions conducive
to the settling of beliefs. But in the absence
of any context-independent principles regulating
all inquirers under all circumstances, we cannot
countenance criteria for the justification of
shifting from settled or unsettled belief or,
for that matter, of shifting from unsettled to
settled belief.

Carnap is an egregious example of someone suffering from the Curse of Frege. To the extent
that some activity is subject to critical appraisal by context-independent objectivist
norms - and only to that extent - it is subject
to critical control. Insofar as such principles
are not operative, "anything goes." As A.F.
Bentley rightly alleged, Carnap tossed "all such
uncomfortable issues as 'gaining and communicat-
ing knowledge' to the garbage bucket of pragma-
tics, while himself pursuing unhampered his
'logical analysis'."[4]

One cannot, of course, blame Dewey or other
contextualists for the fact that Carnap and
other victims of the Curse of Frege read their
writings in such a question-begging manner.
Pragmatists are not obliged to be exorcists.
Still contextualists may be faulted for a certain complacency. They have been so pleased to
realize that there may be alternatives to empty
objectivism and psychologism, sociologism or

historicism, that they have not explained or
explored in much detail how contextual factors
are relevant to the settling or unsettling of
beliefs and how these contextual factors themselves are subject to control if at all.

There is a legitimate worry as to how an investigator who takes some assumption as settled
can legitimately open his mind to its being
doubtful. If he cannot do so legitimately,
historical circumstance has constrained the investigator to be stuck with the assumption.
If he can so open his mind, but there is no
critical control concerning when and how he
should do so, doubtworthiness is a matter of
subjective whim to be explained as a matter of
psychological and social determination but not
to be justified.

What is needed is some account of how, starting with a given body of settled doctrine or
warranted assertions, some items may be removed
justifiably from their status as warranted.
Dewey tended to address more attention to the
problem of the conditions under which items may
legitimately become warranted. It is easy for
the unsympathetic critic to conclude that coming
to doubt is a matter of subjective whim and then
to argue that ceasing to doubt is as well.
Failure to attend to both aspects of the question of doubtworthiness renders Dewey vulnerable
to the condescension of Carnap.

The moral is generalizable. Only when contextualists avoid resting content with smug references to context and begin spelling out how
context controls the legitimacy of revisions of
doctrine may they hope to rebut the charges of
those critics who fail to see a useful difference between contextualism and various forms of
psychologism, sociologism, or historicism.

Sidney Morgenbesser, by his own example,

taught me this lesson a long time ago. Sidney used to talk about questions concerning scientific explanation in ways which seemed orthogonal to efforts to eviscerate science by focusing exclusively on "objective" context-independent aspects of explanation on the one hand or by advocating a form of contextualism about explanation which protected the subject from any serious form of systematic study leaving it in its pristine state as a blooming buzzing confusion.

Thanks to Sidney, I began to think one could indeed take context seriously without being reduced to theoretical or empirical social science. I am sure Sidney thinks I have pushed this line of thinking much too far (although it was he who used to ask "how far is too far?"). I suspect that Sidney himself thinks that full relief from the Curse of Frege is more than he or I or anyone else deserves and should await the advent of the Messiah. In this respect, my restraint is less than he would endorse. Even so, I am deeply grateful to him for having pointed me in directions of philosophical inquiry which, for me at any rate, have been so fruitful and exciting.

Thanks are due to Ernest Nagel and Norbert Hornstein for comments on the first draft of this essay.

1. *Logic, the theory of Inquiry* (N.Y.: Holt, 1938), p. 7
2. For example, E.B. McGilvary, in his 1939 review of Dewey's *Logic*; see Morgenbesser, ed., *Dewey and His Critics* (N.Y.: J. Phil. and Hackett, 1977), pp. 545–549
3. *Logical Foundations of Probability* (Chicago University Press, 2nd ed., 1962).
4. "Vagueness in Logic," in Dewey and Bentley, *Knowing and the Known* (Boston: Beacon, 1949), p. 27.

Hilary Putnam

ON TRUTH

Analytic philosophers today can be divided roughly into two classes. In one class there are
philosophers of a number of different persuasions
who see truth as a substantial notion which still
remains to be philosophically explicated in a
satisfactory way or which cannot be satisfactorily explicated, but must in that case be simply
taken as primitive. Donald Davidson (who takes
the notion of truth as primitive), Michael
Dummett (who wants to identify truth with justification), and many, if not all, metaphysical
realists share the view that truth is what I
shall call a "substantial notion." In the second
class are philosophers who feel that the problem
of truth, if there ever was one, has been solved.
These philosophers tend to call themselves "disquo-
tationalists." Very often, though not always,
they refer to the work of Alfred Tarski and to the
semantical conception of truth. The purpose of
this essay is to refute the views of the philosophers of the second class. The idea that the philosophical problems surrounding the notion of truth
have been solved once and for all either by the
idea of disquotation, or by the semantical conception of truth, or by some combination of these two
is simply an error. It is a very important error,
because if one commits it, and especially if one
appeals to the work of Alfred Tarski, then one is
liable to have the illusion that the major problem
of philosophy - the problem of the way language
and thought "hook on" to the world - has been
solved by modern mathematical logic. It seems to
me a task absolutely essential to repairing many
of the gaping errors and confusions that fill the
literature of contemporary analytical philosophy

to show that this is not the case.

It is not the purpose of this essay to say anything positive about the notion of truth. My aim
here is simply and purely destructive: I hope to
show that a certain attitude toward the significance of scientific results for a major philosophical problem, the classical problem of truth,
is misguided.

One may see the importance of what I am trying
to do by seeing how it affects the argument put
forward by Richard Rorty in a recent book.[1] In
this book Rorty argues that all of the classical
problems of philosophy, at least from the time
of Descartes, are "optional." One of the problems
that he lumps under the general name of the problem of "representation" is precisely the problem
of the nature of truth. Rorty's own solution to
this problem is that what is true is what could
be established to the satisfaction of one's
"cultural peers." I have pointed out elsewhere
that this is a self-refuting view. But one who
believes that Tarski (or the "disquotational
theory," whatever that is) *solved* the problem of
truth might nevertheless agree with Rorty that
all the classical problems were "optional,"
while criticizing the particular argument that
Rorty gave. If neither Rorty's "solution" to the
problem of truth nor any of the alternative
fashionable solutions really works then at least
one major problem in the history of philosophy
is not "optional." But this is enough to destroy
Rorty's entire argument.

Tarski's Theory of Truth

Tarski provided logicians with a method for defining a predicate which is coextensive with the
predicate 'is true', or rather which is coextensive with that predicate when that predicate is

restricted to the sentences of a particular interpreted formalized language. Unfortunately,
Tarski also wrote some philosophical essays in
which he made various philosophical claims about
the significance of his work as a conceptual
analysis of the notion of truth. He claimed, for
example, that it was philosophically neutral,
and also that it explicated the grain of truth
in the classical correspondence theory of truth.
These various claims have resulted in Tarski's
being acclaimed as the solver of the classical
problem of truth by some realists (notably Karl
Popper) and some anti-realists (notably W.V.
Quine). It is these philosophical claims advanced
by Tarski, or advanced by others on behalf of
Tarski, that I wish to refute. I do not deny that
a properly defined "truth predicate" is, indeed,
coextensive with the predicate 'is true' (in the
way just explained), at least in the case when
the object language does not contain any vague
(semantically undecided) sentences. What I deny
is that the so-called "truth predicate" that
Tarski defines is in any way similar in meaning
to the intuitive predicate 'is true'. If there
is a problem of conceptually analyzing our intuitive notion of truth,[2] then Tarski's work does
not speak to it.
   To see why it does not speak to it, it is useful
to ignore the technical complications involved
in the actual construction of a truth definition
for languages with infinitely many sentences, and
see what a Tarskian truth definition looks like
when the language in question has only finitely
many sentences. (This idea was originally suggested to me by Rudolph Carnap, who used to illustrate Tarski's idea in just this way.) Let 'mond-
shaped' be a predicate which applies to all and
only those inscriptions which have the shape "Der
Mond is blau." Let 'schnee-shaped' be a predicate

that applies to all and only those inscriptions
which have the shape "Schnee ist weiss." Call a
sentence *mond-good* if and only if it is the case
both that the sentence in question is mond-shaped
and that the moon is blue. Call a sentence *schnee-
good* if and only it is the case both that the
sentence is schnee-shaped and that snow is white.
Finally, call a sentence *L-true* if and only if
the sentence is either mond-good or schnee-good.

The property of being L-true just defined is
the property that would correspond to the truth
predicate for a language which contained just the
two sentences "Der Mond ist blau" and "Schnee ist
weiss" with their standard German meanings. If we
have a language ML which contains the two sentences that make up the total stock of well-formed
formulas of the object language L and which in
addition contains devices for spelling and for
talking about the shapes of sentences, and has
quantifiers ranging over sentences and standard
truth functions, then in such a language ML we
can easily define the predicates 'mond-shaped',
'schnee-shaped', 'mond-good', 'schnee-good',
and 'L-true'. Such a language ML is "strong
enough to give a truth definition for L" in the
standard Tarskian sense.

In such an ML the following two theorems are
easily proved (assuming standard axioms for syntax and logic):

"Der Mond ist blau" is L-true if and only if
der mond ist blau.

"Schnee ist weiss" is L-true if and only if
schnee ist weiss.

If instead of taking "Schnee ist weiss" and "Der
Mond ist blau" as primitive sentences of ML we
take their translations into English, say "The

moon is blue" and "Snow is white," and modify
the "truth definition" in ML in the obvious way,
then we can prove in ML the two sentences:

  "Der Mond ist blau" is L-true if and only if
  the moon is blue.

  "Schnee ist weiss" is L-true if and only if
  snow is white.

That these two sentences are theorems of ML shows
that the "truth definition" is "adequate," according to Tarski.
  Notice that the property L-true is defined in
a way that makes no reference to *speakers* or to
uses of words. Whether or not an arbitrary string
of letters is or is not "L-true" depends on just
three things: how that string of letters is composed (the *spelling*, in other words) and whether
or not snow is white and whether or not the moon
is blue. If we know the spelling of a string of
letters and we know whether or not snow is white
and whether or not the moon is blue, then we can
decide *in any possible world* whether or not that
string of letters is "L-true." In particular
then, the string of letters "Schnee ist weiss"
has the property of being L-true in all worlds
in which snow is white, *including* worlds in which
what it means is that water is a liquid. The
property "L-true" is not a *semantical* or even a
pragmatic property of utterances (except in Tarski's specially constructed sense of 'semantic').
It is easy to imagine counterfactual situations
in which a sentence would have the property of
being L-true and not be true. Thus the notion of
truth has not been conceptually analyzed at all.
  The same objection applies to the more complicated truth definitions that Tarski's procedure
yields when the object language has infinitely

many sentences. The property "L-true" that we
obtain by the Tarskian procedure always is a property that depends solely on the spelling of the
objects to which it is applied and on facts about
the world describable by the sentences of L. If
the sentence to which the predicate 'L-true' is
applied is one which itself does not talk about
speakers or their use of words, then whether or
not the sentence has the property of being L-true
will be independent of speakers and their use of
words. But 'is true' as that notion is *pre-anal-
ytically understood* is a predicate whose truth
conditions do not depend only on the spelling of
the objects to which it is applied and on such
facts as the color of the moon and the color of
snow, but depend crucially on whether or not
speakers *use* the object to which the predicate
is applied in such a way that it *means*, say,
that the moon is blue or that snow is white. A
property which by its very meaning has nothing
to do with the way speakers use and understand
language cannot be seriously offered as having
the same *intension* as the predicate 'is true',
even if it is coextensive with the predicate 'is
true' in the actual world.[3]

The Convention "T"

So far I have considered the view that it is
the truth definition for an individual language
that is supposed to give us some kind of analysis
or understanding of the notion of truth. It may
be urged however that this is to misunderstand
what Tarski's philosophical claims actually were.
It might be thought that what is supposed to tell
us the meaning of "truth" is not the individual
truth definitions for the various individual
languages, but rather the "criterion of adequacy,"
Tarski's famous "Convention T."

Convention T has, however, experienced remark-
ably little textually faithful philosophical investigation or discussion. Philosophers often
write as if the *following* were the Convention T:
all substitution instances of the following
schema must be *true* if *L-true* is to be an adequate
truth-predicate for a language L:

"*P*" is L-true if and only if *P*.

This however would be flagrantly circular,
since in this form (which is not Tarski's) the
Convention T would itself contain the word 'true'.
If we know that all instances of the above schema
are true, then of course we know the predicate L-
true is coextensive with the predicate 'true in L'.
To say this may be to say something informative
about the notion of truth; but since to say this
we have to use the notion of truth (in the language
ML) we have not really successfully answered any
of the deep philosophical worries about what truth
really comes to.
What Tarski really required was not that the
instances of the above schema should all be true,
but rather that they should all be *theorems* of the
language ML. But this will not do either; if the
language ML is ω-inconsistent,then it may be the
case that some instances of the above schema are
theorems of ML although (in the metametalanguage)
one can easily see that they are not all (in the
intuitive sense) *true*. The fact that all instances
of a schema are provable in some language or other
does not mean that all instances of that schema
are *true*. A third possibility is the following:
it might be held (although Tarski himself never,
as far as I know, suggests this) that we understand the word 'true' by knowing that a predicate
is coextensive with 'true' just in case all instances of the above schema are *assertible*. This

idea would try to combine an idea which often
arises in connection with the so-called "redundancy theory" of truth,[4] or "disquotational theory
of truth," the idea that we understand our language by mastering or "internalizing" assertibility
conditions, rather than truth conditions in the
realist sense, with the idea that the meaning of
the word 'true' is somehow fixed by the Convention
T. Whether or not anyone has actually held it, the
hybrid view just suggested would have two advantages: it would overcome Tarski's own objection to
the "redundancy theory," namely that *that* theory
does not tell one how to use the word 'true' with
variables and quantifiers, in the way suggested
by Tarski himself. We know how to use the word
'true' with variables and quantifiers, because we
know how to find a predicate which is coextensive
with 'true' and which *can* be used with variables
and quantifiers. (Of course this would be very
strange as a description of how the man on the
street uses 'true' in ordinary language.) The objection that the Convention T is either circular
or incorrect (the objection that I just made) would
be overcome by saying that what we really require
is not that all instances of the above schema be
true (which would be circular) and not that all
instances of the above schema should be theorems
(which ignores the possibility that ML is incorrect), but that all instances of the above
schema should be assertible. On this view there
are no philosophical problems with truth; all
the real philosophical problems concern the
notion of *assertibility*.

Asserting as Uttering

That a disquotational account of truth, either
in the sense of Ayer's "redundancy theory" or in
the sense of an attempted combination of the redundancy theory with more or less of Tarski's

work along the lines just sketched, finds its
proper home in an account according to which our
understanding of our language consists in the
mastery (or "internalization") of so-called
"assertibility conditions" is widely recognized.
One might expect, therefore, that there would be
a considerable literature devoted to the analysis of *assertibility*. But one would be disappointed. Notions of "assertibility conditions" appear
here and there in the literature, as if some
agreed-upon account of assertibility existed, but
in fact no such account (no account that is sufficiently clear and noncontroversial to justify
using the notion of an "assertibility condition"
as if this, itself, were an unproblematic notion)
exists. (I am reminded of the situation that once
obtained in the philosophy of science with
respect to the notion of "partial interpretation.")

In fact, at least three notions of "assertibility" seem to be present in contemporary philosophical writing. Sometimes "assertibility" is
used in a very "thin" sense. In the thinnest
possible sense to "assert" something is merely
to *utter* it (without provoking what Quine calls
a "bizarreness reaction"), or, perhaps to "sub-
vocalize" it (if we allow that one can assert
things in thought, without saying them out loud).
If "assertibility" is taken in this thin behaviorist sense, then the idea that the mastery of our
language consists in the internalization of assertibility conditions comes to no more and no less
than the claim that a complete account of our
understanding of our language would simply be a
description of the noises that we utter together
with a description of the actual causal processes by which we produced those noises (or subvocalizations).

Although Quine, in particular, seems tempted

by the idea that such a pure cause-effect story
is a complete scientific *and* philosophical description of the use of a language, the problem
with such a view is obvious. If the cause-effect
description is complete from a philosophical as
well as from a behavioral-scientific point of
view; if all there is to say about language is
that it consists in the production of noises
(and subvocalizations) according to a certain
causal pattern; if the causal story is not to be
and need not be supplemented by a normative
story; if there is no substantive property of
warrant connected with the notion of *assertion*;
if truth itself is not a property (the denial
that truth is a property is, in fact, the
central theme of all disquotational theories);
then there is no way in which the noises we
utter (or the subvocalizations that occur in our
bodies) are more than mere "expressions of our
subjectivity," as Edward Lee put it in a fine
paper describing similar ideas[5] advanced by Protagoras. A human being speaking and thinking
resembles an animal producing various cries in
response to various natural contingencies, or
even a plant putting forth now a leaf and now
a flower, on such a story. Such a story leaves
out that we are *thinkers*. If such a story is
right, then not only is *representation* a myth;
the very idea of *thinking* is a myth.

Can any philosopher think that *so* reductionist a story is really right? Even Quine emphasizes that such a story is right only from the
standpoint of what he calls "our first-class
conceptual scheme"; he has often said in lectures
and conversations that the first-class conceptual
system needs to be supplemented by a vague, informal, but nonetheless indispensable notion of
"justification" or "coherence". (But if these are
indispensable notions, what is the point of call-

ing them "second class"?)

Such a view falls, in fact, before the arguments that Frege deployed against the naturalism
and empiricism of *his* day. On such an account,
we cannot genuinely disagree with one another:
if I produce a noise and you produce the noise
"No, that's wrong", then we have no more dis-
agreed with each other than if I produce a noise
and you produce a groan or a grunt. Nor can we
agree with each other any more than we can disagree with each other: if I produce a noise and
you produce the same noise, then this is no more
agreement than if a bough creaks and then another
creaks in the same way.[6] Frege's point was that
the *data* in philosophy are not limited to *sensations*; my knowledge that, e.g., *I am now thinking the same thought that I thought a little
while ago* or my knowledge that *I disagree with
what you just said*, is also knowledge that is as
sure as any that we have. Such knowledge must be
taken seriously by philosophers; not treated as
an illusion to be explained away.

I am not advocating that we all become metaphysical realists; in fact, I don't agree with
Dummett that *Frege* was a metaphysical (or
"Platonic") realist. What I think is that we
have to recognize that there are *some kind of*
objective properties of rightness and wrongness
associated with speaking and thinking, before we
can even face the question whether we should
take them as primitive, give a metaphysical
realist account of them, give an "idealist" account of them, or seek a new response altogether.
I suspect that most philosophers today would
agree with this and that very few would, accordingly, be willing to regard Tarski's work (or the
disquotational theory) as having "solved" (or
"dissolved") the philosophical problem of truth
if they believed that accepting the solution (or

the "dissolution") required them to accept the
further idea that to say of what another person
says that it is "right" or "warranted" or "justified" or ... is only to express the disposition
to say "yes" to what has been said, or something
of that kind.

"Cultural" Accounts of
Warranted Assertibility

Sometimes the solution to the problem just pointed out is thought to be quite simple. My own past
idea, that psychological states should be identified with functional states of the organism, is
sometimes alleged to solve just about all the
problems there are (the nature of truth, the
nature of reference, the nature of justification,
the nature of explanation ...).[7] In particular,
someone who wants to hold fast to a disquotational account of truth, while avoiding the extreme
behaviorism of Quine's "first-class" account,
might, it is thought, get the sort of account he
is looking for by saying that to "assert" p is
not merely to produce the noise p as the result
of any physical causes whatever, but is rather to
produce the noise p in accordance with a certain
"program," in accordance with the requirements of
a certain "functional organization." (Think of us
as computers and of the "functional organization"
as a program that we are able to instantiate.)
The notion of "functional organization," whatever
its merits in other contexts, is of little help
with these problems, however. In the context of
any deep philosophical worry about truth or justification (warrant) it is fatally ambiguous. Any
actually existing thing, and, in particular, any
actually existing organism, can be viewed as
realizing, and (even more easily) as approximately realizing, infinitely many different "machine

tables". One functional description of any organism (actually, it is not unique) is that which
predicts the actual response probabilities of
the organism in any situation (including those
produced by errors, slips, biological breakdowns,
etc.). Such an assignment of a functional organization to an organism has the property that if
we assign *that* functional organization as the
organism's "conceptual-role semantics," then
everything the organism says is "competent" (and
even "warranted," if being in accordance with
the program is identified with being warranted).
Under such a description, the organism makes no
"performance errors" at all.

This is not, however, the normal way of assigning a functional organization to something - to
look for a "program" that predicts actual behavior. Generally what one looks for is a "machine
table" or whatever, which the actual computer
only approximately obeys. When a speaker, in
particular, performs according to his hypothetical "machine table", then Chomskyans say he is
performing up to his "competence"; when he dis-
obeys the machine table they say he has made a
"performance error."

Clearly there are infinitely many descriptions
of the functional organization of an actual
organism which could be used to divide the actual
behavior of that organism into what is in accordance with competence and what is "performance
error". What singles out the "true" functional
organization of the organism, or the class of
"best" descriptions of or assignments of functional organization?

If we say that the "correct" description of
the functional organization of the organism is
the description that best *explains* what the
organism does, then we have assumed an objective
intentional notion, namely the notion of *explana-*

tion. If our aim, in trying to give an account
of truth, was to avoid the need for unreduced
intentional notions in philosophy, then, in this
respect at least, no progress will have been made.

It is perhaps for this reason that some philosophers have recently suggested that the distinction between what is said *rightly*, either in
the sense of being true or in the sense of being
meaningful or in the sense of being justified,
and what is not said rightly makes no sense in
the case of a single organism considered in iso-
lation from any community to which that organism
belongs. The suggestion is that these "normative"
properties of utterances are properties that
utterances possess only when considered as utterances by a (member of a) linguistic community.
This view has been read into the later Wittgenstein by Saul Kripke in a recent book,[8] and has,
in any case, been explicitly espoused by Richard
Rorty in *Philosophy and the Mirror of Nature*.

On these "cultural" views, what we say has any
kind of rightness or wrongness only when it is
produced in accordance with (respectively,
deviates from) a pattern of speech production
(perhaps a "functional organization") which leads
us to agree with our community sufficiently often
or in sufficiently many paradigmatic cases. There
is, on such views, an objective property of rightness (though not necessarily of *truth*; the predicate "is true" is itself explained disquotational-
ly in the way we have described) and that objective property of rightness is identified with a
culturally relative property.

Meaningfulness in a public language is indeed a
culturally relative property; but warranted assertibility cannot be identified with a culturally
relative property any more than truth can be, for
reasons which I am sure are familiar and which I
shall not rehearse here.[9] I do not believe that

very many philosophers would regard the problem
of truth as *solved* if they had to agree that the
solution involves the notion that rightness (in
any objective sense) is a culturally relative
property. (In particular, the cultural relativists themselves do not stop believing that their
own views are right just because they cannot get
the agreement of *their* "cultural peers" that
their relativist views are right.)

Warranted Assertibility as Degree of Confirmation

The final suggestion I shall consider is that the
assertibility (or the "rightness") of an utterance, to the extent that "rightness" *is* a property, might be identified with its *degree of confirmation*. The idea would be that degree of confirmation is itself an objective property, an
objective degree of rightness or wrongness that
particular utterances enjoy, whereas truth is not
a property. "To say a sentence is true is to reaffirm the sentence," as Quine has put it, whereas to say that a sentence is highly confirmed is
to ascribe a substantive property to the sentence,
on this view (not Quine's).

In part, this view has the same problems that
the "functional organization" view has. There are
many possible definitions of "degree of confirmation" that might be associated with a particular
language, dialect, or idiolect. What singles out
a particular definition of degree of confirmation,
a particular inductive logic or "conceptual role
semantics" as the *right* one?

If the answer is some kind of agreement with
the dispositions of a culture, then we are back
in cultural relativism. In addition, the use of
dispositions in these accounts (cultural accounts,
I mean) involves us in such notions as "similarity of possible worlds" or "cotenability"; and it

seems to me that the notion that some non-actual
situations are "more similar" to the actual
situation than others, or that some non-actual
situations are more "cotenable" with the actual
situation than others, is an intentional notion
on the face of it.

Suppose, however, that the advocate of this
view is willing to just take "degree of confirmation" as an unreduced normative notion. It is
not wholly clear why he would not just take the
notion of *truth* as an unreduced normative notion,
but let that pass. Could such a view - the view
that degree of confirmation is an objective and
substantial property but truth is not - possibly
be the correct view?

Such a view might have a certain attraction.
One can say, as on Tarski's theory, that "snow
is white" is true if and only if snow is white
(this sentence would have degree of confirmation
1 on every evidence *e*); and, by uttering this
sentence, one might claim to have recognized
that what is true "depends on the world." It is
a little more complicated, but one can even give
a sense to "the truth value of 'snow is white'
would be different, even if snow were still
white, if our use of the language were sufficiently different." One might point out that one
has not said, in the account that we described
as a mixture of Tarski's ideas and disquotational ideas, that the Tarski "truth-predicate" for
the language L is *synonymous* with 'true'. One
has said only that Tarski's procedure provides
one with a procedure for discovering a predicate
that is *coextensive* with 'true' as restricted to
L. If one imagines counterfactual situations in
which the words are used differently, then one
has to ask whether the language as used in those
counterfactual situations is to be translated
into our "home language" homophonically or in

some other way. If the use is sufficiently different from the use in the actual world, then we
will not translate the words "snow is white"
homophonically any more. We might even translate
them by the words "the kettle is on the stove."
If we adopt this translation, then the criterion
of adequacy (in this special case) becomes that
we should not accept a predicate "L-true" as a
"truth predicate" for L *as used in the situation*
unless we are willing to accept the sentence

"Snow is white" is L-true if and only if
the kettle is on the stove.

Since one can say that "snow is white" would
not be true if the world were different (if snow
were not white), and one can say that "snow is
white" would not be true if the use of the
language were different (if the translation of
that sentence into our actual language were "the
kettle is on the stove"), then can we not say
everything that a "realist" should want us to say?

In a sense, yes, and yet this account cannot,
I think, be accepted either. For one thing, the
account contains no answer to the question, What
is the nature of the property *truth*? Rather, we
are told that although the question, What is the
nature of the property *electrical charge*? is a
perfectly legitimate question, the question, What
is the nature of the property *truth*? is a confused question. The description of the assertibility conditions (in the sense of confirmation
conditions) for sentences containing the word
'true' tells us all there is to know about truth,
although a description of the assertibility conditions for sentences containing the words 'electrical charge' would not (unless we are opera-
tionalists) tell us all there is to know about
electrical charge. In this way, the account,

whether it asserts or denies the sentence "truth is a property," reveals that truth is still not thought of as any kind of *substantive* property of the things we say.

But if truth is not a substantive property of some of the things that we say, if "to say that a sentence is true is just to reaffirm the sentence," then is the picture not like the picture that Reichenbach once flirted with[10] in which everything that we say is built up from a reduction basis of the experience of a single speaker at a single instant? The *picture* is, after all, that a language speaker is a device which says things and which appraises the things that it says and hears at each instant for a property (degree of confirmation) that *depends only on the present memory and experience of the speaker*. Even if the speaker says "the truth or falsity of a sentence does not depend, in general, only on my present memory and experience," that too is a *noise* which the speaker processes by ascertaining whether it (the noise) possesses a sufficiently high "degree of confirmation" (possesses a property which depends only on the present memory and experience of the speaker). If the noise in question (the noise that sounds like the avowal of a "realistic" philosophy) possesses the property (the methodologically solipsist property, the one which depends only on the present memory and experience of the speaker), then it possesses the only kind of objective rightness the view allows for. Such a picture of language speaking, leaving out, as it does, any property of rightness that goes *beyond* methodological solipsism is simply disastrous.[11] And one cannot turn a solipsistic picture into a realistic picture by merely adding a "disquotation scheme."

To recapitulate, the idea that there is such a thing as an "assertibility-conditions" account

of language falls before the simple fact that
nobody has ever given a theory of what "assertibility conditions" are. The only candidates I
have been able to find in the literature plunge
us at once into the disastrous picture of Skin-
nerian behaviorism or the disastrous picture of
cultural relativism or the disastrous picture of
methodological solipsism of the present instant.
That any of the exhibits in this philosophical
horror show constitutes a solution to the
problem of the nature of truth, cannot be and
should not be believed.

Footnotes:

Sidney Morgenbesser, when he was himself a
graduate student, was my first teacher in the
Philosophy of Science. Two of the ideas that he
made a living reality for me were the idea that
the responsible discussion of philosophical
problems requires an adequate familiarity with
modern logic, and the idea that fashionable solutions to philosophical problems are to be viewed
with a certain cynicism. If the present paper is
not directly about the work of Sidney Morgenbesser, I hope that the attitude of mind that it
expresses is one that is still congenial to him.
It is a great pleasure to contribute this paper
to the Festschrift for my teacher and friend.

1. *Philosophy and the Mirror of Nature* (Princeton, N.J.: University Press, 1979) I criticize
Rorty's relativism in "Why Reason Can't be
Naturalized", in my *Realism and Reason: Philosophical Papers,* Vol. 3, New York: Cambridge, 1983).

2. A philosopher who has denied that there is
is Charles Chihara, who in "The Semantic Paradoxes: A Diagnostic Investigation" [*Philosophical Review*, LXXXVIII, 4 (October 1979): 590-618]
opts for the view that our intuitive notion of
truth is simply inconsistent. The argument of
the present paper leads me to respond that if
the intuitive notion *is* inconsistent, then I don't
know just what notion Tarski is supposed to have
put in its place. Just as Tarski's "truth-predi-
cates" are properties that do not depend on the
speaker's *use* of the language in any way, so
Tarski's reference relations ("satisfaction" relations) likewise do not depend on the speaker's
use of the language in any way. But then, how
any one of these is singled out as the way the
language "hooks on" to the world is left a mystery. Perhaps the idea of a world/language dicho-
tomy is what leads us astray; but *this* is a deep
philosophical issue to which Tarski's "truth
definitions" hardly speak.

3. I use the traditional terminology of 'intensions', 'conceptual analysis', etc., here for
simplicity of exposition. Even if these notions
are not well defined (and I don't think they are
well defined), there is still a difference between
an account of a predicate which intends to give a
perspicuous picture of the way the predicate is
employed in practice, an account which should also
be correct in hypothetical situations we have some
handle on (even if we don't believe in a definite
totality of *all* "possible worlds"), and an account
which merely aims at specifying the extension the
predicate happens to have in the actual world in
any way whatsoever. Giving up the analytic/syn-
thetic distinction isn't the same thing as giving
up the distinction between a philosophical analysis of a notion and a description of its extension, or, at least, it isn't giving up *that* distinction altogether.

4. The "redundancy theory", as put forward by A.J. Ayer in *Language, Truth and Logic*, is that 'is true' is "redundant" in such sentences as *"Snow is white" is true*; i.e., *"Snow is white" is true* just *means* "Snow is white."

5. "Hoist with His Own Petard" in *Exegesis and Argument: Studies in Greek Philosophy Presented to Gregory Vlastos*, edited by E.N. Lee, A.P.D. Mourelatos, and Richard Rorty (Assen: Van Gorcum, 1973), pp. 23]-278.

6. Another way of making the same point is that what makes two utterances, say, "snow is white" and "snow isn't white" *contradict* each other is that there are various *rightness-properties* that the two utterances cannot both have simultaneously. For instance, if one is true then the other can't be; if one is justified, then the other can't be; if one has probability greater than .5, then the other can't have ... The fact that Quine has to take 'assent' and 'dissent' as primitive in what is supposed to be a behaviorist account is a symptom of his inability to give an account of agreement and disagreement in judgment.

7. For example, Gilbert Harman argues that the competence/performance distinction solves the problem of the nature of *justification* in his "Metaphysical Realism and Moral Relativism: Reflections on Hilary Putnam's *Reason, Truth and History*", *The Journal of Philosophy*, LXXIX, 10 October 1982): 568-574.

8. *Wittgenstein on Rules and Private Language* (Cambridge, Mass: Harvard, 1982).

9. In this connection, see my article mentioned in No. 1.

10. I should emphasize that Reichenbach flirted with this solipsistic reduction basis ("reports about our personal macroscopic environment (concreta) at a certain moment") in only one place

("The Verifiability Theory of Meaning", reprinted in *Readings in the Philosophy of Science*, ed.
H. Feigl and M. Brodbeck (New York: Appleton-
Century-Crofts, 1953), pp. 93-102. In his major
works he is much more realistically inclined
than this.

11. Another way of putting the point is that
there is a realist intuition, namely that there
is a substantive kind of rightness (or wrongness)
that my statement that I had cereal for breakfast
this morning possesses as a consequence of what
happened this morning, and not as a consequence
of my present memory and experience, which must
be preserved even if one finds *metaphysical*
realism unintelligible (as I do). Preserving
this philosophical intuition is not, of course,
just a matter of making it right to utter this
noise.

BELIEF, DISPOSITION, AND RATIONALITY

Henry E.
Kyburg, Jr.

In an unjustly neglected article that appeared
some years ago[1] Isaac Levi and Sidney Morgenbesser
discussed in detail the pros and cons of construing beliefs as dispositions to act. They
concluded that if we construe dispositions generally as place-holders - as promissory notes
that can, at least potentially, be cashed in for
an explanatory theory - then the proposal to regard beliefs as dispositions to act does "not
solve a philosophical problem, but [raises] a
scientific one" (p. 12). In general, this is
true: to characterize the continuing or standing
state of having a belief in terms of a disposition to act, is, as the authors point out, to
call for answers to the questions: Act how?
Under what circumstances? Given what boundary
conditions? And in accord with what general
laws? But we may also raise another question,
more appropriate to philosophers than to psychol-
ogists or neurologists: how *ought* belief and
action to be related? Or, more deeply, we may
raise a pair of questions:
   (1) How is rational belief distinguished from
       irrational belief, and, assuming that we
       ought to strive for the former, how can we
       do so? and
   (2) How are rational action and rational belief
       related?
To focus on rational belief and rational action
is not to belittle the scientific question to
which the authors drew attention, nor is it even
to suggest - I do not believe the authors meant
to suggest this - that the analysis of belief
simpliciter is something to which philosophers
cannot contribute. But it does bring up normative

57

as well as factual issues and thus philosophical
as well as scientific problems. These philosophical problems are important because we wish not
merely to know the good (the rational), nor
merely to strive for it, but, knowing it, to be
able to strive for it with some degree of success. The scientific questions are relevant,
too: a goal that such beings as we cannot
approach is inappropriate; a goal that we cannot help but achieve is empty. If we are seeking the improvement of the understanding, there
must be room for improvement, and deliberate improvement must be possible. We must therefore
steer a judicious line in developing norms for
rationality that reflects both the abilities and
propensities of people we are willing to regard
as relatively rational, and that embodies standards that we can strive toward.

I. Full and Partial Belief

The usual contemporary analysis of partial belief
falls quite naturally into the pattern suggested
by a dispositional analysis. In its simplest
form it amounts to the claim that the agent has
a partial degree of belief p in a statement S
just in case he would be just willing to offer a
stake of P units of utility for a unit return in
case S turns out to be true. This is intended
to be a clear-cut disposition to behave in a certain way, and it is equally clearly intended to
be a place-holder for a set of psychological laws
(presumably involving both A's particular genetic
heritage and his particular history) which would
explain how such dispositions came to be formed
and to characterize A at a certain time, and for
a set of neurological laws that would explain
how such dispositions are embodied in our flesh,
and for a set of biological laws which would
explain the evolutionary development of the

second-order disposition of *homo sapiens* (and
cats and dogs) to form such first order dispositions. We don't have all these explanations,
but we don't have the full quantum-mechanical
explanation of solubility, either.

Of course it isn't always easy to tell when a
person has the disposition in question. Maybe
he doesn't like to gamble, or maybe he doesn't
understand what you're asking. But we should not
let ourselves be overwhelmed by these difficulties. The solubility of table sugar isn't
completely straightforward either. The sugar in
your iced tea doesn't dissolve instantaneously -
you have to stir. For how long? How vigor-
ously? How much sugar do you put in your iced
tea, anyway?

But there is a significant disanalogy between
being disposed to dissolve under certain conditions and being disposed to buy a lottery ticket
under certain conditions. Solubility is a permanent characteristic of certain kinds of chemical compounds. Having a certain degree of belief
in S is a relatively evanescent property of A.
A's degrees of belief not only do change, but
should change. Not only is his store of past
experience constantly increasing, but he is also
forgetting, remembering, thinking, and reflect-
ing. He is also listening to other people, sometimes learning from their experience, examining
their arguments, offering arguments of his own.
Just to add to the difficulties, the utility
function in terms of which we want to say that
A is willing to pay p units for a ticket on the
truth of S is also changing over time, in response
to various stimuli, and perhaps in response to
mere reflection or to argument.

This is not to say that the dispositional analysis of belief is completely wrong-headed; we
might construe temperature as dispositional, even

though the temperatures of bodies are constantly
changing. But it does suggest that the model of
paying p for a lottery ticket on S is seriously
incomplete. We require a dynamics of belief,
even to get at a characterization of A's beliefs
at a particular instant in time. Given a characterization of A's degrees of belief at t, we
need a dynamics of belief in order to know what
A will *do* at $t + 1$. And we also need a dynamics
of value.

How about *rational* partial belief? This has
been the focus of most philosophical discussion
of degrees of belief. If we construe the measure
of partial belief in the usual way as the frac-
tion of a unit of utility that a person will exchange for a ticket yielding a unit of utility
if S is true, then it is customary to say that a
set of such exchange ratios at a given time t
represents a set of *rational* beliefs at that time
only if it satisfies the usual probability axioms.
Note that *rationality* thus construed is so far
only being taken to characterize a *set* of partial
beliefs collectively, rather than each partial
belief individually, and furthermore is merely
a synchronic notion.

Let us for the moment suppose that this constraint makes sense as it stands, and ask whether
there are other constraints that should be imposed on beliefs. There are two kinds of constraints we might consider: one is a diachronic
constraint, again characterizing sets of beliefs
collectively, that characterizes how sets of partial degrees of belief ought to change; the other
is a more ambitious constraint that applies to
individual beliefs as well as to sets of beliefs.

The diachronic constraint most often proposed
is the principle of temporal conditionalization.[2]
If P is the agent's partial belief function at t,
and between t and t' the agent comes to have full

belief in S, then the partial belief function
the agent *should* have at t' is $P'(T) = P(T/S) =$
$P(S \wedge T)/P(S)$. There are technical problems
with this suggestion, apart from Levi's concern
with the distinction between temporal and confirmational conditionalization. We must demand
that "coming to have full belief in S" is the
only epistemic thing that happens to the agent -
but is this possible? What does it mean?[3] What
are we to say if $P(S) = 0$?[4] How are we to
handle epistemic changes like those considered
by Richard Jeffrey, in which, on the basis of
sensory input, we change from $P(S) = p$ to $P'(S) =$
p'?[5] But the point I want to focus on here is
that the recipes for rational diachronic change
of belief depend on the credal effects of achieving *full belief* in some evidential statement E.
(This is as true on Jeffrey's view as on any
other, for, where P' is the new and P the old
probability function, and the probability of S
is shifted from $P(S)$ to $P'(S)$, the probability
of T is shifted from $P(T)$ to $P'(T) =$
$f(P(T), P(S), P(T/S), P(T/{\sim}S))$, where $P(X/Y)$ is the
conditionalization of X on the *acceptance* of Y.)
In short, any principle of temporal conditionalization requires that we consider the effects of
full belief, of acceptance, of credence = 1.
This is so, even on those controversial views,
like Jeffrey's, that allow the initiation of
diachronic change to consist in a shift of
partial belief in a statement.

The other, vaguer, constraint that one might
expect *rational*, as opposed to *mere*, beliefs to
satisfy is that the degree of belief in statement S on the part of the agent A should be that
degree of belief justified or warranted by the
evidence A actually has. There are a number of
ways - all of them controversial - of fleshing
this out. The most straightforward - accepted as

realistic by nobody - is to suppose that there
is a *measure m*, a là Carnap or Hintikka, on the
sentences of the agent's language, and that the
agent's degree of belief in S *should* be $P(S) =$
$m(S \wedge E)/m(E)$, where m is this probabilistic
measure, and E the lifetime conjunction, up to
now, of those sentences to which the agent has
rationally accorded full belief, presumably as
a result of experience in some sense of
"experience." It is obviously not sufficient
for the agent whimsically or without warrant, to
accord full belief to only some of the sentences
of E; or to sentences not included in E; that
would mean that one could render one's belief
rational by tailoring one's evidence. This procedure thus clearly involves a notion of rational
full belief - of belief of the highest degree.
But even less formal requirements - indeed any
requirement that demands of rational belief that
it be based on and appropriate to the evidence
in the agent's possession and relevant to it -
implicitly requires a notion of rational acceptance. The evidence consists of statements that
are accorded, on some ground or other, full
belief, belief corresponding to probability 1.

We must therefore in any case consider the
question of full belief. Can we give an analysis
of full belief along the lines of the proposed
analysis of partial belief? Is to have full
belief in S to be willing to pay a unit of
utility for a ticket that will pay a unit of
utility if S is true? Or to be indifferent
between a ticket that pays a prize P in any case
and one that pays a prize P only if S is true?
If it is logically possible that S should be
false, one would think the natural response
would be: Why take the chance?

There is a fair amount of empirical data to the
effect that when dealing with events whose rela-

tive frequencies are close to 0 or to 1, people's
choices between alternative gambles no longer
seem to fit the general pattern of maximizing
expected subjective utility.[6] The deviations
suggest that in the experimental situation events
with frequencies that are very close to 1 are
simply assumed to occur, and events with relative
frequencies very close to 0 are simply assumed
not to occur. This leads to conflicts with the
Bayesian model of deliberation, but that is not
my concern here. What I am concerned with is
the fact that if "full belief" is to to be considered a limiting case of "partial belief,"
then we should suppose that partial beliefs progress in an orderly way toward this limit. Empirically, this does not seem to be the case. To be
sure, our object is a theory of *rational* belief,
rather than an empirical descriptive theory of
belief, and we *might* say that people tend to be
irrational about events with extremely high or
extremely low relative frequencies. But we
should not with unseemly haste conclude that our
fellowmen uniformly leap into irrationality under
the same uniform circumstances. It may be that
there is an intuitively acceptable notion of
rationality within which this general tendency
can be accounted for, and perhaps even regarded
as rational.

   R. B. Braithwaite[7] offers an alternative and at
first sight more useful dispositional interpretation of full belief. It is (roughly) that a
person has full belief in *S* if he acts as if *S*
were true. The difficulty is that whether or not
a person "acts as if *S* were true" depends on what
is at stake. A man may act as if a certain vaccine is nontoxic when it comes to vaccinating
monkeys, but not when it comes to vaccinating
children.[8] Braithwaite requires that full belief
in *S* be represented as a disposition to act as if

S were true under *any* circumstances to which the truth of S is relevant. But as Levi and Morgenbesser point out, "for any contingent proposition p on which action can be taken, there is at least one objective relative to which a non-suicidal, rational agent would refuse to act as if p were true. Consider, for example, the following gamble on the truth of p: If the agent bets on p and p is true, he wins some paltry prize, and if p is false he forfeits his life. However, if he bets on not-p, he stands to win or lose some minor stake. ... Hence ... the agent could not rationally and sincerely believe that p where p is contingent" (p. 3).

Levi and Morgenbesser go on to consider more complicated reconstructions, in which actions are taken to depend on circumstances, motives, and stimulus, as well as beliefs, and show that what is involved is more like a promissory book than a promissory note. My concern here, however, is not with the general problem of construing beliefs dispositionally - a very knotty problem indeed - but with the far simpler partial problem of making sense of full belief *presupposing* an understanding of such parameters as motives, stimuli, external circumstances, and the like. In particular we shall presuppose, what is itself transparently (I should say, rather, "opaquely") dispositional: a cardinal utility function for the agent over states of the world.

II. Full (r/s) Belief

Let us begin by looking more closely at the matter of "acting as if" S were true. If I bet at even money on heads on the fall of a coin, it might appear as if I were acting as if "The coin will fall heads," were true. The appearance is misleading. My *action* is that of making a bet, and making a bet is not acting as if the proposition

that is the subject of the bet were true. On the
contrary, it is acting as if a certain relative
frequency or propensity characterized the *kind*
of event at issue. Thus betting at even money
on heads *is* acting as if at least half the
tosses of coins yielded heads. This much, at
least, seems relatively straightforward, though
in detail we would have to take account of my
aversion to risk, or my pleasure in excitement.
In fact, we can no doubt characterize my betting
behavior concerning coin tosses in general by
saying that *in ordinary circumstances* I act as
if the relative frequency of propensity of heads
were a half, or, more precisely, as if the distribution of heads among coin tosses were binomial
with $p = 1/2$.

But this claim concerning the relative frequency
or propensity of heads is surely a contingent
claim, and subject to the considerations raised
by Levi and Morgenbesser. Would you risk your
life in exchange for a paltry prize on the proposition that the propensity of this coin to yield
heads was a half? Or even "close" to a half?
Hardly. But we can easily enough imagine bets
and stakes concerning the long-run behavior of
the coin that would strike us as reasonable. (I'll
give you odds of ten to one that if we flip the
coin until it wears out, the relative frequency
of heads will end up between .48 and .52.) Now,
of course, I am "acting as if" almost all coins
and flippings are symmetrical enough to yield
that result.

On the other hand, let us suppose that I am
willing to act as if "half the tosses of coins
yield heads" is true - i.e., to bet at even money
on heads on a toss of a coin. From "half the
tosses of coins yield heads" it follows that (let
us suppose) 1/1,346,451 of the sets of 10,000
tosses fail to yield a relative frequency of

heads between 4,000 and 6,000.[9] (The exact
numbers are irrelevant.) Then should I not
be willing to offer or receive odds of $1 to
$1,346,452 against this outcome in a particular
case? It seems to me that I should not.

One might think that this is a reflection of
the size of the stake involved – a million seems
large. This feeling is reinforced by the
example of the possibly toxic vaccine: so much
more is at stake in innoculation children than
in innoculating monkeys that we should have much
more evidence that the vaccine is nontoxic
before we innoculate children than before we
innoculate monkeys. But I think this intuition
is mistaken, and that we are being misled by our
background knowledge of the frequencies of
disease and the function of vaccination. Suppose
that it is not a new vaccine at issue, but a new
antibiotic, which is demonstrably effective
against disease D in pigs. Humans are also subject to D (though only rarely); but whereas pigs
rarely fail to recover from this disease, humans
almost always succumb to it. We have some evidence regarding the toxicity of this drug in both
humans and pigs; to fix our ideas, suppose we can
say that the probability that it is nontoxic to
pigs and the probability that it is nontoxic to
humans is about the same – say about .8. It seems
quite clear that one would give the drug to a
group of children known to have D, but that one
would not give it to a group of pigs known to
have D. That is, with respect to the children,
one would act as if the drug were nontoxic,
despite the high stakes involved, but with
respect to the pigs, one would not act as if the
drug were nontoxic.

This and similar examples suggest that what is
crucial in whether or not a person "acts as if S
were true" is not the total magnitude of the

stake involved, but the ratio of the amount risked to the amount gained. Let us take this as our basic idea: A fully believes S in the sense of the ratio (r/s) just in case in any situation in which the ratio of risk to reward is less than $r:s$, A simply acts as if S were true. Symmetrically, A will then also fully disbelieve ~S - i.e., in any situation in which the ratio of the risk of counting on ~S to the benefit if S is true is less than $s:r$, A will simply act as if S were true. Putting the matter more formally, we have:

B1 A fully (r/s) believes S if and only if for every action that A takes to cost r' if S is false and to yield s' if S is true, where $r'/s' < r/s$, A acts as if S were true, and for any action that A takes to cost s' if S is true, and to yield r' if S is false, where $s'/r' < s/r$, A acts as if S were false.

A number of consequences of B1 follow:

T1 A fully (r/s) believes S if and only if there is a $p \in [0,1]$ such that A fully $(p/(1-p))$ believes S.

[Because if $p = r/(r+s)$, then $r'/s' < r/s$ if and only if $r'/s' < p/(1-p)$.]

T2 If A fully (r/s) believes S and $1 < r'/s' < r/s$, then A fully (r'/s') believes S.

A cannot act both as if S were true and as if ~S were true, though of course A can simultaneously bet on both S and ~S - indeed, this is just how a bookmaker makes his living. From this it follows that if $r/s < 1$, A cannot fully (r/s) believe S.

T3 If A cannot both act as if S is true and act as if $\sim S$ is true, then if A fully (r/s) believes S, $r/s > 1$.

T4 If A is logically omniscient and $S \vdash S'$, then if A fully (r/s) believes S, A fully (r/s) believes S'.

Clearly it need not be the case that if A fully (r/s) believes S and fully (r/s) believes S', then A fully (r/s) believes $S \wedge S'$. The ratio of stakes involved in acting as if both S and S' were true may no longer be less than r/s.[10]

Suppose that P is an epistemic probability function defined relative to what A fully (r/s) believes. I am supposing here that probability is a lgoical relation of the sort I have described elsewhere. By calling it a logical relation, I mean that the probability of S relative to any other set of statements is logically determinate (it won't be bothersome if there are a few peculiar circumstances under which it is not defined), and has a certain value regardless of what anyone whose body of full beliefs corresponds to that set of evidence statements does believe or would believe.

B2 If $P(S) = p < r/(r + s) = p'$ and Bd is the act of paying d for a unit return contingent on S, then A will rationally perform Bd if $d < p$; A will rationally refrain from Bd if $p < d$, and if $p = d$, then the rationality of A cannot be faulted whether or not he performs Bd.

So far as it goes, this principle conforms to the principle of maximizing expected utility. But now suppose that $p \geq p' = r/(r + s)$. Then according to the generally accepted scheme,

the previous analysis should still apply: if
$p > d$, it is worth buying a ticket for d that
will return a unit if S is true, even if $d > p'$.
But this is equivalent to staking a possible
gain of $1- d$ against a possible loss of d on the
truth of S. This is not in the range of stakes
contemplated in the sense of "full (r/s) belief,"
unless $d/(1-d) < r/s = p'/(1-p')$. Since $d > p'$,
$d/(1-d) < r/s$ is impossible and the ratio of
stakes in Bd is not among those contemplated.
Similar considerations govern a bet against S.

Thus the conventional Bayesian wisdom breaks
down. If we are interpreting full belief as full
(r/s) belief, then probabilities greater than
$p' = r/(r+s)$ or smaller than $1-p' = s/(r+s)$ are
not fit subjects for bets; but neither are such
statements whose probabilities relative to the
set of A's full (r/s) beliefs are greater than p'
necessarily fit subjects for full belief (r/s).

This appears to represent a gap in our normative
theory of full and partial belief. A statement S
may neither qualify for full belief (r/s) nor
for full disbelief (r/s), nor be such that the
Bayesian principle of maximizing expected utility
always gives us guidance for actions depending on
S. But we can fill this gap, and at the same
time achieve a unification and generalization of
our theory, by recalling that the parameter r/s
characterizing full (r/s) belief is adjustable.
Thus S, which presents a problem relative to full
(r/s) belief, may not present a problem relative
to a higher or lower level of full belief.

Let us write the index r/s in the normalized
form $p'/(1-p')$, or, better yet, as a single number
$p' = r/(r+s)$. If S is anomalous for full (p')
belief, then it should be acceptable as worthy of
full (p) belief for some lower level. And at
some higher level, it may be a fit subject for
Bayesian guidance. All that is required is to

make full (p') belief depend on having a probability of at least p' relative to a body of
knowledge whose index is higher than p'.   More
precisely, we adopt a third principle of rationality:

B3 A should give full (p) belief to S if and only
    if for some $p' > p$, the probability of S, rela-
    tive to A's full (p') beliefs, is greater than
    p, or S is obtained by observation, and rela-
    tive to A's full (p') beliefs the probability
    that S is in error is less than $1 - p$.[11]

This principle leads immediately to the result
that by shifting the ratio r/s slightly, we can
always resolve the anomalies in at least one way:

T5 If S is anomalous relative to A's full (p)
    beliefs - i.e., if its probability is greater
    than p, but it is not a member of A's full (p)
    beliefs - then A should give full (p') belief
    to S where $1/2 < p' < p$. (This holds in vir-
    tue of theorem T3, which requires that $p > 1/2$.)

    It is also possible to resolve anomalies the
other way - i.e., to move to a level p' such that
the Bayesian maxim does apply. (As we shall see,
this need not be the case when we generalize the
notion of probability slightly.)

T6 If S is anomalous relative to A's full (p)
    beliefs, then there exists a p' such that
    relative to A's full (p') beliefs, the
    probability of S is less than p', and there-
    fore the Bayesian maxim is appropriate for
    bets on S relative to A's full (p') beliefs.

[Suppose there is no such p'. Then, relative to
every one of A's full (p') beliefs, where $p' > p$,

S has probability greater than or equal to p'. In
particular this applies to A's set of full (1)
beliefs – i.e., A's beliefs concerning mathematical and logical truths. But then there is a p'–
namely 1 – such that the probability of S relative
to A's full (p') beliefs is greater than p, where
p' is greater than p. But this contradicts the
assumption that S not be fully (p) believed by A.]

A final generalization will allow us to construe
the probability of a statement S, relative to a set
set of full (p) beliefs as an interval rather than
a real number. Then B2 and B3 are to be construed
as requiring that the *minimum* or lower probability
of S relative to the set of full p' beliefs be
greater than p. This creates a problem for the
second way of resolving anomalies. Suppose that
relative to A's full (p) beliefs, the probability
of S is $[p',q']$, where $p' < p < q'$. It need not
be the case that there is a $p* > p$, such that the
upper probability of S is less than $p*$ relative
to A's full ($p*$) beliefs. Again the Bayesian
principle will not guide us. This situation will
be discussed shortly. Theorem 5, however, still
holds.

III. Partial Belief

Let us see how this framework can be taken to impose constraints on rational belief and rational
degrees of belief. One of the relevant factors
in the dispositional analysis of belief, however
we go from there, is the set of circumstances in
which the agent finds himself. But although this
is a relevant factor, it is not one that should
lead to despair; we do not want to say that we
can provide a dispositional analysis of rational
belief only if we know the circumstances of the
agent in infinite detail. Indeed, this would
preclude our being able to assess the rationality

of others or to improve the rationality of ourselves, for we can never articulate our circumstances in infinite detail. What is required is
that we be able to characterize a broad *class* of
circumstances under which our analysis is to
apply. Within the framework suggested here, this
class of circumstances is characterized precisely
by the range of ratios of stakes that the agent
has (implicitly) in mind. It is easy enough to
alter the circumstances so that they lie outside
this range - at least hypothetically. This is
precisely what Levi and Morgenbesser are doing
when they point out that, whatever the evidence
for S, there are circumstances under which the
agent A will not act as if S were true - e.g.,
when his honor is on the line against a paltry
prize. But this is precisely because this represents a ratio of stakes outside the range implicitly and initially contemplated by A. Often this
shift can be accomplished relatively easily and
realistically by means of the simple query:
"Wanna bet?"

According to the framework, we could consider a
notion of full belief in which the ratio of stakes
was very close to unity - full $(1/2 + \varepsilon)$ belief.
This is just what is done, sometimes, by episte-
mologists who require of S merely that it be
"more probable than not" in order to be worthy
of belief. But this is not a very interesting
sense of "full belief." Ordinarily we want our
beliefs to remain fixed through a relatively
wide range of circumstances - i.e., to be suitable for a relatively wide range of ratios of
stakes. A range from 10:1 to 1:10 might seem
more plausible.

Now the actual stakes, in any circumstnace,
depend on the agent's utility function; therefore
so also does their range. The set of circumstances relative to which our analysis is to be

performed should thus be represented by a function of both the Agent's utility function and a ratio of stakes: $C(A, r/s)$.

Consider full belief first. We say that A has full (r/s) belief in S, just in case for any circumstance $c \in C(A, r/s)$ A acts as if S were true. Note that for A to act as if S were true is not for A to perform any particular action (in any ordinary sense of 'particular') as Levi and Morgenbesser seem to suggest (p. 6, fn 30). This is not the place to attempt a characterization of action, but it nevertheless seems clear that there is a certain class of "deliberate behaviors" that are ruled out by A's "acting as if S were true," and a certain class that are required. It seems to me that this is all that is needed to give content to the notion.

A's full (r/s) belief in S is *rational*, according to the framework principle B3, just in case the *probability* of S, relative to A's full (r'/s') set of beliefs, is at least $r/(r+s)$ where r'/s' is smaller than r/s, and A's (r'/s') beliefs are themselves rational in turn. This raises a problem to which we shall return shortly.

Now let us consider A's partial (r/s) belief in S. If A's degree of belief in S is to be characterized by a real number p, it will be exactly that number p such that if A is compelled to take one side or the other of a bet at odds of $p:1-p$ on S, he will be indifferent as to which side he takes. But this seems unnatural, and foreign to the notion of the set of ordinary circumstances $C(A, r/s)$; we should seek a gentler characterization of degree of partial belief. We can get at this by supposing that there is a *range* of ratios, say from $p:1-p$ to $p'/1-p'$, such that A would be indifferent about taking either side of the bet. (Remember that the bets are in utilities; so A's enthusiasms for gambling and his reluctance to

take chances are already taken into account.)
A's partial degree of belief then comes to be
characterized by the interval $[p,p']$. Put
another way, if he is offered the opportunity
to bet against S at odds less than $(1-p'):p'$, he
will take it; and if he is offered the opportunity to bet on S at odds less than $p:(1-p)$, he
will take it.

When is A's partial (r/s) belief in S rational?
Clearly when, relative to A's body of full (r/s)
rational beliefs, the probability of S is $[p,p']$.
This means that, under any circumstances
$c \in C(A,r/s)$, A ought to bet on S at odds lower
than $p:1-p$, and ought to bet against S at odds
lower than $1-p':p'$. Note, however, that, if the
odds do not lie in the range $[r:s,s:r]$, then A
is not in the circumstances $C(A,r/s)$ envisaged by
the analysis. Suppose that A is offered a bet on
S at odds between $p:1-p$ and $p':1-p'$. Then he is
under no rational constraint either to accept or
to reject the bet. But this is all right. We
still have perfectly good characterizations of
A's partial (r/s) belief and of the constraints
that this belief must satisfy in order to be
rational:

For any $c \in C(A,r/s)$, if A is offered a bet at
stakes r'/s' on S or s'/r' against S, where
$r/s > r'/s'$,
   (1) he will (ought to) accept the bet on S if
   r'/s' is less than $p:1-p$, where p is the lower
   bound of his (r/s) degree of (rational) belief
   in S;
   (2) he will (ought to) accept the bet against S
   if r'/s' is greater than $p':1-p'$, where p' is
   the upper bound of his (r/s) degree of rational
   belief in S; and
   (3) he may or may not accept either bet otherwise, where 'may' has its customary English
   ambiguity.

There are several difficulties, both apparent
and real, with this framework. Suppose that,
relative to A's rational full (r/s) beliefs, the
probability of S is $[p,q]$, where p is greater
than $r/(r+s)$. Then for no $c \in C(A,r/s)$ could A
rationally bet against S, but if S is not a member of A's full (r/s) beliefs, neither can we
demand that A act as if S were true under any
$c \in C(A,r/s)$. What should A's doxastic attitude
toward S be? It seems perfectly natural to say
both that S is not a statement that A believes
and also that it is not a statement against which
he would bet under any circumstance in $C(A,r/s)$.
This seems to be a perfectly natural (and indeed
familiar) circumstance to be in. But we may also
suppose that the possibility of a *serious* bet on
S would change the circumstances contemplated
from $C(A,r/s)$ to $C(A,r'/s')$ where $r'/s' < r/s$,
and the odds of this possible serious bet are
such that they fall in the range $r'/s',s'/r'$.
Then the previous analysis would hold. I do not,
therefore regard this as a real difficulty.

Another nonserious difficulty arises from our
treatment of probability as interval-valued.
Suppose that, relative to A's (r/s) rational
beliefs, the probability of S is $[p,q]$, where
$r/s \in [p,q]$. Then A should bet on S at odds less
than $p:1-p$, but there are no odds at which he
should bet against S. But the ratio of stakes
contemplated, r/s, includes some at which A
could rationally bet against S. I think this
situation will be found anomalous only by those
who think that A's doxastic state should be represented by a single classical Bayesian distribution.

The most serious difficulty of the analysis is
raised by B3 itself: B3 requires only that there
exist a set of full $(p':1-p')$ rational beliefs

relative to which the probability of S is at
least p ($p < p'$) in order that S ought to be
counted among A's full (p:$1-p$) beliefs. This
threatens serious anomaly: what if S were
probable to at least degree p relative to A's
full (p') beliefs, and $\sim S$ were probable to at
least degree p relative to A's full (p'') beliefs?
We have no guarantee that this will not happen,
in which case the whole scheme blows up in self-
contradiction. Furthermore, if p' may be as
close as you please to p, one might suspect that
probabilities might mount toward the level of
acceptance with unseemly rapidity. It is for
these reasons, as well as others, that I have in
other places required that we not merely consider
as full (p) beliefs those more probable than p
relative to *some* set of full p' beliefs where
$p' > p$, but rather consider as full (p) beliefs -
the set of practical certainties - only those
statements more probable than p relative to a
specified level p' of full beliefs - what I have
called the "moral certainties" (p', of course, is
to be greater than p). But then we have what may
be the slight awkwardness of two parameters
floating about, where there seems to be need for
only one, barring the difficulties I have just
alluded to.

IV. Dispositions Again

Now let us see to what extent this is a dispositional analysis of belief or rational belief, and
what sort of dispositional analysis it is. In the
first place, it is perfectly clear that the analysis is not free of dispositional talk; dispositions have not been elimitated, since the whole
analysis depends on a utility function for A, and
no hint has been given as to how to eliminate
those dispositions. On the other hand, if preferences are the only dispositions left in the

analysis, then we have succeeded in removing at least one layer of dispositions from the analysis of belief.

Concerning actual belief, it seems to me that we have failed. We would have succeeded in reducing the number of promissory notes only if we could characterize the circumstances $C(A,r/s)$ - even if we were to do so in terms of dispositions to prefer - in such a way that we could emerge with truly universal laws of the form: for all $c \in C(A,r/s)$ A will perform an action of the class Q. It is quite clear that we have no such laws - even if we allow *ceteris paribus* clauses - if only because people do not always behave rationally or consistently.

But concerning rational belief, it seems to me that we have accomplished the reduction in question. Of course we still have the promissory note implied by our characterization of $C(A,r/s)$, but, given that characterization, I think we have a universal constraint on rational belief in terms of possible actions. A's beliefs are rational in the class of circumstances $C(A,r/s)$ if and only if, for every $c \in C(A,r/s)$, A performs (would perform) one of a certain class of actions and refrains from (would refrain from) another class of actions, where the circumstances determine a classification of actions into the rationally obligatory, the rationally prohibited, and a class of actions which are neither obligatory nor prohibited.

Given a knowledge of an agent's preferential dispositions, we can characterize sets of circumstances $C(A,r/s)$. Then, given a knowledge of the agent's full (r/s) rational beliefs, we can divide the actions he might contemplate into those he ought rationally to perform; those he ought rationally to refrain from, and those concerning which there are no rational constraints.

If we wish to assess the rationality of his full
(r/s) beliefs, we may do so by considering the
probabilities of the statements fully (r/s)
believed, relative to the agent's full (r'/s')
beliefs, where $r'/s' > r/s$. We may do this for
any set of circumstances $c(A,r/s)$. This serves,
I maintain, to give us a complete handle on both
the agent's rational beliefs and his rational
actions, subject only to the characterization of
his utility function - obviously a nontrivial
matter, and one that itself involves dispositional
interpretation. Thus although the dispositional
characterization of *actual* belief does seem to
open up a Pandora's box of confederate notes, and
thus to represent a research program rather than
an enlightenment, the dispositional characterization of *rational* belief calls for only one blank
check (to be filled out in A's utilities), and
otherwise admits of relatively clear-cut prescriptions. As in many other areas of endeavor
(in geometry, for example) it turns out to be
easier to prescribe the ideal (the rational) than
to describe the real (the actual). But the ideal
is not without relevance to the real. The constraints on rationality are those we should try
to embody.

Footnotes:

    Support for research relevant to this
article was provided by grant SES 8023005
from the National Science Foundation.

    1. Isaac Levi and Sidney Morgenbesser, "Belief
and Disposition," *American Philosophical
Quarterly*, I, 1 (1964): p. 1-12.
    2. Levi makes the distinction between temporal
conditionalization and confirmational condition-

alization in "Direct Inference," *Journal of Philosophy*, LXXIV, 1 (January 1977): 5-29, as well as other places.

3. Paul Weirich, "Conditionalization and Evidence," *Journal of Critical Analysis*, VIII, 1 (1979): 15-18.

4. See, for example, William Harper, "Rational Conceptual Change," *PSA 1976*, Asquith and Hacking, eds., for an attempt to deal sensibly with evidence whose prior probability is 0, together with the references therein.

5. Richard Jeffrey, *The Logic of Decision* (New York: McGraw-Hill, 1965), especially ch. 11.

6. See Ward Edwards, "Subjective Probabilities Inferred from Decisions," *Psychological Review*, LXIX (1972): 109-135, and references therein; see also C. Stäel von Holstein, ed., *The Concept of Probability in Psychological Experiments* (Dordrecht: Reidel, 1974).

7. R.B. Braithwaite, "Belief and Action," *Proceedings of the Aristotelian Society*, XX (1946): 1-19.

8. The example comes from Levi and Morgenbesser, *op. cit.*, pp. 2, 3.

9. I refer here literally to a *set* of tosses, not a sequence of 10,000 tosses; hence there is no requirement of "independence."

10. Since $r'/s' < r/s$ and $r''/s'' < r/s$ imply $(r' + r'')/(s' + s'') < r/s$, one might think not. But the risk is in fact $r' + r'' + r'''$, where r''' is the additional cost of both S and S' being false.

11. More principles are required to work this out in detail – see my forthcoming *Theory and Measurement* – but this statement suggests sensibly that it is possible to come to fully (p) believe something on the basis of observation without having to stake one's life or one's honor on it.

QUANTITY AND SUPERVENIENCE

Arnold Koslow

We have described elsewhere[1] what might be
called a "double-component" account of theories
of measurable empirical attributes. One component studies various quantitative and qualitative
relations of the theory: the second considers
the empirical attribute – the target, subject,
or topic of the theory. In the first component
we consider what it means to say that "x is
twice as long as y" is a quantitative relation.
In the second, we try to explain in what sense
such a quantitative relation is about the empirical attribute length. For various reasons suggested below, we do not regard attributes like mass,
length, and charge as identifiable with any quantitative terms of the theory: thus the idea of
two components. We hope the brief review that
follows will make it credible that such an
account has some merit worth exploring. The principal purpose of our present remarks, however,
is to show that there is a connection between
these components and certain philosophically
interesting distinctions in the literature.

According to our account, empirical attributes
like mass, length, and charge stand in a very
special relation to quantitative relations. Given
these conditions, we can then show that they are
very like the determinables of the determinate/
determinable distinction first formulated by W.
E. Johnson.[2] Thus a convenient way of expressing
this result is that measurable empirical attributes are determinables, demonstrably so, even
though this interesting distinction is usually
exemplified by "color" and "shape" – distinctly
nonmeasurable attributes. Moreover, although our
brief review of the two components exhibits the

relation that underlying empirical attributes
have to quantitative relations, it turns out that
this relation too is an instance of another powerful distinction in the literature: if an attribute
P is an underlying empirical attribute of some
quantitative relation R, then R is supervenient
on P, and demonstrably so. We shall also consider
certain arresting theorems about the supervenience
relation, which were first proved by Jaegwon Kim[3],
and evaluate their significance in the special
case of theories of measurable attributes.

I. The Double-Component Theory

When we say that x is twice as long as y, we usually intend not only to assert a quantitative relation between x and y, but also to suggest that
that relation is somehow about a specific empirical attribute: length. We think of the attribution
of length, not as a mere way of talking, but as
conveying a sifnificant thought. What I would like
to do is to try to give some expression to that
thought. In each of a large variety of examples,
there seems to be a concern both with quantitative relations and with what those relations are
about. This concern runs deep. Explicating what
those theories are about is not an exercise in
the semantics of the theories or a study of the
intricacies of "about" - important as those problems are. The assumption that a quantitative term
or a family of quantitative terms has an underlying attribute has very specific consequences for
the extension of those terms to new domains and
for the possibility of representation theorems
for them. We have already noted some of these
consequences elsewhere, and shall pass over them
briefly.

   On one view which is widely shared, the problem has been solved. Once a theory of length or

mass, with its qualitative relations and axioms
has been set forth, one seeks representation and
uniqueness theorems. What is mass then? It is,
on this view, just the representing function ϕ
(or the family of equivalent functions determined
by the relevant uniqueness theorem) which maps
the objects of the domain into the non-negative
real numbers, and is a homomorphism of a relational structure to a numerical relational structure.

There are several reasons against identifying
mass (say) with a representing function, or even
a set of equivalent representing functions. Each
of these mini-theories has a certain domain of
objects, over which the representing function is
defined. If there is a shift in the domain, we
want to think of the theory over the new domain
as still concerned with mass. But that is a difficulty for the identification of mass with representing functions. The representing functions
over the two domains have to be different, since
there is a difference in their domains. Therefore, a direct identification of mass with a
representing function or a set of such functions,
is not suitable, given an extensional account of
functions. Furthermore, if there were a domain
on which two relations were coextensive, say
"x is at least as long as y" and "x is at least
as massive as y", then their representing functions would have to be the same. Therefore there
would be no difference between mass and charge
over that domain.

These problems are not cause for either rejecting or abandoning any part of the Suppes program
for theories about measurable empirical attributes.
All the hard-won results remain intact. The difficulties, however, provide some reason for supplementing those theories with additional distinctions. The difficulties we have mentioned concern
the identification of the empirical attributes

like length, mass, and charge with any of the
quantitative terms of the relational system for
(say) mass. Representing functions, however, can
be proved to be uniquely associated with (many-
sorted[4]) quantitative relations. In that sense,
they are quantitative. But they are quantitative
relations and are different from the empirical
attributes that underlie those relations. We do
not think it is impossible to attend to these
issues within the type of approach outlined, for
example, by Suppes. We are concerned here with
supplementing the usual considerations associated with such an approach, so that the empirical
attributes are explicitly recognized as different
from, but related to the quantitative relations
they underlie.

2. The First Component:
Quantitative and Qualitative Relations

Relations, on our account, are classificatory,
comparative, or quantitative, relative to a partition of the domain on which they are defined.
If the partition is discrete (each member of the
partition itself has just one member), then the
traditional notions of classificatory and comparative relations coincide with the relativized
versions. Thus there is some assurance that despite the relativization of quantitative and qualitative relations to partitions, most of the old
has been incorporated. Let us briefly review this
relativized account.

Comparative Relations. We shall use a two-place
relation term for convenience of exposition (the
general n-place case requires that every pair of
variables (x_i, x_j) $(i \neq j)$ satisfy the conditions
below: 'Rxy' is comparative over D with respect
to the partition π, if and only if (1) If Rxy,
and x and x' belong to the same π_i of π, then $Rx'y$.

(2) If Rxy, and y and y' belong to the same π_j of π, then Rxy'.   (3) 'Rxy' is weakly connected in D: for any x and y in D, either Rxy or Ryx. (4) 'Rxy' is strictly transitive: R is transitive, but it is not anti-transitive (anti-transitivity requires that if Rxy and Ryz, then not-Rxz).

Quantitative Relations. Again, for convenience we use only a two-place relation. For an n-place relation '$Rx_1 \ldots x_n$', the following conditions are required of each component x_i. Let 'Rxy' be a relation over a domain D, and let π be a non-discrete partition of D. R is quantitative over D, with respect to π if and only if (1) Rxy and $Rx'y$ together imply that x and x' both belong to some member π_i of π.   (2) Rxy and Rxy' together imply that y and y' both belong to some member π_j.   (3) If x and x' both belong to some member of the partition, then Rxy if and only if $Rx'y$. (4) If y and y' both belong to some member of the partition, then Rxy if and only if Rxy'. We shall also allow relations to be quantitative with respect to a discrete partition under this condition: 'Rxy' is quantitative over D with respect to the discrete partition π, if and only if 'Rxy' is the restriction of some relation R^*, which is quantitative according to conditions (1)-(4).

The general idea is that there is a grouping of the objects in the domain into subsets whose members are "alike" (Helmholtz). The idea of using such a partition for the study of quantitative relations seems to have originated with Helmholtz.[5] The third and fourth conditions require that any members that are "alike" and belong to the same member of the partition are substitutable one for the other, in any relation that is quantitative with respect to such an organization of the domain. Conditions (1) and (2) require of the quantitative relation that it is so "tight" that if two objects of the domain are both related in

the same way by it to some objects, then the two
have to be in the same member of the partition -
they have to be "alike". Relativization of clasi-
ficatory, comparative, and quantitative relations
yields an account of these three types of relations which permits a proof that, except for certain pathological situations, classificatory,
comparative, and quantitative relations are
mutually exclusive types of relations. Further,
we can also show that, if a relation R is comparative with respect to a partition, then it is also
comparative with respect to a maximum partition,
the minimum (discrete) partition, and all partitions that lie between the two (the 'between'
refers to the usual ordering by refinement: one
partition is a refinement of another if and only
if every member of the first is a subset of some
member of the other). Quantitative relations
have the theoretically interesting property that,
if a relation is quantitative with respect to a
partition of its domain, then there is only one
such partition of its domain with respect to
which it is quantitative. *Quantitative relations
therefore uniquely determine their partitions.*

There are a host of traditional as well as new
examples that are covered by this notion of a
quantitative relation. They range from utterly
simple examples like "x is twice as long as y"
(for which the partition is those sets of equally
long objects), to fairly sophisticated ones like
"X is in one-to-one correspondance with the power
set of Y" (the partition consists of those sets
which have the same cardinality), or "Z is the
union of (disjoint) X and Y". Included also are
intermediate examples from modular arithmetic,
"$x + y$" = 12 (mod n)" (the partition is the set
of n residue classes), and geometric examples
like "z is the hypotenuse of a right triangle
whose arms are x and y" (the partition is the

set of congruent segments). The range partially
illustrates one striking aspect of the characterization of quantitative relations: it makes no
reference to numbers, numerical functions, ordering relations, or concatenation operations. This
is a virtue rather than a vice. It permits applications to a range of cases where a numerically
oriented approach would be inappropriate. If
quantitative relations are treated in this non-
numerical manner, it appears that nothing quantitative is lost and that perhaps a theoretical
simplicity is gained. Some numerical functions
and relations are quantitative, but, to be quantitative, a relation need not be numerical. Our
characterization doesn't force the issue either
way, but is intended to cover those cases which
are numerical as well as those which are not.
Quantitative relations are the business of the
first component. The business of the second concerns the notion of an underlying empirical attribute and the systematic way in which it links up
with quantitative relations.

4. Underlying Empirical Attributes

We have already suggested several reasons why an
empirical attribute such as length is not directly identifiable with any of the quantitative
relations such as "x is twice as long as y", or
"x is longer than y, by z", or "thirteen x's are
as long as seventeen y's". We are not suggesting
that a term cannot be quantitative unless it has
an underlying attribute. In fact, our characterization of quantitative relations suggests otherwise. However, when a quantitative relation, or
family of such relations, is thought to be about
some empirical attribute, then it seems to me to
be important to try to characterize that belief.
We suggest that the empirical attribute that

underlies a quantitative relation, the attribute
it is "about", consists of a family of predicates,
which, among other things, specifies or "fixes"
the unique partition of the quantitative relation.
It is interesting to note that the idea of taking
the empirical attribute to be a set of predicates
(or properties) seems close to what Norman Campbell once expressed when he wrote that when "we
have assigned numerals to represent the property
we shall know that the body with the property 2
(sic) added to that with the property 3 will have
the same property as that with the property 5, or
as the combination of the bodies with the properties 4 and 1."[6] Although this view is similar to
the view we wish to propose, we should note that
it doesn't represent a final view of Campbell,
and should not be pressed too closely.

Let $P = \{P_\lambda\}$ be a set of predicates. We shall
say that *P is an underlying attribute for the*
quantitative term 'Rxy' (with domain D and par-
tition π) if and only if (1) $Rxy \Rightarrow P_\lambda x$ and $P_\mu y$,
for some P_λ and P_μ in P; (2) for every P_λ in
P, the restriction of P_λ to the domain D is some
member of P's partition (i.e., $P_\lambda | D = \pi_i$ for some
member π_i of R's partition); (3) For every π_j
in π, there is a P_μ in P, such that $P_\mu | D = \pi_j$.
Thus, if P is an underlying attribute for "x is
twice as long as y", then we refer to P as "length,
given P", and by length (simpliciter) we mean the
weakest of such families P. The fact that P is a
set of predicates rather than a single predicate
doesn't preclude attributing it to the members of
the domain. We shall say that *x has P* (length)
just in case some P_λ holds true of x, and we shall
say that *x and x' have the same P* (length) if and
only if there is some P_μ that holds of both x and
x'. According to (1), if P underlies 'Rxy', then
it follows from Rxy that x has P, and so too does
y. Condition (2) states that, when each P_λ is

restricted to the domain D, it determines exactly
one member of R's partition, and (3) states that
every member of R's partition is the restriction
of some member of P to the domain of R.

The assumption that a quantitative relation has
an underlying empirical attribute is not a piece
of useless colloquialism, scientific or commonplace. One interesting consequence of the assumption is that, if R has an underlying attribute P,
then one can prove that there is a representation
theorem for R (there is another quantitative term,
$R^{\#}$, over a domain $D^{\#}$, with a partition $\pi^{\#}$, and a
mapping ϕ of D to $\pi^{\#}$ such that $Rx_1 \ldots x_n$ if and
only if $R^{\#}\phi x_1, \ldots, \phi x_n$). Another consequence is
this: if R is quantitative over a domain D, with
partition π, and R^* is quantitative over a domain
D^* that includes D, with partition π^*, and R and
R^* have an underlying empirical attribute in
common, then the partition π is a refinement of
the partition π^*. This is a stability theorem of
a sort. Even though the quantitative terms R and
R^* may be very different, if they share an underlying attribute, then things grouped as "alike"
by the partition of R will continue to be grouped
as "alike" by the partition of R^* on the super
domain. It follows immediately that if two quantitative relations partition the same domain differently, then they have no underlying empirical
attribute in common. Thus the assumption that
there are underlying empirical attributes for
quantitative relations has a theoretical force
to it. The present account leaves open the possible sources for such families of predicates. They
could be furnished by some background theory, or
they could be put forth as an i.o.u., upon which
some quantitative theory is constructed and together with which it is tested.

5. Determinables and Underlying Empirical Attributes

This completes our sketch of the two components: qualitative and quantitative relations on the one hand; underlying attributes on the other. It is obvious that the notion of an underlying attribute and the relation of an underlying attribute to a quantitative relation are hardly familiar philosophical fare. In the next two sections, we shall try to establish some connections between these notions and some more familiar philosophical distinctions. We do not think that every underlying attribute is a determinable. The connection between the two is not that direct. A special class of underlying attributes can be proved to be determinables. They are those which are the weakest of all those which underly a given quantitative relation. Thus, length (simpliciter), as we described it above, is a determinable.

The description of a special kind of adjective, the notion of a determinable and its determinates, was first introduced by W. E. Johnson. The most familiar examples are 'color' and 'shape', but 'pitch', 'feeling tone', and 'pressure' also qualify. 'Color' is a determinable, having 'red', 'orange', 'green', and 'blue' as determinates, and 'shape' is a determinable, with 'triangular', 'circular', 'square', and 'octagonal' among its determinates. The original occasion for the distinction concerned a difference in logical form between "Plato is a man", and "Red is a color". The distinction was also used by Johnson for a variety of other problems, which ranged from the genus-species distinction, and comparability under sortals, to issues about causality, change and continuity, absolute and relational theories of space and time, and inductive inference. There

is no doubt that the distinction has a vitality
and interest beyond its origin in semantic theory.

We can now list some of the characteristic
theses that Johnson used to elucidate the deter-
minable/determinate distinction. We state them
briefly, and then indicate why empirical attributes like length and mass can be shown to satisfy them, or in some cases, a reasonable variant.
(J1) Any instance of a determinate of a determinable is also an instance of that determinable.
(J2) Any two determinates of a determinable are
exclusive. (J3) The determinates of a determinable are exhaustive. (J4) Determinates are
"ultimately *different*", according to Johnson, in
the sense that no two determinables can be subsumed under a higher determinable. He seems also
to have held that any two determinates of a determinable are comparable, and that any adjective
that is comparable with a determinate of a determinable must also be a determinate of that determinable. Unfortunately, there is no explanation
of the crucial notion of comparability between
adjectives; there is the non-example which he
offers: "color" and "shape" are noncomparable.
It follows from (J4) that no determinables are
comparable; otherwise they would be determinates
of the same determinable, and that is incompatible with the fourth condition. (J5) There is
an ordering relation for the determinates of a
determinable. Although there is no comparability
between determinables, all the determinates of a
determinable are supposed to satisfy some ordering relation. The specific relation may vary from
determinable to determinable, but Johnson thought
that all the orderings were examples of a betweenness relation. Johnson is rather vague on the
details of this particular requirement. Finally,
(J6) If two objects have the same determinate of
some determinable, then they share all the adjec-

tives and relations definable in terms of that
determinable. He offers the example of two objects
that are the same shade of yellow. Although they
may differ in shape or size, any color property
of the one will also, he claims, agree with the
color property of the other. Johnson seems to
have thought of this condition as showing that
there are generalizations that can be produced
which have the determinates as antecedents: all
objects having such and such a determinate also
have such and such a property definable in terms
of the appropriate determinable. There is a parallel, he thinks, with Fechner's laws correlating
differences in the intensity or quality of sensations with quantitative differences in physical
stimuli. Generalization is possible, he thought,
using determinates from an intensive scale, just
as it is possible using determinates in a quantitative science. This raises the interesting possibility of there being generalizations in non-
quantitative disciplines, as long as there are
determinates and determinables in those disciplines. However, as we shall see below, the generalizations that are based on determinates as
antecedents turn out to be transparent common-
places or else singular statements, and not
genuine generalizations at all.

This is the theory, in rough form, of a certain
kind of adjective. It is, despite the unfinished
state of its theses, capable of a wide number of
applications. It may even, we believe, be transferred to situations where it is not adjectives,
but theories themselves, which exemplify the
determinable/determinate distinction. Our present
concern is not the construction of a satisfactory
account of the distinction. We shall assume that
the usual examples go a long way towards convincing the reader that there is something here which

ought to be given a better description. We are
concerned instead with noting that it is reasonable to think of a special type of underlying
attribute, $P = \{ P_\lambda \}$ as a determinable, with
the various P_λ s as its determinates.

Let us first say that if P is an underlying
attribute of a quantitative relation R, then P_λ
is nonredundant if and only if no predicate P_λ
has an extension that is a proper subset of (the
extension of) any other predicate P_μ of P. It
follows immediately that, if P and Q are nonredundant underlying attributes and each is a
refinement of the other, then they are identical.
With this minor formal adjustment in place, we
can proceed to look at the determinable character of underlying attributes of quantitative relations. We also suppose, for the rest of the discussion, that P is not only an underlying attribute of some quantitative term R, it is also the
weakest of all such (i.e., any underlying attribute of R is a refinement of P), and that P is
nonredundant (although this assumption is needed
for the demonstration of only one of the following six conditions (J3).

The first condition (J1) is automatically satisfied as a consequence of the proposal that 'x has
P' holds just in case there is some predicate in
P which holds true of x. For the same obvious
reason, (J3) (exhaustiveness) is also satisfied.
The second condition (J2) concerns the exclusiveness of the determinates of a determinable. In
general, we do not have the exclusiveness of any
two predicates of P; we have their disjointness
over the domain D. This seems fair enough. D is
the domain of R, which P underlies. If P underlay
any other quantitative relation, say S, then the
predicates of P would also be disjoint over the
domain of S. Since we are concerned with P and
the quantitative relations it underlies, we know

that different members of P will be disjoint as
far as the domains under study are concerned. The
proof of disjointness over the domain of R is
somewhat intricate. Suppose that P_λ and P_μ have
some member of D in common - say x. Then x is in
the restriction of P_λ to D, and also in the restriction of P_μ to D. Since P is an underlying
attribute of a quantitative relation R, whose
partition is π, it follows that these restrictions to D are members of R's partition - say π_λ
and π_μ, respectively. Since π is a partition, it
follows that $\pi_\lambda = \pi_\mu$, since each contains x. Therefore the restrictions of P_λ and P_μ to D, are
identical. Now consider a new family of predi-
cates: $P^+ = P \cup \{(P_\lambda \cup P_\mu)\}$. It is easy to verify that P^+ is an underlying attribute for R, if
P is. Since P is the weakest attribute underlying R, it follows that P^+ is a refinement of P.
Consequently, every member of P^+ is a subset of
some member of P. Therefore $(P_\lambda \cup P_\mu)$ is a subset of some P_ξ. Therefore P_λ is a subset of P_ξ,
and so too is P_μ. But P is nonredundant. Thus
P_λ is identical with P_ξ, and so too is P_μ.
Therefore $P_\lambda = P_\mu$. Consequently, if P is the
weakest attribute underlying R and is nonredundant, then any two predicates of P are disjoint
over the domain of R.

We now turn to the remaining three conditions:
(J4) the incomparability of determinables, (J5)
the ordering of determinates of a determinable,
and (J6) the generalization thesis.

First, (J4). It is not generally true that, if
P and Q are attributes underlying quantitative
terms, neither of which is a refinement of the
other, then they are not subsumable under some
other underlying attribute. In general the empirical attributes that underlie a quantitative relation have a lattice structure. However, *if P is
the weakest empirical attribute underlying a*

*quantitative term R (and is nonredundant), and Q
is the weakest empirical attribute that underlies
a quantitative relation S (and is nonredundant),
and neither is a refinement of the other, then
there is no (nonredundant) empirical attribute,
U, weakest or not, which underlies either R or S
and which subsumes both P and Q under it.* Here,
'*P is subsumed under U*' is taken to mean that *P*
is a refinement of *U*. Thus, if length underlies
"*x* is twice as long as *y*" and charge underlies
"*x* is twice as charged as *y*", and it is granted
that neither length nor charge is a refinement
of the other, then there is no empirical attribute underlying either of these quantitative relations such that both length and charge are
refinements of it.

The reason is just that, if *P* is a refinement
of *U* and *Q* is a refinement of *U*, then *U* cannot
underlie either *R* or *S*. There are two cases: if
U underlies the quantitative relation *R*, then *U*
and *P* both underlie the term *R*. In that case,
since *P* is the weakest of those attributes which
underlie *R*, it follows that *U* is a refinement of
P. But *P* is also, by hypothesis, a refinement of
U. Since both are assumed to be nonredundant, it
follows that they are identical. The second case
assumes that *U* underlies the quantitative relation *S*. By a similar argument, *U* is identical
with *Q*. Thus, roughly put, no attribute that subsumes both *P* and *Q* (where neither is a refinement
of the other), can underlie any relation which *P*
underlies or which *Q* underlies. We do not have an
unqualified conclusion that these special underlying attributes are never subsumable under others.
We have instead, the qualified result. It is
interesting to note in this connection that something like noncomparability has been assumed in
the proof on nonsubsumability, but it is not the
notion that Johnson appealed to, but didn't ex-

plain. It is the perfectly standard idea that P and Q are noncomparable if and only if neither is a refinement of the other.

The fifth condition (J5) also has its support. It required that the determinates of any determinable satisfy some betweenness ordering. Now we cannot justify the fifth condition in just this form. However, given our concern with quantitative relations, we do have a reasonable rendition: *the determinates have some quantitative relation definable for them*. The reason is that, if P is an underlying empirical attribute for a quantitative relation R, then there is a representation of R by a quantitative relation S, defined over the set of indices of P.[7] We can therefore think of the determinates of P, i.e., P_λ, P_μ, P_ξ, ..., as standing in the quantitative relation $S*$ if and only if the indices λ, μ, ξ, ... stand in the relation S. The determinates thus have a quantitative structure provided for them, though it will not necessarily yield a betweenness ordering. Although we haven't provided any more structure for the determinables than that which comes from a representation of R over the set of indices of P, something more can be said about ordering relations. Under certain conditions, quantitative relations can be used to define a canonical ordering relation. The idea originated with Helmholtz and was later developed by Karl Menger.[8] It can be shown that any representing function for such special quantitative relations R will also be a representing function for the canonical ordering based upon R. The determinates of P can then be provided with an ordering relation, by using a representing function - it doesn't matter which.

The sixth condition (J6) is supposed to indicate how generalizations can be based upon determinates, whether those determinates are drawn from a qualitative discipline or from a quantitative science.

There are at least two ways of understanding Johnson's claim that there are generalizations whose antecedents are determinates and whose consequents are those terms definable in terms of their determinables. The first way is true enough, but not at all interesting. If every instance of a determinate is also an instance of its determinable (J1), then it is hard to see how any two instances of (say) the same shade of yellow can fail to share all the adjectives and relations that are definable in terms of the term 'color'. The sixth condition, on this reading, is just a platitude. On a second reading, instead of taking 'color-word' to mean just those words definable on the basis of 'color' (a funny proposal anyway), it is proposed that there is a class C of adjectives and relations such that any two objects that share any determinate of 'color' will also share all the predicates belonging to C. It then becomes an interesting open problem how such a class is to be described in a noncircular way. This question can be raised for any determinable and its determinates. We shall consider it in the special case where the determinable is P, an underlying attribute for some quantiative relation R, which has domain D and partition π. The Johnsonian question then becomes: What is the class of relations S for which any relation of S holds of any two objects if they have some determinate P_λ of P in common. Even in this particular case, we do not have a complete answer. We do, however, have a noncircular partial solution for a special class of quantitative relations. Let P be an underlying attribute of a quantitative relation R, whose domain is D and partition is π. If '$Tx_1...x_n$' is a quantitative relation, defined over a superset D^T of D, with a partition π^T, such that T covers the subdomain D (i.e., for any α in D there is an ordered n-tuple $< x_1,\ldots,x_n >$ in D^T, such that $\alpha = x_i$ and '$Tx_1,\ldots, x_n$' holds), then *T is invariant with respect to the substitution of any objects belonging to any determinate P_λ of P, if and only if R's partition is a refinement of T's partition;* i.e., for any x and y in D and for any P_λ in P,

$$(*) \quad (P_\lambda x \ \& \ P_\lambda y \ \rightarrow \ (Tx_1\ldots x\ldots x_n \ \leftrightarrow \ Tx_1\ldots y\, x_n))$$

   if and only if $\pi \preceq \pi^T$

This solution is partial because it concerns only invariant *quantitative* relations, not invariant relations in general. Thus it says nothing about when an *ordering* relation is invariant under substitution of codeterminates, and that, of course, represents a situation of great interest. Nevertheless, given the emphasis of the present study on quantitative relations, it is nice to have at least this information about invariant quantitative relations on the super domains of D. The proof is simple. From right to left, suppose that the partition of R is a refinement of the partition of T. Let x and x' be members of D such that $P_\lambda x$ and $P_\lambda x'$. Therefore, x and x' both belong to some member of R's partition. But R's partition is a refinement of T's. Therefore x and x' both belong to some member of T's partition. Since T is quantitative, it follows that $Tx_1\ldots x\ldots x_n$ if and only if $Tx_1\ldots x'\ldots x_n$. From left to right is a little more complicated. Assume that the left-hand side of (*) holds. Let π_i be any member of R's partition, and let x be any member of it. Now x must also be in some member $\pi_j{}^T$ of T's partition, since x is in D and D is a subset of D^T. We want to show that π_i is a subset of $\pi_j{}^T$. Let x' be any member of π_i. Since x and x' both belong to π_i and π_i is the restriction of some P_λ to D, it follows that $P_\lambda x$ and $P_\lambda x'$. It holds, by hypothesis, that $'Tx_1...x...x_n'^\lambda$ holds for $< x_1, ..., x_n >$ with $x = x_i$. From (*) we conclude that $Tx_1...x...x_n$ if and only if $Tx_1...x'...x_n$. Therefore $'Tx_1...x'...x_n'$ holds. Since we have both $Tx_1...x...x_n$ and $Tx_1...x'...x_n$, and T is quantitative, it follows that x and x' both belong to the same member of the partition of T. But x belongs to π_j^T. Therefore x' belongs to it. Therefore $\pi_i \subseteq \pi_j^T$. Consequently, π is a refinement of π^T.

We are now in a position to see the truth in Johnson's claim about the possibility of generalizations based upon determinates. If a quantitative relation $'Tx_1...x_n'$ satisfies the conditions mentioned in the proof of (*) and, in addition, has a partition that π refines, then the left-hand side of (*) holds - i.e., roughly, T (and in particular R) is invariant under the codeterminates of P. However, if the left-hand side of (*) holds for any quantitative relation T, then we have, as a consequence, the following generalization for T:,

$$(**) \quad (x) \ (P_\lambda x \rightarrow Tx_1...x...x_n)$$

where quantification is over the domain D, and the x_i denote specific objects in T's domain. To see this, one just notes that we have assumed that $'Tx_1...\alpha...x_n'$ holds for some α in D and that $'P_\lambda \alpha'$ also holds. Now let x be any object in D such that $P_\lambda x$. Since α and x are both in D and P_λ holds of both, it follows that $Tx_1...\alpha...x_n$ if and only if $Tx_1...x...x_n$. Since the former holds by hypothesis, we obtain $Tx_1...x...x_n$. Thus (**) *yields a host of generalizations whose antecedents are the determinates of P and whose consequents employ any of a large set of quantitative relations (including R itself).*

The confidence that (**) provides significant
generalizations is short-lived. *On plausible
grounds, it follows that each case of (**) is
equivalent to a singular statement.* Suppose that
a background theory Θ includes the description
of quantitative relations and underlying attributes, together with the information that P_λ
holds of some object α in D. Then it follows
that:

$$\Theta \vdash (x) (P_\lambda x \to Tx_1 \ldots x \ldots x_n) \leftrightarrow Tx_1 \ldots \alpha \ldots x_n.$$

Here is a proof of the biconditional. Assume Θ.
If $(x) (P_\lambda \to Tx_1 \ldots x \ldots x_n)$, then, since $P_\lambda \alpha$ follows from Θ, we have $P_\lambda \alpha \to Tx_1 \ldots \alpha \ldots x_n$, and,
hence, $Tx_1 \ldots \alpha \ldots x_n$. This completes the proof
from left to right. Conversely, suppose Θ and Tx_1
$\ldots \alpha \ldots x_n$. Let x be any object in D such that $P_\lambda x$.
Then $P_\lambda x$ and $P_\lambda \alpha$. Therefore x and α belong to
the restriction of P_λ to D. Since P is an underlying attribute of R, it follows that they both
belong to some member of the partition of R. But
the partition of R is a refinement of the partition of T, and so they both belong to some member
of T's partition. Since T is quantitative, it
follows that $Tx_1 \ldots \alpha \ldots x_n \leftrightarrow Tx_1 \ldots x \ldots x_n$. But
we have $Tx_1 \ldots \alpha \ldots x_n$ by hypothesis. Consequent-
ly, $Tx_1 \ldots x \ldots x_n$. That is, $\Theta \vdash Tx_1 \ldots \ldots x_n$
$\to (x) (P_\lambda \to Tx_1 \ldots x \ldots x_n)$.
Thus the generalizations obtained from (**)
have almost no power as generaltizations: given
the information that some object α in D has the
determinate P_λ, it follows that the generalization is equivalent to the singular statement Tx_1
$\ldots \alpha \ldots x_n$. This last result can be summarized:
the sixth condition on determinables is basically
sound. There are interesting classes of relations
that are invariant under substitution of codeterminates. But there are no generalizations of any

merit which arise in this way.

We hope that the preceding remarks will serve to make the notion of a weakest underlying attribute more familiar to the reader. We now want to consider the special conditions that describe when an attribute underlies a quantitative relation. This is also an unfamiliar set of conditions, but it falls under a special type of relation which is more familiar: supervenience. In the next section we shall show that *if an attribute* $P = \{ P_\lambda \}$ *underlies a set of quantitative relations* $\{ R_\sigma \}$, *then the set* $\{ R_\sigma \}$ *is supervenient upon the set* $\{ P_\lambda \}$.

6. Supervenience and Underlying Empirical Attributes

Recently Jaegwon Kim (*op. cit.*) has called attention to a special relation, supervenience, which holds between families of predicates (or properties), and has provided a clear description of this relation: M and N are two sets of properties, and M^* and N^* are the sets of properties definable via the Ms and Ns respectively, then M is said to be *supervenient upon* N if and only if, whenever x and y are indistinguishable by any property in N^*, then they are indistinguishable by any property in M^*. Thus, if a set of mental properties M is supervenient upon a set of physical properties P, there is no way in which two things can differ in some mental property (definable over M), without differing in some physical property (definable over P). In other words, if two objects x and y share all the physical properties of P^*, then they also share all the mental properties of M^*.

For many writers, one of the most useful features of this distinction is that it seems to permit the expression of a dependency between two sets of properties, without requiring that there be any reduction or definitional equivalence between any property definable over one set, with any property definable over the other. It was thought that there could be a supervenience relation between two sets of properties without any properties of the one set being necessary, sufficient, or necessary and sufficient for any property of the other. Dependency, without dependents, as it were.

Kim, with the first of a series of theorems, has challenged the claim that supervenience really does have such an advantage. He argued that under certain conditions, which he regarded as plausible, the relation of supervenience will guarantee that there are sufficient, or necessary, or necessary and sufficient conditions that hold between properties of the two sets. One conclusion drawn by Kim is that Donald Davidson's claim that there are no psychophysical laws, cannot be correct. We shall say something about this conclusion below. Our principal aim, however, is to establish the claim that the relation between quantitative relations and the empirical attributes that underly them, is an example of supervenience.

Let P be an underlying attribute for each of the quantitative relation R_1, R_2, ... , which are all defined over the same domain. The set of quantitative relations $\{ R_\sigma \}$ is supervenient upon the set of determinates $\{ P_\lambda \}$ of P. The argument is fairly direct: if the objects x and y in D are codeterminates of P, then there is some R_i which they both have. Since P is an underlying attribute of each of the R_i, it follows that both x and y are in the restriction of that P_λ to the domain D. Consider any R_i. Since P underlies R_i, the restriction of P_λ to D is just a member of R_i's partition. Since R_i is quantitative, it does not distinguish between them. This holds true for each R_i; thus supervenience holds.

There is one interesting question which we alluded to and which can now be raised. Kim has shown that if M is supervenient on N, then for any property P of M (which has an instance α), there is a property Q of N^* such that $Q \rightarrow P$ (closure is over D), where Q is an N-maximal property (of α) (any objects sharing Q, share all the properties of N^*). In our case, the Qs are just the P_λs of P. Therefore, the Kim conditional '$Q \rightarrow P$' becomes '$P_\lambda \rightarrow R_i$' (closure over D). In the quantitative case these conditionals are no great news; they simply restate the ways in which a quantitative relation is related to its partition. They are not daring, but dull. However, if Kim is correct, they are not dull, but damaging. Supervenience plus some weak assumptions yields a psychophysical conditional that Kim believes to be lawlike. So, we might ask, is the conditional in the quantitative case lawlike? How nomic is '$P_\lambda \rightarrow R_i$'? Unfortunately, as we noted in the discussion of (J6), the conditional is, given that $P_\lambda\alpha$, equivalent to the singular statement '$Rx_1...\alpha...x_n$'.

Why does there seem to be a difference between the two cases? Why is the conditional equivalent to a singular statement in the quantitative case, but supposedly lawlike in the mental/physical example? The conditional '$P_\lambda \rightarrow R_i$' gives the true picture of things. Contrary to Kim's claim, his conditional '$Q \rightarrow P$' is not lawlike. It too is equivalent, under the assumption of supervenience, and $Q\alpha$, to the singular statement '$P\alpha$'. There are several arguments that can be given, but, unfortunately, they are too long for inclusion here.[10]

Although the application to Davidson's claim of certain theorems about supervenience seems dubious, nevertheless, the concept of supervenience has great resourcefulness and power, and the relation between a quantitative relation and its underlying attribute falls within its scope.

Footnotes:

1. "Quantity and Quality: Some Aspects of Measurement," *Philosophy of Science Association, Proceedings,* I (1982); 183-198.
2. *Logic, Demonstrative Inference: Deductive and Inductive*, Part I (Cambridge: University Press, 1921; reprinted New York: Dover, 1964).
3. "Supervenience and Nomological Incommensurables," *American Philosophical Quarterly*, XV, 2 (April 1978): 149-156.
4. The many-sorted quantitative relations are just those relations $Rx_1...x_n$, defined over the cartesian product of n mutually exclusive sets (at most), D_1, ..., D_n, each with its own partition, for which the four conditions on quantitative relations hold with respect to each component (where x_i ranges over D_i).
5. "Numbers and Measuring from an Epistemological Viewpoint" (1887), as translated and reprinted in R. S. Cohen and Y. Elkana, eds., *Hermann von Helmholtz: Epistemological Writings* (Boston, Reidel, 1977).
6. *What Is Science?* (London: Methuen, 1921).
7. A proof is sketched in my "Quantity and Quality", *op. cit.*
8. "Mensuration and Other Mathematical Connections of Observable Material," in C. W. Churchman and P. Ratoosh, eds., *Measurement: Definitions and Theories* (New York: Wiley, 1959), pp. 97-128.
9. This qualification is necessary since the P_λ of P are supposed to hold or fail to hold over a set of objects that includes but is not restricted to the domain of R.

10. There are in fact several concepts of super-venience in the literature for which our conclusions hold. For example, in a recent article, "Psychophysical Supervenience as a Mind-Body Problem" [*Cognition and Brain Theory*, V, 2 (1982): 129-147], Jaegwon Kim distinguishes between a concept of weak supervenience - the concept described by us above - and strong supervenience, according to which a family of predicates M is (strongly) supervenient on a family of predicates N, if and only if, whenever P is a predicate belonging to M and α is any object in the domain D such that $P\alpha$, then there is a predicate Q belonging to N such that $Q\alpha$, and, for all objects y in the domain D, necessarily if Qy, then Py.

It is also easy to verify that our conclusions for (weak) supervenience also hold for the strong version. That is, (1) the set of quantitative relations $\{R_\sigma\}$ is strongly supervenient on the set of determinables $\{P_\lambda\}$ of any attribute that underlies the R_σs , and (2) it still holds that the Kim conditional '$Q \to P$' is equivalent to the singular statement $P\alpha$, given that strong supervenience holds, and that $Q\alpha$, so that the conditional seems to have no nomic import. We hope to communicate the details of this simple result shortly.

SIMPLICITY AS FALL-OUT

Robert
Nozick

If an indefinite number of hypotheses fit our
data, we need some way to select which one to
accept. Merely fitting the data is not sufficient; the additional criterion philosophers put
forth most prominently is simplicity: we should
believe the simplest of the hypotheses (we can
formulate) that fit (and would explain) our data.

Why believe the simplest? Convenience in mani-
pulating, remembering, transferring, and teaching
the theory or hypothesis would lead us, perhaps,
to utilize the simplest, but why *believe* it? Why
think that, of the otherwise equally satisfactory
explanatory theories, the simplest is most likely
to be true? If simplicity is "relative to the
texture of a conceptual scheme"[1], to the kind of
"graph paper" on which we plot the world, then
to show this connection between simplicity and
truth would involve the unpromising task of
establishing our conceptual scheme or coordinate
system as privileged.

The question about simplicity is not merely a
skeptical conundrum. It is difficult to think of
any reasonable explanation for why including such
a simplicity maxim should help (and should have
helped) make the institution of science successful or more likely to arrive at the truth. To
explain how a simplicity maxim contributes to
the success of science by saying that the world
is simple, says little, if indeed it says anything other than that there is some simple true
theory of the world. (Of *all* of it? And why think
any particular simple theory, which explains only
some things, will be a component of the over-all
simplest theory?) So the maxim of simplicity and
its connection with truth puzzles us.

W. V. Quine and Joseph Ullian[2] find that natural
selection "offers a causal connection between
subjective simplicity and objective truth...Innate
subjective standards of simplicity that make
people prefer some hypotheses to others will have
survival value insofar as they favor successful
prediction. Those who predict best are likeliest
to survive and reproduce their kind...and so
their innate standards of simplicity are handed
down" (p. 47). But maxims of simplicity direct
us to choose the simplest of hypotheses in areas
and at levels in physics, chemistry, cosmology,
molecular biology, none of which were believed
or chosen by our ancestors. What explains why
their subjective standards of simplicity, which
have stood the evolutionary test for hypotheses
about middle-sized macro phenomena, also connect
with truths about cosmology or microphenomena?
(Or is there no "connection between subjective
simplicity and objective truth" in these areas?)
Perhaps the fact that nature is uniform, here
interpreted as meaning that the same type of
simplicity obtains throughout. *If* one could turn
this into a precise statement about *the world*,
the requisite sort of explanatory link between
our standards of simplicity and truth would be
forged. Quine and Ullian further note that "Such
standards will also change in the light of experience, becoming still better adapted to the growing body of science in the course of the individual's lifetime. (But these improvements do not
get handed down genetically)" (p. 47). However,
they do get handed down in the education of
scientists. If scientists' standards of simplicity change to fit the theories they develop and
accept, then these theories will seem to them
and to later generations, who judge by these
changed standards, simple.
  In "On Simple Theories of a Complex World",

Quine artfully side-stepped the issue of simplicity's connection with truth by connecting it
not with truth but with confirmation. A preference for simplicity is, so to speak, an *artifact*
of our procedures of confirmation, so that the
simpler of two theories is more likely to be confirmed and to hold up under the way we investigate theories. The question Quine raises, what
the artifacts of our procedures are, is of extreme importance. However, to raise the question
of whether something is an artifact of our procedures of confirmation is to raise the question
of whether, in that respect, those procedures
should determine our beliefs. If people who
learn science (strangely) got headaches when they
considered a hypothesis containing three words
beginning with the letter "d", then no such hypothesis could get confirmed. That would be an
artifact of the man-scientific-procedures combination, but surely no reason to disbelieve such
a hypothesis. Thus, questions of the justification, and not merely the causes, of our beliefs
would be raised. Put somewhat differently,
noticing the artifact and knowing the artifactual
causal story might lead us to change our (artifactual) beliefs.

Simplicity is usually introduced as an additional factor to help decide among the different
hypotheses that fit (or would explain) the data
D_1 in hand at time t_1. Another way to decide
would be to gather more data. But this seems not
to solve the current problem, for however much
new data D_2 we gather, and however many old hypotheses D_2 eliminates, there will still be an
indefinite number of hypotheses that fit D_1+D_2.
And how are we to choose among them?

The feeling that no progress has been made by
collecting new data - to be sure some old hypotheses are refuted - should set us to wondering

whether the situation is being misconceived. Instead of thinking of a temporal cross section of hypotheses and data, consider the following very simple model of an ongoing process.[4] At time t_1 there are data D_1 and already formulated hypotheses $H_1 \ldots H_m$ which fit D_1. New data D_2 are gathered *to select among* these hypotheses. If only one hypothesis survives, believe it (tentatively), and go on to gather new data to test it against other hypotheses you now think up which fit $D_1 + D_2$.

"But how can it matter that a particular hypothesis was actually thought of earlier and tested? If another hypothesis H_{23} which we have just now thought of and which also fits $D_1 + D_2$ had been thought of earlier, then it would fit all the data we now have. Surely which hypothesis the data support cannot depend upon which hypothesis we happened to be thinking about as we gathered the data." If H_{23} had been thought of earlier it would fit $D_1 + D_2$ now, but we *don't* know that it would fit all the data we would have now, for if H_{23} had been thought of earlier, we would have gathered *different* data. Our process of data gathering is selective. Given hypotheses $H_j: y = f_j(x)$ we gather data at values of x where the hypotheses differ, and at a sufficient number of points x so as to leave only one of the original hypotheses surviving. If H_{23} had been one of that original number, we would have gathered data at some additional points x.

Granted that the counterfactual that purports to make the sequential procedure look ridiculous is *not* known to be true, still the question arises of why we should (tentatively) believe the surviving hypothesis rather than another that fits those data just as well. The answer depends on the way the underdetermination of theory appears to make it difficult to (strongly) support a hypo-

thesis. Hypothesis *H* fits data *D*. But an infinite
number do. We expect many to, and this is one of
those which do. Whatever the data we found, we
could dream up many hypotheses afterwards to fit
them, and so with *D* we dreamed up *H*; is this any
reason to believe *H*?

Suppose someone says he will show you that he
is a very skilled archer. If an arrow is shot at
random at a large target, the probability of its
hitting a particular point is *very* small (has
measure zero). And that's true for each point.
"So", he says, "if I shoot and succeed in getting
the arrow to a particular point, it will show I
am very skilled." He shoots, the arrow lands,
and he says, "See how skilled I am; the probability that the arrow would have landed precisely there at random was minuscule." "Hold on",
we say, "the arrow had to land *somewhere*, and it
landed there. Wherever it landed would have been
an unlikely place. We'll believe you're a skilled
archer if you *first specify* the minuscule area
your arrow is going to hit, and *then* succeed in
hitting it." Similarly the data are going to land
somewhere. That they land in a particular place
is a reason for thinking a specification of that
place is significant only if *that* specification
was offered beforehand.

Suppose the archer shot at random at a wall,
and then went to where the arrow had landed,
drew a circle around it, and said "Bull's eye!"
Suppose when the data land somewhere, we draw
a curve through it and say "Bull's eye." A bull's
eye is when the data hit the hypothesis, not the
other way around. Since bull's eyes give support,
to believe the best supported hypothesis is (some
complications aside) to adopt the method of tenacity.[5]

Now to connect simplicity with the sequential
selective data gathering and testing procedure.

We (tend to) think of the simpler hypotheses,
relative to *our* conceptual scheme. So the simpler
hypotheses get into the fray early. Suppose only
one hypothesis H_S from the initial batch of hypotheses we formulated survives our gathering
of data D and, in accordance with the procedure,
we tentatively believe it. Either:

(1) The initial hypotheses[6] were the simplest
possible which would fit D_1; no other possible
hypothesis that fits D_1 is simpler than any one
of these. With all but one of the original hypotheses eliminated by D_2, H_S is the simplest possible uneliminated hypothesis that fits D_1. Since
whatever fits the large data set D_1+D_2 must also
fit D_1, H_S is the simplest possible hypothesis
that fits D_1+D_2. So we *already* are (tentatively)
believing the simplest hypothesis compatible
with our data.

or (2) We did not originally formulate the simplest hypotheses that fit D_1, and there are hypotheses simpler than H_S compatible with D_1+D_2. We
formulate further hypotheses, and enter the next
stage, gathering the (selective) data D_3, and we
(tentatively) believe the surviving hypothesis.
Either it's now like case 1 above: our formulated
hypotheses were the simplest that fit D_1+D_2 (that
is, their subset bounded by this stage's survivor
contained the simplest), and so we're now believing the simplest hypothesis compatible with all
of our data, or else (loop) case 2 again.

This sequential testing procedure fails to get
us believing the simplest hypothesis (of those
we can formulate) compatible with our data only
if there is an infinite descending sequence of
more and more simple hypotheses, and we start up
on it and move slowly down. If we sequentially
test hypotheses that we've thought of, tentatively believing the survivor, and if we do (tend to)
think of simple hypotheses (judged relative to

our conceptual scheme), then the result will
soon be that we are believing the simplest hypothesis (of those we can formulate) which is compatible with all the data we have. (Even simpler
hypotheses, of course, may have been eliminated
earlier.)

We need no rule or maxim that bids us to believe
the simplest hypothesis compatible with our data.
It's just a consequence of the operation of *that*
sequential procedure that we *will* end up doing
so. And the fact that simplicity seems relative
to our own conceptual scheme, to our background
concepts, coordinate system, type of conceptual
graph paper, etc. - a fact that blocks attempts
to connect simplicity with truth - fits naturally
into *this* story. The more simplicity fits however
we happen to tend to think, the more likely it is
that we *will* think that way, and early. To *guarantee* we'll end up believing the simplest hypothesis compatible with the data, it would have
to be assumed, not merely that we tend to think
up simple hypotheses, but that by some time we
have thought up *all* the simplest. This assumption is too strong, but then again science provides no guarantee of convergence to the simplest. It is no defect for our theory of simplicity to explain no more than the facts.

Simplicity is not called in as an additional
criterion for hypothesis selection which is made
necessary by underdetermination of theories. Rather, underdetermination of theories makes necessary, in order to have hypotheses supported, a
sequential process of data gathering and testing,
and out of that process drops simplicity (as
judged by us).[7] But what is the explanation of
the fact that we do find hypotheses that fit the
data at all, and that not all those we think up
are always eliminated at the very next stage?
Scientists choose to work on problems and in

areas where they think they can get results, and leave intractable problems aside. It would need explaining if they were never able to succeed!

Our argument about how simplicity precipitates out of the sequential process would apply to any situation in which:

1. Instances of some type of thing T are generated.
2. The instances can be ordered along some dimension D.
3. Those T's which are generated early tend to cluster around and eventually exhaust one end of the dimension; they are D-er than any T's not yet generated.
4. At each stage, T's that fail to satisfy some criterion C are eliminated.
5. The ordering of the T's along the dimension D does not depend upon their relation to the criterion C.

Since these conditions do not focus especially upon simplicity, any process with a dimension D that satisfies 1 to 5 will eventuate in the survival of the D-est.[8]

The theory we have presented yields simplicity as fall-out from the process, but it gives simplicity, qua simplicity, no role as input, and so does not account for the way we utilize simplicity, seek it, and consciously favor it. For example, the sequential process may involve rejecting previous data on grounds of simplicity, if there is a relatively simple hypothesis that fits D_2 and most of D_1, and only very complicated hypotheses fit D_2 and all of D_1. Some of D_1 may be rejected in order to accept the simpler hypothesis. Or suppose we came upon beings on another planet with a different simplicity ordering and, hence, with a different history of hypothesis testing. They had never tried out what (to us) is the simplest hypothesis about the opera-

tion of their environment. Would we be impressed
by the history of one of their hypotheses? Before we tested theirs against the simplest one
of ours that fit their data, which would we believe? If ours, even though it hadn't yet been
tested by them or us, that also would show that
there's something more to simplicity than merely
the fall-out result of the sequential procedure.

Our story about simplicity as fall-out can be
elabotated to give simplicity some role as input
to the process as well. Once we notice that we
are believing the simplest hypothesis that fits
the data, we can come to pursue a policy of doing
so. The fall-out provides the basis of an induction. Here Quine and Ullian's natural-selection
argument serves. We find ourselves having simple
beliefs about ordinary middle-sized natural
macro objects and situations because those (who
were contemporaries of our ancestors) to whom
these truths seemed complicated left no descen-
dants among our contemporaries. Also, since the
process of sequential testing and tentative acceptance leads us to end up believing the simplest hypothesis compatible with our data, a
retrospective look will find that simplicity is
successful, that the successful are simple. Even
more so because, as Quine and Ullian note, our
culturally transmitted standards of simplicity
tend to change so as to fit more neatly what we
actually have ended up accepting.[9]

Since the past exhibits a correlation between
the simplicity and the success of a hypothesis,
a modest induction - to be sure, a simple one,
but that's how we tend to think - leads us to
conclude that these do go together and, hence,
to rely upon simplicity. There are various ways
to imagine the induction; one is as an inference
to the best explanation.[10] We start with an observed connection between simplicity and accep-

tance by scientific procedures, and we explain
this by positing connections between each of
these and truth: we posit that acceptance of hypotheses by scientific procedures is correlated
with their truth (there is independent reason to
believe this, since scientific procedures eliminate *false* hypotheses that conflict with the data)
and that the simplicity of hypotheses is connected with their truth (that the simpler of competing hypotheses is more likely to be true). These
last two connections, if sufficiently tight, would
imply and explain the observed correlation. One,
therefore, might be led, in order to explain the
observed connection, to infer a real connection
of simplicity with truth. This account is admit-
tedly rough, but fortunately we require no precise and rigorous inference for a plausible account of how one might actually arrive at a
trust in simplicity. It might appear, however,
that this account is vitiated by circularity. For
the conclusion that simplicity and truth really
are connected is inferred in order to explain
the observed connection of simplicity with acceptance by scientific procedures. Yet there are
other more complicated explanations of this observed connection. So in making the inference to
the connection of simplicity with truth (and not
some inference to a more complicated explanation)
isn't a simplicity maxim already being used? A
simple inference was made, but simplicity was not
consciously pursued. Since our purpose is not to
justify simplicity but to explain how it might
come to be consciously pursued as a goal, we
legitimately may place the wisdom of pursuing
simplicity as the conclusion of an inference
which instances simplicity without itself pursuing it.

    Starting only with simplicity as fall-out, we
end up trusting in simplicity and using it in

the process. Seeking simplicity affects the sequential procedure in two ways: first, we try to
think up especially simple hypotheses, and second
we consciously use simplicity as a criterion in
selecting among hypotheses. Thereby the sequential process even more effectively yields simplicity.[11]

This lovely picture, unfortunately, is marred
by the fact that our fall-out explanation of
simplicity, if correct, undercuts the induction
that leads to trusting in simplicity. If the
fall-out tale is the best explanation of the observed correlation between success and simplicity, then the inductive extrapolation that leads
to trust in simplicity is blocked; that is, it
is unreasonable. But still, it may have occurred
(and *not* unreasonably then, since no one then
had the fall-out explanation), and that induction may be the actual explanation of our current trust in simplicity.

Does and should accepting all this undermine
trust in simplicity? It would be pleasant to
bring things full circle by having the trust
tenaciously hang on. After all, the hypothesis
that there is a real connection between the simplicity and the success of a hypothesis entered
the field before my explanation did; that hypothesis fit past data, and new data were gathered
which the hypothesis also fit, and so that hypothesis came to be accepted. In accordance with
the method of tenacity, that hypothesis and the
accompanying trust in simplicity will and should
continue; that hypothesis should not be displaced
merely because some new hypothesis has been
thought up which also fits the data.

But even if we granted this application of the
method of tenacity, our confidence in simplicity
might well be short-lived; for the next step,
now that another hypothesis has entered the field,

would be to use the hypothesis to generate different predictions, to test them selectively, to
discover which survives, and to end up believing
that one.

However, I find myself *already* believing the
explanation I have offered. This might be because
the two explanations, mine and the one positing
a real connection between simplicity and truth,
do not fit exactly the same currently available
data, because mine already explains more. But
another view of the matter is more fun.

My explanation involving fall-out and the induction based upon the fall-out is, I believe,
simple, elegant, forceful, and lovely. More so,
surely, than the reigning hypothesis of a real
connection between simplicity and truth. The
simplest and most elegant hypothesis is that
there is no real connection between simplicity
(and elegance) and truth. Now if I accept this
hypothesis as true (partly) *because* it is so
simple and elegant, and the proponent of a real
connection between simplicity (and elegance) on
the one hand and truth on the other rejects this
hypothesis as true because it denies any such
connection, with whose petard is each of us
hoist?

Footnotes:

This essay is part of a larger one written
in 1974 to appear in *The Philosophy of W.V. Quine*
(La Salle, Ill.: Open Court, forthcoming), and
has been deleted from that one in order to appear
separately here. It is especially appropriate
that it appear in a volume of essays in honor of
Sidney Morgenbesser, since it was in his classes
that I first encountered the writings of Quine
and issues about simplicity.

1. W.V. Quine, "On Simple Theories of a Complex World," in his *The Ways of Paradox* (Cambridge, Mass.; Harvard, 1976), p. 255.

2. *The Web of Belief* (New York: Random House, 1970), p. 47.

3. I doubt whether Quine is correct in his particular claims about how simplicity might artifactually be favored by our procedures. Some experimental setups allow us to get evidence for similarities but not for differences. Do none work in the reverse direction? And Quine's claim that if we add a parameter we have modified a hypothesis whereas if we change a parameter the hypothesis is refuted, seems merely verbal (is it "refuted" or "altered"?), and too fragile to support or produce even an artifact of the procedures.

4. See Hilary Putnam, "'Degree of Confirmation' and Inductive Logic", in P.A. Schilpp ed., *The Philosophy of Rudolf Carnap* (La Salle, Ill.: Open Court, 1963), esp. pp. 770-774. Refinements of our approach to simplicity, I hope, would apply to more complicated and intricate versions of this simple model.

5. It is an oversimplification to say that only data gathered *after* a hypothesis is formulated support it. (Even the oversimplification should be put more accurately so that it ignores *when* the hypothesis was formulated, and concentrates on whether or not the hypothesis was *designed* to fit the data.) A newly accepted hypothesis (accepted on the basis of independent data gathered after its formulation) will *inherit* as support the data of the hypothesis it supplants, even though the new hypothesis was geared to explain the previously known data. So there is a historical *change* in whether data support a hypothesis; data that don't at one time support a hypothesis (because the hypothesis was dreamed up to fit those data) may come later to support it, when that hy-

pothesis is accepted because it also fits new
data that refute the previously reigning hypothesis. This phenomenon of inherited support makes
it (even more) likely that the method of tenacity will yield much of the maxim of conservatism
about theory change.

6. More accurately, that subset of the original batch containing all those as simple as H_S,
including H_S itself.

7. Note that we have presented, thus far, an
invisible-hand explanation of simplicity. [See
my *Anarchy, State, and Utopia*, (New York: Basic
Books, 1974), pp. 18–22.] There may be still
another connection between simplicity and underdetermination of theories. Underdetermination of
theories makes it too easy to find a hypothesis
that fits the data, and so the fact that one
fits isn't (much) support for it. Whereas being
a hypothesis that data gathered afterwards fit
is harder. But there might be yet other hard
conditions to fulfill. Is a hypothesis supported
if it fulfills *any* hard-to-fulfill previously
formulated condition C, or must something independently be said for C as connected with truth?
To whatever extent the former gives support,
then, having a certain degree of simplicity will
count for a hypothesis, if it is not easy
to find a simple hypothesis that fits the
data.

8. If "simpler than" was not merely some
structural relationship between hypotheses or
theories, but also depended upon the way the hypotheses handled the data at hand, then the argument would not go through. For in *this* case H_1,
..., H_m might each be simpler than *any* other
hypothesis to explain data D_1, yet at the second
stage still another hypothesis could be simpler
than any one of these in relation to the data
$D_1 + D_2$. (I owe this observation to Walter Gil-

bert.) Thus the argument applies only to notions
of simplicity which satisfy 5. Note also that
the conditions do not mention or require multiple generation of T's at any stage. Though presumably the more there are, the quicker there
will be convergence to the D-est.

9. Might the *whole* truth about simplicity be
that standards of simplicity change to fit what
we believe? No, for we still think some hypotheses that were rejected earlier (e.g., circular
planetary orbits) are simpler than what we currently believe. There is no psychological process
that creates a simplicity gradient that peaks at
our current beliefs.

10. Gilbert Harman, "The Inference to the Best
Explanation," *Philosophical Review*, LXXIV, 1
(January 1965): 88-95.

11. When we seek simplicity in this way, the
total process whereby we end up with simplicity
is no longer merely an invisible-hand process,
though it is based on one. The invisible-hand
character of even the original fall-out process
would be undermined if part of the explanation
of why (in that process) we think up the hypotheses we do is that they are simple; that is,
if we tend to think them up *because* they're
simple. On the view we have presented, we think
them simple because we tend to think them up.

I need hardly mention that I do not claim
that the view presented here is the *complete*
story about simplicity. But so intractable is
the topic of the real connection between simplicity and truth that it is progress, I think, to
chip away at simplicity, reducing what remains
for a (metaphysical?) theory to explain.

"UNDER A DESCRIPTION"

Mark
Steiner

One of the important insights I gained from Sidney Morgenbesser's teaching is that *all explanation is relative to description*. By this Morgenbesser meant that by redescribing the explanans and the explanandum (the "explainer" and the "explained") of an explanation one can turn it into a nonexplanation. And the opposite is also true. Whether *A* explains *B* depends on how they are described. (I am being deliberately vague meanwhile about what kind of variables '*A*' and '*B*' are.) Of course, literally speaking, one doesn't describe or redescribe the explanans and explanandum, since these are usually understood to be sentences, which are used in an explanation - not described. What Morgenbesser meant was that by redescribing entities, *realia*, mentioned in an explanation we can nullify its explanatory power - and vice versa, by redescribing we can restore or invest a nonexplanation with explanatory power.

Morgenbesser's insight was corroborated for me by Donald Davidson's masterful essay, "Causal Relations."[1] Davidson here asserted that what are real, what are redescribable, are *events*. Events stand to one another, or do not stand to one another, in a causal relation, which is a logically primitive, two-place relation. If *a* and *b* are events such that *a* causes *b*, then *a* causes *b* under any description - the causal relation is thoroughly extensional. If Galbraith was right in saying that the Depression was caused by the Great Crash, and the Great Crash was in fact the most ridiculous event in the 20's, then the most ridiculous event in the 20's caused the Depression. On the other hand, how one describes the

cause and the effect can determine whether or
not we have causally explained the effect *under
the descriptions*. And here the views of Morgenbesser and Davidson converge. So from here on in
I shall refer to the "Morgenbesser/Davidson insight" - only because it was impressed upon me by
these two philosophers.

Though the Morgenbesser/Davidson insight can
sound simple enough, it is often ignored. Here
are two examples.

Consider, first, the thesis of universal determinism. Often quantum-mechanical phenomena are
said to refute it. Imagine, for example, a black
box with a door, an apparatus to measure the
"spin" of an incoming electron ("up" or "down"),
and two lights, red and green, which go on if
the spin is found to be "up" or "down," respectively. Introduce an electron at the proverbial
"time *t*" and watch the lights. Suppose the red
light lights. Physics says that if the electron
had been "prepared" to have a 50-50 chance that
the spin will be "up", then there is no way to
have predicted the outcome. Determinism is thus
refuted.

But is it? From the Morgenbesser/Davidson thesis, it follows that determinism can be formulated in two nonequivalent ways:

(a) every event has a cause.

(b) every event, under any description, has
an explanation.

If we adopt formulation (a), our experiment, if
anything, *confirms* determinism! For the event
of the red light going on at "time *t*" could be
redescribed "light going on at 'time *t*'" - and
under that description, which is the redescrip-
tion of the same event, the event could have
been predicted. If we adopt (b), of course, then
determinism *is* refuted by our "experiment." But
thesis (b) is in any event implausible in the

extreme and would in any case have to be tamed.
I shall not attempt to tame it here.

Now there may be other experiments in quantum
mechanics that refute determinism even in formulation (a). Such an experiment[2] might simply be
to observe a heavy atom to see if anything causes it to break up. In fact, it decays spontaneously. True, a *statistical* explanation could
be given, based on the uncertainty principle,
according to which the probability of decay in-
creases with the length of time we wait. But no
antecedent event occurs to trigger it off; it
just happens. I protest not against the conclusion that quantum mechanics refutes determinism,
but against obliviousness to how the refutation
goes, obliviousness which is apparently related
to ignoring the Morganbesser/Davidson insight.

A second application of our insight is, again,
a criticism of an argument, rather than of a
conclusion. I speak of Carl Hempel's argument[3]
that the door must be opened to statistical explanation, because we refer to explanation when
"deductive-nomological" explanation is not in
the cards. His example: a patient gets the measles upon exposure to the disease. There is no
doubt what caused the disease in our patient;
yet at best we have only a "statistical covering law" to the effect that a high percentage
of patients exposed to the measles get the disease.

Now aside from the objection, made by Isaac
Levi,[4] that there is really no such thing as a
"statistical covering law", there is the more
elementary point that we can know that one's
exposure to a disease caused the disease even
if the observed percentage of illness upon exposure has been negligible. When we say that a
certain event, such as exposure to the disease
at "time *t*," caused the illness, we don't mean

that that event, *under the description* "exposure," etc., causally explains the disease at a
later time. What we mean is that both the cause
and the effect here *can be* redescribed in such a
way that under their new descriptions the cause
and effect exemplify an invariable regularity.
Hempel, then, errs in not distinguishing cause
from causal explanation. But, again, my complaint
is against Hempel's argument, not his conclusion.
Undoubtedly there are statistical explanations,
such as the quantum-mechanical explanation of the
heavy atom mentioned earlier. (Of course, if Levi
is right - and I am persuaded that he is - Hempel
may be mistaken also about the nature of such
statistical explanation, since he invokes non-
existent "statistical covering laws.")

We can see from the above that the "dispute"
between Hempel and Michael Scriven[5] concerning
the necessity of including laws in an explanation
of a particular event, was totally unnecessary.
Scriven, citing everyday ascriptions of cause and
effect, argued that we can know the explanation
of, say, the stain on the carpet (I knocked over
a bottle of ink) knowing no laws whatever. Hempel,
responding, maintained that such "explanations"
lose their plausibility as soon as we make precise their explanans and explanandum. In fact,
Scriven and Hempel are talking about two different things. Scriven illustrates our ability to
ascribe causal relations between events without
being able to specify the appropriate descriptions under which the cause would explain the
effect, not merely cause it. Hempel invokes explanation, not causation, in stressing the importance of the descriptions of the explanans and
the explanandum. What Hempel should have said
was that Scriven's argument, though valid, is
irrelevant to the controversy over criteria for
explanation.

A more subtle fallacy concerning explanation, descriptions, and causality, is to be found in a recent work, Bas C. van Fraassen's *The Scientific Image*.[6] In the course of a polemic against a certain type of realist argument favored by Hilary Putnam, J.J.C. Smart, and others - namely, that the nonrealist has no explanation for certain "coincidences" or regularities in observable phenomena, van Fraassen remarks:

> In any case, it seems to me that it is illegitimate to equate being a lucky accident, or a coincidence, with having no explanation. It was by coincidence that I met my friend in the market - but I can explain why he came, so together we can explain how this meeting happened. We call it a coincidence, not because the occurrence was inexplicable, but because we did not severally go to the market in order to meet.

The win over realism is too easy, however. Our meeting in the market, first, is a coincidence not because there is no *explanation* for it, but because the meeting has no *cause*. That is, there is no antecedent event that stands to the meeting as cause to effect. [If we insist upon the term 'explanation' here, we may say that the meeting has no "causal explanation," where a causal explanation is an explanation of an event in which (one of) its cause(s) is cited.] For the event of our meeting at the market at 9:00 a.m. today is the "sum" of two events: my arriving at the market today at 9:00 a.m. and your arriving there then. My arriving at the market at 9:00 a.m. today may have had a cause, and your arriving there at 9:00 a.m. may also have had a cause. But the "sum" of these two causes does not necessarily give us a cause for the "sum" of the two effects, i.e., a cause of our meeting.

There well may be no pair of descriptions under which the "sum" of the causes and the "sum" of the effects, respectively, exemplify a natural law.

In any event, the kind of "coincidence" the realists are talking about is not a one-shot affair, such as our meeting today at the market. Instead, the realists are referring to *regularities* that have no explanation, though each individual "coincidence" may have one. Suppose, for example, we note that a_1 is followed by b_1, a_2 by b_2, and so on. Suppose that, for each n, there are descriptions of a and of b such that under those descriptions the occurrence of a_n explains the occurrence of b_n. It does not follow that we have explained why the b's always follow the a's, at least where the a's and the b's are actually or even potentially infinite in number. For we may have no pair of predicates applicable to the a's and to the b's, respectively, such that each pair (a_n, b_n) exemplifies the *same* natural law.

A fascinating example of just this situation is furnished by the Heisenberg uncertainty principle. When this principle is illustrated in textbooks, students often get the idea that the principle is trivial, in that it adds no new ideas to classical mechanics. For imaginary experiments are set up in an attempt to measure simultaneously the position and the momentum of a particle, and, every time, no matter how ingenious the experiment, the apparatus behaves, classically, like a bull in a china shop, destroying the evidence. What is inexplicable however (without quantum mechanics) is why interactions of totally different kinds should introduce uncertainties related to Planck's constant, for example. The most astonishing example of this was furnished by Bohr in his confrontation with Einstein at the Solvay Conference. Einstein attempted to refute the uncertainty principle by a thought experiment concerning a clock in a box attached to a spring. With this apparatus, he claimed, one could measure simultaneously the exact time and the exact energy of the system. After long hours of thought, Bohr realized that Einstein's own General Theory of Relativity would account for an uncertainty in our knowledge of the time, since, according to that theory, the inhomogeneous gravitational field of the earth would influence the motion of a clock. The Heisenberg principle unifies an otherwise unrelated set of causes under the description 'measurement', and an otherwise unrelated set of effects under the description 'uncertainty', in one natural law. (This argument would seem to favor a realistic interpretation of quantum mechanics, supposing the realist argument in general were valid; whether the realist argument *is* valid, or whether its application to this case is warranted, are subjects too broad to discuss here.)

II

In this section, I shall restrict my remarks to a further elaboration of Davidson's position which I have no reason to believe Morgenbesser would accept. This is Davidson's conception of a "causal law" and of the relationship between causal laws and singular causal statements.

Davidson says that a causal law is a conjunction of two types of generalization, which he calls "S" and "N".[7] An "S" generalization says that every event of type (say) F is followed by an event of type G *which it causes*. An "N" generalization says that every event of type G is preceded, and caused, by an event of type F. (We shall not discuss "N" generalizations in the sequel.)

It is true, of course, that the primitive predicate 'causes' thus appears in the very statement
of the form of the causal law, but Davidson is
not interested in the (legitimate) problem of
analyzing what causality is; he merely wants to
find the logical form of causal laws. This separate task has its own rewards. For, aside from
making progress in Davidson's general program to
discover the "truth conditions," in Tarski's
sense, for yet another realm of English discourse,
Davidson would like to shed light on the relationship between singular causal judgments and general
causal laws:

> The relation in general is...this: if 'a
> caused b' is true, then there are descrip-
> tions of a and b such that the result of
> substituting them for 'a' and 'b' in 'a
> caused b' is entailed by true premises of
> the form of (L) and (P).[8]

In other words, to know that a caused b is to
know that there exist descriptions of these
events so that under these descriptions, a and b
exemplify a causal law. It is not necessary to
know what the law is, just that there is one.
And since a causal law is exceptionless, it will
generally be the case that we cannot cite descriptions under which two events exemplify invariable causal regularities, even when we know that
one of the events caused the other. Nevertheless,
Davidson reasons, we can know that the descriptions exist.

In a footnote (8, p.160), Davidson draws attention to the pitfalls of "quantifying over"
descriptions or, in general, linguistic expressions - "of what language?" he asks. To admit
properties into the universe, and say then that
if a causes b there must exist properties F and G,

such that *Fa* and *Gb* and such that *Fs* are followed by *Gs* - such a position would contradict Davidson's nominalism with respect to properties. I
shall not discuss its motivation here. Yet I
doubt whether nominalism can work here - the elaboration of this doubt is the burden of what follows. For Davidson seems to think that the only
problem with quantifying over expressions is the
"inherent vagueness" of such quantification,
since the language has not been specified.   I
shall argue that there are more serious problems.

Suppose somebody just dropped a bottle on the
sidewalk and it broke. Clearly, the breaking
was caused by the dropping. I know this; hence,
according to Davidson, I know that there exist
appropriate descriptions of these two events
under which the events exemplify a universal,
causal law. Now these descriptions, known by me
to exist, are *not* known by me to exist in present-
day English, even when supplemented by all the
scientific argot presently current. Revisions in
the jargon will undoubtedly be necessary.

Now we could specify an extension of English
that would do the causal trick if we again were
allowed to speak of properties, Ramsey style. We
could just stipulate some new predicate into the
language in order to express whatever property
we need. But then, we might as well go back to
our second-order statement above,which we said
Davidson cannot accept.

The only way out, so far as I can see, is to
affirm - what some linguists would assert anyhow
- that contemporary English already has the expressive power to describe anything worth describing. Any new terms needed to describe something new can be introduced by definition into
the language. Just as, it might be claimed, one
could explain quantum mechanics to an ancient
Greek - so are we certain that we can define any

new terms using the linguistic resources we already have.

But suppose the following assumption to be true, an assumption I find reasonable: the ability of a linguistic community to expand its own vocabulary is sometimes contingent on the occurrence of certain events in the environment. This would be true, for example, if an indexical or demonstrative element were necessarily present at least some of the time where a new term is introduced. It is plausible, for example, that if certain experiments had not been observed, certain samples not been seen, modern scientific English could not have evolved in the way it has. And this could very well be true of future developments. On that assumption, no one today could say, while remaining as before a nominalist with respect to properties, that he *knows* that there are descriptions under which the dropping of the bottle and its breaking exemplify a universal causal law. For he cannot know that the requisite events for introducing the elements of those descriptions will occur. Hence he cannot know that any actual language, strong enough to provide those descriptions, exists. Possible languages there are, of course, but these would hardly make Davidson jump for joy. He'd probably prefer admitting properties. (As Hilary Putnam has pointed out, properties, though intensional in the sense that two different properties may have the same extension, are extensional in that one may identify in science properties from independent theories; witness the identification of heat with mean kinetic energy.)

No allegiance to the theories of Saul Kripke[9] or of Hilary Putnam[10] is necessary for accepting my assumption that the history of the world plays an essential role in the growth of language. But on their theories, mine is a natural assumption to make, even though neither Kripke nor Putnam makes any claims about how terms *must* be introduced. They merely claim to describe how they are introduced.

Yet, on their theories, how could we introduce a term like 'gold' without demonstratives? By its atomic number? But how can we introduce atomic theory without introducing the concept of positive and negative charge? These charges are introduced by specifying what happens to certain substances when they are rubbed by other substances. And how could we specify the substances without samples?

I conclude, then, that we can describe possible histories of the world in which a term like 'gold' could not have been introduced: no sample of the stuff was ever found, and observations necessary for the introduction of the atomic definition of gold were not made. And thus there are serious difficulties in the way of a purely nominalistic theory of the relationship between singular causality and general law, along the lines suggested by Davidson.[11]

Footnotes:

1. *The Journal of Philosophy*, LXIV, 21 (Nov. 9, 1967): 691-703; reprinted in *Essays on Actions and Events* (New York: Oxford, 1980), pp. 149-162. Page references are to the latter source.
2. I am indebted to Yemima Ben-Menahem for this example.
3. *Philosophy of Natural Science* (Englewood Cliffs: Prentice Hall, 1966), p. 58.
4. "Are Statistical Hypotheses Covering Laws?"

Synthese, XX (1969): 297–307.

5. See Hempel, *Aspects of Scientific Explanation* (New York: Macmillan, 1965), pp. 359–364.

6. New York: Oxford, 1980; p. 25.

7. Davidson, p. 158. "S" evidently for "sufficient"; "N" for "necessary."

8. Davidson, pp. 159/60. "(L)" premises are conjunctions of "S" and "N" generalizations, in other words, general laws; "(P)" premises assert that particular events occur(red).

9. *Naming and Necessity* (Cambridge, Mass.: Harvard, 1980).

10. "Explanation and Reference," reprinted in *Mind, Language, and Reality* (New York: Cambridge, 1975).

11. The idea for this paper arose during a conversation with Igal Kvart. I have learned much about the topics of the paper from discussions with Morgenbesser, Charles Parsons, Isaac Levi, and James Higginbotham.

THE IMPREDICATIVITY
OF INDUCTION

Charles
Parsons

According to Gottlob Frege and many logicists
since his time, the principle of mathematical
induction is a consequence of the definition of
natural number. Let 'Na' mean " is a natural
number" and let $A(x)$ be an open sentence. Then
we can take the principle as a rule of inference
that enables us to go from the premises

$$A(0) \qquad Na \rightarrow [A(a) \rightarrow A(Sa)] \qquad Nt$$

to the conclusion $A(t)$, for any term t. In effect,
Frege defined 'Na' as

$$\forall F \ \{[F0 \wedge \forall x(Fx \ \rightarrow \ F(Sx))] \rightarrow Fa\}$$

and then, given his logic (a form of second-
order logic), the principle of induction is indeed a derived rule.

A frequently voiced objection to Frege's view
of induction is that the application of his
definition requires the second-order logic to
be impredicative. It must allow the instantia-
tion of predicates containing second-order
quantifiers for F in the definition of 'N'. We
can see this if we reflect that, in order to
carry out even elementary proofs in number theory,
we need to apply induction in cases where the
predicate $A(x)$ contains the predicate 'N', which,
ex hypothesi, has been defined by second-order
quantification.

I shall use the term 'second-order entity' as
a neutral term for whatever our second-order
variables range over. Different interpretations
will make them Fregean concepts, propositional
functions, sets, classes, or attributes. The

point is that a logic in which Frege's definition yields the instances of induction needed
even for elementary arithmetic must allow instan-
tiation for a universal quantifier of predicates
containing quantification over all second-order
entities; thus these entities are taken to include some defined in terms of quantification
over all of them, a totality to which they themselves belong.

Different attitudes have been taken concerning
the force of this objection, depending on one's
view of impredicativity in general. The most
widely held view is perhaps that it is an objection to taking full second-order logic to be truly
logic, in the sense of consisting of rules that
are basic to all reasoning about objects in
general. Such second-order logic includes, implicitly or explicitly, assumptions as to when a
predicate expresses or stands for a second-order
entity. In particular, it assumes that predicates
containing quantifiers over such entities do so.
Such assumptions are in effect comprehension
axioms and have an existential character; they
are not essentially different from existence
axioms for sets or classes.

The thesis of the present note is that the impredicativity that arises in Frege's attempt to
reduce mathematical induction to a definition is
not a mere artifact of Frege's strategy of reduction. The impredicativity - though not necessarily impredicative second-order logic - remains
if we regard induction in a looser way, as part
of the explanation of the term 'natural number'.
If one explains the notion of natural number in
such a way that induction falls out of the explanation, then one will be left with a similar
impredicativity. The same holds for other domains
of objects obtained by iteration of operations
yielding new objects, beginning with certain

initial objects. It seems that the impredicativity will lose its significance only from points of view that leave it mysterious why mathematical induction is evident. A conclusion I wish to draw from this simple observation is that some impredicativity is inevitable in mathematical concept formation. This contradicts the once-influential view deriving from Poincaré, that it is a clear sign of a vicious circle. At the end of the paper I will comment on some recent views of predicativity, particularly those of Lorenzen and Feferman.

Induction appears to be implicit in our concept of natural number, but there are other ways of capturing this idea than Frege's explicit definition. One way that avoids some of the difficulties of Frege's is viewing the predicate 'natural number' as introduced by an inductive definition. Some would find the term 'definition' inappropriate here, and it is not essential. What we have is a system of rules which serves to explain a newly introduced predicate. Unlike an explicit definition, these rules do not lead to the eliminability in principle of the predicate from contexts in which it occurs, but other arguments can be given for their adequacy. We will assume that we understand the term '0' and an operation S leading from x to its successor Sx. Terms of the form 'SS ... S0' behave like singular terms, but I do not wish to take this too strictly, since I want my remarks to apply to a situation where variables for numbers are substitutional. Moreover, where such variables are understood objectually, nothing is to turn on any claim to the effect that what these terms denote are really natural numbers rather than elements of some other model of arithmetic. My remarks should apply to any instance of the structure of natural

numbers, in particular intuitive models such as
Hilbert's strings of strokes.[1] This is in keeping with the widely held view that the natural
numbers are given only by their structure.

Our conception of the natural numbers is of what
is obtained by beginning with 0 and iterating the
successor operation. Frege tried to capture this
by an explicit definition; the present approach
undertakes to capture it by rules. Obviously it
allows us to assert that 0 is a natural number
and that Sx is a number if x is. Hence we have
the following "introduction rules":

$$N0$$

From Nx infer $N(Sx)$.

Now these rules are understood as the canonical way of arriving at statements to the effect
that something is a natural number; it is only
by virtue of them that something is a natural
number. Thus a common way of stating inductive
definitions is by giving rules like these and
then saying something like, "Nothing is a number
except by these rules." That amounts to taking N
to be *minimal* so that the introduction rules hold.
But now suppose $A(a)$ is a predicate for which the
introduction rules hold:

$$A(0)$$

$$A(x) \rightarrow A(Sx)$$

Then $A(a)$ must be true of any natural number. But
that is just the induction principle. It can be
given the form of an "elimination rule" for N,
that is, a rule of inference that from the above
two premises with the additional premise Nt allows inference of $A(t)$.[2]

There is a very natural picture that arises here: If x is a number, then it is "constructed" by the introduction rules: if we begin with 0, then by a succession of steps from y to Sy we reach x. Then by a parallel succession of steps, we can show that $A(y)$ holds for each y figuring in the construction, and therefore that $A(x)$ holds. In fact, for each x we can construct a *proof* of $A(x)$ by beginning with $A(0)$ and building up by modus ponens, using $A(x) \rightarrow A(Sx)$. As a *proof* of induction, this is circular: the "construction" of x by a *succession* of steps is itself inductively defined, and it is by a corresponding induction that it is established that A holds at each point in the construction. Nonetheless, it is still useful for metamathematical arguments concerning induction in formalized theories, and it is no worse than arguments for the validity of elementary logical rules.

Now evidently the state of affairs that made Frege's definition require impredicative logic also obtains in the present setting: In order to apply the induction rule to prove significant generalizations about numbers, we will have to use predicates containing the predicate 'N'. As originally offered, as a principle cashing in our intention that the numbers should be what is obtained by the introduction rules and those alone, the principle refers to arbitrary predicates, without any assumptions having been made about what counts as a predicate. Like the principles of predicate logic itself, we have a purely formal generalization about predicates, which is not a generalization over a given *domain* of entities and could not be, since it is not determined what predicates will or can be constructed and understood. If our explanation of the natural numbers is successful, then we do understand 'N' as a predicate and indeed as describing a possible

domain for quantification; that is, we are able
to understand quantifiers restricted to N. But
this means that the impredicativity of Frege's
definition survives in the present setting,
since we have explained 'N' in part by a formal
generalization about predicates, which has to
admit as instances predicates containing 'N'
itself.

Our situation can be described as follows:
The alternative to something like the inductive-
definition model of the concept of natural number
(with or without the Fregean reduction) would be
to give it an explanation that is blatantly
circular, such as: the natural numbers are what
is obtained by beginning with 0 and iterating the
successor operation an *arbitrary finite number*
of times, or to take the concept of natural
number as given and the principle of induction
as evident without any explication connecting it
with the concept of natural number. Either alternative seems to me a counsel of philosophical
despair that leaves us with no motivation for the
principle of induction. The explanation we have
includes a generalization about predicates that
includes the predicate 'N' in its scope.

In interpreting both Frege's definition and
our characterization by rules of the predicate
'N', one can ask what is the range of the *first*-
order variables. In some applications of inductive definitions, all the definition aspires to
do is to define a predicate of objects of a
previously given domain, and so we can take first-
order quantifiers to be understood in some independent way. Frege himself seems to have as-
similated his own case to this one in assuming
that first-order quantification is quantification
over *all* objects, in an absolute sense independent of the particular context of inquiry. Such a
view is not very persuasive now. Should we still

interpret our explanation of the notion of natural number as picking out the natural numbers from a previously given domain? One might reply that our conception of the natural numbers is that of a *structure* and therefore does not give individual identities to the objects playing the role of 0, 1, 2, etc.; therefore there should be no unique answer to the question from what domain the natural numbers are picked out or even whether there is one. The generality with which we have proceeded is in keeping with this structuralist view and, therefore, cannot exclude the case where there is a previously given domain: Some instances of the structure of natural numbers are substructures of others, and we might describe such substructures by inductive definitions.

However, to assume that this is always the case is to assume that some infinite structure is given to us independently of our knowledge of the kind of structure the natural numbers instantiate. This may be a domain of mathematical objects such as sets. Or one may, as in nominalist views, claim that one can find in the physical world a realization of the structure of natural numbers, which is therefore to be described by quantifiers ranging over some domain of physical objects. Either of these alternatives has its difficulties, which it would take us too far to go into. My main point concerning the impredicativity of induction is independent of whether the natural numbers (or a representative of their structure that is of some basic significance) are a class of previously given objects.

If there is no such previously given infinite structure, then it is as if we had arrived at the concept of natural number by pulling ourselves up by our conceptual bootstraps, so as to understand the notion of some such structure and convince ourselves of its possibility without having in advance the conception of a domain of objects from which the objects of the structure are picked out.

In my view this is possible for an intuitive model such as the Hilbertian one. Let us suppose for the moment that '0' denotes the symbol '1' (as a type, understood as a spatial configuration), and that, for a given x, Sx is the result of adding another '1' on the right. Then the objects of the model are strings such as

$$1111111111$$

Now evidently this interpretation presupposes that every such string can be extended by the addition of another '1'. In my earlier discussion ("Intuition" 156–158) I argued that this is intuitively evident. Both this proposition and the statement that for any x, $Nx \rightarrow N(Sx)$, obtained from the second introduction rule, are general statements about strings, but they are not obtained by induction. The variable in the second introduction rule is in a way more inclusive than variables over numbers. The thought-experiment that verifies that every string can be extended does not depend on any insight into the specific totality of such strings; this is shown by the fact that in the sense in which a new '1' can be added to any string, it can be added to any bounded geometric configuration.

Although the generality of the variable 'x' in the second introduction rule is more inclusive than a variable over numbers (in the present setting, strings), I do not want to say that it ranges over a more inclusive *totality of objects*. There would not be a convincing answer to the question what that totality is. We could specify the range as something like "object given in space or time." But this very general rubric might go with quite different ways of *individuating* such objects. The generality is akin to the kind of generality Husserl called "formal," characteristic of formal logic. In a sense, we used free variables with a generality interpretation without yet knowing what they ranged over.

If this is our situation, then the impredicativity of induction arises more sharply than before, because it is induction that cashes in our conception of the totality of strings and therefore gives us a predicate that can serve to define the range of variables of quantification that can be used in the formation of predicates. Stated as a general principle, induction is about "all predicates." The predicates that we use are defined by means of basic relations, logical connectives, and quantification over N and other domains that we might come to subsequently. Induction is thus inherently impredicative, because without it we do not have a definite domain for our quantifiers, but we cannot apply it without taking predicates involving quantification over this domain as instances.[3]

It will no doubt occur to the reader that as an "inductive definition" of 'N' the introduction rules and the induction principle are incomplete, no matter what resources are deployed for the formation of predicates. Even to obtain the elementary theory of 0 and S, we need the two additional axioms

$$Sx \neq 0$$

$$Sx = Sy \rightarrow x = y$$

which intuitively express the fact that if the successor operation has been applied a number of times beginning with 0, then its application will still yield something *new*. Evidently, since they

contain identity, they are bound up with the individuation of the objects of the domain. In the
Hilbertian intuitive model, the notion of type
provides the principle of individuation ("Intuition" 153-156), and these axioms seem evident
enough on intuitive grounds. But other points of
view about them are possible, such as Lorenzen's
that they are admissible rules once one has introduced the equality predicate in a similar inductive way.[4] These axioms raise many questions,
but space does not permit going into them here.

We must not take the impredicativity of induction as implying the legitimacy or unavoidability of full second-order logic. Given a
domain D for individual variables, full second-
order logic is naturally understood by taking
second-order variables to range over all subsets
of D. It requires that the "predicates" of objects in D should be closed under second-order
quantification. Nothing we have said implies
this; indeed our picture should suggest rather
the opposite, that the "predicates" talked of in
the induction rule are a quite open-ended and indefinite totality, depending on linguistic and
conceptual resources of whose limits we have no
real conception. That would raise a question
whether second-order quantifiers, in particular
their use to define new predicates as in second-
order logic, can have a definite sense. My own
view is that any such sense that would license
impredicative logic must derive from the concept
of set.[5] That such second-order logic is not
forced upon us at this point is shown by the
fact that a mathematics that assumes the concept
of natural number but from there on is strictly
predicative is perfectly coherent.

Up to now our main argument has consisted essentially in applying to the case of the natural

numbers a well-known argument for the impredicativity of inductive definitions, in particular
so-called "generalized inductive definitions" in
which the introduction rules for an inductively
defined predicate P may contain general statements involving P. For example, in the course of
presenting his own analysis of predicativity,
Solomon Feferman offers such an argument for the
impredicativity of the usual definitions of
Kleene's set O of recursive ordinal notations.[6]
A simpler example to illustrate the same point
is the notion of accessibility for a relation R
of natural numbers, which we will assume to be
a linear ordering. Intuitively, 'Acc(a)' means
that transfinite induction holds for the relation $\{<x, y>: xRa \wedge xRy\}$; it can therefore be
given an obvious second-order explicit definition. In the inductive definition, the introduction rule takes the form

From $xRa \rightarrow$ Acc(x) infer Acc(a).

whereas the elimination rule or induction principle says that if $A(x)$ satisfies the above
closure condition, then it holds for all acces-
sible numbers, i.e.,

From $\forall y[yRx \rightarrow A(y)] \rightarrow A(x)$ and Acc(t)

infer $A(t)$.

If R is one of the primitive recursive orderings
used in proof theory, the notion of accessibility
can be used for formal derivations of transfinite
induction; standard derivations in texts on proof
theory can be recast in this form.[7] One comes
rather quickly to need to use instances of the induction schema where the formula $A(a)$ contains
'Acc', and for longer orderings this cannot be re-

placed by other means that can be recognized as predicative.[8]

The sense of "predicative" in which this last remark holds is captured by the beautiful and persuasive analysis of predicative provability of Feferman and Schütte.[9] According to this analysis, generalized inductive definitions like that of 'Acc' and O are impredicative principles of proof. I shall not enter here into the details of the analysis, which are complex. It turns on looking at transfinite iterations of different methods of enlarging the means of expression and proof of formal systems. At no point is any restriction placed on ordinary induction on natural numbers. The considerations advanced above might suggest a doubt as to whether what is predicative according to this analysis really is so. However, in one respect pressing this point would misconstrue the intent of the analysis. What it is intended to capture is predicativity *given the natural numbers*, where the problem of predicativity is raised in the first instance about reasoning about sets of natural numbers, and then perhaps extended to further reasoning about sets and functions. Thus Feferman writes:

> According to this [the predicative conception], only the natural numbers can be regarded as "given" to us.... In contrast, sets are created by man to act as convenient abstractions ... from particular conditions or definitions ("Systems," 1/2).[10]

Feferman and others have suggested that an analysis of predicativity should describe the concepts and principles that are in some way implicit in the conception of natural number. The manner in which reasoning about classes, sets, or functions is allowed is based on the conception of classes as extensions of predicates, and so a generalization about classes (or sets) must be cashable as a generalization about the predicates of which the classes are the extensions. Such generalizations about predicates will be semantical in character, involving satisfaction or truth. Thus semantic reflection, or what Lorenzen some years ago called "logical reflection," is the manner in which second-order entities are understood.[11] One can obtain considerable strength by iterating such reflection into the transfinite, as in the construction of the ramified hierarchy. But on the Feferman-Schütte conception, the iteration is constrained by the requirement that its stages (ordinals) be given in advance as well-founded. In contrast, a generalized inductive definition like that of 0 or 'Acc' allows objects to fall into the extension of the introduced predicate by iteration of the introduction rule, but the stages needed are described only by the definition itself or another comparable one. This is exactly parallel to the situation with the natural numbers.

The Feferman-Schütte conception of predicative mathematics is constructed from elements that are very basic and deeply entrenched parts of our conceptual apparatus: either first-order logic or a second-order logic with quite minimal comprehension assumptions, the notion of natural number, and semantic reflection. Describing the limits of what can be accomplished by these means not only was a technical achievement but served to delineate a natural conceptual boundary. Some of the discussion of constructivity and predicativity in the immediately preceding period shows the lack of a clear distinction between this apparatus and a more generous conception that would extend it at least by certain generalized inductive definitions. Feferman's criticism of

Lorenzen and Wang on this point is justified
("Systems" 5). However, I shall argue that the
distinction can be seen as one between two senses
of predicativity.

If one grants a certain impredicative character
to ordinary induction, the issue between Feferman
and the earlier writers appears in a somewhat
different light. It is hard to see how a mode of
concept formation which involves a "vicious
circle" in the case of generalized inductive
definitions does not involve such a circle in the
case of the natural numbers themselves. Granted,
then, that Feferman has correctly characterized
the limits of predicativity relative to the
natural numbers, the case that the traditional
arguments deriving from Poincaré show that this
is the limit of acceptable mathematics is weak-
ened.

Lorenzen usually characterized his position as
"constructivist" or "critical" (in the writings
cited in notes 4, 11, and 12) and to that extent
did not depend on a particular interpretation of
predicativity. However, he did specifically claim
that generalized inductive definitions are predicative, though to be sure in a joint paper. [12]
Clearly, my view is that this claim is mistaken.
However, at this point one should make another
distinction. The primary sense of impredicativity
applies to sets or classes, and they are said to
be impredicatively defined if they are given by
abstracts involving quantification over some
totality of sets to which they themselves belong.
This extends readily to other cases; for example
Russell's diagnosis of the semantical paradoxes
involves pointing out that sentences such as 'The
proposition expressed by my present utterance is
false' or 'Every proposition asserted by a
Cretan is false', asserted by Epimenides the
Cretan, will, when taken naively, express propo-

sitions that are in the range of their own quantifiers. In the present case, inductive definitions are said to be impredicative because they involve introducing a predicate by rules or axiom schemata such that expressions containing the predicate itself have to be admitted as within their scope. All these cases are of the type where the question of a vicious circle was raised by Poincaré, Russell, and Weyl.

However, if we reflect on the motives of the original critique of impredicativity, an underlying conception was that classes or sets are extensions of predicates and, therefore, that the circle lay in speaking of sets that could not be the extensions of predicates antecedently understood. This conception is quite clear in the writings of Poincaré and Weyl.[13] In the case of Russell it is perhaps not so clear because of his unclear conception of the relation of propositional functions to language. However, his original adoption of a vicious-circle principle was as a guiding principle in the construction of a "no-class" theory, in which classes were to be eliminable by contextual definition, and propositional functions were treated in a completely predicative way.

Historically, ~~what has~~ served to defuse the critique of impredicativity is set-theoretic realism, with its attendant abandonment of the idea that sets are extensions of predicates in a given language, so that the domain of sets one can quantify over has to be seen as potential, expanding as one's linguistic resources expand, in particular by quantifying over totalities of sets previously arrived at. Russell took the realistic attitude in a somewhat half-hearted way in introducing his axiom of reducibility, of which he said that it accomplishes "what common sense effects by the admission of classes."[14]

To return to Lorenzen, it is quite clear that
he is especially concerned to avoid this set-
theoretic realism, what he calls "naive" concepts
of set, relation, and function.[15] His concept of
set is just the one that underlies the critique
of Poincaré and Weyl, even though the issue of a
"vicious circle" does not occupy the center of
his attention.

Since it is generally agreed that there is a
coherent conception of "constructive" mathematics
which goes beyond the predicative as characterized by Feferman and incorporates theories of
generalized inductive definitions but which still
does not presuppose set-theoretic realism, it
might seem that our discussion can just end with
the observation that Lorenzen held such a constructive conception. However, in my view there
is still a remark worth making, which justifies
to some extent the use of the word 'predicative'
by Lorenzen and Myhill. Constructivists have not
always been very explicit about the relation of
higher-order entities to language; indeed Brou-
wer's own radical view that mathematics is essentially independent of language works against
such clarity, particularly in his notion of
species (i.e., class). The term 'impredicative'
was coined by Poincaré because of his view of
sets or classes as essentially extensions of
predicates; in a terminology I have used elsewhere, the language of classes serves as a means
of generalizing predicate places in a language.
But then that the classes in the range of a
generalization should be the extensions of predicates antecedently understood is entirely natural.
Now if we call "predicative" such a view of
classes, the question arises whether it is violated by inductive definitions. If it is not, it
will give a sense in which Lorenzen's view is
predicative, and a divergence of two possible

meanings of predicativity.

Now it is characteristic of the inductive definitions we have been considering that they are introductions of *predicates* and not in the first instance definitions or characterizations of *sets*. Because semantic reflection comes so readily to us, once we have understood such a predicate as the natural-number predicate or an accessibility predicate we will almost immediately talk of its extension. However, there is an essential conceptual order here, which places the understanding of the predicate before the apprehension of its extension as an object. There is, to be sure, a subtle difference between the situation we are envisaging, where we eschew set-theoretic realism and treat the inductive rules themselves as giving us understanding of the predicate, and a situation where one assumes set theory and where moreover what is being introduced is a predicate of objects in a domain that has been recognized to be a set. In the latter case the axiom of separation implies that there *is* a set that is its extension; there is therefore a proof of its existence which does not use any semantic concept. At least if one is prepared to hold that particular instances of a schema like the axiom of separation can be seen to be true independently of the general principle, it follows that semantic reflection does not enter into one's insight that there is such a set as $\{x: Nx \land Acc(x)\}$. However, this does not change the essential point: that one's understanding of the predicate is prior to the insight that the set exists.

Thus in my opinion Lorenzen does not violate the limitations of his own concept in admitting generalized inductive definitions, and the divergence of two senses of predicativity does indeed exist. Though this observation is a partial

defense of Lorenzen against Feferman, clearly the
meaning of the term 'impredicative' underlying
both Feferman's analysis and the earlier part of
this paper is so firmly entrenched that it is now
the more appropriate way to use the term, particularly since there is no ready alternative term
for the same idea.

In these remarks I have bypassed an issue about
the status of higher-order entities in constructive mathematics. According to many constructivists,
the notion of *function* enters essentially into
the interpretations of quantifiers, even over such
objects as numbers. The context in which the issue
arises is explanation of the meaning of statements
in intuitionistic theories in terms of what would
count as a proof of them, worked out formally in
theories of constructions.[16] In intuitionistic
mathematics, we no longer have the mutual reducibility of the notions of set and function which
obtains in classical mathematics. A theory may
be compatible with the idea of sets and classes
as arising by semantic reflection and still
depend on a notion of function of a different
nature. In my view this issue primarily affects
the claim of the sort of conception I have been
discussing to be constructive, which has not
been a primary concern in the present paper. At
all events the conception of function that on
this view would be required is weaker than the
set-theoretic conception in that the functions
that would have to be assumed are intuitively
effectively calculable.

Finally, since this paper is being written for
Sidney Morgenbesser, I cannot evade completely a
nagging doubt that I am sure would arise in his
mind. My argument has rested on a model in which
induction is constitutive of the meaning of the
term 'natural number'. But, one will ask, is
there even a fact of the matter as to what

belongs to the meaning of 'natural number' as opposed to merely being true (even if necessarily) of all natural numbers? Does not my discussion flirt rather dangerously with the notion of "conceptual truth" or "meaning postulate"?

A proper reply to this objection would require a paper in itself. I will confine myself to two brief remarks. First, even if this model is taken literally it still does not remove every "factual" aspect from the principles of arithmetic: that we *understand* a concept explained in this way and have consistency in its applications is not something we could establish by other more evident or fundamental principles; our possession of a concept of number is a sort of *Faktum der Vernunft*. Second, in the present context a purely dialectical reply to the objection is possible: if there is no such fact of the matter in the case of the concept of natural number itself, then on the same grounds there should be no such fact of the matter in the case of notions introduced by generalized inductive definitions. Thus the main thesis of this paper, that as far as the specific issue of impredicativity goes ordinary induction is in the same boat as these higher inductions, still stands.[17]

Footnotes:

1. D. Hilbert and P. Bernays, *Grundlagen der Mathematik I* (Berlin: Springer, 1934, 2nd ed., 1968), §2. The sense in which this model is intuitive is discussed in my "Mathematical Intuition," *Proceedings of the Aristotelian Society*, LXXX (1979/80): 145–168. Cited hereafter as "Intuition."

2. As our terminology suggests, the introduction rules and induction can serve as introduction and elimination rules for 'N' in a natural-deduction formalization of arithmetic. In such a formulation, the antecedent $A(x)$ in the second premise of induction can be replaced by a premise to be discharged.

3. This seems to be the view of Michael Dummett, who says that "the notion of 'natural number' ... is impredicative," for the reasons we have given. See "The Philosophical Significance of Gödel's Theorem," in *Truth and Other Enigmas* (Cambridge, Mass.: Harvard, 1978), p. 199. Dummett does not apply his viewpoint to issues concerning predicativity and inductive definitions in general.

4. Paul Lorenzen, *Einführung in die operative Logik und Mathematik* (Berlin etc.: Springer, 1955), p. 134.

5. "Sets and Classes," *Noûs*, VIII, 1 (March 1974): 1-12, pp. 8/9.

6. "Systems of Predicative Analysis," *The Journal of Symbolic Logic*, XXIX, 1 (March 1964): 1-30, p. 5. Cited hereafter as "Systems."

7. For example, this is true of the work of §21 of Kurt Schütte, *Proof Theory* (Berlin etc.: Springer, 1977), which is predicative by the Feferman-Schütte criterion discussed below, or of §22 of Schütte, *Beweistheorie* (Berlin etc.: Springer, 1960), which is not. On the latter, cf. his "Logische Abgrenzungen des Transfiniten," in Max Käsbauer and Franz von Kutschera (eds.), *Logik und Logikkalkül* (Freiburg and München: Alber, 1962), pp. 105-114, at p. 110. To handle the ordering dealt with in §29 of *Proof Theory*, one needs arbitrary finite iteration of inductive definitions.

8. If the inductive definition of accessibility is our only means of proof beyond arithmetic, we need to use the elimination rule with predi-

cates containing 'Acc' even in some cases that
are clearly predicative given the natural
numbers. Does this cast doubt on our argument
for the impredicativity of ordinary induction?
In the present situation, such prima facie im-
predicativities can be replaced by other methods
of proof such as ramified second-order reasoning
with levels already established as well-founded.
No such alternatives are in sight in the case of
ordinary induction. Nonetheless, some further
logical analysis to reinforce the point would be
desirable.

9. Feferman, "Systems." This is still the best
source for his motivating ideas and for the statement of the most basic technical results, although
his analysis is refined and extended in later
papers.

Schütte offered an analysis based on the same
basic ideas and obtained independently some of
the relevant technical results but did not carry
the matter as far as Feferman, mainly because
the only form of predicative analysis that he
considered was based on the ramified hierarchy.
In "Logische Abgrenzungen" (see note 7) he
presents his ideas very clearly and describes
his results informally.

10. Schütte is not so explicit on this point.

11. Lorenzen, "Logical Reflection and Formalism," *The Journal of Symbolic Logic*, XXIII, 3
(September 1958): 241-249, p. 244. Cf. Feferman's
recent characterization of predicative analysis
as the "strong reflective closure" of first-
order arithmetic, in "Gödel's Incompleteness
Theorems and the Reflective Closure of Theories,"
forthcoming in *The Journal of Symbolic Logic*.

12. Lorenzen and John Myhill, "Constructive
Definition of Certain Analytic Sets of Numbers,"
The Journal of Symbolic Logic, XXIV, 1 (March
1959): 37-49, pp. 47/8. Hao Wang also proposes

that generalized inductive definitions be included in predicative theories, for example, in *A Survey of Mathematical Logic* (Peking: Science Press, and Amsterdam: North Holland, 1962), ch. XXV, §5. On p. 644, there is intimation of a *ceteris paribus* argument like that of the present note.

13. Though I find it clear enough, in Poincaré it is not quite so explicit, or so clearly disengaged from other considerations such as rejection of the actual infinite, perhaps because of his negative attitude toward symbolic logic. But he makes quite clear that he expects sets to be definable, most explicitly in the first essay of *Dernières Pensées* (Paris: Flammarion, 1913, 2nd ed. 1926); see especially the criticism of Cantor's diagonal argument in §6.

For Weyl, see the analysis of the concept of set in *Das Kontinuum* (Leipzig: Veit, 1918), §5, and its polemical use in "Der *circulus vitiosus* in der heutigen Begründung der Analysis," *Jahresbericht der Deutschen Mathematiker-Vereinigung*, XXVIII (1919): 85-92.

14. "Mathematical Logic as Based on the Theory of Types," in *Logic and Knowledge* (London: Allen & Unwin, 1956), p. 81.

15. "Logical Reflection and Formalism," pp. 246/7.

16. One sees this clearly in W.W. Tait's characterization of the mathematics that can be obtained *without* presupposing a general concept of function. See "Finitism," *The Journal of Philosophy*, LXXVIII, 9 (September 1981): 524-546.

17. I wish to thank Isaac Levi and Wilfried Sieg for helpful comments.

SOME CONCEPTUAL SHIFTS IN THE STUDY OF LANGUAGE

Noam Chomsky

The study of generative grammar, initiated
about 25-30 years ago in its modern form, of
course has many antecedents. Nevertheless, the
research program then initiated was based on a
significant shift in focus in the study of
language, leading to many new questions and new
versions of older ones. Since then, this program has been running its course - in many
directions, in fact, of which I will consider
only one. There are indications that a new
shift of focus is now taking place, one that is
narrower, more technical, more theory-internal,
but, I think, rich in promise. It seems an
appropriate moment for an attempt to evaluate
what has been achieved and what went wrong,
exploiting the advantages of hindsight to clarify the issues that have been at stake. That
would be an ambitious project. Here, I will
keep to some preliminary observations.

The first shift in focus was from the study
of language regarded as an externalized object
to the study of grammar regarded as a state of
the mind, a relatively stable component of
transitory mental states of the mature speaker.
Structural and descriptive linguistics,
behavioral psychology, and other contemporary
approaches tended to view a language as a collection of actions, or utterances ("the totality of utterances that can be made in a
speech-community"; Bloomfield, 1926), or
linguistic forms paired with meanings or in a
stimulus-response nexus, or as a system of
linguistic forms or events. From this point of
view, a grammar is a collection of descriptive
statements concerning the externalized

language, which is the real object of study
(or, taking grammar to be a feature of externalized language, "the meaningful arrangements
of forms in a language constitute its grammar";
Bloomfield, 1933, p. 163). Grammar is a
derivative notion; the linguist may select the
grammar one way or another as long as its
statements are true of the objects that constitute the externalized language. The problem of
accounting for the unbounded character of the
externalized language was not squarely
addressed. As for universal grammar (UG), to
the extent that such a study was recognized as
legitimate, UG would consist of "inductive generalizations" true of many or all languages
(Bloomfield, 1933, p. 26). Some appeared to
deny the possibility of the enterprise, for
example, Martin Joos, who advocated what he
called "the American (Boas) tradition that
languages could differ from each other without
limit and in unpredictable ways" (Joos, 1957).
Earlier, Edward Sapir had characterized
"speech" (or "language," used interchangeably
in this context) as "a human activity that
varies without assignable limit," "a merely
conventional system of sound symbols" (Sapir,
1933, p. 4). While such formulations can hardly
have been intended literally, they do express a
widespread attitude of the time, though there
certainly were major contributions to what we
might call UG, for example, the theory of distinctive features in phonology, which greatly
influenced structuralist studies in other
fields.

Generative grammar shifted the focus of study
from actual or potential behavior, or the products of behavior, to the system of knowledge
that underlies the use and understanding of
language, and more deeply, to the innate

endowment that makes it possible for humans to
attain such knowledge. A generative grammar is
not a set of statements about externalized
objects selected in some manner; rather it purports to depict what one knows when one knows a
language (or, to be more exact, one central
aspect of such knowledge): that is, what has
been learned, as supplemented by innate principles. And UG is a characterization of these
innate, biologically determined principles,
which constitute one component of the human
mind. We may think of a particular grammar,
say, of English, as assigning a status to every
relevant physical event. From these, the externalized language can be selected in various
ways; how one chooses to draw its boundaries is
not a very significant question, so it appears.
Its status is similar to that of other derived
objects, say, the set R of rhyming pairs, an
"externalized object" which is determined by
the internalized grammar that constitutes the
knowledge attained. In fact, the status of the
externalized language L is even less clear than
that of R, since the latter is determinate,
while the bounds of L are rather arbitrary.

This shift of focus was very much in order,
for two main reasons. First, externalized
languages, however characterized, are not real
world objects, but are artificial, somewhat
arbitrary, and perhaps not very interesting
constructs. In contrast, a mentally represented
grammar and UG are real objects, part of the
physical world, where we understand mental
states and representations to be physically
encoded in some manner. Statements about particular grammars or about UG are true or false
statements about steady states attained or the
initial state (assumed fixed for the species),
each of which is a definite real-world object,

situated in space-time and entering into causal
relations. UG, given experience, becomes a
particular grammar; the latter enters into
various systems of language use. (Note that
the thrust of these remarks would not be
changed if one were to assume a less direct
relation between a grammar representing
knowledge attained and the computational systems proposed as theoretical models for various
aspects of language use). Statements about the
externalized language, however it is characterized, have a status that is much less clear,
since there is no corresponding real-world
object. To put it differently, externalized
language, however construed, is at a further
remove from mechanisms than particular grammar
or UG, at a higher level of abstraction.
Correspondingly, the concept raises a host of
new problems, and it is not clear that they are
worth addressing given the artificial nature of
the construct.

With this shift of focus, linguistics becomes
in principle part of biology. As a discipline,
linguistics is defined by its attention to a
certain type of data - for example, informant
judgments - which happen to be readily accessi-
ble and considerably more informative than
other kinds of data now available. It should
sooner or later disappear as a discipline as
new kinds of data become available, remaining
distinct only in that its concern is a particular faculty of the mind, ultimately, the human
brain: its initial state and its various
attainable mature states.

Secondly, it should be noted that the concept
"knowledge of grammar" in the technical sense
approximates fairly closely to what we call
"knowledge of language" in normal usage.
Specifically, the concept "language" of

informal pre-theoretic usage is much closer to
the technical concept "grammar" than it is to
the technical concept "language" taken as an
externalized object. When we speak informally
of a person knowing a language, we do not mean
that the person "knows" a system of linguistic
forms, or acts, or pairings of sound and meaning, or a totality of possible utterances.
Rather, what we mean is that the person knows
what makes sounds and meanings relate to one
another in a specific way, what makes them
"hang together." In short, the person knows a
grammar. Similarly, when we say informally
that such and such is a rule of English (i.e.,
of the English language), we are referring to
an element of the grammar, not the externalized
language in the technical sense of these terms.

Thus the shift of perspective noted is a
shift toward realism in two respects: toward
the study of real objects rather than abstract
constructs, and toward the study of what we
really mean by "a language" or "knowledge of a
language" or "rules of language" in informal
usage.

It would have been preferable, in the earliest stages of this work, to use the term
'language' as a technical term in place of
'(generative) grammar' while adopting some
other term (perhaps 'externalized language')
for what was called "language." Much confusion
might have been spared in this way, in particular, the erroneous idea that the study of
(internalized) grammar raises new, complex, and
perhaps intractable philosophical issues as
compared with the study of externalized
language. Exactly the opposite is true.

The misleading choice of terms was in part a
historical accident. The study of generative
grammar developed from the confluence of two

intellectual traditions: (1) traditional and
structuralist grammar, and (2) the study of
formal systems. Although there are many pre-
cursors, it was not until the mid-1950s that
these intellectual currents truly merged, as
ideas adapted from the study of formal systems
came to be applied to the far more complex systems of natural language in something like
their actual richness, and in subsequent years,
their actual variety. But in each of these
traditions, the term 'language' was commonly
used in the sense of 'externalized language.'
Consider, e.g., the definition given by Bloomfield, quoted above, or the normal usage in the
study of formal languages. In the latter case
it is reasonable to think of, say, the set of
well-formed sentences of arithmetic in some
notation as being given in terms of some external criterion, whereas the "grammar" is some
characterization of this infinite set of
objects, a construct that may be selected one
way or another depending on convenience or some
other extraneous consideration. To adopt a
similar view in the case of natural language
makes no sense, however. One may think of some
finite set of expressions as "given" (say, a
corpus, or the body of someone's experience),
with the externalized language taken as a projection of this set. The projection, however,
is mediated by the grammar attained, the latter
a real-world object, as noted. A misleading
choice of terminology, based on the immediate
historical precedents, has helped to engender
much pointless discussion.

If this is so, then it is quite appropriate
to speak of knowledge of the system of rules
and principles constituting the grammar, and
even knowledge of these rules and principles,
just as in informal usage we speak of knowledge

of language and knowledge of the rules of
language. Suppose, for example, that R is the
rule that objects must directly follow verbs,
and R' the rule that unvoiced stop consonants
are aspirated in certain positions; R and R'
are rules of English (when properly formulated), but not of French. Then one would, I
think, have no hesitation in saying that John,
a native speaker of English, knows R and R',
and knows that R and that R' (not troubling
here to distinguish between a rule and its contents). That is, we would say that John knows
that objects must directly follow verbs, etc.,
as shown by his judgments and speech behavior,
whereas Pierre, who is learning English, has
not yet learned and does not know these rules,
as shown by his use of such expressions as "I
read often the books" (as in his native
French), his pronunciation, and so on. Of
course, John presumably does not know that
these rules hold, though he knows the rules;
and the person who makes such statements,
attributing knowledge to John and Pierre, must
understand the terms that enter into them
(though John and Pierre need not). But these
are different questions, leading into difficult
terrain.

It has often been argued that it is wrong, or
even "outrageous" (McGinn, 1981), to speak of
knowledge of rules in this way. As a general
statement, this cannot be true, at least if the
term 'know' is understood in something like its
normal sense, as the preceding example illustrates. There are other cases to consider, and
intuitions are not always clear, but it does
seem to me fair enough to regard 'knowledge of
grammar', knowledge that R' (R a rule of grammar), etc. as reasonable reconstructions of
informal usage, and to regard the concept of

knowledge as it develops in this theoretical
inquiry as the appropriate concept for the
study of what we know and how we come to attain
this knowledge, even if comes to depart in some
respects from informal usage.

Knowledge of grammar, or of the rules and
principles of grammar, entails ordinary propositional knowledge of fact, e.g., John's
knowledge that the sentence ... means such and
such rather than something else. How did John
attain this knowledge? The answer seems to be
that John's biological endowment includes the
system characterized by UG (or, we could say,
includes UG, using the term with the familiar
systematic ambiguity), and that under the
triggering and partially shaping effect of
experience, his mind/brain passed through a
series of states reaching the steady state S,
which is characterized by the grammar G (or, in
the same usage, which contains G). The grammar
G is the language that John knows (the
linguist's grammar purports to characterize the
internalized grammar). It is a system of rules
and principles from which the propositional
knowledge in question derives. This latter
knowledge is not grounded in or warranted by
experience in any generally useful sense of
these terms, though it is partially determined
by experience. An organism differently endowed
would have reached a different cognitive state,
or no cognitive state, given comparable experience, and would thus not share John's knowledge
that so and so. Similar observations hold of
other domains of our knowledge, a conclusion
with consequences that I will not pursue here
(cf. Chomsky, 1980a,b).

Given the shift of focus from externalized
language to grammar and UG, and the corresponding interpretation of the study of language as

the study of systems of mental representations
and computations, a number of questions arise.
Some relate to the legitimacy or proper bounds
of this move; these I will put aside. Others
arise internally to the research program that
develops naturally from this shift of focus.
Let us consider these questions.

The central task is to find the basic elements of grammar. One must, in the first
place, show that these are adequate to the
descriptive task at hand - that is, that they
are rich enough to account for the properties
and attested variety of language systems, and
indeed for their possible variety, an empirical
question, surely. A second task is to show
that these devices are meager enough so that
very few grammars are available in principle,
given the kinds of data that suffice for
language acquisition, in technical terms, grammar acquisition. The transition from the initial to the steady state takes place in a
determinate fashion, with no conscious attention or choice, with no specific training being
necessary, and, it seems, on the basis of
"positive evidence" only in general - that is,
evidence that something is not a sentence or
has been improperly used (e.g., corrections by
the speech community) appears superfluous. The
transition is essentially uniform for individuals in a given speech community despite diverse
experience. The state attained is highly arti-
culated and very rich, providing a specific
interpretation for a vast array of sentences
lacking close models in experience. The problem is one of "poverty of the stimulus," a
variant of what we might call "Plato's problem," expressed by Russell when he asked: "How
comes it that human beings, whose contacts with
the world are brief and personal and limited,

are nevertheless able to know as much as they do know" (Russell, 1948).

The two tasks mentioned are in conflict. To achieve descriptive adequacy, it seems necessary to enrich the system of available devices, whereas to solve our case of Plato's problem (to achieve what is often called "explanatory adequacy") we must restrict these devices so that only a few grammars, or just one, are available, given data that vastly underdetermine the choice of grammar in terms of any principle of induction, generalization, association, or the like. It is the tension between these two tasks that makes the field intellectually interesting, in my view. Let us consider briefly how this problem has been faced in the research program that was initiated with the shift of focus just discussed.

The earliest work was devoted to determining the permissible format for the rule systems of grammar, that is, determining the types of rules and how they interact. The basic idea was that UG consists of a format for rule systems and an evaluation metric. Presented with data, the child's mind selects the highest-valued grammar of a permissible form, which constitutes the system of knowledge attained. Along these lines, our case of Plato's problem might be solved. The proposed rule format, adapted from traditional descriptive and historical grammar and reformulated in terms derived from the study of formal systems, included phrase structure, transformational and phonological rules, and (in later work), rules mapping abstract syntactic structures to representations in a level of LF ("logical form," with familiar provisos) in which scope and perhaps other properties are expressed. The output of phonological rules and LF

constitute the interface with other systems of
the mind/brain. These systems of grammar, it
was hoped, would provide descriptive adequacy.
Systems of the permissible type would be sufficiently scattered in terms of an evaluation
metric so as to solve the problem of explanatory adequacy. The format for rule systems and
the evaluation metric constitute UG, the biologically given endowment.

But there were, from the start, serious problems, relating to the tension between the
requirements of descriptive and explanatory
adequacy. These problems did not arise for
traditional grammar, which simply assumed an
"intelligent reader" - just what the study of
generative grammar attempted to understand and
characterize - or for structural grammar, with
its narrow limitations of scope. But they
arise as soon as we face seriously the task of
accounting explicitly for the unbounded range
of sentence structures in a particular
language, the variety of languages, and Plato's
problem. Accepting these challenges, we soon
discover many properties of language which were
previously unnoticed or ignored, including some
quite simple ones. The problem of dealing with
them appropriately is far from trivial.

The earliest efforts simply extended the
available descriptive devices so that the facts
observed could be correctly stated. Though
descriptive adequacy could be attained in this
way in many cases, the problem of explanatory
adequacy is brought into prominence: How does
the child know to select complex rules, rather
than much simpler (but factually wrong) rules
derived by a natural inductive process from the
simple sentences of actual experience? From
the early 1960s, problems of this sort - which
are numerous - were approached by formulation

of general conditions on rule application.
Whenever such a principle is formulated, the
class of permissible rules can be restricted,
since it is no longer necessary to incorporate
within the rule itself the conditions on its
application; in effect, these conditions are
factored out of many rules and assigned to UG.
Formulation of such principles, then, is a step
toward explanatory adequacy - assuming, of
course, that the variety of actual language
structures is not improperly limited.

In the past ten years, this kind of work has
taken a new and promising turn. It was found
that general principles of this sort often
cluster, and can be derived from rather reasonable conditions governing the properties of
expressions that are "anaphoric," in that their
referential possibilities (in a loose sense of
this term) depend on antecedents to which they
are related. Among these anaphoric expressions
we include crucially so-called "empty
categories," that is, categories that have no
direct physical realization but are present in
mental representation as determined by a "projection principle" that states, informally,
that the lexical properties of particular items
are categorially represented at each syntactic
level (e.g., if "kill" is a verb that takes an
object, then this object must be represented as
a noun phrase; an empty noun phrase if there is
no overt noun phrase in the proper position, as
in such sentences as "John was killed e," "who
did John kill e," e being the empty noun
phrase). In this way, UG begins to have a certain deductive structure. Furthermore, small
changes in the underlying principles may proli-
ferate through the system, yielding what appear
to be large-scale differences in the grammars
(i.e., in informal usage, languages)

determined.

In the course of this work, it has been shown, I think quite successfully, that the inventory of possible transformational rules can be sharply restricted, ultimately, perhaps, to the single rule Move-X, X an arbitrary category; i.e., move anything anywhere. Independently valid principles that govern structures of anaphora and the like overcome the vast overgeneration permitted by this simplification of the rule system. At the same time, various general principles of phrase structure have been proposed which substantially reduce the richness and variety of systems of phrase structure rules; there would, of course, be no gain in simplifying one component of the rule system at the cost of enriching other systems. In fact, it now appears that there may be no phrase structure rules at all in the grammar, where by the 'grammar', now, we mean the specification of what has in fact been learned. Rather, the phrase structure and transformational rules are determined by specification of other properties that may vary across languages.

In the past two or three years, this work has greatly accelerated and has fallen together in interesting ways, yielding a rather new conception of the nature of grammar (cf. Chomsky, 1981, 1982; Rizzi, 1982; and references cited there, among others). The general format of the so-called "Extended standard theory" (cf. Chomsky, 1980a, chapter 4) is preserved, with approximately the same "distribution of effort" among its various components, but in a rather different conceptual framework. Rule systems are of an extremely limited variety. A modular theory of subsystems of UG has been developed, each consisting of certain general principles.

Each of these in turn has certain parameters
that can be set one way or another by experience, in fact, by data from very simple sentences. For example, the head of a construction may be first or last, the subject of a
sentence may have to be overtly expressed or an
empty category may suffice, etc. The rule systems are thereby fixed without further specification. UG consists of these systems of principles and parameters and the principles that
determine the interactions among them.

This brings us to the second major shift of
focus that I mentioned. When the parameters of
UG are set, in terms of simple data, we derive
a "core grammar." Normally, a language will
have a periphery of "marked constructions,"
which must be learned, often from more complex
data. Rule systems are rudimentary at least
for the core, and the periphery too is no doubt
also limited in possible variety. The core
grammar is simply the set of values for the
parameters of UG (where again, by "grammar" we
refer here to what is learned). The interac-
tion of principles and parameters yields a wide
variety of highly complex phenomena, facts that
are known without direct experience. We can,
in effect, deduce the phenomena of particular
externalized languages by setting the parameters of UG, and, given the interactions of the
various modules of grammar, a few changes of
parameters may yield what appear to be radi-
cally different externalized languages.

This shift of focus, just now becoming clear
in its character and import, promises to carry
us a long way toward dealing with the fundamental problem of explanatory adequacy, I believe.
At the same time, there has in recent years
been quite an explosion in the range and complexity of empirical materials in a variety of

languages which have been submitted to investigation from this point of view; and the same,
incidentally, is true of other approaches
(e.g., relational and lexical-functional grammar), offering the opportunity to fuse results
obtained from a number of approaches into a
more comprehensive and deeper theory of UG (cf.
Marantz, 1981). The quality of current work is
quite new in the depth and scope of explanatory
power, I believe, as well as in descriptive
range. This is what accounts for an unmistake-
able sense of energy and anticipation - and
also uncertainty - which to me is reminiscent
of the period of the origins of generative
grammar.

Are there general principles of learning that
enter into the process of language acquisition?
According to the conception just outlined,
these would be principles that guide the setting of parameters. A plausible example is the
"subset principle" suggested by Robert Berwick
(1982). Let us accept the simplifying assumption that parameters can be set independently.
Suppose further that each parameter has two
values, + and -, and that choice of + yields a
set of generated sentences (by whatever criterion) which properly includes the set determined by choice of -. Then the child sets the
value at -, unless presented with evidence that
this choice is incorrect: expressions that are
not generated if the value - is chosen.
Presumably, such evidence would have to be sufficiently dense in experience to require choice
of the more marked value. The subset principle
is necessary and sufficient to ensure that
knowledge can be acquired on the basis of positive evidence only and seems to incorporate a
number of specific proposals that have been put
forth to explain apparent facts of language

Errata: The material below should have appeared
as page 170 of this book; it attaches to Noam
Chomsky's article, "Some Conceptual Shifts in
the Study of Language," pp. 154-169.
 Also, two pages have been reversed: 409 and 410
(both ending in "required") of James J. Walsh,
"Justice and the Virtues: A Medieval Problem,"
pp. 396-421. The editors regret these errors.

Bibliography

Berwick, R.C. (1982), *Locality Principles and
the Acquisition of Syntactic Knowledge,* MIT
PhD Dissertation.

Bloomfield, L. (1926), "A Set of Postulates
for the Science of Language," *Language* 2.153-
164; reprinted in Joos (1957).

----- (1933), *Language* (Holt, New York).

Chomsky, N. (1980a), *Rules and Representations*
(Columbia, New York).

----- (1980b), "Response," *Behavioral and Brain
Sciences* 3.1.

----- (1981), *Lectures on Government and
Binding* (Foris, Dordrecht).

----- (1982), *Some Concepts and Consequences
of the Theory of Government and Binding* (MIT,
Cambridge, Mass.).

Joos, M. (1957), comments in M. Joos, ed.,
Readings in Linguistics (ACLS, Washington, D.C.).

Marantz, A. (1981), *On the Nature of Grammatical Relations*, MIT PhD Dissertation.

McGinn, C. (1981), "Review of Chomsky" (1980a),
J. Phil. 78.5, 288-298.

Rizzi, L. (1982), *Issues in Italian Syntax*
(Foris, Dordrecht).

Russell, B. (1948), *Human Knowledge: Its
Scope and Limits* (Simon & Schuster, New York).

Sapir, E. (1921), *Knowledge* (Harcourt, Brace
& World, New York).

acquisition. It is therefore a plausible candidate for what might be called "general learning theory," one of very few such. Note that
the term 'general' should not be misunderstood.
The principle has some plausibility on the
assumption that there is a highly structured
device of special design, UG, as a specific
faculty of mind with its own internal modular-
ity.   I think this is to be expected. The
idea that there might be generalized learning
mechanisms that in themselves account for any
substantial part of our knowledge seems to me
an illusion. It also seems to me that in the
areas where something is known about the character and growth of cognitive capacities -
language, vision, and a few other domains - the
idea is highly implausible.

Much of the interest of the study of
language, in my opinion, lies in the fact that
it offers an approach to the classical problem
of explaining how we can know what we do know,
while also raising questions about familiar
paradigms for the character of knowledge. If
the recent developments just very briefly
sketched are on the right track, we might well
ask whether other systems of knowledge have a
similar design, though we would hardly expect
to find similar principles or possibilities of
parametric variation. We might also ask
whether a reconsideration of the nature of
knowledge systems is required elsewhere, as
seems to me to be the case in connection with
knowledge of language.

It is within this larger framework, I think,
that the technical developments within the
field of generative grammar should be understood. And it is this range of questions,
still on the horizon, that gives them a broader
significance in the study of human nature and
its specific manifestations.

IS GRAMMAR PSYCHOLOGICAL?

James Higginbotham

In his class lectures Sidney Morgenbesser deplored the fascination exerted by questions of disciplinary boundaries. This fascination has shown itself, I think, in recent discussions of whether linguistic theory is or is not part of psychology, and rather extreme positions have been taken on the question. In this note I will argue that its importance is minimal, once terminology is straightened out and the dimensions of the theoretical linguistics advocated especially by Chomsky are made plain. My aim, therefore, is clarificatory, rather than speculative; if I succeed even partially, this note may exemplify part of what I think I learned from Sidney.

Our question concerns the relations between linguistic theory and the psychology of language. Linguistic psychology needn't tie itself to any particular apparatus; it needn't, because it often doesn't. Inversely, linguistics may be pursued independently of psychological considerations of any sort; it may be, because it has been. The chief architect of the view that theoretical linguistics is a chapter of psychology, and more particularly that it is concerned with the acquisition of language, namely Noam Chomsky, has advanced detailed views on linguistics and psychology; but I will appeal here only to the broadest outline of his basic ideas.

One argument against the psychological interpretation of linguistic theory is that offered by Jerrold Katz in his recent book *Language and Other Abstract Objects*.[1] His considerations appear to me to reduce ultimately to a question of terminology; but in so reducing them I hope to raise a significant issue. Katz advances two

170

theses: (i) that linguistics is not psychology, but the science of language, and (ii) that languages are *abstracta*, akin to the objects of mathematics. The first thesis is expressed on page 76 in the statement that "linguistics is not a psychological science, ..., but about sentences and languages directly." The second thesis constitutes Katz's "Platonism" toward language - the view that languages are independent abstract objects, having no ontic dependence upon the material world, including the human beings that speak them.

My belief is that the second thesis, Katz's Platonism, is at least as reasonable a position as Platonism in mathematics (or Platonic views about the nature of scientific theories, which don't require that the theories *belong* to any practising scientist), and that the first thesis, to the degree that it is not *merely* terminological, admits a response that emerges if we consider how the Platonic objects can figure in empirical investigation. Hence, I will consider them in reverse order.

Languages are abstract objects; in our contemporary way of looking at things, they are in fact bipartite structures (S,S'), where S is a formal syntax and S' is a semantics for S. Their existence is independent of whether there are in any region of space and time any speakers of them, or inscriptions of their syntactic designs, and it is in fact trivial to describe languages that are instanced nowhere. However, it must not be forgotten that *abstract* objects have *empirical* descriptions.[2] Thus take the description 'Jones's language'. If Jones has just one language, so that the description is proper, then this very language is among the abstract objects (S,S'), in just the way that the number of books that Jones has read is among the natural numbers. Now, one *may* investigate the objects (S,S') in abstraction from all empirical considerations (or at least, in an abstraction comparable to that of mathematics). But one may also be interested questions like (1):

(1) For which (S,S') is Jones's language = (S,S'), and why?

(1) is an empirical issue: Jones's language got to be whatever it is through his linguistic capacities and ambient experience. In this simple way, the abstract objects (S,S') are involved in an empirical question.

Consider now Katz's first thesis, that linguistics is "about sentences and languages directly." Defense of this thesis Katz appears to take as entirely straightforward, once we distinguish between theories of a domain *D* and theories of the *knowledge* of *D*. The science of language, that is, linguistics, is then to be distinguished from the science of the knowledge of language in the way that arithmetic, the science of numbers, is to be distinguished from a psychological inquiry into the nature of arithmetic knowledge (a comparison Katz uses, p. 77 *passim*).

Katz's *distinction* is impeccable; but his appropriation of the term 'linguistics' to denote one side of it is just stipulation. Why should a science that calls itself "linguistics" be "about" objects (S,S') "directly," rather than about the proper answers to questions of the form (1)? In fact, there *is* a discipline that studies pairs (S,S') directly, by mathematical means, namely the theory of models. One might complain that Katz confuses linguistics with model theory; but this complaint would have no foundation, and is in fact the other side of the dubious stipulative coin.

There is, then, room for two distinct enter-
prises, namely linguistics in the sense of question (1), an empirical inquiry into the identities of human languages, and their etiologies in
individuals and in the species, and linguistics
in the Katzian sense, which is concerned to describe the systems (S,S'), abstracting from empirical considerations. Obviously, the explicit
description of the systems that are the languages
of human beings is of crucial interest for the
first type of linguistics. It is not clear, however, why these objects should be of any special
interest to Katz.

Suppose we distinguished two conceptions of
the study of space. On one of these, spaces are
studied directly as abstract structures; on the
other, the interest would be in the question
which of these abstract objects are instanced in
the physical world. The Katzian conception of
linguistics is like the first conception of the
study of space, it would seem; whereas the conception of linguistics sketched above is analogous to the question which abstract spaces are
realized in the world. But in the abstract study
of space, that *our* space should have certain
definite properties is of no interest in itself,
even if these very properties turn out to be
mathematically interesting on other grounds. Pursuing the analogy, we might ask whether English,
for the Katzian linguist, is a more interesting
object of study than, say, second-order arithmetic; and we might question the appropriateness
of calling the abstract study of symbolic systems
"linguistics," insofar as that terminology would
equally license calling the abstract study of
space, that is, general topology, a branch of
physics.

If Katz's thesis that "linguistics is not a
psychological science" reduces, as I have argued,

to stipulation, still our response, if correct, does highlight the sense in which linguistics is highly abstract. The reason is that conjectures about the answers to questions like (1) do require the formal manipulation of the systems (S, S'), because it is only by seeing the consequences of the attribution of such systems to persons that linguistic theory can be tested. This degree of abstraction has been a source of disquiet, both within the field of linguistics and outside it. An appraisal of some of the disturbing features of the abstract theory will be our next topic.

An interesting paper by Scott Soames pinpoints a source of widely shared skepticism about linguistics as a chapter of psychology.[3] The skepticism stems from an apparent divergence between the ways in which linguistic theories are formulated, argued about, and modified, on the one hand, and the ways in which accounts of cognitive states and processes are pursued, on the other. The divergence leads Soames to suggest that "the formal structures utilized by optimal linguistic theories are not isomorphic to the internal representations posited by cognitive theories in psychology." Furthermore, he argues, even if by some coincidence the formal structures given in linguistic theories *should* bear some intimate relation to internal representations, that would not undermine the point that linguistic theory is "conceptually distinct" from cognitive psychology.

The force of Soames's thesis does not depend upon departmental traditions as to what is "linguistics" and what "psychology," nor upon the (probably confused) conceptions of the practitioners of these disciplines about what they are doing. A fair amount of Soames's paper nevertheless appeals to traditional conceptions of disci-

plinary identity; but, since I think that his
most forceful considerations do not depend on
such matters, I will pass over them.

I suggested above that there was a discipline,
which I will call "linguistic theory," that seeks
to answer questions of the form of (1), and more
generally seeks to determine which abstract systems (S,S') will constitute the languages of
human beings under which experiential conditions.
It is Chomsky whose work is most closely associated with this type of inquiry. But the *singular*
feature that Chomsky introduced is the conjecture
that the epistemological question of the growth
of knowledge of language can be formulated and
at least partially answered within the theory of
grammar, using just the means made available by
formal descriptions themselves. In other words:
the child acquiring language can be viewed as
constructing a theory, for which his or her linguistic experience constitutes evidence. It is
this feature of theory that detaches it from the
more familiar aspects of psychology.

I believe that the thesis I have just stated
can be documented in detail from the critical
literature of the past several years; but I will
not attempt such documentation here. Instead,
returning to Soames's contention that linguistic
theories do not provide mental representations,
or structures isomorphic to them, I will try to
bring out the point in more detail, by briefly
indicating the type of work that extends the
picture of the child as theorist into the construction of hypotheses about the structure of
language and its acquisition.

Linguistic theory, I have said, seeks to determine which abstract systems (S,S') are the languages of human beings. In so doing, it must
provide formal explications of linguistic predicates and relations that present themselves

empirically -- explications, for instance, of notions such as "sentence," "syntactic category," "word," "passive-of," and so forth. There is a good bit of interplay between theory and evidence here: various of the notions, and the grasp of their extensions, are not given in advance of the theory itself. More significantly, however, the formal explications themselves surely cannot be said *immediately* to provide an account of mental representations or cognitive processes. Consider, for instance, the notion "x is a sentence (of Jones's language)" and how this notion is explicated in a standard form of linguistic theory that recognizes abstract linguistic levels, with conditions on well-formedness and principles relating the descriptions at the various levels. In this case, the notion of sentencehood is explicated roughly as in (2):

(2) x is a sentence in (S,S') if and only if there are well-formed abstract descriptions underlying x at the several linguistic levels, and a derivation admitted by the rules R of S.

If we were actually to write out a definition of the form (2), we would find a long description, bristling with existential quantifiers. The explication of other linguistic notions proceeds along similar lines.

Attribution of systems (S,S') to Jones can be checked by empirical means - typically, by asking Jones for his pre-theoretic judgments, or "intuitions" about linguistic matters, but in other ways as well (the theory, of course, is not *about* Jones's linguistic intuitions, which may be quite poor, or unavailable). Clearly, however, the correct attribution of (S,S') to Jones leaves it entirely open how the abstract system is in fact

employed, as well as the precise way in which
the correct attribution of (S,S') is realized in
his physical or psychological state. Hence, if
one takes psychology of language to be the theory
of these states, linguistics "is not" psychology.

The conclusion just reached is a weak one, however, since, if taken literally, it would classi-
fy much actual research in psychology departments
as "not" psychology either. To see this, one has
only to consider cases where a feature of cognition is revealed by experiment in advance of any
clear conception of the mechanisms responsible
for it. It is known, for instance, that occlusion
is a depth cue, where occlusion refers to "inferred" dimensions of the stimulus, so that if you
see a drawing of half a gorilla atop an elephant,
you will suppose a huge gorilla behind an elephant. Here is a fact about cognition known in
advance of the mechanisms that realize it. It
seems pointless to say that it "is not" psychological.

The substance of the point we have just made
about linguistic theory remains, however: that
linguistic theory is not, or at least not immediately, a theory about the way in which languages are physically or psychologically instantiated, but about their *identities*, independent
of such matters.

Let us now extend the point just made, taking
into account the idea that linguistic theory
should try not only to solve the descriptive
problem, of finding the right abstract systems
to attribute to persons, but also to contribute
to a solution of the problem of the basis of
the acquisition of language. The child is viewed
as selecting a system (S,S') on the basis of evidence presented. Since convergence upon a system
is known to be rapid, the principles of selection
must have great deductive power. Consequently, an

optimal linguistic theory will seek to reduce the
systems as far as possible, so that small amounts
of linguistic evidence will settle a host of questions about grammatical organization. The resulting theory, evidently, will not *directly* concern
the cognitive states or mechanisms of sentence
perception, whatever these may be. It is this consequence, I think, that supports Soames's point
that optimal linguistic theories are not theories
of mental representation.

Of course, we expect linguistic theory to enter
into the description of psychological processes
somehow, and the position has been advocated that
the representations at linguistic levels that a
linguistic theory provides are in fact present as
percepts in sentence perception. The conception
that I would like to advance here (in contradis-
tinction to Chomsky's, I believe) is that, however these matters may turn out, the linguistic
theory that seeks to identify the abstract objects that constitute human languages, and to explain their acquisition on the model of theory
construction, is not closely bound up with the
question whether these objects are "mentally
represented" in any stronger sense than simply
being the languages of the persons to whom they
are correctly ascribed. Linguistic theory may
turn out to be "about" states and processes in
the brain only in a remote sense, perhaps as the
theory of chemical valence turned out in the end
to be "about" configurations of elementary particles in the atom. The prospects for such an
eventuality do not undermine the coherence of the
theoretical pursuit, in my opinion. If the program of research is on the right track, then it
will be increasingly possible to see the variety
of human languages as stemming from individually
small, but collectively consequential, specifica-
tions of abstract features from among those which

are available for human languages. Otherwise,
the program will fail on internal grounds.

In this note, I have commented on two writings
that seem to me representative of the current
discussion of questions concerning the relation
of linguistic theory to psychology, and I have
also insinuated at least an interpretation of
linguistics as currently practised. To summarize:
linguistic theory as I have characterized it is
concerned to answer the question which abstract
languages are the languages of human beings, and
to explain how persons are able rapidly to select
a system from among those which are logically
conceivable, on the basis of their experience.
Is this inquiry "psychological"? Since it is
empirical, the question does not seem significant. The more important question, I think, is
whether it can make progress in its own terms,
abstracting as it does from the question of the
physical or psychological basis for its identification of human languages with certain formal
systems. And to this question, there is only
the usual answer: time will tell.

Footnotes:

1. Totowa, N.J.: Rowman and Littlefield, 1981.
2. Lectures by Saul Kripke at Columbia University in 1971 first made me aware of the significance of this point for the philosophy of language. Kripke discussed the point in connection
with examples like:
Horses are called "horses" in English.
which may be understood as necessary or as contingent, depending upon how one unpacks the expressions 'called' and 'English'.
3. "Linguistics and Psychology," ms., Princeton University.

LINGUISTIC GRAMMAR AND LOGICAL GRAMMAR

Fred Sommers

Peter Geach has pointed out that Frege's conception of the atomic sentence as composed of one or more subjects (object words) and a predicate (concept word) has its roots in Plato's analysis in the *Sophist*:

> Plato there put forward the view that the simplest form of proposition is composed of two heterogeneous elements, a noun (onoma) and a verb (rhema); for example 'Man walks', 'Theaetetus flies' (*Logic Matters*, p. 45).

Geach goes on to hold Aristotle responsible for having abandoned this mode of analysis of elementary sentences in favor of a two-term analysis according to which each elementary sentence is composed of two homogeneous (because interchangeable) terms connected by a functor such as 'some is' or 'every is'. Geach assumes, and the assumption is commonly accepted, that this Aristotelian doctrine had two harmful effects. First by classifying singular sentences such as 'Theaetetus flies' with general sentences such as 'Some man flies' it treats 'Theaetetus' and 'some man' as expressions of the same syntactic category, thereby obscuring the difference of logical form of the two sentences. Second it makes impossible the development of a logic that can handle arguments with relational sentences, since such sentences do not conform to the two-term pattern.

180

I

As it happens, the accepted view of term logic
as essentially inferior to modern predicate
logic (hereafter "MPL") is incorrect; we have
in fact two healthy rivals for the constituent
analysis of elementary sentences. We have on the
one hand the Platonist theory of logical grammar
later adopted by Priscian and Chomsky in linguistics and by Frege in logic, which analyzes the
elementary sentence into a noun-phrase subject
and a verb-phrase predicate. We have, on the
other hand, the Aristotelian theory of logical
grammar according to which the elementary
sentence is composed of two terms joined by a
functor (the old A, E, I, and O functors of
syllogistic logic). The latter analysis held
sway in what Geach and a majority of contemporary philosophers judge to be a corrupt tradition until the recent Fregean revolution in
logic.
 Aristotle came after Plato but before Frege,
whose logical grammar is dominant today. So I
shall call a grammar that takes the Platonist
mode of constituent analysis to be fundamental
a modern logical grammar (MLG). MLG's more
recent incarnation in Frege's concept script
takes the simplest sentence to be of subject-
predicate form. An example is 'Peter lives' in
which the proper name 'Peter' is the subject, or
Object Word, and the verb 'lives' is the predicate, or Concept Word. We note several features
of MLG:

1. Predication takes place exclusively in
   atomic sentences.

2. Predication is asymmetric. The parties in
   predication are two categorematic expres-

sions that are not interchangeable.

3. Predication is unmediated. It takes place
   between the parties without the aid of a
   third (syncategorematic) element that
   connects them to each other.

4. The parties in predication are simple,
   and unanalyzable. Just as 'Peter'is a
   seamless noun, so is 'lives' a seamless
   verb. From the standpoint of logical syntax there is no point in thinking of the
   predicate as composed of a copula followed
   by a term, just as there is no point in
   thinking of the subject as a name preceded
   by a word of quantity such as 'some'. The
   categoremata of MLG are predicates (verbs)
   and individual symbols (names and pronouns).
   Terms play no role in the logical syntax
   of MLG.

5. The MLG analysis of predications coincides
   with the constituent analysis into Noun
   Phrase and Verb Phrase which the modern
   linguist gives to sentences of a natural
   language. Applied to nonatomic sentences,
   the Noun Phrase/Verb Phrase analysis may
   be considered as an extension of the analysis of the simple sentences where Noun
   Phrase coincides with logical subject and
   Verb Phrase coincides with logical predicate. Strawson argues for the legitimacy
   of the extension; Geach rejects it.

I shall refer to the grammar of traditional
term logic (TTL) as traditional logical grammar
(TLG). In TLG every sentence has a subject of
form 'some S' or 'every S' and a predicate of
form 'is P'. But analysis into subject and predi-

cate is not the basic TLG mode of constituent
analysis, since we may better construe the sentence as divided into terms and functor. The
functor 'some is' connects the terms in '(some)
Peter is (a) living (thing)'. Thus TLG distinguishes the subject from the subject term and
the predicate from the predicate term. The terms
are interchangeable grammatically; one may say
'some living thing is Peter'. The parsing of
'Peter lives' as 'some Peter is a living thing'
is suggested by Leibniz. Leibniz notes that
where '*S*' is a singular term known to have unique
denotation, 'some *S* is *P*' will entail 'every *S*
is *P*' (there being no more than one *S*). In this
way TLG views Frege's atomic sentences as having
the same form as general categoricals.

I have mentioned Priscian and Chomsky as linguists who adopted the constituent analysis of
MLG. It might be thought that TLG has no linguistic counterpart and that it is merely a logical
grammar. The case of the *Port Royal Grammar*
shows this to be a mistake. In both the *Port
Royal Grammar* and the *Port Royal Logic* we find
the same term-functor analysis of 'Peter lives'
and other elementary sentences:

> To say 'Peter lives' is to say 'Peter is
> alive'. Because men use verbs both to
> indicate assertion and to express ideas
> each language has many verbs rather than
> just one copulative verb.

Here Arnauld says that the predicate 'lives' is
a hybrid consisting of the essential verb 'is'
and a term denoting living things. The copula
does not denote and in this sense is not a word
that expresses an idea. Its role is that of term
connective:

We say a verb's essential function is to connect the two terms of a sentence so that the sentence indicates a connection between ideas.

These passages are from the *Art of Thinking*, but the same is found in the *General and Rational Grammar*.

Let me now summarize the contrasting theses of TLG:

1. Predication takes place in categorical sentences of form 'some/every *S* is *P*' where *S* may be a general or a uniquely denoting "definite singular" term.

2. Predication is symmetric. The parties in predication are interchangeable.

3. Predication is mediated by a syncategorematic expression which joins the two categoremata.

4. Subjects and predicates are hybrid expressions; the subject consists of a word of quantity followed by a subject term, the predicate of a word of copulation followed by the predicate term. Predication is best construed as taking place between two terms connected by a unitary functor.

5. The TLG analysis of categoricals coincides with the constituent analysis of Cartesian Linguistics. The mode of analysis characteristic of Cartesian Linguistics is Term-Functor; it is not Noun Phrase/Verb Phrase.

II

In this brief discussion of the contrast between MLG and TLG I am emphasizing what is most impor-

tant: the primacy in TLG of the distinction
between categorematic and syncategorematic expressions in constituent analysis. As is well
known, it was the logistic failure of TTL in
handling inferences with relational sentences
that spelled the doom of traditional logic; the
failure was responsible for the eclipse of the
term-functor mode of constituent analysis. We
shall see, however, that the analysis of TLG can
be applied to relational sentences in a very
straightforward manner. Moreover, this does not
entail a loss of inference power (but that cannot be shown in the compass of this paper). The
next paragraphs introduce a notation for TLG
which makes its extension to relational sentences
perspicuous and which enables TTL to cope with
inferences involving relations and multiple
generality. The primary concern here however is
not with inference but with syntax.

A subject in TLG is an expression of form
'some S' or 'every S'. A sentence will be said
to be in Subject-predicate Normal Form (SNF) if
each of its subjects is to the left of its predicate. For example, if (1) 'A sailor is giving
every child a toy' is construed as having a
single subject, then it is in SNF. But if it is
read with three subjects, then its SNF is 'a
sailor every child a toy is giving' in which
giving to (every child a toy) is predicated of a
sailor, getting (a toy) is predicated of every
child and being given is predicated of a toy.
The SNF of (2) 'Paris is a lover of Helen' is
'Paris Helen loves'. On one reading of (2) 'lover-
of-Helen' is its predicate term in which case (2)
is already in SNF. On another reading (2) contains
three terms, 'Paris', 'lover', and 'Helen'. Its
SNF may then be understood as 'Paris is what
Helen is loved by'. This analyzes (2) as a subject-predicate sentence that contains 'Helen is

loved' as a subsentence. The idea of analyzing relational sentences as sentences that nest subsentences is first found in Leibniz. We discuss this presently.

An elementary sentence consists of a subject followed by a predicate. Equivalently and more to the point, it consists of two terms and a connective such as the functor 'some is'. The categoremata of TLG are positive or negative terms or positive or negative sentences. Term letters will be upper case, sentence letters, lower case. If A is a term, $-A$ is its contrary; if s is a sentence, $-s$ is its contradictory.

The basic formulas of TLG are dyads of two terms or two sentences joined by a functor such as 'some is' or 'and'. The binary term functor 'some is' and the binary sentence functor 'and' are both commutative. We may therefore represent the elementary sentence 'some A is B' as '$+A+B$', reading the first plus sign as 'some', the second as 'is'. We represent the compound sentence 'both p and q' as '$+p+q$', reading the first plus sign as 'both', the second as 'and'. The position of a sign and the convention to use upper-case letters for terms, lower-case letters for sentences, prevents confusion in reading the algebraic signs. Since 'and' is used to conjoin terms as well as sentences, we adopt the further convention of representing a compound term such as 'both a gentleman and a scholar' as '$<+G+S>$', encasing compound terms in angular brackets. Yet another convention is the use of square brackets for sentences that occur as elements in compound sentences. For example, the sentence 'some farmers are boors and some farmers are gentlemen and scholars' is transcribed as '$+[+F+B]+[\ +F\ +\ <+G+S>\ ]$'. The use of signs that are disambiguated by position and context affords logical power to the term calculus. Analogously, the ambiguity of the arabic numerals (in, say, '222') is an advantage

over Roman numeration (in which 222 is represented unambiguously as 'CCXXII').

Our notation so far covers 'some is' (+..+...),
'not' (-), and 'and' (+..+...). We define representations for 'every is' and 'if then' as follows:

every A is $B =_{df}$ not some A is not-B; $-A+B =$
$-(+A+(-B))$

if p then $q =_{df}$ not both p and not q;
$-p+q = -(+p+(-q))$

The definition of 'every is' reveals that the
words of quantity 'some' and 'every' are opposed
as positive and negative signs. This is due to
the negative valence of universal propositions
('every is' being defined by way of 'not some
is'). Similarly disjunctions and conditionals
are negative in valence, being defined as nega-
tions of conjunctions which are positive in
valence. To be equivalent is to be convalent and
equal. The general form of sentence is now

$\pm(\pm(\pm X)$ $\pm(\pm Y)$

where X and Y are two term letters or two
sentence letters. The valence of a sentence is
determined by looking at the first two signs. If
they are the same, the valence is positive; if
they differ, the valence is negative. Our algebraic notation for term logic still lacks representations for 'or' and other logical words.
These can be defined. But we have enough for
making the point that a termist constituent analysis sees sentences as dyads that may nest other
dyads as terms. This applies also to relational
sentences which again are transcribed in a
straightforward way using '+' for 'some' and '-'
for 'every'. The following transcriptions illus-

trate the expressive range of the algebraic way
of representing sentences in term logic. We use
'⟹' for 'transcribes as'.

some student is a favorite of every teacher ⟹
+S+F−T.

if every A is B then some C is D ⟹ −[−A+B] +
[+C+D].

some sailor is giving every child a toy ⟹
+S+G−C+T.

some boy envies every owner of a dog ⟹
+B+E−(O+D).

The subject expressions of the first sentence
are 'some student' and 'every teacher'. There are
three terms: 'student', 'favorite', and 'teacher'.
Note that both subject terms pair with 'favorite'
as their predicate term. According to Leibniz,
each pairs with it in a different way. Thus Leibniz analyzes 'Paris loves Helen' as 'Paris loves
and *eo ipso* Helen is loved'. He would similarly
construe the student sentence to say that some
student is favored and *eo ipso* every teacher is
favoring. The idea is to give each subject its
own predicate by treating a relational expression
of form 'R to some/every Y' as a subsentence of
the sentence that contains it. This enables
Leibniz to proceed "monadically", construing a
relative term like 'lover (of)' as a Janus-faced
expression 'lover (of)-beloved (by)' which turns
one face to one subject and another face to another subject. To see better what Leibniz is
about, let us represent 'Paris loves' as 'pL'
and 'Helen is loved' as 'Lh'. The conjunction
'pL&Lh' does not capture the crucial "eo ipso";
'pL&Lh' could be true if Paris loved someone
other than Helen. Leibniz's point is that when a
single 'L' pairs with two subjects in one sentence
then 'Lh' has the meaning 'Helen is thereby loved'.

This happens in 'pLh' which can be construed as
'(pL)h' -- 'Helen is what Paris loves' -- or as
'p(Lh)' -- 'Paris is what Helen is loved by'.
The analysis preserves the essential feature of
termist grammar: that each sentence be parsed
with two categorematic elements and a syncategorematic connective. In effect this means that
a relational sentence has at least one term that
pairs two or more times with other terms; and it
also means that we must parse the relational
sentence as a sentence containing at least one
subsentence. In term logic, the "adicity" of a
term is not fixed but varies from sentence to
sentence depending on the number of pairings it
makes with other terms. Thus 'lover' is monadic
in 'Paris is a lover'; the same term is dyadic
in 'Paris is a lover of Helen'. Davidson has
shown how we may derive 'Helen is loved' from
'Paris loves Helen' at the price of construing
it to be about a loving by Paris of Helen.
Leibniz would have no initial difficulty with
the inference, since he construes 'loves' as a
monadic term in each of its pairings. The
termist way here seems altogether more natural
and plausible.

The termist doctrine that relational sentences
of the vernacular are analyzable as dyads nesting other dyads as subsentences is perspicuous
in the SNF paraphrases of relational sentences
where all the subject-predicate relations are
rendered explicit. Directly transcribed, 'some
sailor gives every child a toy' is '$+S+G-C+T$'.
Its SNF is '$+S+(-C+(+T+G))$'. The envious-boy
sentence transcribes as '$+B+E-(O+D)$' whose SNF
is '$+B + (-(+D+O)+E)$' which may be read as 'some
boy everyone (who) some dog is owner of is
envying'. Its MPL translation is $\exists x(Bx \& (y) (\exists z
(Dz \& Oyz \to Exy))$. Note that the order of predi-
cates in the MPL form is the order of the terms

in the SNF form. This suggests, what is in fact
the case, that we can apply mechanical rules to
the SNF form to arrive at its MPL counterpart.
(For details see Appendix A of my book *The Logic
of Natural Language*.) Teachers of logic who have
wrestled with the problem of getting students to
translate from the vernacular into the artificial
language of MPL will welcome a mechanical procedure. Oddly enough the only available procedure
uses the termist idea of a subject-predicate
normal form based on the termist idea of (nested)
two-term (sub)sentences rejected by Geach and
other Fregeans.

The following rules for translating SNF formulas into MPL may be applied:

1. $+A + B$ maps as $\exists x(Ax \& Bx)$
2. $-A + B$ maps as $(x)(Ax \to Bx)$
3. $(...R)x$ rewrites as $(...Rx)$

Applying these to the SNF of the sailor sentence,
we take the following steps:

$\exists x(Sx \& (-W + (+F + Gx)))$ Rules 1 and 3
$\exists x(Sx \& ((y)(Wy \to (+F + Gxy)))$ Rules 2 and 3
$\exists x(Sx \& ((y)(Wy \to (\exists z \& (Fz \& Gxyz)))$ Rules 2 and 3

The last formula is a canonical MPL translation
of the original vernacular sentence. The terms
paired are explicitly shown by the variables; the
"adicity" of each term is explicitly given by the
number of variable subscripts. The formula shows
that S pairs with G in its first place, W pairs
with G in its second place, and F pairs with G
in its third place.

The envious-boy sentence contains a relational
product 'envious of an owner of'. Its SNF is '$+B$
$+ (-(+D + O) + E)$'. Applying the mapping rules
in the order R1, R3, R2, R3, R2 results in the

translation '∃x(*Bx* & ((*y*) (∃z (*Dz&Oyz*)) → *Exy*)'
in which *B* pairs with *E* (A boy is envious), *O*
pairs with *E* (An owner is envied), and *D* pairs
with *O* (A dog is owned). These pairings are explicit in the MPL formula but they are implicit
in the SNF form and may be read directly from it
by pairing the rightmost letter of each predicate
expression with the rightmost letter of its subject. Thus the letter *E* pairs with *B* and the
letter *E* again pairs with *O* of the subject
'-(+*D* + *O*)'. The letter *O* again pairs with *D*.

III

I have throughout been attending to the difference between the syntax of a logical language
and the syntax of a natural language, between
"logical" and "linguistic" grammar. For Chomsky
and for Frege linguistic grammar and logical
grammar coincide at the level of atomic sentences.
For Leibniz and Arnauld they coincide for any
sentence of natural language that transcribes as
a dyad of form '±(±(±*X*)+(±*Y*))' whose categorematic elements, when complex, must also be of that
canonical form. Thus the logical syntax of
natural language has a precise meaning for TTL;
it is the syntax of that fragment of natural
language whose sentences transcribe directly into
algebraic notation. Nor is the fragment logically
insignificant. It is a central thesis of termist
logical theory that any statement entering into
deductive reasoning has a canonical paraphrase.
For example 'The whale is a mammal' paraphrases
as 'every whale is a mammal' and (B) 'only the
brave deserve the fair' paraphrases as (Bt) 'not
some nonbrave one is deserving of some fair one'.
The latter is canonical, transcribable, and
mechanically translatable (via '-(+(-*B*) +*D+F*)'
whose SNF is '-(+(-*B*) + (+*F+D*))') into a formula

of modern predicate logic (MPL). The former is
not.

TLG is both a logical and a linguistic grammar,
at least for the canonical fragment whose sentences have the dyadic structure of classical
two-term analysis. Since this comprehends relational as well as monadic sentences, the status
of TLG as a logical syntax of sentences of
natural language is unproblematic. By contrast,
the idea that MLG is a logical syntax of vernacular sentences is shrouded in obscurity. Above
the level of atomic sentences, the modern logician does not pretend to give the logical syntax
of sentences from the natural languages. Even so
simple a sentence form as 'some A is B' must be
construed as containing a truth function such as
'and' and a pronoun in the form of a bound variable. In short, MLG cannot transcribe such sentences; it must "translate" them, transforming
subject and predicate into function and argument.
Just here the practitioner of MPL who wants to
apply it to sentences of the vernacular will
make his appeal to the idea of their "logical
form". Looking at (B) or (Bt), he cannot but
grant that their syntax differs. This, however,
is overridden by the fact that their logical
form as represented by their common translation,
$-\exists x(-Bx \& \exists y(Fy \& Dxy))$, is the same. The idea of
logical form is by no means clear, since no rules
for translation are given. As we have seen, such
rules as can be had operate on the fragment of
natural-language sentences that are canonical in
TLG. Ironically, the very possibility of applying MPL to sentences of natural language attests
to the primacy of TLG over MLG.

Think of statements as answers to questions.
In natural language the question is apt to be
about some given thing or person under consideration; e.g., the "answer" 'Socrates is wise' is

about Socrates and the question might be 'Is
Socrates wise (or not)?'. Similarly we might
wonder whether violets are blue and be told they
are. Less often the question is about some given
property or condition specified by a predicate.
Blue: what, if anything, is blue? Wise: who, if
anyone, is that? Frege's open sentences may be
thought of as sentences of this second kind and
his closed sentences as the answers: Socrates it
is who is wise; There is someone who is wise .
Such questions and such answers are the norm in
mathematics. An equation "asks" whether anything
has a certain property or satisfies a certain
condition and if so what. The solution to the
equation is an atomic closed sentence. Or we may
"answer" the equation by saying that no number
satisfies the condition in question. Frege's syntax of function and argument is peculiarly appropriate to the kind of sentences that are characteristic of mathematics (whose formal characterization was Frege's primary concern as a logician). It is far less appropriate as a way of
construing the statement sentences of natural
language. Frege himself has taught us the value
of constructing a logical grammar without regard
to the syntax of the vernacular sentences that
are used in common reasoning. In so doing he
abandoned the classical enterprise of specifying the logical syntax of natural-language
sentences begun by Aristotle and carried on by
"Cartesians" such as Leibniz and Arnauld and indeed by most logicians before Frege's revolutionary work.
   We have taken note of the tension between the
modern logician and the modern linguist with
regard to general (nonatomic) sentences. The
linguist continues to treat 'some man' as a Noun
Phrase on par with 'Socrates', but the logician
balks. This is Geach's Fregean objection to

modern linguistics, and, indeed, if the syntax
of function and argument were the only alternative available for a logic of adequate inference
power, the objection would be well taken. For it
is surely imperative that linguists conform to
what logicians can tell them about the form of
the sentences they seek to construe. To some
this has meant that the contemporary linguist
has the task of showing how the logical form of
a sentence is related to its surface form. But
does he? We have seen that the termist logician
can dispense with the idea of logical form by
dealing directly with the fragment of natural
language that has a logical syntax. In that
fragment 'Socrates' and 'some man' are members
of the same substitution class of grammatical
expressions serving as noun phrases. Thus the
linguist can be at home with a termist grammar
for sentences used in reasoning even if he does
not make use of this syntax as the primary mode
of constituent analysis, preferring MLG to TLG.

He may, on the other hand, choose to deploy
the term-functor analysis for linguistic grammar.
This was Arnauld's style of linguistics, what we
have called TLG. TLG is literally Cartesian, and
Cartesian Linguistics in this historically faithful sense has had no contemporary development.
This is surely unfortunate. The contemporary
linguist who is probing the natural languages
for significant cognitive structure will get nowhere slowly and intricately if he continues to
ignore those structures of language which can
be isolated as constituting its logical syntax.

WHAT THE TORTOISE TOLD TERTULLIAN

Avishai
Margalit

> God sets us nothing but riddles. Here the
> boundaries meet and all contradictions
> exist side by side.   Dostoevski

Can one understand an overt contradiction and
yet believe it to be true? A strange question,
no doubt, but not an unimportant one. "Just because it is absurd it is to be believed" preached
Tertullian, the first Latin father of the church,
thus contriving a most astonishing "paradox" in
religious discourse.[1] Our question is related to
this "paradox". If it is absurd, can it be believed? Tertullian's 'it' refers to the central
creeds of Christianity, those claimed by Marcion
("the butcher of the truth") to lead to overt
contradictions. Our 'it' refers to contradictions in general. But I shall concentrate on
oxymorons, paradoxes, and contradictions used
by mystics.

The title of my paper results from grafting
Tertullian onto Lewis Carroll's trunk: "What
the Tortoise Said to Achilles".[2] The title suggests that there is a connection between the
problem presented by Carroll's puzzle and that
posed by the Tertullian paradox. The real issue
in Carroll's puzzle is the relation between deduction on the one hand and belief and acceptance of a conclusion on the other.

Ours is a parallel problem, namely, What is
the relation between the stark falsity of a
contradiction and its being recognized as such
by the speaker?

The tone in which I pose my question is that
referred to by Wittgenstein as the "anthropological" way rather than the mathematical-logical

195

way. This approach, Wittgenstein assures us, which involves the examination of the actual occurrences and uses of contradictions, sheds new light on contradictions. It is different from that of the logician, who considers an inconsistency in a calculus to be a major catastrophe, a cancerous growth in the tissues of the calculus. For Wittgenstein to expose a contradiction in mathematics is like revealing an inconsistency in the rules of a game: the game can still be played: likewise the calculus can still be used.[3]

My own concern is not with inconsistency in mathematics: it is with Saint Teresa rather than with Tarski. Miss Anscombe tells us that Wittgenstein once quoted St. Augustine as saying "He moves without moving".[4] Wittgenstein on her account meant to take the contradiction literally, as it had been intended, and yet treat it with utmost respect.

In religion more than in mathematics his idea was to handle contradictions as they come: one at a time. My approach on that score differs from his. I shall not treat contradictions on a retail basis.

The claim I would like to advance is that there are evident falsities; that is, there are sentences that cannot be understood without being recognized as false. Surface contradictions of the form 'p and not p' are paradigms of such evident falsities. What I am saying is that it is not merely irrational to believe an overt contradiction to be true, it is (in a sense yet to be explained) impossible. If you don't see that it is false you cannot understand it. There is no other criterion for understanding surface contradictions than seeing their falsity. To be sure, you can understand them in a nonliteral manner - say 'It rains and it does

not rain' in the sense of 'it drizzles'. But
this, of course, is another matter. I deliberately confine myself to surface contradictions. Surface contradictions are such that
there is no need to apply logical operations
to bring them to a logical form in which it is
explicit that a sentence and its negation are
asserted simultaneously. Deep contradictions
are not perspicuous in that sense, especially
not mathematical falsities.

Thus Goldbach may have believed that the
statement "Every even number is the sum of
two primes" is true. Yet it might one day be
proved to be false. Moreover: necessarily false.
But Goldbach most certainly understood this
statement. There were many ways for him to
manifest his understanding: knowledge of the
relevant computations, of the role the statement may play in various proofs of what makes
the statement plausible (e.g., the fact that
all the numbers checked by Goldbach confirmed
his conjecture), and so on.

The upshot of this example seems to be that,
even with necessarily false sentences, there are
more ways than one to manifest one's understanding of them without recognizing them as false.

I also take the Goldbach example as a reason
to reject the suggested claim that "If S believes
that p, then p is possible".[5] Goldbach on my
intuitions believed his conjecture, even if it
turns out to be necessarily false.

Anyhow, I stick to overt contradictions in the
same spirit in which Hilary Putnam defends the
claim that there is at least one a priori truth.[6]
I try to make room for at least one kind of evident sentences, sentences that we do not understand unless we know them to be false.

The problem of understanding and believing an
overt contradiction dips into the general prob-

lem of the relation between meaning and understanding. An influential philosophical position has it that the theory of meaning is a theory of understanding. As a catch phrase this is likely to be misleading. There is more to the understanding of a sentence than knowing its meaning; the "more" having to do, simply, with knowing something about the subject matter. The theory of meaning is thus not a theory of understanding simpliciter, but rather a theory of *understanding the meaning*.

The circularity is considered to be blessed once understanding of a sentence is rendered in terms of knowing its truth *conditions*. Our case is different. We require that understanding an overt contradiction involve knowing its truth *value*, i.e., knowing it to be false.[7] But can't we imagine a Sheffer kndergarten, where the first connective that toddlers learn to master is the joint denial (neither ... nor ...)? For these children 'p and not p' will be a "deep" contradiction, one they may understand and yet believe to be true; for them 'p and not p' is derived from Neither (neither p nor (neither p nor p)). So might they not, on occasion, get the truth value of 'p and not p' wrong?

Understanding (English) is for us a concept with explanatory power. This is precisely why we reject the normative sense of 'understanding' in which understanding an "analytical" statement always involves knowing its truth value.

If children could be reared in a Sheffer kindergarten we would most certainly be forced to change our empirical notion of understanding. The little monsters in this (inhuman?) nursery would have a psychology rather different from that to which our notion of understanding of language and logic applies.

The importance of the Sheffer-kindergarten

thought-experiment is that it makes us aware of the sense of the modality involved in "no one can understand the English sentence 'p and not p' and believe it to be true". It is more akin to impossibilities due to complexity than to those due to unsolvability-in-principle.

Logic and Mysticism

A common feature of mystical discourse is the extensive use of oxymorons ("dazzling darkness") and contradictions ("it moves and it doesn't move"). There is a common explanation for this phenomenon: the peak experiences of the mystic are alleged encounters with the highest religious existence. That which is encountered is ineffable. Oxymorons and paradoxes (contradictions) are the only linguistic substitute for such ineffability. For they trespass the boundaries of what can be said in a language. As Maugham has it, the mystic sees the ineffable and the psychopathologist the unspeakable.

For my part I would like to try a different move for treating contradictions in mystical discourse.

Suppose we encounter a Meistermystic who cares deeply about logic. He takes full responsibility for his use of language. He claims that he understands what he says, even when it is a contradiction, and believes it to be literally true in its proper context – namely the context of the mystical experience. When he utters, in the same vein as T.S. Eliot, "What I do not know is the only thing I know and where I am is where I am not", he means it in the most literal sense ascribable to this sentence, and he believes it to be true. At the same time he assures us that the occasions on which he asserts such things are rare and special indeed. But special occasions, even deviant ones, through pushing language to its boundaries, do not, he maintains, necessarily result in deviant uses of language. Before there were telephones in the world the utterance 'I am talking to you from two thousand miles away' was highly irregular. Since Bell's invention there is nothing unusual about it. The context has changed, not the meaning of the words involved. True, talking to The Almighty requires more than a telephone, but here too, claims our Meister-mystic, the context does not affect the meaning of the words.

The mystic does not regard all or most of the sentences of the form 'p and not p' as true. He argues that he knows very well that in "ordinary" contexts such sentences are plainly false. The fact that he focuses on a few, very special utterances, makes his claim poignant, since the more focused the conflict as to the truth or falsity of some sentences, the more likely it is that the conflict arises from genuine disagreement rather than general misunderstanding. "I manifest my understanding of the nature of contradictions," says Meistermystic. "It is not logic refuted by reality that I'm arguing for, but rather logic refuted by supra-reality. It is here that logic fails." He goes on: "When I say, at the right moment, that I see Eternity and I don't see it, I choose my words carefully and use them in their current and literal sense. But it so happens that on the occasions when I utter it, it is true. There is no other way to describe what I see. My utterance passes the severest test: the criterion of direct verification. Let me explain. The mystical experience needs preparation, but so does seeing through a telescope or a microscope. Once you are ready to see the light, however, it is open to you to verify the truth of my contradictions in as straightforward a manner as any ordinary ob-

servational sentence. My utterances, in sum, are
esoteric only in the sense that they require
preparation for having the right experience, not
in any other occult sense."

All in all, our Meistermystic makes the following four claims:

(1) The literal use of a contradiction in the
    context of the *unio mystica* is apt, and
    its content can be believed on such occa-
    sions to be true.

(2) The use of contradictions on such occa-
    sions is by no means metaphorical, since
    there is no way to describe what is
    grasped, other than by paradoxes.

(3) There is no meaning change involved in
    the pertinent contradictions, since the
    criterion for a meaning change is the
    need to learn anew an old word with a
    new meaning, and this does not happen
    in our case.

(4) There is nothing noncommunicative or
    private (in principle) about the use
    of contradictions in the context of
    mystical experience. After all, paral-
    lel contradictions occur in such con-
    texts in various unconnected cultures
    and traditions.

How can we meet these somewhat obnoxious claims?
To the first claim: An expression can be apt without being literal. If we descend from the wuther-
ing heights of peak experiences to the vanity
fair of ordinary human affairs, we shall be able
to discover oxymorons on the very shelves of our
supermarkets. Epithets like 'soap without soap'

or 'coffeeless coffee' (for decaffeinated coffee)
can be found there. These may indeed be apt for
conveying the idea that an active substance with
undesirable side-effects is lacking from those
commodities. But one thing is clear: no one is
going to be mistaken and take such titles as informing the buyer, e.g., about a new kind of
soap which is a soap and at the very same time
and in the very same meaning also not a soap.

Aptness and literalness, then do not always
converge.

As for the second claim, let me first restate
it. The claim is that the mystic's contradictions
should be taken literally since he cannot say
what he wants to say in any other way. And of
course if there is no way of expressing something differently, no metaphoricity is to be
ascribed to the expression. Thus Rimbaud's
famous line "A noire E blanc I rouge U vert O bleu"
is on this account a literal line. This in any
case is Wittgenstein's view (*ibid*.) The underlying principle here, according to which a metaphor presupposes the possibility of paraphrase,
so the impossibility of paraphrase is an indicator of literalness, is a dubious principle.

Let me remind you that many have argued for
the opposite claim, namely that metaphor - unlike literal expression - is not amenable to
paraphrase.

The claim that the mystic cannot say what he
says in any other way may amount to the claim
that the mystic cannot preserve the heightened
poetic function of his language by more mundane
modes of expression. But this is more a sign of
his contradiction's being nonliteral than of its
being literal. Nonparaphrasability is no indication of literalness; perhaps it calls for a
third category, such as Wittgenstein's "secondary
sense."

As to the third claim, which is about the need
to learn anew any old word that acquires a new
meaning: our Meister, we recall, claimed that,
since we have nothing new to learn for our use
of contradictions, there is no room for talk of
new meanings. The criterion of learning anew as
a criterion of meaning change is, however, highly
problematic. True enough, knowing the meaning of
'division' in its mathematical sense gives one
no clue as to its military sense. One has to
learn each meaning separately. But the case of
metaphors or "secondary senses" (healthy food)
is different: here the meaning changes are such
that one can compute the new meanings on the
basis of the old ones.

As to the last claim, ubiquity of contradictions, it lends very little support to the notion
that contradictions should be taken in the assert-
ive rather than the expressive mood. It lends no
support at all to the claim that these expressions,
in their respective cultures, are meant literally;
for they can just be universal metaphors. And so
they are. After all, besides contradictions, mystical discourse also contains erotic expressions,
to express mystical rapture; yet one hardly takes
literally the love affair between the soul and
the Almighty.

It may be charged against me that my account,
far from refuting the Meistermystic's, merely restates it in different terms. Whereas he reports
"seeing" something that is truly depicted by a
literal contradiction, I render it in terms of
an experience that is aptly described by a metaphorical contradiction.

But my counterclaims amount to more than mere
paraphrase. I actually deny the possibility of
one's *seeing* something that is truly and literally described by 'p and not p'. Moreover, I claim
that this denial is constitutive of the very understanding of the sentence 'p and not p'.

The tortoise who was willing to accept p and also 'if p then q' but refused to accept q surely displayed misapprehension rather than disbelief (or misbelief). Analogously, refusal to accept that a (surface) contradiction is false under all assignments of truth values amounts to not understanding the sentence as a contradiction, that is, to not taking it in its literal sense.

Monsieur Ouine, professor of living languages, is the hero of a novel written by Bernanos. ("Monsieur Ouine", in English translation: *The Open Mind*.) The name 'Ouine' is a fusion of 'Oui' and 'Non'. In the context of the book 'Oui'-and-'Non' means the absolute desolation of a soul which has lost interest in itself and is slowly rotting away. This of course is not a literal interpretation of what 'yes'-and-'no' means. It falls in line with what another professor with a keen interest in living languages says: "Thus when to our querying of an English sentence an English speaker answers 'Yes and No', we assume that the queried sentence is meant differently in the affirmation and negation; this rather than that he would be so silly as to affirm and deny the same thing".[8]

The writer here is not Professor Ouine but Professor Quine. My claim, however, is that, even if one is silly, one cannot sincerely affirm and deny the same sentence, because one just cannot understand what one is talking about in doing so. Thus, we must interpret the apparent contradiction nonliterally, and not out of charity, as Quine does, but objectively. There is no type of behavior that can manifest an understanding and a belief in an overt contradiction. The issue now turns from what constitutes understanding, to what manifests understanding. That is, what type of behavior is to indicate that the utterer of a contradiction understands it lit-

erally yet believes it to be true? "I can see
that our contemplative behavior won't count as
such a manifestation," says our Meister. So let
me convince you of the possibility of such
behavior, drawn from a more homely scene.

The Charade of Contradictions

Imagine a game of charades in which you are told
to act out in pantomime the contradiction "It is
raining and it is not raining". You must produce
a pantomime that displays the meaning of the
sentence as a whole. Can you produce an act that
will allow the spectators to guess the sentence?
Suppose you appear with an umbrella and a rain-
coat in one hand and a sunshade and sun-tan lo-
tion in another, and that you wear a thick jumper
and skimpy shorts. You hug yourself to escape the
rain and immediately stretch your neck to catch
the sun. Can this sort of behavior lead the
spectators to come up with the right contradictory sentence? Of course, the behavior thus
described is a behavior of "let's pretend". But
"let's pretend" presupposes the possibility of a
sincere behavior of that kind, say by a madman.
Does it follow, then, that a mad man or a mad
woman can believe the contradiction to be true
and that this can be manifested by the kind of
behavior just described?
　I do not accept that the pantomime in this
thought-experiment displays an understanding of a
contradiction. Even if the described behavior
does yield the right guess, it does not mean that
the guessed sentence was guessed in its literal
sense. To appreciate the point, think of the
following case in which you act out the expression 'take to heart'. The meaning that will be
displayed will no doubt be the literal meaning,
not the idiomatic one; but the meaning that will
be guessed if the act succeeds will be the idio-

matic one. In the case of "it rains and it doesn't rain" the rain-sun-behavior I described manifests what the sentence suggests - vacillation, erratic manners, indecision in face of rain, but not what the sentence asserts. There is no behavior that manifests both understanding of a contradiction and belief in it.

A true story has it that a dialectically minded student once asked Sidney Morgenbesser in class whether formal logic is not flawed in that it upholds the law of contradiction though reality is so full of contradictions. "Well, yes and no," was Morgenbesser's retort.

As for the tortoise, it should have told Tertullian that, if it is really absurd, you cannot believe it.

Footnotes:

1. Bernard Williams, "Tertullian's Paradox," in Antony Flew and Alasdair McIntyre, eds., *New Essays in Philosophical Theology* (London: Macmillan, 1955), pp. 187-211.

2. Lewis Carroll, "What the Tortoise Said to Achilles", *Mind* (1895).

3. Crispin Wright, *Wittgenstein on the Foundations of Mathematics* (London: Duckworth, 1980), chap. XVI.

4. G.E.M. Anscombe, "Linguistic Idealism," in Jaakko Hintikka, ed., *Essays on Wittgenstein in Honour of G.H. Von Wright, Acta Philosophica Fennica* (1976): 200.

5. Ruth Barcan Marcus, "A Proposed Solution to a Puzzle about Belief," *Midwest Studies in Philosophy*, VI (1981): 501-510.

6. "There Is at Least One A Priori Truth", *Erkenntnis* XIII, 1 (July 1978): 153-170.

7. Ludwig Wittgenstein, *Philosophical Investigations,* Anscombe, ed.   (New York: Macmillan, 1953).

8. W.V. Quine, *Word and Object* (Cambridge, Mass: MIT Press, 1960), p. 59.

SOME NOTES ON "WHAT CAN'T BE SAID"

Mary Mothersill

Sidney Morgenbesser once told me about a class in which there was an encouraging show of hands when he asked how many knew what their unconscious wishes were. A joke, no doubt, but also an ancient riddle. How can you say anything about what you don't know? That is the question that Meno puts to Socrates:

> How will you enquire, Socrates, into that which you do not know? What will you put forth as the subject of enquiry? And how, if you find what you want, will you ever know that this is the thing which you did not know? (*Meno*, 80)

Although he complains that Meno has introduced "a tiresome dispute", Socrates shows that a slave-boy, who knows no geometry (although he speaks Greek and can count) will understand the Pythagorean problem and, with a certain amount of coaching, recognize that the most obvious solutions don't work. When a solution is sketched for him, he sees at once that it is correct. So you can come to know what you didn't know if you have a trustworthy teacher and guide. But how do you manage if, like Socrates himself, you are on your own? If you don't know what virtue is, how can you be sure that Gorgias isn't right in saying that it is "the power of governing mankind"? Socrates has to call on the testimony of "priests, priestesses and poets" who speak "by inspiration" in order to sketch an answer. It was in another, better, brighter world that he was acquainted with Virtue and could describe it, just as here and now, being acquainted with Meno, he can say

whether Meno is or is not "fair, rich, and noble".
All that remains is a recollection, but that is
enough - enough at least for a Socrates. Although
he can no longer give the true account, he can
see that the simulacra of virtue, praised by the
other cave-dwellers, are images and lies. Like
the slave-boy, he can rule out wrong answers
without being able to formulate the right one.

I

Is this the way it was with Morgenbesser's students? The story Freud tells is not so different
from Plato's: at one time our murderous and erotic wishes were poignantly compelling; then they
were repressed. The trauma that forced them
underground was not the trauma of being born
into the world of becoming, but having to face
the fact that the wishes were nonviable. Now
they are shades that lurk just beyond the circle
of light from the campfire - troubling though
barely discernible. But Morgenbesser's students
were not hesitant; they said that they *knew*.
What did they know and how? The answer is surely
that they had learned (from reading books) what
those wishes are. (If someone wants to cavil at
the phrase 'unconscious wishes', then he has to
take it up with Freud.) Is there anything mysterious in this? I know that, e.g., I have kidneys and roughly what they do. Such knowledge
is based on book learning, not experience. A
lower-back pain has to be diagnosed: it might be
kidneys, or a pulled muscle, even the extrusion
of an unconscious wish. But a wish (you might
say), even an unconscious one, is a propositional attitude, whereas a kidney is just a filter-

210 SOME NOTES ON "WHAT CAN'T BE SAID"

ing device. So I could *become* aware of my unconscious wishes but not of my (operational)
kidneys. But unless the distinction is made by
definitional fiat, it seems not to hold. By paying attention I become aware of my breathing and
my heartbeat; isn't it an accident that I can't
detect any renal hums and gurgles? As for unconscious wishes, I believe the hypothesis is that,
if the barriers are breached, the ego is swamped
by unmanageable affect. Is an awareness that entails psychosis to be counted as knowledge?

What I can say about my unconscious wishes (or
my kidneys) is based on what I have been told. To
the extent that I trust the authorities, I take
the generalizations they put forward to apply to
my own case *a fortiori*. In fact, inner states
bodily or mental aside, *most* of what I claim as
knowledge is second hand. The items that, with
their various properties, make my true beliefs
true are, by and large, items I have never encountered. In part this may be because I am unob-
servant, don't get around much, and so forth, but
there is much that is ineluctably beyond my ken
- things that are too large, too small, moving
at too great a speed, too far away, etc., to be
as much as candidates for acquaintance. Nonetheless I speak of such things with confidence.

What of the items that *do* in one way or another
cross my path? Some are quite surprising and bi-
zarre, but none defies description. Of course, I
may be too scared or too thrilled to speak co-
herently. Alternatively, my description, though
coherent, may be so boring that nobody cares to
hear it. Certain things I keep to myself: an in-
cident may be so embarrassing that I don't want
to dwell on the details even long enough to
write an account in my secret diary. Still, there
is nothing that I know at first hand of which I
cannot speak.

II

A good way to study the history of philosophy
would be to consider the ways in which "what
can't be said" has been used in arguments. Since
one can string together words and sentences as
one wishes, it would be a matter of finding what
constraints and prohibitions each philosopher
takes to be in force. In everyday life what can't
be said is what would be tactless, disloyal, a
violation of protocol: in learning a new language
one finds that some reasonable-sounding locutions
are ruled out - e.g., in German. Philosophical
leverage comes from the connection between what
can't be said and what can't be thought, conceived, imagined, known, and finally what flatly
can't *be*. In her book on the *Tractatus*, Elizabeth
Anscombe remarks that appeal to such notions is
central to philosophical debate. A scientist may
attack a rival theory on a variety of grounds -
the evidence is inadequate, the reasoning flawed,
the experiments inconclusive - but if other
things are in order, a certain amount of what
looks like incoherence is tolerated. How could
anything be somewhat like a particle and at the
same time somewhat like a wave? Still, if that's
how it seems with the transmission of light,
then while waiting for a better account we have
to live with it. In philosophy, since the data
are, as it were, all in, a theory that becomes
at some point unintelligible may be viewed as
fatally flawed.

How do the limits of intelligibility, of what
can and can't be said, get fixed? A hard question.
Every original philosopher is apt to strike his
contemporaries as difficult and enigmatic. Think
of Kant or Wittgenstein. And every serious philosopher *wants* to be understood, at least to be

understandable. No one wittingly crosses the border-line between sense and nonsense, but it is not, on the other hand, clear how one could do so *un*wittingly. (Rhetoricians don't recognize a border or don't care; they are carried away by the sound of their own voices.) Well, what are the possibilities? An explicit contradiction is hard to overlook, but perhaps "p & $-p$" will crop up in the unconsidered consequences of my theory. (That would be as if I had *authorized* the saying of what can't be said.) Another possibility: one might not notice that the steps needed to establish a particular claim were infinite in number (what can't be said because it would take too long). Or what Wittgenstein suggests: we are mesmerized by one favored idiom and forget the variety and specificity of functions that the terms of our language serve. So one might be led to speculate about the distinctive characteristics of Non-being. Anyone can make a mistake or fall for an invalid argument, but to be told or, worse still, *shown* that one's whole project lacks sense is very humiliating. Hence the rancor of philosophical debate.

Not all arguments that appeal to "what can't be said" are negative and deflationary. Parmenides, e.g., manages to extract from his critical thesis grounds for proving that the world is necessarily spherical and solid - like a cannon-ball. In some of its versions, the Ontological Argument depends on the claim that "God does not exist" is something that can't be said - only a fool would try. Since what can't be said can't be true and since God either does or doesn't exist, it follows (so the story goes) that God exists necessarily. Tricky modalities! "It must be said (must be true) that God exists" is the contrary, not the contradictory of "It can't be said (can't be true) that God doesn't exist".

The contradictory, as Hume says, is that one *may*
say (it may be true) that God doesn't exist.
(Then it's up to the believer to make out his
case via, say, the Argument from Design.) Of
course Hume also thought the premise false, i.e.,
thought "God doesn't exist" is *not* something that
can't be said.

> Whatever *is* may not be. No negation of a fact
> can involve a contradiction. The non-existence
> of any being without exception, is as clear
> and distinct an idea as its existence. The
> proposition, which affirms it not to be, how-
> ever false, is no less conceivable and intelli-
> gible than that which affirms it to be (*An
> Inquiry concerning Human Understanding*,
> Section XII).

An impasse: what can't be said on Descartes's
view, Hume purports to say. Should this be counted
as a "refutation"? Is it like Dr. Johnson kicking
a stone or G. E. Moore holding up his hand? Probably we would do better to declare a moratorium on
all appeals to "what can't be said (or known)";
then when a philosopher wanted to make such an
appeal, he would have to set out the principles
that he takes to be limiting. In that way we
could see what we thought of the rules as well
as of the alleged violations.

One thing that helps is a good notation: what
Hume and Kant saw clearly enough might still
remain as a nagging doubt if it hadn't been for
Frege, Russell, and the existential quantifier
put to use in the Theory of Descriptions. (Of
course a die-hard could say that the Theory of
Descriptions itself begs the question, but then
he would have to say what the question *is* and
make his formulation as perspicuous as Russell's
- not an easy task.

III

Large-scale, dramatic contrasts are pleasing. A
rhetorical tradition that goes back to Longinus
has it that we ought to be impressed by the vast-
ness of the universe and the insignificance of
man. In the same spirit, scientists and educators
like to dwell on the thought of how much there
is that we don't know. The nominal point of such
homiletics is to defeat intellectual arrogance
and foster humility, but they are well received,
no matter how often repeated, for a more homely
reason: if I have gone through life learning
nothing and missing every opportunity to learn,
I feel less remorse if I consider that, after
all, Einstein knew very little compared to what
there *is* to know. An innocent sophistry per-
suades us that we know what we're talking about
when we make such comparisons of magnitude. There
is, however, one striking contrast that is genuine, namely that between what is known to someone or other and what any single person knows.
The advances of the past century have brought a
degree of specialization undreamed of by the
Victorians, Some think this a pity but it is not
clear why. Breadth of erudition and wide-ranging
interests are pleasant in themselves and useful
to art historians, social scientists, and literary critics. But someone in the sciences, given
talent, diligence, and a long life may actually
master a field. That the field is a small province of algebra or set theory or microbiology
does not diminish his achievement. (Think of the
dimwits who complain about Jane Austen's "narrow-
ness of focus.") It is a fact - whatever its
weight - that we (distributively) know and can
say very little compared with what we (collectively) know and can say.

IV

Philosophers have been interested in the idea that
the range of what is knowable has limits that can
be set a priori; Locke, Descartes, Hume, and Kant
are examples. They differ with respect to the
question of what, if anything, may be supposed
to lie beyond the limits, as also in the attitude
or spirit in which they see what they take to be
our confinement. Locke remarks petulantly that
"our knowledge reaches very little farther than
our experience," but of course he was the one who
began by insisting that the mind is, as it were,
a blank tablet and went on to ask "whence comes
it to be so furnished"? Descartes, of all the
great speculative philosophers the least (as one
might say) romantic, reasons as follows: although
my will is untrammeled (like God's), my intellect
is imperfect, as witness the fact that I make
mistakes. Of course if I were circumspect and
patient, I wouldn't, but even so, my knowledge
would fall short of omniscience. For one thing,
there is this body that "I call my own"; furthermore, for reasons that might be described as technical, there can be only one supreme being and it
can be demonstrated that I am not He. Anyone who
thinks it requires a proof to establish that he
is necessarily nonomniscient is unlikely to re-
pine about the limits of knowledge. (Perhaps Descartes's aplomb is connected with the fact that
he viewed the science of his day not as an is-
land in a sea of ignorance but as virtually complete – the interesting problems had been set and
resolved in principle; it remained only to clear
up the details.)

 Hume, more clear-headed in this respect than
Locke, recognized that a theory that allows no
more than impressions, ideas, and the gentle

force of custom is one that will have to disallow questions about the ultimate nature of reality. But Hume, like Descartes, seems quite comfortable: there is no hint of pathos in his talk about the "narrow confines." On the contrary:

> ...nothing is more certain than that despair has almost the same effect upon us as enjoyment...When we see that we have arrived at the utmost extent of human reason, we sit down contented; though we be perfectly satisfied in the main of our ignorance, and perceive that we can give no reason for our most general and refined principles besides our experience of their reality (*A Treatise of Human Nature*, Introduction).

Kant is a difficult case: he argues that to have grasped the conditions under which we can say everything that *can* be said is to realize that there must *be* something further of which nothing can be said. He thinks of this as a hard lesson that has to be learned anew by each generation.

> ...human reason has this peculiar fate that in one species of knowledge, it is burdened by questions which...it is not able to ignore, but which...it is also not able to answer (*The Critique of Pure Reason*, Preface to First Edition, A vii).

Kant, like Freud, is a "negative" thinker: each believes that certain very deeply rooted desires are doomed to frustration and that our intellectual integrity (or our sanity) requires that we face the unwelcome truth squarely. Kant's successors, like Freudian revisionists, persuade themselves that they have "transcended" their original - which means, in effect, that they borrow what they can

use and edit out such elements of doctrine as are
found dispiriting or distasteful.

I think that Kant is right (or anyway closer to
the truth than Hume) about the pertinacity of
cosmic yearnings and about our inclination to believe that our chronic nostalgia would be allevia-
ted if only we could discover the answers to questions which, as Kant successfully shows, can't be
asked. (It is from this standpoint that what Hegel
offers is optimistic and vulgar in a degree that
overshadows even the parodies of Leibniz in, e.g.,
Candide.) But why did Kant insist on the noumenal
world - the "transcendental Object = x" of which
nothing can be said? Nothing seems to depend on
it: if it were deleted, wouldn't everything in the
First Critique remain in place? Kant's mistakes
are never simple, but it does look as though he had
fallen into thinking of synthetic a priori truths,
such as, e.g., that our common world is spatiotemporal and subject to causal laws, as if they
were like admission requirements for a school -
requirements that would be pointless unless there
were applicant candidates. (If the "transcendental
Object = x" were spatiotemporal and had a determinate causal role, then it would already *be* "in" and
hence not a candidate.) In a way it is natural to
think that, if necessary conditions are designed
to exclude, then there must be something to be excluded. But where what is characterized is a totality - our one and only intelligible world - then
(as Kant himself taught us) homely parallels fail.
The way things are (and have to be) may be thought
of as a "domain" only if we cancel the suggestion
that there are neighboring provinces, an encircl-
ing wilderness, barbarian hordes, and the like.

Perhaps Kant is paving the way for the second
Critique, and "supersensible reality" should be
thought of as required by practical reason. But of
the noumenal self, in contrast with the "Ding-an-

sich", there is *much* that can be said, such as,
e.g., that it defeats inclination and contravenes
psychological laws in the name of the Categorial
Imperative. That does happen in the phenomenal
world, and it may be that we can give a satisfactory account that does not postulate any other
world. The "good will" presents somewhat the
same difficulty for philosophical psychology as
does the "weak will": an agent, *x*, as he appears
to us and to himself, has "every reason" to ϕ in
circumstances *C*, and yet when the moment comes,
he does something else. Given standard patterns
of explanation, both *akrasia* and moral purity
are anomalies. For the morally pure person there
is, to be sure, a *nomos*, so to speak, in the
background, but, as Kant admits, he need not be
aware of it, need not, e.g., review his maxim in
the light of the universalizability criterion.
Does it help to locate the authority in the noumenal world? Isn't it like offering, as a blanket
explanation of *akrasia*, some subconscious slow
drag on rationality - original sin, perhaps, or
in Kant's phrase, man's "innate predisposition
to evil"?

V

Although nothing that is noticed *defies* description, there are many items, some of them very
familiar, e.g., my left foot, which I have never
been called on to describe. Theories of perception tend to make us sound more intellectually
active than we are. If I look up from my type-
writer, I see nothing that I can't identify, but
it doesn't follow that I am busy filing percepts
under concepts. Not that I am in a daze or a
reverie or concentrating very hard on a problem.
It isn't that I don't "notice" my bookcase. (How
could I not notice it?   It takes up a whole

wall.) But it would be odd to say that I "recognize" it and false to imagine that I am reciting
sub voce, "Top shelf: fat red book, then thin
green book, then two ratty paperbacks...". In describing *x*, I try to say something true of *x*, but
describing is a species of intentional action and
so must have a *point*, and the point determines
what I say and how I say it. Suppose I am asked,
as an exercise, say, to test my "powers of observation," to describe my left foot: I would have a
hard time. ("Well, in the first place, it's a *foot*
and has, er, toes...".) How can I describe my *foot*
when I don't know whom I'm talking to or what their
interests are or what they are supposed to know?

Philosophers have claimed that although we can't
say what it is for something to be blue or to
sound like an oboe, such features can be "shown".
The negative thesis - that perceptual properties
can neither be described nor defined - seems to be
either trivial or false. Color predicates describe
colors, and any color can be defined by locating
it in the color-cone, alternatively in terms of
lightwaves, absorption, refraction, and so forth.
There are discriminable shades of blue that have
no names, but where names are needed, they are
assigned, as in decorators' samples. It is true
that blue is a color and that color, as Aristotle
says, is the "proper object" of sight. So a man
blind from birth will not be able to recognize
colors, and whatever sense he attaches to "*x* is
blue" will depend on associations he is able to
pick up, e.g., "like some people's eyes", "like
the sky on cloudless days", etc. But as far as
making oneself understood is concerned, is there
any systematic difference between color, sound,
and taste predicates and other terms? I, e.g.,
have only the sketchiest idea of an internal com-
bustion engine and can neither distinguish nor
remember the difference between the carburetor

and the distributor. I can listen to a discussion
among experts, but it has "no meaning for me". I
could learn: I am neither blind nor deaf, but what
is involved in learning, whether it's hard or easy,
when it is or isn't helpful to have someone point
- "See, it's that black thing with the wires coming
out of it" - is surely something that differs from
case to case. Unexpected obstacles can crop up anywhere. The blind can't see (which is sad), but
what does that tell us about the distinctive features of colors or color predicates?

The last stronghold of what can't be said but
can be shown is the aesthetic. What makes it sad
to be blind is as much the emotional deprivation
as the practical hazards. There are many whose
faculties are unimpaired but who are too anxious
or self-preoccupied to notice the beauties of art
and nature. That too is sad, but at least they
have something to hope for. A work of art can be
described more or less accurately, in greater or
less detail. What is it that can't be said? Won't
this claim too turn out to be trivial? A musical
composition consists of audible elements; the
beauty of a piece of music either lies in or super-
venes on those elements as they are ordered. Hence
to appreciate music, it is necessary to hear it.
Is *that* all? It has been claimed that what makes
a particular piece of music beautiful is something
that can't be said. That would be true if you
thought that such explanation required reference
to laws or principles of taste, but no one who
cares about the arts makes that supposition. The
critics we value are, nonetheless, those who *do*
lead us to see what it is that makes a particular
work beautiful. But their saying is also a showing - in a literal sense, a demonstration. The
qualities that distinguish a successful work of
art are picked out only by indexical predicates.
What it means to speak of, e.g., Haydn's chroma-

ticism is evident only to someone who listens
carefully to Haydn. You may or may not agree
with what a critic says by way of explanation,
but, to make any but the thinnest sense of what
he says, you must have first-hand knowledge of
the work he is talking about. Arnold Isenberg
puts the point as follows:

> Reading criticism, otherwise than in the
> presence, or with the direct recollection,
> of the objects discussed is a blank and
> senseless employment - a fact which is
> concealed from us by the cooperation, in
> our reading, of many non-critical purposes
> for which the information offered by the
> critic is material and useful.[1]

My conjecture is that all cases in which it
seems both interesting and true to say of something that it can be shown, though not said,
will conform to the aesthetic model. Consider
truth: Kant derides attempts at definition, and
Wittgenstein (in the *Tractatus*) thinks of the
relation of language to the world as a central
example of what can be shown but not otherwise
conveyed. What could such a "showing" be, if not
an invitation to appreciate a certain fitness -
the concinnity between, e.g., the sentence, "The
cat is on the mat", uttered in appropriate circumstances, and the cat's *being* plainly on the
mat? Or think of Plato's Forms: they are hard to
describe not because they are abstract entities
- one could go on at great length about the properties of a triangle - but because they are
conceived as *beautiful*. One has recourse to Diotima and her ilk just as, on a more mundane
level, one consults a critic whom one trusts
about a difficult work of art. What Diotima has
to say about the Forms, although couched in lan-

guage that is figurative and obscure, may nonetheless serve to indicate - which is to say,
remind us, since we all remember *something* -
wherein their beauty lies.

What about the mystic's vision? I have, let
us say, an experience that I take to be revela-
tory - my desire to understand *everything* has
been for a moment gratified. But although some
important secret has been disclosed, I am unable
to say what the secret *is*. Alternatively, what I
can say sounds, even to me, somewhat fatuous.
("How marvelous that the world should be exactly
as it is!") In a way, we are on familiar terri-
tory: to see the world *sub specie aeternitatis*
is to see it as beautiful. Why should it surprise
me that I am inarticulate when a simple melody
or a field of daisies can reduce me to the same
state? One can recognize and appreciate what,
because of lack of talent, training, and practice,
one is unable to show. I am stymied - but Vermeer
wasn't, or Bach, or Emily Dickenson.

I conclude that it is proper to challenge any
philosophical claim about what can't be said in
two ways: the first question is "Why not?" and an
acceptable answer would be that the putative
"saying" leads to contradiction or to an infinite
regress. The second is to ask *what* it is that
can't be said, and an acceptable answer would be
a showing. If neither question can be answered
(as in the imagined case of my cosmic *aperçu*)
then, although what I thought I suddenly understood may be of great importance to me, I can
hardly expect it to interest anyone else.

Footnotes:
1. "Critical Communication," in William Callag-
han *et al.*, eds., *Aesthetics and the Theory of
Criticism: Selected Essays of Arnold Isenberg*
(Chicago: University Press, 1973), p. 164.

LOCKE AND THE ISSUE OVER INNATENESS

Margaret
Atherton

Empiricism is a position often linked with the
rejection of innate ideas. Indeed, not believing
in the possibility of innate ideas is sometimes
taken to be a defining characteristic of an empiricist: an empiricist is one who believes that
all knowledge comes from experience and, hence,
rejects innate ideas. John Locke is a key figure
in the development of empiricism because he believed that the mind is a blank tablet on which
experience writes, and, for that reason, argued
against the possibility of innate ideas and principles. Although this account of Locke's role in
the development of empiricism is a familiar one,[1]
it has disguised rather than uncovered the impulses that led to Locke's empiricism. It is true
that lately the nature of Locke's empiricism has
been recognized to be such a clouded issue that
it is sometimes thought better not to call him
an empiricist at all. But this heroic step will
not be necessary if we can be a little clearer
about the actual nature of Locke's arguments. For
the standard view gets the order of Locke's argument wrong in suggesting that his rejection of
innateness is a consequence of his empiricism. In
fact, Locke's demonstration of where our ideas
come from depends upon his rejection of the possibility of innateness, which, in turn, stems
from a picture of what mentality is like and what
mental states consist in.

The interpretation of Locke that I am calling
the *standard view*, the view that takes Locke's
rejection of innateness to follow from his adoption of empiricism, supposes his empiricism to
be constituted by a set of basic commitments
about the origin of ideas. On this sort of

account, empiricists are held to be committed to
a highly economical theory of the structure of
the mind. They are thought to believe that a mind
is endowed only with simple combinatorial networks, and so to reject explanations of mental
phenomena that would suggest that it possesses
any richer kinds of mental structure. On this
version of Locke's program, the most important
feature of his empiricism is his claim that the
furniture of the mind consists in a stock of simple ideas from which the rest, the complex ideas,
are constructed by means of a few principles of
association. His line of reasoning with respect
to innateness is thought to be that, since he has
shown that all our ideas are either simple or
built out of simples and since this construction
can be accomplished without any appeal to innate
ideas, there will be no reason to suppose that
there are any. So conceived, Locke's attack on
innateness is thought to be open to several
counterarguments. Defenders of innateness claim
that Locke's rejection of innate ideas and principles depends upon the success of his own constructive program, but that his program does not
in and of itself provide sufficient reason to reject innateness. For, even if Locke's program
were successful, it too must depend upon innate
principles, inasmuch as the combinatorial rules
by means of which complex ideas are put together
from simple ideas amount to innate principles.
The success of such a program would not show that
all our knowledge can be acquired without innateness. Empiricists like Locke are not really opposed to innateness at all, it is said; they just
have a prejudice in favor of simpler as opposed to
richer mental processes. And, the argument continues, Locke's program is not actually successful. He could claim to have succeeded only if he
had really shown that any complex idea has been

constructed in the appropriate manner. But since
Locke has not actually considered all ideas, it
is possible that someone could produce an example
of an idea we have, but could not have acquired
as a construction out of simple ideas. That is,
this sort of argument places the burden of proof
on Locke. Locke is thought to be putting forward
a rival theory to one that includes innateness,
which he takes to be preferable because it is
simpler and just as powerful. But this approach
to Locke's views on innateness presupposes that
a theory with innateness will be justified so
long as there is no successful rival. If an
"empiricist" theory, one that constructs ideas
from simples by associative principles, can't do
the job, then there must be innate ideas or principles.

All these arguments against Locke, however,
rely on an approach to what divides empiricists
from rationalists which is not particularly helpful in understanding Locke. In the end the arguments encouraged by such an approach get the relationships among Locke's claims quite wrong. It is
not in the least necessary for Locke to develop
a successful or a complete program of constructing
complex ideas, for his arguments against innate
ideas or principles to hold. His arguments against
innateness are not only independent of his own or
any other constructive program; they in no sense
reflect a predilection for the metaphysical economy of associative networks. Instead, Locke was
worried about quite different issues, issues
which more readily reflect difficulties in the
theories appealing to innateness he would have
been familiar with, such as Descartes's.

Locke did not, after all, begin his *Essay* by
laying out his views on simple and complex ideas.
Instead, he began with an extended attack on innate ideas and principles. But these arguments

in Book I against innateness have frequently received short shrift. Locke is often accused of
attacking a straw man and of failing to do justice to any interesting version of innateness.[2]
Such charges, however, are based on a misunderstanding of the nature and scope of Locke's
arguments. Locke talks a great deal about what
is said to be a very naive version of the innateness claim, namely, that innate knowledge is
knowledge we are born with, in the sense that we
are born consciously apprehending and assenting
to such knowledge. And since theories of innateness, typically, are not intended to make this
naive and indeed absurd claim, it is supposed
that Locke's arguments fail to touch on any
interesting version of innateness.[3] Theories of
innateness generally are committed to a much
weaker claim: that innate ideas or principles
are present tacitly, or as dispositions or capacities. Even when it is recognized that Locke
does seem inclined to reject this dispositional
version of innateness as well, his rejection is
not taken seriously, because Locke himself makes
claims about capacities and faculties. To put
the Book I arguments in proper perspective, however, requires that Locke's enterprise there be
understood as a demonstration that theories of
innateness are either unintelligible or, if intelligible, obviously false or trivially true.[4]
He produces the "naive" version as an example of
an innateness claim that succeeds in being intelligible, but is clearly false, while those theories making reference to capacities which he finds
intelligible are, he argues, trivial as theories
of innateness.

The argument Locke proposes to discuss is one
that he says is "commonly taken for granted." It
claims that there are certain practical and speculative principles to which all persons give assent,

and says that this universal assent would be too
great a coincidence except on the assumption that
the principles are innate (1.2.2.).[5] Locke points
out that this argument is unconvincing in and of
itself because universal assent would not imply
innateness unless there were no other means by
which such assent could be gained. But the real
flaw in the argument, as Locke sees it, is that
there are no principles to which everyone gives
assent. This is a serious flaw, not just because
the absence of universal assent constitutes a
lack of evidence for innateness. Locke's argument
is that someone who claims there are principles
that everyone is born knowing is in fact committed to claiming there is universal assent to these
principles. For to call these principles *innate*
is precisely to say they are part of the equipment
we are born with. And to call these principles innate *knowledge* is to say the principles we are
born with are known to us. If they are known to
us, we are aware of them, and in being aware of
them, will have perceived their truth and have
assented to them. Locke says: "If therefore these
two Propositions, *Whatsoever is, is*; and *It is
impossible for the same Thing to be, and not to
be*, are by Nature imprinted, Children cannot be
ignorant of them: Infants, and all that have
Souls must necessarily have them in their Under-
standings, know the Truth of them, and assent"
(1.2.5). What Locke is saying is that the claim
that people, by virtue of their native endowment,
from birth all assent to innate principles is a
false claim which nativists (possibly unbeknownst
to themselves) are committed to making.

So stated, Locke's argument escapes the charge
that he is attacking a straw man, but rests instead on a premise that has been considered highly implausible. For this argument of Locke's now
requires the claim that if we were born with in-

nate knowledge, we would be born conscious of
this knowledge. It seems to insist that if we
want to say that someone knows something, we
must be willing to say that that person is in a
state of consciously knowing that something. His
reason for making such a claim is that it seems
nonsensical "to say, that there are Truths imprinted on the Soul, which it perceives or understands not; imprinting, if it signify any thing,
being nothing else, but the making certain
Truths to be perceived. For to imprint any thing
on the Mind without the Mind's perceiving it,
seems to me hardly intelligible" (1.2.5). So
Locke's reason for rejecting innate ideas rests
on a conviction that having ideas requires that
we be conscious of them.

That Locke's attitudes with respect to innateness depend so heavily on his perception of a
strong connection between "being in the mind"
and "being in consciousness" has sometimes been
overlooked, in part perhaps because such a view
seems to be quite unnaturally restrictive. Jonathan Barnes, for example, wants to save Locke
from the consequences of saying that the only
ideas or propositions people can be said to have
in their minds are those they are conscious of
by suggesting that Locke never intended to make
such a claim. "Locke's language is careless," he
says, "but all he requires, and all he means to
maintain is that being 'in the mind' consists in,
or at least entails, being believed: innate principles are innately *believed*."[6] But Locke's language is not careless, if he would not have accepted any account of believing that did not tie
it closely to conscious episodes of entertaining
and consenting. Locke would certainly reject an
account of believing that says that we believe a
proposition if we are disposed to act as if it
were true, whether or not we had ever conscious-

ly considered such a proposition. His argument, for example, which occurs in several places (e.g., 2.2.23) that young children know "that sweet is not bitter" before they know "that it is impossible for the same thing to be and not to be" depends upon the assumption that we know or believe only ideas we find in our minds and would be nonsense if Locke had any inclination to allow that we can be said to believe a proposition if we merely act as if it were true. Nor does it seem that Locke would be willing to attribute to people as beliefs propositions they *would* assent to, when such propositions were presented to them. His discussion of the possible innateness of self-evident propositions makes clear that he considers it quite empty to claim that a person has implicit knowledge of a self-evident proposition before that proposition has been consciously considered. He says: "This cannot be deny'd, that Men grow first acquainted with many of these self-evident Truths, upon their being proposed: But it is clear, that whosoever does so, finds in himself, that he then begins to know a Proposition which he knew not before; and which from thenceforth he never questions: not because it was innate; but, because the consideration of the Nature of the things contained in those Words, would not suffer him to think otherwise, now, or whensoever he is brought to reflect on them" (1.2.21). It seems reasonable to conclude from this that Locke would not want to say that a person has actually come to believe a proposition, whether self-evident or very easy to reason to, until such time as it has been consciously considered.

Locke, however, does not need to be saved from what many consider to be the most serious consequence of linking what is in the mind with what is being consciously entertained, for he is not committed to the claim that only those beliefs

can be attributed to people that they happen to
be consciously considering at a particular
moment. In discussing what he calls "habitual
knowledge," Locke specifically rules this out
(4.1.8). What he does do is develop an account
of habitual knowledge which maintains the connection between being in mind and being in consciousness. He makes clear that habitual knowledge
of propositions we have once come to believe and
hence assent to upon presentation, is a species
of memory. The only sort of beliefs, moreover,
Locke is willing to say a person has when not
conscious of them are memories, beliefs that have
at one time been consciously considered. He lays
strict constraints on what it means to continue
to attribute these propositions to a person when
they are not thought of. He says:

> But our *Ideas* being nothing, but actual
> Perceptions in the Mind, which cease to
> be anything, when there is no perception
> of them, this *laying up* of our Ideas in
> the Repository of the Memory, signifies
> no more but this, that the Mind has a
> Power, in many cases, to revive Percep-
> tions, which it once had with the addi-
> tional Perception annexed to them, that
> it has had them before. And in this Sense
> it is, that our *Ideas* are said to be in
> our Memories, when indeed, they are actual-
> ly no where, but only there is an ability
> in the Mind, when it will, to revive them
> again (2.10.2).

A memory is literally "in the mind" just when we
are conscious of it; otherwise, we have only an
ability to think of it again. On the basis of
this ability we continue to attribute a belief
in a proposition to a person who is not think-

ing of it, but it is a confusion to suppose that
this means that the memory is stored somewhere,
in propositional form.

Locke's treatment of memory, therefore, is consistent with an identification of being in the
mind and being consciously in the mind. The only
sorts of thing that can literally be in the *mind*
are things we think of as mental, ideas or propositions, and they must be in the mind through
our being conscious of them. Something of which
we are not conscious, like a memory we are not
remembering, is in the mind only in a derivative
sense. Since Locke is opposed to the suggestion
that there could be anything ideational or propositional in the mind unless it is being consciously thought, memories are mental only in the
sense that they can be linked with episodes of
conscious thought. What is unconscious is not
something mental at all, but only an ability or
power.

Locke insists, therefore, that an innate idea
could only be an idea we are conscious of from
birth, because he thinks it makes no sense to
suppose someone could have an idea but have it
unconsciously. As his discussion of memory makes
clear, Locke thinks that something with the characteristics of an idea gets into a mind only by
being perceived, that is, when we are sensible or
aware of it. He says: "*To ask at what time a Man
has first any* Ideas is to ask, when he begins to
perceive; having Ideas and Perception being one
and the same thing" (2.1.9). An idea, for Locke,
just is a way of perceiving; so to have an idea
is to perceive in some manner or other. Ideas,
that is, have a specific content. Having an idea
of water is different from having one of H_2O or
having one of a colorless liquid or having one of
something to drink. These ideas differ one from
another because each is a different kind of aware-

ness. The idea that a person has is the one that
person is aware of, and if we want to know what
kinds of ideas a mind can have, the answer will
be in terms of the kinds of things it can be
aware of. For something with the particular content characteristic of ideas comes about through
awareness of that content. So it is nonsensical
to attribute ideas to minds unless those minds
are sensible of them. Locke says: "Our being
sensible of it is not necessary to anything but
to our thoughts; and to them it is, and to them
it will always be necessary, till we can think
without being conscious of it" (2.1.10). The
claim that there are ideas we are born with can
be made intelligible as a claim that there are
ideas we are conscious of from birth, but, in
this form, is clearly false. Locke's argument
with respect to innateness lays the burden of
proof on the proponent of innate ideas to show
in what sense such ideas can belong to minds
who are not having - that is, being aware of -
them.

Locke's discussion of memory also shows, however, that he is willing to talk of a capacity
or faculty of memory, in addition to episodes of
remembering. Advocates of innateness have argued
that innate ideas are to be thought of as no
more than tendencies or dispositions, in the way
diseases run in families, or as veins in a block
of marble, predisposing the shape of the statue
to come.[7] And since Locke is prepared to talk
about any number of mental capacities, in addition to memory, it is argued that his theory
does not really differ from that of nativists.[8]
This claim, however, overlooks an important
aspect of Locke's approach. His argument is addressed to the claim that mental capacities can
be *explained* in terms of innate ideas or principles. Explanations of capacities are to be dis-

tinguished, he points out, from the considerably less interesting claim that the mind has capacities or tendencies. If, by calling a principle innate, all we mean is that we are capable of recognizing that it is true, then this will fail to distinguish innate principles from any principle whose truth we have recognized, since we are clearly capable of recognizing all such principles as true. He says: "So that if the Capacity of knowing be the natural Impression contended for, all the Truths a Man ever comes to know, will, by this Account, be, every one of them, innate; and this great Point will amount to no more, but only to a very improper way of speaking; which whilst it pretends to assert the contrary, says nothing different from those, who deny innate Principles" (1.2.5). To say that we have a capacity and to say that we have an innate capacity is to say one and the same thing, in the sense that we are and have been from birth capable of doing whatever we end up doing. Since no one could possibly want to deny this, it cannot be that, simply by talking about capacities, Locke has ended up committing himself to innateness.

Someone who says that innate ideas are present as dispositions is typically intending to say more than that humans have the capacity to perform in one way or another. To identify someone as having abilities or psychological dispositions is, according to a recent claim of Chomsky's "merely a promissory note."[9] Talking about innate knowledge is a way of cashing in on the promissory note. Capacities are to be explained by referring to ideas or propositions, the innate knowledge of which is supposed to account for the capacity. It is this move, which assumes that a capacity can be explained by talk of the possession of unconscious knowledge, to which Locke takes exception. In the same way that he objected to explaining a capacity to

remember in terms of the possession of the proposition that is to be remembered, Locke wants
to reject, for example, attempts to explain a
capacity to assent to self-evident propositions
by attributing a knowledge of some such proposition as "whatever is, is." Since having an idea
is an act of awareness, ideas are not available
to explain capacities unless they are ideas we
are aware of. Locke is not objecting to claims
that humans are predisposed toward some states
or behaviors and not others. He says he sees nothing wrong with saying that humans have a natural tendency to seek happiness and avoid misery,
so long as these tendencies are not understood
to be represented in the form of ideas:

> I deny not, [he says] that there are
> natural tendencies imprinted on the
> Minds of Men; and that, from the very
> first instances of Sense and Perception
> there are some things, that are grateful,
> and others unwelcome to them; some things
> that they incline to, and others that
> they fly: But this makes nothing for in-
> nate Characters on the Mind, which are
> to be the Principles of Knowledge,
> regulating our Practice (1.3.3).

Locke's arguments are addressed only to theories
that try to account for our predispositions and
tendencies in mentalistic terms, that is, in terms
of ideas and principles present to the mind, but
unconsciously. Locke is objecting to attempts, on
the level of explanation, to use words like 'idea',
which make sense, he thinks, only on the conscious
level.

Locke's discussion of the reality of simple
ideas (2.30) makes it especially clear that his
objection is to attempts to explain capacities in

terms of knowledge of ideas and principles, and
not to the claim that our mental states are highly determined by an inborn constitution. What he
says there suggests that he believes we are
"wired up" by nature to have simple ideas in the
way that we do. He argues that we are entitled
to take simple ideas as reflective of real qualities in nature just because such ideas are nothing
more than the effects of the powers of bodies to
work changes in us of which we can be sensible.

> But though Whiteness and Coldness are no
> more in Snow, than Pain is; yet those *Ideas*
> of Whiteness, and Coldness, Pain, etc.,
> being in us the Effects of Powers in Things,
> without us, ordained by our Maker, to pro-
> duce in us such Sensations; they are real
> *Ideas* in us, whereby we distinguish the
> Qualities, that are really in things them-
> selves (2.30.2).

But in arguing that our simple ideas are effects
in us whose nature is in part due to the way our
inner constitution is ordained by God, Locke is
not committing himself to the sort of innateness
claim he has argued against. This would be the
case only if he had wanted to argue that our
ability to, for example, receive color ideas
ought to be explained in terms of an innate knowledge of color categories. But Locke's actual
position is that we are ignorant of the nature
of the mechanism by means of which outside events
result in sensations in us.[10]
Locke therefore has no objection to talk of
capacities dependent upon an inborn constitution.
But he would certainly deny that in either case
he is making a concession that commits him to the
use of innate ideas or principles. For he will
not accept any account of capacities or any des-

cription of an inborn constitution that says
that what we are born with is "in our minds" or
has ideational content. This does not mean that
Locke thinks that capacities or dispositions
don't require further explanation. But the conclusion he wants to draw about these capacities
has to do with limitations on the kinds of explanations available to us. Here, as in many
other places, Locke's attitude is one of agnosticism. He thinks that we simply do not always
know what accounts for our mental capacities.
His quarrel with the nativist stems from the
fact that the nativist gives an explanation in
terms of innate ideas on occasions when Locke
thinks it is appropriate to give none, preferring to talk of "something or other" underlying
or accounting for some capacity.

It is true that if Locke indeed believed that
our mental capacities amounted to a series of
simple combinatorial principles, then there might
be some justice to the charge that he, too, is
committed to some kind of nativism. But Locke
does not have any interest in showing that all
complex ideas can be accounted for on the basis
of a few principles of association. Although he
introduced the phrase, 'association of ideas',
into the literature, it was as a pejorative term,
so that he could warn against associations made
by custom as a source of prejudice. Locke's
theory of the relation between simple and complex
ideas is difficult to understand, but it does
seem, at the very least, that he thinks complex
ideas can be the result of several mental operations, which include combining, but also discern-
ing and abstracting. What is clear, however, is
that he is not rejecting innateness because he is
committed to a simpler rival. Rather, having ruled
out theories that appeal to innateness on grounds
of unintelligibility, he is calling our attention

to the explanatory power of mental operations of whose presence within us we can be aware. But though Locke thinks we can understand a good deal about our mental capacities by paying attention to the mental operations we find within ourselves, there is no reason to suppose that he would think that, by pursuing such a method, we ought to be able to offer an explanation for everything a nativist claims to be able to explain.

It is in fact the emphasis Locke places on the possibility of uncovering limitations on our knowledge that creates an important area of difference between his approach and that of someone like Descartes, who is committed to the use of innate ideas. Descartes thought there could be no knowledge at all unless we could know some things with certainty. Descartes also thought that whatever we learn from experience is probable only, and, therefore, that anything we know with certainty is unlearned and due to our faculty of knowing. On these sorts of grounds, Descartes supported claims about innateness. Locke, on the other hand, thought it must remain a question pending investigation whether or to what extent we can know anything with certainty (1.1.5). He is opposed to an approach that first claims there is some kind of knowledge we must have and then constructs hypotheses about what the faculties that deliver this knowledge must be like. Rather, Locke thinks the correct order of investigation is first to establish what our cognitive faculties are like and only then to go on to find out what we can and can't be said to know, using these faculties. Locke's demonstration that it is unintelligible to suppose that our faculties are endowed with innate knowledge constitutes one such investigation of the nature of our cognitive faculties. His further investigations into what we can or cannot know will make use of this demonstration to rule out the possibility of our having knowledge that could only have been acquired with the help of innate ideas or principles. Locke cannot be seen as putting forward his constructive program as an independent piece of evidence against nativism or as a way of showing that he can do everything the nativist thinks needs doing. Rather, Locke is able to undertake his positive exploration of what our faculties can do on the assumption that one thing they can't do is have innate knowledge, and he is willing to accept as a consequence that there are some ideas we can't have. The arguments against innateness in Book I constitute a necessary first step in the development of Locke's theory.

It is a mistake, therefore, to see Locke as arguing for the nonexistence of innate ideas from the success of his own constructive program. For Locke has no commitment at all to showing that his account of how we construct our ideas describes a system that is just as powerful as that of the nativist, and he feels no need to say that he can explain whatever the nativist seeks to explain. His position is that explanations in terms of innate ideas or principles can be rejected out of hand on grounds of incoherence. This is because he believes there is no way to have such mental states as ideas or principles except through being aware of them, so that the mark of the mental is that mental states are conscious states. Thus, it is quite inappropriate to talk about anything having ideational content as existing in an unconscious form. If a capacity is to be explained by talking about such underlying ideas or principles, then, at the very least, we are owed an account of some alternative way, other than being aware of them, of "having" these

ideas or principles. Such an account, however,
Locke thinks cannot be forthcoming.

Whether or not Locke intended his arguments to
be directed against Descartes or against some
other target, in fact they raise a serious problem for Descartes. Descartes is, of course, the
locus classicus for the doctrine that mental
states can be distinguished from physical states
because mental states are transparent to their
possessor. Consciousness for Descartes, as for
Locke, is the distinguishing characteristic of
thought. But, as Margaret Wilson points out,[11]
in grounding knowledge in innate ideas, Descartes
is acknowledging a "hidden structure" to thought,
a structure of ideas we have but are not aware
of. Descartes is apparently driven to this inconsistency because he wants to hold both that the
distinguishing feature of mentality is consciousness and that whatever is responsible for thought
will itself be a kind of thought, rather than,
for example, something physical. Locke avoids
this inconsistency by rejecting the possibility
of thoughts we have but are not aware of and
adopts an agnostic rather than an explicitly
dualistic attitude toward the nature of what it
is that is responsible for thought.

Thus Locke's reasons for rejecting innateness
cannot be understood as following in some direct
manner from assumptions about an empiricist program. They are independent of any account of how
complex ideas are to be constructed out of simple
ones. Nor are they focused on issues of metaphysical simplicity or economy. It might be appropriate to look at, say, the issue dividing
Hume from Kant in that light, and to argue that
what distinguishes Hume's associative principles
from Kant's categories is the simplicity of the
former. There is no reason, however, to identify
Hume's position with Locke's. Locke's quarrel

with an innateness theory such as Descartes's is over a different issue, although one that is central to any innateness claim: the issue of whether it is justifiable to give a description of the hidden structure underlying thought which identifies this structure as itself something mental, something that can be thought of as knowledge of ideas or principles. It is Locke's negative decision with respect to this issue that motivates the story he wants to tell about how ideas are constructed. Thus, Locke's empiricism, his account of how the ideas we have derive from experience, follows from his rejection of innate ideas, which, in turn, depends upon his theory of the nature of mentality.

Footnotes:

I learned a lot about the issues with which this paper is concerned in a seminar Robert Schwartz and I taught with Sidney Morgenbesser on problems concerning the analysis of mental states. I would also like to thank David Rosenthal and Stephen Nathanson for their help with earlier versions.

1. What I am trying to present here is a kind of "common knowledge" picture of Locke and his relationship to empiricism. This is the version of Locke that has entered the psychological literature, for example, and the version that has informed the view of empiricism in the contemporary debate on innateness in the work of Noam Chomsky and Jerrold J. Katz and others; see, for example, *Aspects of the Theory of Syn-*

tax (Cambridge, Mass.: MIT Press, 1965); *Cartes-*
ian Linguistics (New York: Harper & Row, 1966);
Language and Mind (New York: Harcourt Brace,
1968); *Reflections on Language* (New York: Pan-
theon, 1975); Katz, *Philosophy of Language* (New
York: Harper & Row, 1966); Chomsky and Katz, "On
Innateness: A Reply to Cooper," *Philosophical Re-*
view, LXXXIV, 1 (January 1975): 70-87. An excellent bibliography of contemporary work about innateness can be found in Stephen P. Stich, ed.,
Innate Ideas (Berkeley: Univ. of California Press,
1976).

2. Many of these arguments occur in the literature cited above. The contemporary complaints
about Locke, in some cases, echo earlier ones.
Thomas Webb, writing in the middle of the nine-
teenth century, reports that Cousin regarded
Locke's polemic as a "mere chimera", Coleridge
said he was attacking a "man of straw," and Hamil-
ton considered Locke to have been led astray by an
"ignis fatuus" (*The Intellectualism of Locke*, New
York: Burt Franklin, 1973, reprint of 1857 ed.).

3. See, for example, Robert Merrihew Adams,
"Where Do Our Ideas Come from?" in *Innate Ideas*,
op. cit.; Roy Edgley, "Innate Ideas", in Godfrey
Vesey, ed., *Knowledge and Necessity* (New York: St.
Martin's, 1970).

4. Nelson Goodman calls attention to this reading of Locke's arguments in "The Epistemological
Argument," *Synthese*, XVII, 1 (March 1967): 23-28.

5. All references are to the Clarendon edition
of *An Essay concerning Human Understanding*,
edited by P. H. Nidditch, Oxford, 1975.

6. "Mr. Locke's Darling Notion," *Philosophical*
Quarterly, XXII, 88 (July 1972): 193-2]4, p.200.

7. This approach is to be found among supporters
of innate ideas in Locke's own era, such as Descartes, *Notes against a Certain Programme*, ed. &
trans. Haldane and Ross, Cambridge, 1911, re-

printed 1969: Leibniz, *New Essays on Human Understanding*, ed. & trans. Peter Remnant and Jonathan Bennett (Cambridge, 1981), as well as in Chomsky, *Language, and Mind*, *op. cit.*

8. H. M. Bracken, "Innate Ideas - Then and Now," *Dialogue*, VI, 3 (December 1967): 334-346. It is also common in contemporary claims about innateness to suppose there is no real issue about innateness, since both nativists and empiricists admit the existence of dispositions and tendencies. See John Searle, "Chomsky's Linguistics", *New York Review of Books* (22 February 1973).

9. *Rules and Representations* (New York: Columbia, 1980), p. 48.

10. Locke, therefore, would not be inclined to accept a way Hume proposes of understanding the innateness controversy. Hume says that since we show ideas are not innate by showing they are derived from impressions and since impressions are natural and copied from nothing else, then we can say that all impressions are innate and no ideas are innate (*Treatise*, 1.1.2; *Enquiry*, sec. 2). Hume's way of talking about the issue presupposes that the way to go about showing whether or not an idea is innate is just to find out whether it can be learned. That Hume talks in this way has been cited by Jerry Fodor ["The Present Status of the Innateness Controversy," in *Representations* (Cambridge, Mass.: MIT Press, 1981), p. 276] as a reason for saying that nativists differ from empiricists only in the kind of ideas they take to be innate. But to Locke, no one has any simple idea until he is conscious of it, so that which ideas are in our minds is a matter of our histories. That we are born with the capacity to become conscious of simple ideas does not single them out from any other idea we end up with.

11. *Descartes* (London: Routledge & Kegan Paul, 1978), p. 164.

TOWARD A RETENTIVE MATERIALISM

Arthur C. Danto

The structure of controversy over the question
whether a fundamental boundary divides the natural sciences from the human sciences - the *Geist-
wissenschaften* so-called - is complicated by a
further controversy over how the line is to be
erased by philosophers who reject its indelibi-
lity. Defenders of the boundary, whom I shall
call Dualists here, have in consequence various
sorts of Anti-Dualist to contend with, who happen,
fortunately for the Dualist, to be as irreconcilable with one another as with their sworn common
enemy. As elsewhere in philosophy, one's allies
are often as bad if not worse than one's foes,
and the structure of this particular controversy is as ramified, accordingly, as is that Middle-
east of philosophical warfare, the mind-body problem - not surprisingly, I suppose, since the
issues turn in part on how the language of psychology is to be construed.

An audacious form of Anti-Dualist offensive in
recent times has consisted in an effort to socio-
logize the natural sciences, depicting science-
makers as engaged in an essentially political activity, imposing in the name of truth some favored
paradigm upon the world. The natural sciences then
consitute a form of life, are as much subject to
sociohistorical description and deconstruction as
the sexual or ritual comportments of Melanesians,
between whom and the tribe of science-makers the
distinctions are as deep, but no deeper, than the
distinctions between Melanesians and, say, Tro-
brianders or, for the matter, the Ik. Nor is there
much to differentiate the scientific revolution
from the French or the Russian revolutions, all
of them involving a new elite which seeks to se-

244 TOWARD A RETENTIVE MATERIALISM

cure its ascendancy by ideology, scientific theories being instances of this. The anti-realist, not to say nihilist consequences drawn from this move make plain, from the somewhat olympian perspective under which I am seeking to view things, that we are dealing with another of the myriad forms of philosophical idealism, since idealism, as I understand it, is the view that the structure of reality is in the end but the structure of mind – so the natural sciences are disarmed through being treated as subjects for applied political psychology. The differences between this new and the older forms of achieving the unity of science are, if I may be deconstructive in my own right, but surface transforms of a deep philosophical thought. It is not an accident that Kuhn's influential and ultimately dissolutive monograph should have first appeared in the same format with Carnap's "Logical Foundations of the Unity of Science" in *The International Encyclopedia of Unified Science*. Unity of Science, hence Anti-Dualism, is the fulcrum of strategy, which has, of course, shifted from earlier times. Hempel famously sought unity at the price of overcoming alleged differences between historical explanation and explanations in the natural sciences in favor of the latter. The new posture seeks unity by subjecting the natural sciences to a form of historical or hermeneutical explanation or, if you wish, interpretation. But it is still warfare, whatever form it takes. The disguises of Idealism are myriad and philosophical ingenuity tireless. And as Idealism disguises itself from itself, notoriously so in the case of Logical Positivism, it is difficult to pin down, much less eliminate, and what often happens is that it is declared an enemy by something that is only another form of itself.

There is, however, a strategy available to Dual-

ists these days, which consists in pitting Idealism, whatever its form, against its own and lat-
terly Dualism's enemy, namely Materialism. I have
in mind that form of Materialism which maintains
that the entirety of human conduct can be represented, ultimately, within the framework of a
projected neuroscience. This strong Neuro-Mater-
ialism has been truculently defended by the
Churchlands, and it is their version I wish to
draw upon, since the moment we pit it against
Idealism in the version of it the Sociology of
Natural Science makes available, the contest becomes abruptly comical, like a struggle between
two snakes with their tails in each other's
mouths, each seeking to swallow the other, which
either of them can do only by swallowing itself.
For nothing prevents the Sociologizer of tomorrow from ideologizing tomorrow's neuroscientist,
as nothing will prevent tomorrow's neuroscientist
from representing even the Sociologizer's conduct
in the chill and neutral discourse of advanced
neuroscience. The contest is inevitable and ir-
resoluble, for the idealist under whatever dis-
guise (There he is, made up like Professor
Quine!) will seek to assimilate matters of fact
to matters of meaning, while the materialist
will seek to assimilate matters of meaning to
matters of fact. It is the deep assumption of
Dualism that the "untenable dualism" each of
these unificational usurpations promotes is
pretty much the boundary he himself is committed to defend. And he may derive from the comical struggle just sketched a model for dealing
with the materialist, who is a considerably
simpler fellow than the Idealist, having no
taste for masquerade.

Here is his insight. If we are speaking of
tomorrow's *science*, then we are really speaking
after all of an enterprise of representation.

For representation is just what a science does.
It does this even if in fact the Sociologizer is
right and representations are but ideologies and
vehicles for the Will to Power. So even if we
represent ourselves in a language that has no
room for representational categories, well, *we*
are still representing ourselves that way. And
by a para-Cartesian sort of argument we arrive
at a conclusion inescapable through the fact
that we *arrive* at it, namely that we are *ens representans* no matter how we represent ourselves -
falsely in case, with the materialist, curiously
given over to the jesuitical prejudice that matter cannot think - we represent ourselves as not
representing at all. I say "falsely," because
the neuroscientists of the future, however they
may represent their subjects, themselves included, will surely be doing such things as performing experiments, the outcomes of which can be
negative in a sense that presupposes a representation that is wrong. They will be drawing inferences from whatever outcomes they do arrive at -
and nothing counts as inference which is not to
be evaluated in terms of validity, and hence of
truth and falsity, which again presuppose representations. And they will arrive at some more or
less warranted beliefs about neurostructure. At
least they will if the neuroscience of the future
has, as science, any continuity with the sciences
of today. The semantical components expelled from
the content of their representations will reap-
pear as parts of their representations of these
a-representational contents. And so they will
have two ways of representing themselves - as
scientists who represent and as subjects that do
not - which shows how negligible philosophical
progress will have been since the originating
insights of Descartes.

It is not, I think, surprising that scientific

materialism, at least the materialism epitomized
in a clever parody of Protagoras by Wilfred Sellars, that science is the measure of all things,
would, in drawing its ontology from the content
of scientific theory, leave no room in it for
science itself, treated, so to speak, as ontolo-
gically weightless. This is perhaps because science is so rarely part of its own subject matter:
because predicates sensibly applicable to scientific representations are not the predicates used
in those representations at all. And they are
never so, I dare say, in the representations of
the most basic sciences - chemistry and physics
- favored by materialists of this persuasion.
Since there is no room in the lexical resources
of these sciences to represent the sciences
whose lexical resources they are, it is easy for
those fixated upon that vocabulary to lose sight
of the fact that it *is* a vocabulary, and that
there must be a vocabulary for treating it as
such. Since it is a vocabulary, it forms part of
a representational system, the representational
system of science itself - and where is this to
be housed in a world given only through the lexical resources of the basic science? For me, science itself has to be part of the world, not
something outside and epiphenomenal.
   But, in treating it as outside, the Sellarsian
philosophers but follow the linguistic philosophers of the time, who have made transformations
into questions of language the touchmark of their
practice and have then gone on to forget that
something has to be done with language itself.
The most notorious example of this is doubtless
Wittgenstein, in the *Tractatus*, in which he
designed a conception of the world that left no
room for its representation, since the language
in which it was to be represented had no way of
representing the facts of representation, regar-

ding which we must be silent. Since the representation of the world Wittgenstein is disposed to countenance is what he terms "the total natural science", meta-representational questions, which are of course the questions the *Tractatus* itself deals with, are not part of science, hence not part of the world – they are "outside the world" – it is plain that Wittgenstein there treats language as if it were as transparent as consciousness is sometimes thought to be, *presenting* the world but not a datum for itself. And when the *Tractatus* goes up in philosophical smoke, leaving "not a wrack behind" we will regain a lost innocence and nevermore think of representation or have the means to construe ourselves as *ens representans* or frame philosophical questions.

Much the same forgetfulness is to be found in a more immediately relevant theory, that of Eliminative Materialism, as defended by Richard Rorty. As nearly as I understand it, this is the view that terms referring to sensations in fact refer to physiological states in whose description the predicates of sensation have no locus, so that such terms as 'pain' refer to perturbations of C-fibers, and we could eliminate the former term in favor of the latter and, as Rorty puts it "at no greater cost than an inconvenient linguistic reform, we could drop [mentalistic] terms from our vocabulary" this because "what we call sensations are nothing but brain processes," so why not call things by the names that science gives them? And in his recent book Rorty tells a pretty tale about a culture in which in fact this is done. Something that can be eliminated so effortlessly cannot have much connection with the world, I suppose, but what Rorty appears to have forgotten is that, however interesting it is that one set of terms should

through reform have been eliminated in favor of
another, the fact remains that these still are
terms, terms which by his own criterion occur in
scientific theories - and where are these to be
housed? No doubt we could represent ourselves
with the contents of neurophysiology, so long as
we forgot that we were representing ourselves. I
want therefore to move to the center of discussion what has been so much at the periphery of
it as to have been treated as Wittgenstein says
the boundaries of the visual field are, namely,
as not part of the field. And if indeed the
periphery of the visual field cannot be seen,
well, we then will have paid too high a price
for allowing seeing to specify the contents of
believing. We have to expand the wherewithal
of representation to represent the fact that we
represent.

I can see no way of doing this consistent with
materialist principles, which I find on other
grounds uniquely sensible, other than by rejecting the jesuitical principle I alluded to and by
supposing that matter itself in some instances
has representational properties, nervous tissue
being perhaps a kind that does, so that we could
be representation and matter at once. After all,
our galleries and libraries are filled with
things that are at once about something, hence
representational, and material, if paint and
paper are matter. States of our nervous system
differ from these cases, which are brought forward only to make the principle clear, through
the fact that they are dynamic, in entering causal relationships. But they are not uniquely
dynamic either, if functionalism is a good theory
and other modes of embodiment are feasible, as
when we replace ravaged protein with cerbical
chips, enabling mental functioning to continue
unimpaired or even enhanced. I shall call this

view *retentive* materialism, to preserve the intestinal metaphor that *eliminative* materialism gives us. My view is that mentalistic terms may indeed refer to physiological states or processes, but we cannot eliminate these terms unless we allow that the physiological states or processes retain the representational properties attributed to us when we attribute such mental states as believing, wishing, hoping, or the like. There is, in brief, matter and matter, some being representational and some not, and it is finally a scientific question where the line between them is to be drawn. The line, which doubtless bisects us, does not divide us from the surrounding world as neatly as thinkers like Descartes would have it, since animals clearly are as much representational engines as we are. The line in any case must pretty closely coincide with that which defines the dualism I began by considering, marking a basis for distinguishing the natural not so much from the human, narrowly speaking, but from the representational sciences. In part the difference is marked by a difference in the kinds of laws, which I can but sketch out here.

It has not been observed, or not frequently at least, that there are no such things as *pure* representations, so that whichever representation R one chooses, it will always be embodied and so possess those properties, call them (M), something that sort of matter normally possesses. "The cat is on the mat," which represents a cat as being on a mat, which is *about* the cat and the mat, and the relationship between them, has such chemical and topological properties as a typed or written sentence would have, and were I to intone it, it would retain unaltered its representational properties while undergoing a

seachange into perturbations of the air. The
fact that language is written *and* spoken, that
for handed creatures it *can* be gestured, directly entails one part of the functionalist theory,
namely that according to which representations
underdetermine the stuff of their embodiment,
the same meanings, as it were, appearing in different media. The relationship of meaning to medium has few parallels, inasmuch as mediumless
meanings are not to be had; so the mode of embodiment is not like some form of clothing which can
be exchanged for clothing of some other kind,
since there is no naked meaning to cover. In any
case retentive materialism extends the domain of
embodiments to nervous tissue. It takes seriously
Aristotle's fine observation that as speech is to
writing, writing is to thought, and it asks what
the embodiment of thought would be, giving an acceptably materialist answer.

Underdetermination of medium by meaning - in
writing we can scribble in ink, in water, in milk,
in vegetable juices, in pencil, on any suitable
surface, or no surface at all, as when Picasso
draws in light against the night air, or the air-
plane writes in smoke against the blue skies of
Bellport, and in shapes which differ as uncial
from cursive, roman from italic, cyrillic from
latin, or as spencerian script differs from my
own eccentric and illegible scrawl - implies the
absence of what we may term "graphophysical laws."
Further, take any set of material properties a particular written message may have. Then it is possible to imagine something that possesses exactly
the same material properties so as to be indiscern-
able from the written message, but which is no representation at all - as when the ink leaks out of
my rapidograph to form a set of shapes which, had
they been written, would say "Aristotle is confused" but, since not written, say nothing at all.

Since a set of material properties (M) may embody or not embody a given representation, depending upon a variety of factors, some of them causal, there are no physicographic laws either. And this is perfectly general for all media and all representations. I surmise it is no different with nervous tissue, at least in the direction from representation to medium, for the same representation may find different neural embodiments even within the same individual at the same or different times. If this is what Davidson meant by his singularly obscure doctrine of anomalism, then indeed there are no psychophysical laws and probably no physicopsychic laws, even if it is true, in whatever sense that it is true that the representation *is* the embodied thing, i.e., the message *is* the medium. There are none for the same reason that there are no madonna-pigmental laws, though each painted madonna "is" the actual complex of paint in which she is embodied, though painted madonnas - or paintings of madonnas - all look different, all are different, one from another. But this is clearly not going to drive the psychophysical laboratory out of business, as the psychophysical laws they seek are of a different order, standing to the laws Davidson impugns as efficient causation stands to formal and material causation in that still useful schematism. I want to outline certain logical features of these.

Retentive materialism recognizes four main types of causal episode, depending upon whether cause or effect or neither or both have representational properties significantly (all of them obviously have what I am terming material properties, in consequence of there being nothing that is purely representational, i.e., whose only properties are representational). Abstracting for subjects, times, and places if relevant, the types of episode are (1) R-R, (2) $\not{R}$-R; (3) R-$\not{R}$; and (4) $\not{R}$-$\not{R}$, where 'R' attributes a representational property and '$\not{R}$' is understood to mean that there is no relevant representational property. By 'no relevant representational property' I mean that if there is one, it does not figure as explanandum or explanans in the episode in question. Thus I may break a tooth on a fortune cookie which bears the message "Only a fool bites hard" - but I take it the tooth would have broken even had the confection contained the usual chopstick wisdom, e.g., "Look before you leap", and that the "content" of the fortune cookie in this instance is gratuitous. $\not{R}$-$\not{R}$ episodes (physicophysic in the appropriate domain) are illustrated by the colliding billiard balls of classroom tradition. R-$\not{R}$ episodes are exemplified in the standard basic action, e.g., a reason explains an arm-rise, supposing the latter to be simply a physical movement and not representational in its own right, the way signals are. $\not{R}$-R episodes find their philosophically most useful examples in simple cognitions: the sun shines, causing me to believe that it does. If perception is representational, my perceiving the sun shining because it does shine is a further instance. So (2) and (3) cover psychophysical and physicopsychic episodes of causation, and (4) will cover psychopsychic episodes, as when I think of Swann because I think of Combray, or believe Max a crook because I believe (falsely as it happens) that he picked my pocket. I shall suppose that attribution of causality implies the existence of a general law, following White and Davidson in this, so that there will be psychophysical laws if there are type (3) causal episodes. But there are connections between cause and effect in types (1), (2), (3), and lacking in (4), and these are more pertinent

to the theory I am sketching than the long-moot-
ed questions of covering laws. It is these further connections which make representation "relevant" in explanation and, hence, in the human
sciences, where explanation of and through representations is one distinguishing mark.

These are *semantical* or *logical* connections.
Thus the effect in (2) is an action and not just
the consequence of a representation, only if it
satisfies the latter; the effect in (3) is a
cognition only if its cause satisfies it; and in
(4) it is an inference if someone represents
someone as a thief because he represents a pick-
pocket only if he also represents pickpockets as
thieves. So in (4) there are logical as well as
causal connections, and it is the former that
Hume meant to extrude from causal episodes of
type (4), opposing the theory that the world
holds together the way our minds do (it is a defect in his account that it opposes the thesis
that our minds hold together that way too, Hume
having no room for intentionality in his system).
Obviously a more detailed analysis than I can
give here is needed to close up, if indeed they
can be closed up, the sorts of gaps in each of
the relevant sorts of episodes in which Gettier-
style counterinstances flourish. But it is the
presence of these semantical conditions in certain central descriptions of cognition, action,
and ratiocination which make a further basis for
distinguishing the human, or at least the representational sciences from the nonrepresentational ones. It is through these relations that we
ourselves, as *ens representans*, relate differently to the world, to one another, and finally
to ourselves than mere things do. Indeed, it is
these "nonnatural" relations that must doubtless
be invoked in explaining how we come, evolution-
arily, to fit the world because our representa-

tions of it do. The contingencies of adaptation give a shape to our responses congruent with the shape of stimuli.

Beyond this it would be imprudent to trespass in the present paper. But the line that has emerged, between the representational and the nonrepresentational sciences, perhaps better answers to the true cleavages of the world than the line I began by retracing, between the so-called "human" and the so-called "natural" sciences. To be sure, we, as humans, are not segregated by this line from the balance of creation, as representationality is something shared by our fellow animals, and how deeply into the realms of matter representationality will be found is hardly something that can be decided in advance, or on the basis of philosophical arguments. For the rest, retentive materialism is a kind of scientific theory, at the crudest possible level, since it makes a truth claim against the world. But if it is at that level science, so is that controversy which has seemed at the heart of philosophy a scientific controversy, and the various postures on the mind-body problem but forms of anticipatory science. All philosophy can do is to work out the logical structure of the laws of representation.

THE CONCEPT OF INTELLIGENCE

Robert
Schwartz

Research on intelligence is in a peculiar state.
Debates rage over whether IQ tests really test
intelligence, whether intelligence is inherited
or acquired, whether intelligence consists of
one factor or many, whether creativity and
motivational factors are part of intelligence
or incidental to it, etc., etc. At the same time,
it is widely admitted that we have no clear idea
of what intelligence is. A.J. Edwards sums up
matters nicely: "Probably no phenomenon in human
society creates the interest that is generated
over intelligence. Though what the term means
might vary from person to person there is common
agreement that we observe the effects of intelligence in ourselves and others. Beyond this
general point there is inconsistency."[1] But it
is hard to see how many of the debates about intelligence can be satisfactorily resolved unless
we do move beyond such inconsistency. Without a
better understanding of the nature of intelligence, it is even obscure what sorts of evidence
would be relevant to supplying adequate answers
to these problems. The purpose of this paper is
to take some beginning steps toward an explication and clarification of the concept of intelligence. What I intend to do is isolate an
important sense of the concept's use, make some
basic distinctions using this analysis, and then
show how this analysis may be used to enhance
our understanding of related issues.

In searching for a fundamental sense of intelligence, I think it profitable to turn our backs
on the noun 'intelligence' and focus on the adverb

'intelligently'. For if we are to get to a prin-
cipled grip on the concept, we must pay attention
to how it may function in theory. And if intelligence is to play a significant role in psychological explanation, the obvious place for it to show
up would be in accounting for how we act intelligently. The more intelligent we are, the more intelligently we should be capable of behaving, defects in intelligence should be a hindrance to
intelligent behavior, and aspects of our intelligence should be correlated with aspects of intelligently performed activity. This, then, shifts
our concern to examining what it means for an
activity to be intelligently done, and, here perhaps the best starting point is still Gilbert
Ryle's *The Concept of Mind*.[2]

The main burden Ryle assumes in his discussion
of intelligence is to dissolve and dispel the so-
called "intellectualist's legend." The legend,
as Ryle sees it, arises from assuming that intelligent performance involves prior intellectual contemplation or adherence to propositions
entertained - from assimilating knowing how to
knowing that. But, Ryle argues, this view of
mind is mistaken. There are many skills or things
we may be said to know how to do for which we do
not know propositions describing relevant performance features. And even if we did, it would
not guarantee that we had the skill - knowing
the physical laws that describe balance points
is not the same as being able to ride a bicycle.
Further, Ryle points out a certain incoherence
in the intellectualist's position. He notes that
"the consideration of propositions is itself an
operation the execution of which can be more or
less intelligent, less or more stupid. But if
for any operation to be intelligently executed
a prior theoretical operation had first to be
performed and performed intelligently, it would

be a logical impossibility to break into the circle" (30). *Intelligent* cannot be equated with
intellectual, nor can *knowing how* be defined in
terms of *knowing that.* In place of the intellectualist's legend Ryle comments "What is involved
in our descriptions of people as knowing how...?
Part of what is meant is that, when they perform
these operations they tend to perform them well,
i.e., correctly or efficiently or successfully.
Their performances come up to certain standards
or satisfy certain criteria. But this is not
enough. The well-regulated clock keeps good time
and the well-drilled circus seal performs its
tricks flawlessly, yet we do not call them 'intelligent'...To be intelligent is not merely to
satisfy criteria, but to apply them; to regulate
one's actions and not merely be well-regulated.
A person's performance is described as careful
or skillful, if in his operations he is ready to
detect and correct lapses, to repeat and improve
upon successes, to profit from the examples of
others and so forth" (28/29). To demonstrate skill
or know-how in an activity is not to do two
things but to do one thing in a particular *way.*
For Ryle it is to do something well or successfully while being mindful of what you are doing,
ready to make corrections, adjustments, and
adaptations.

  With much of what Ryle says here I am in agreement, but I think there is a certain running together of issues in his account, which blurs distinctions important to our project. The problem
is that on Ryle's account there is a tendency to
assimilate *knowing how* to *being capable of intelligent performance* and to assume that *being capable of intelligent performance* entails *being good
or successful at the activity.* Israel Scheffler
in *Conditions of Knowledge* has taken Ryle to task
for linking knowing how too closely with intelli-

gent performance.[3] He argues that Ryle has been
led astray by his own analysis. Ryle wants to distinguish cases of knowing how from reflexes and
habits without claiming that knowing how requires
knowing that. To be said to know how to do something is to have acquired a level of proficiency
that demands training and practice. These concepts
of proficiency, training, and practice, Ryle feels,
do not apply to reflexes and habits. But then
Ryle goes on to assimilate knowing how to skilled
performance involving critical assessment and the
exercise of care. This, Scheffler notes, does not
follow. First, not all cases of know-how are
cases of skills that require critical assessment
or judgment. Second, it is a mistake to equate
knowing how with being good at the activity. In
most cases we distinguish between knowing how to
do something and doing it well. True, proficiency
does play a role in determining what we may be
said to know. For example, were we thoroughly
incompetent - could never get a ball over the net -
we would not know how to play tennis. Knowing
how to do something is to have a minimal proficiency or ability to succeed, but that is only
part of the story. Within the class of people who
know how to do X we observe gradations of skill,
proficiency, and success. And, as Scheffler shows,
running together knowing how and doing well ob-
scures important distinctions concerning learning,
teaching, and developing skills.

Now I maintain that the concept of intelligence
is also somewhat obscured on this analysis. The
connection between doing something intelligently
and doing it well or successfully is in important
ways looser than the Rylean analysis (and, I think,
even Scheffler's modified account) would suggest.
On both their accounts, there is the implication
or suggestion that to perform intelligently is
to be skilled, successful, or good at the activity,

and I do not think that this is entirely correct.
Ryle in part accepts this when he says that pre-
cision performance is not *sufficient* to make an
act intelligently done, what is further required
is a certain heed or mindfulness in the way it is
accomplished. What makes an act intelligent is
how it is done, the way it is brought about. But,
I would argue, these ways do not always entail
high achievement, advanced ability, success, or
expertise. To do X intelligently is not necessarily
to succeed at X-ing, to perform better than most,
or to be particularly skilled at doing X.

When we say that John is a more intelligent
tennis player than James we are not claiming that
John can beat James or that John is more skillful
than James - in fact the reverse may be true. To
play intelligently is to use your skills and abilities effectively, to have a reasoned game plan,
to be ready to adjust to changing conditions, to
take advantage of your own strengths and your
opponent's weaknesses. All this may improve your
game, but using your own abilities wisely is not
the same as being successful or attaining high
achievement. James may mindlessly and unintelli-
gently run John off the court. Intelligence has
more to do with the budgeting of our abilities,
with how we employ our abilities, than directly
with skill itself. The intelligent player is not
necessarily the best but rather the one who gets
the most mileage out of what he has got - and
gets this mileage because of efficient planning,
adaptation, and judgment. Similarly, the most
intelligent singer need not be the singer with
the best voice or the one whose performances are
most acclaimed. Rather the singer shows his intelligence in how he adapts to his limitations
and adjusts his performance so as to get the
most out of his voice.

This same distinction between success or achieve-

ment and intelligence holds for more intellectual
activities as well. Two people may both succeed
in proving a theorem, but the more intelligent of
the proofs is the one done with more economy of
method and axioms, with wise adoption of existing
lemmas, and lack of superfluous steps. To repeat
Ryle, intellectual activities can themselves be
done more or less intelligently. And, I would add,
intelligent performances may turn out more or less
successful. This of course is not to deny that
intelligence is often a component of achievement,
for the more intelligently people use their abilities, the better off they will usually be. Given
two people with the same skills, information, and
opportunities, we would expect the person who uses
them more intelligently to accomplish more.[4]

To summarize: Ryle, I think, is right in his
refusal simply to equate intelligence with the
intellectual. This not only enables us to avoid
certain mistakes in the philosophy of mind, but
has the further advantage of enabling us to apply the concept of intelligence more naturally to
a wider range of activities. For example, it does
not limit us arbitrarily to taking only traditional
school subjects as falling within the range of
the concept. Playing tennis, singing, doing carpentry are not excluded; they can all be done more
or less intelligently. Also, the concept can be
applied with less strain to animals and prelin-
guistic children. Doing well on intellectual tasks
is not seen as the only way to manifest intelligence, nor does excellence in just any intellectual task automatically entail high intelligence.
Finally, since intelligent performance need not
mean success, we cannot assume that lower levels
of achievement reflect lesser intelligence.

The Intellect
Denying the strong assimilation of intelligence

with the intellectual in order to emphasize its
links with economy, adaptation, and integration
of abilities leaves us, though, with many loose
ends. In particular, much more needs to be said
about the relationship between intellectual capacities and intelligently performed activity.[5]
Once intelligence has been severed from intellectual achievement, the next step is to initi-
ate some form of reconciliation. For there is
something essentially right in stressing the importance of certain intellectual competences
in describing and evaluating intelligence. Moreover, to accept the view that any capacity is
as constitutive of intelligence as any other not
only would do violence to our intuitions concerning intelligent activity but would render
the concept useless as an explanatory tool.
Nevertheless, I think distinguishing intelligence from the intellectual, in the way we did,
is a necessary step if we are to justify the
special importance of the intellectual in a non-
ad-hoc manner.

The wedge into these matters is to be found
in examining the way specific abilities may be
related to the intelligent guidance of activity.
By doing this, we can start to see grounds for
sustaining some of our intuitive claims about
the relevance and importance of certain skills
and capacities. For notice that, in refusing to
identify intelligence with the intellectual, we
have not committed ourselves to the position that
intellectual abilities are no more important to
intelligence than any others. The reason is that
some skills, in particular some intellectual
skills, enable us to use our other abilities and
competences more intelligently. Although these
intellectual skills are not identical with intelligence and although they themselves may be
employed stupidly or intelligently, they can and

do play an important role when it comes to planning, adjusting, and adapting other activities.

Verbal or symbolic proficiency is an obvious example. It has frequently been remarked that it is difficult to conceive how an organism lacking symbolic competence could have very complex thoughts or take account of spatially or temporally remote events or actions. Yet such complex interrelating of relevant variables, such allowing for changing conditions and mental testting of alternatives, are part and parcel of what we mean by acting intelligently. Where the farmer shows her intelligence over the lion or monkey is not in her native food-gathering abilities or particular successes. Rather she shows her intelligence in planning for future crops, adjusting to changing soil and climate conditions, profiting by her own mistakes and those of others, in ways far surpassing the animals'. But these are ways hardly conceivable as available to an organism that lacks symbolic skills. Competence in reasoning and use of logical concepts play a similar role. Our ability to understand logical relations, to see analogies, to make complex inferences, vastly enrich our minds in ways that enable us to use our native capacities and acquired competences more wisely. Memory capacity is another mental property that is of obvious importance to intelligent behavior. In order to plan, to adjust, and to adapt we must be able to recall past successes and failures, keep in mind our strategies, and store relevant information. These abilities require memory, and a severely limited memory capacity will limit how intelligently we can guide our activities.

With symbolic and logical skill and memory capacity we see a good deal of transfer and enrichment of our behavior patterns in general. These skills and capacities have a significant place in

the economy and guidance of our activities. The
same type of transfer and enrichment cannot be
seen to hold for many of our other skills and capacities. Being able to ride a bicycle or being
strong do not help very much in enabling us to
perform *intelligently* in other areas. Such skills
and capacities may enable us to perform better or
more successfully but not necessarily more intelligently.

So our analysis provides a preliminary basis for
separating competences and capacities in terms
of their contributions to intelligent activity.
A skill or capacity is more basic to intelligence
to the extent that it enhances the intelligent
guidance of our activities. This analysis fits in
nicely with David Weschler's position that "so far
as general intelligence is concerned intellectual
ability, per se, merely enters as a minimum."[6]
High levels of achievement on a mental or intellectual task will not be pertinent to intelligence unless the underlying competence is har-
nessed to enhance the wise organization of our
activities. Weschler's example of superior achievement on memory tasks may be a case in point. He
claims that whereas an immediate memory span of
around seven items seems important for intelligent functioning, having a span of twenty-five
may have little if any effect in promoting intelligent behavior.[7]

Another Aspect

Thus far we have sought to associate the intelligence ranking of a skill or capacity with its
contribution or potential contribution to the intelligent guidance of activity. But this way of
structuring matters does not do justice to some
further intuitions about intelligent skills. We do
feel that skill at chess is a more intelligent

skill than, say, skill at balancing a bicycle.
Still, being able to play chess may not enable
us to do very much else more wisely and so would
not meet our primary requirement for intelligence.

A resolution of this difficulty, though, is not
hard to find. Although skill at chess may not itself contribute to intelligence, reasonable skill
at chess usually is a manifestation of those abilities which we do feel are important for intelligent activity. The essence of chess is to plan,
to probe weaknesses, use strengths, and employ
strategy. Skill at chess requires a reasonably
good memory, facility with logical relationships,
and the ability to think up, keep in mind, and
evaluate alternative possibilities. And, since all
these skills and capacities are crucial for intelligent behavior in general, we see chess playing, as opposed to bicycle riding, as a manifestation of intelligence. In fact an even closer
connection between knowing how and intelligence
may be found in the case of competences like chess.
To know how to play chess (other than in the
sense of just knowing the rules) is to have a
minimal competence at the game, for example, not
to be mated always within four moves. This minimal competence, however, requires some ability to
plan, to evaluate alternative possibilities, to
adjust to the unexpected. To know how to play
chess is to an extent to play intelligently, and
doing well in chess usually requires playing intelligently.[8]

The link between skill and intelligence is even
stronger in certain other areas. Consider the
ability to read well. By reading well we mean
reading with comprehension and understanding, seeing the significance of points, drawing appropriate inferences, relating information presented to
previous beliefs, zeroing in on the essential and
skipping the unimportant. In short, to read well

is to read intelligently. Although one may be a
good but unintelligent tennis player, it is much
harder to make sense out of the distinction between a good reader and an intelligent reader.
   This last point serves to strengthen further
the ties between symbolic capacities and intelligence. As we noted, although symbolic competence may be necessary for very intelligent
behavior, it is obvious that merely being able
to speak is no safeguard against stupidity.
There is a sense, however, in which mastery of
any rich symbol system not only provides a potential for intelligent behavior but necessarily
manifests it. For mastering a language requires
more than the ability to parrot words or merely
recognize allowable syntactic patterns. To understand a language involves a whole constellation of interrelated skills and organizations.
As Gilbert Harman puts it, "meaning has to do
with evidence, inference and reasoning, including
the impact sensory experience has on what one
believes, the way in which inference and reasoning modify one's beliefs and plans and the way
beliefs and plans are reflected in action".[9]
Language skill requires and is evaluated in
terms of one's competence in the so-called "evidence, inference, action game." But if this is
so, linguistic competence cannot very easily be
separated from intelligence. Intelligent use of
language is necessary for the attribution of
linguistic competence at all. To use words too
stupidly or inappropriately is to fall below the
minimal level of mastery required for us to say
one knows how to speak the language.

Learning and Intelligence

One very common definition of intelligence identifies the concept with learning. It is claimed

that intelligence is a measure of the general
capacity to learn or learn quickly.   Like many
of the other prominent definitions of intelligence, this proposal captures a significant aspect of the concept.   Nevertheless, the simple
identification of intelligence with learning will
not do. A brief examination of this proposal and
comparison with our analysis will be instructive.

We have seen certain skills and abilities are
more closely linked with intelligence than others.
Symbolic competence affords a potential for en-
hancing the intelligent guidance of activity in
ways that swimming skills do not.   Bicycling ability is not a good indicator of intelligence; chess
and reading are. But if intelligence is merely
equated with learning capacity, there would be no
grounds for drawing such distinctions.   The capacity to acquire one skill would be on a par
with the capacity to acquire any other. Without
some additional principle for sorting out or
ranking learning tasks, equating intelligence
with learning will provide little purchase on
anything of psychological interest.

The relationship of learning speed to intelligence is another matter requiring clarification.
Although the capacity to learn certain things
quickly will often be a sign of intelligence,
the connection is not direct. Learning, like
other activities, is something that can be done
more or less intelligently; we may be stupid or
intelligent learners. We may learn by amassing
enormous numbers of instances, by tedious trial
and error, or we may take judicious shortcuts -
shrewdly eliminating unhelpful routes and wisely
transferring existing skills and information.
Intelligence in learning behavior is primarily
a matter of how the task is accomplished, or *how*
we learn.   A thoughtless rote procedure may prove
quite successful, without being the intelligent

way to learn. Rapid learning, in and of itself,
however, does not mean that intelligent learning
has taken place. Rate of acquisition will always
be a function of what capacities, other competences, and information are at hand. A child
with limited knowledge and experience may require
great ingenuity to learn slowly what an adult
may acquire readily, with little thought or
enterprise. Moreover, some skills may be acquired
quickly because they are genetically prefigured,
innately fixed to appear in full bloom with little
experience. Mastering such skills will not provide any real occasion for intelligent learning.
The fact that the resulting competence might be
highly organized and complex does not entail
that the learning process demanded much intelligence. The rapid development of nesting or
mating patterns does not show that the bird is
an intelligent learner. Speed of acquisition
amounts to intelligent learning only when such
speed is due to insight, efficient planning, and
other "intelligent" uses of strategy and materials.
    These considerations serve to bring out a cer-
tain ambiguity in the notion of intelligent
learning. We must distinguish between the intelligence shown in how we learn from the intelligence
demonstrated by what we learn. Human linguistic
competence provides an interesting case. Were
Noam Chomsky and others correct in claiming that
language competence is innately wired in and
merely triggered or "grown" by experience, language acquisition would not require intelligent
learning. Nevertheless, linguistic capacity and
its product, linguistic competence, are marks of
intelligence no matter how acquisition proceeds
and would be even if no learning were required.
The very nature of symbolic competence makes it
an intelligent skill; for where performance lacks
signs of intelligence we do not attribute the

competence.
   Our final qualm with the learning-intelligence
equation is that it is unnecessarily restrictive.
Along with Ryle, we argued that almost any activity can be performed with more or less intelligence. We saw no reason to limit application
of the concept to school subjects or mental tasks.
Nor do we see any reason why the concept should
be restricted to activities that involve learning.
People may demonstrate intelligence in carpentry,
reading, tennis playing, and singing long after
they have learned these skills. Of course, the
intelligent performer is the performer who continues to learn, who seeks out and is sensitive
to opportunities to improve, who learns from
past successes and failures. But the question
whether a given performance exhibits intelligence is not solely a matter of what has been
learned or whether learning has been successful. Insight, adjustment to new conditions,
effective planning, inventive problem-solving
are all features of intelligent behavior which
are not readily described as feats of learning.

Machines and Intelligence

Typically, then, intelligence manifests itself
in different ways, and these give rise to related but somewhat different usages of the term
'intelligence'. On the one hand, to perform intelligently is to use one's abilities wisely -
to adapt and adjust as the need arises and circumstances demand. On the other hand, certain
capacities and skills in and of themselves are
strongly linked to and usually are manifestations
of intelligence. Now paying attention to this
distinction will serve to highlight some complications in discussions about the intelligence
of machines.[10] The inclination to call some

machines "intelligent" is more closely connected
with our second usage. The question of intelligence never seriously arises with most of the
machines we daily come in contact with; it is
over computers, not water pumps or automobiles,
that the issue is debated. And the obvious reason is that the skills and capacities of computers, on the surface at least, resemble the very
abilities and functions we associate with intelligence. Computers play chess, make economic
forecasts, order the comings and goings of rail-
road freight – activities that are typically
signs of intelligence when performed by humans.
Their activities in fact are tasks formerly done
only by beings that display intelligence. Further, computer processes are typically described
in terms of capacities and competences that are
richly linked with intelligent performance.
Computers are said to manipulate symbols, have
memories, follow plans, and perform assorted
logical tasks. In contrast, the functions of
water pumps or automobiles are little if at all
related to the types of skills and capacities
essential for intelligence.
    But as alluring as it may be to attribute in-
telligence to machines, there is much that
argues against it. Perhaps the strongest argument derives from what we have been taking to
be the primary sense of intelligence – activity
intelligently done. For though the office computer does, say, arithmetical tasks, and may do
them more accurately than a mathematician, it
does not manifest signs of intelligence in its
computations. It does not try out new methods,
profit from errors, see short cuts, form habits
based on past successes, or generalize to related
cases. Also, if the machine is completely pro-
grammed to do its tasks, it will not show any
learning behavior. And if it does not learn at

all, it will not show signs of intelligent learning. Furthermore, symbolic and logical competence
are crucially associated with intelligence through
the importance of these skills in organizing and
guiding other activities. But in the case of the
computer there usually is no such transfer or
carry-over. The typical machine does not have a
life of goals and activities that must be coor-
dinated and planned. Nor does it have the need
or the ability to adapt to changes of environment
and scarcity of resources. Indeed, unless it is
specifically reprogrammed to do so, the computer
will not use the mathematical competence it displays for one task in handling quite similar
tasks where its capacities would be highly suited.

So there are countervailing pulls informing
our assessment of machine intelligence. Recent
machines, like the computer, are capable of doing
things that resemble human intellectual skills,
and some of these skills in turn are richly
linked with intelligence. However, as long as
the computer does not use its skill intelligently,
does not learn, and does not show transfer of
its competences in guiding and adapting its activities, there is a strong pull the other way.
What's more, considerations of this latter sort
are the basis for a reluctance to treat the computer's manipulation of marks or impulses as
exhibiting symbolic competence at all. For the
computer typically lacks many of the prerequi-
sites for being said to "understand" its symbols.
Understanding involves mastering to a reasonable
degree the role of the symbol in inference, action, and evidence relations - and integrating
the symbol into a whole range of activities. It
is closely tied to the symbols' intelligent use.
But, barring the computer's having a life of
purpose and having the need and capacity to adjust
to new environments, such use is not readily in

the offing. Human-like symbolic competence thus
represents the mastery and interrelating of a
more elaborate constellation of activities than
our ordinary machine can display in its use of
marks.

Intelligence, IQ, and Cultural Relativity

Our analysis of intelligence may also find application in another area of current debate. In
the much heated controversy over heritability
and IQ, the issue whether our concept of intelligence and our tests for intelligence are culturally biased has loomed large. Opponents of IQ
testing have maintained that the skills and capacities IQ tests attempt to measure are not independently motivated items, but represent a selection guided by social, economic, and cultural
biases. Perhaps surprisingly, many proponents of
IQ testing have also been willing to voice rela-
tivistic views about intelligence and intelligence
measures. For example, Arthur Jensen approvingly
quotes O.D. Duncan: "*intelligence* is a socially
defined quality...Had the first IQ tests been
devised in a hunting culture, *general intelligence*
might well have turned out to involve visual
acuity and running speed, rather than vocabulary
and symbol manipulation" (*op. cit.*, p. 14).
Similarly, but more moderately, Richard Herrnstein
says, "we would reject any intelligence test
that totally discounted verbal ability or logical
power, but how about athletic prowess or manual
dexterity or the ability to carry a tune or qualities of heart and character? More data are not
the final answer, for at bottom, subjective judgment must decide what we want the measure of intelligence to measure... In the case of intelligence, common expectations center around the
common purpose of intelligence testing - predict-
ing success in school, suitability for various

occupations, intellectual achievement in life.[11]

Now surely these theorists are correct when
they claim that IQ tests and the way they are
employed frequently reflect cultural interests.
They are also right in pointing out that social
and economic institutions influence which mental
traits are highly valued and rewarded. Still,
these sorts of claims may serve to foster confusions about intelligence and its role in psychological theory. For from the fact that different
abilities are rewarded in different cultures it
does not follow that what intelligence is is
merely a relative matter. That conclusion might
follow if we were to equate intelligence with
success or see intelligence as entailing high
achievement, but we have argued throughout that
this is mistaken. Intelligence does not imply
success in one's environment. Nor are intelligent skills necessarily the most prized; rather
they are those competences which most enhance
our ability to act intelligently. Speed afoot
is not in any obvious sense an intelligent
capacity and should not be regarded as such even
in a culture that highly rewarded swiftness.
There is still a difference between fleetness of
foot and the ability to run a race intelligently.
However, even in a culture where symbolic competence is not well regarded, having that skill
should enable people to function more intelligently.

This, of course, is not to support standard
IQ tests, student tracking, or any of the hoard
of other unpleasantnesses surrounding the IQ
testing industry. In fact, our analysis strongly
questions the simple identification of intelligence = IQ = social, educational or economic
success that is sometimes urged by defenders
of IQ testing. For suppose IQ tests do accurately
predict social, educational, or economic success,

or even suppose that factors IQ tests measure are causally relevant to such success, this just shows that they measure well the competences needed in a particular environment. It doesn't imply that they test intelligence. Justification of this latter claim would require evidence that the test measured those capacities and abilities we have seen to be important to intelligent behavior.

Footnotes:

Sidney has had a long-standing interest in the family of concepts concerned with human powers and dispositions; I have profited much from talking with him and reading his views on these topics. A while back we discussed some aspects of the concept of intelligence; he raised a batch of problems, and I suspect he will still have qualms with what I say. But Sidney without probing intellectual questions and helpful comments wouldn't be Sidney. So I look forward to continued inter-change with him on these issues. (The work presented here is a much condensed version of an unpublished study on intelligence which was supported by an N.E.H. summer grant.)

1. *Individual Mental Testing*, Part I (Scranton, Pa.: Intext, 1971), p. 1. Any perusal of the literature on intelligence will bear out Edwards' point. For some main trends see L. Tyler, ed., *Intelligence* (New York: Van Nostrand, 1969). See also the plethora of literature that has sprung from A. Jensen, "How Much Can We Boost I.Q. and Scholastic Achievement," in *Environment, Heredity and Intelligence* (Cambridge, Mass.: Harvard Educational Review, 1969).

2. New York: Barnes & Noble, 1949.

3. Chicago: Scott-Foresman, 1965, chap. 5.

4. There is thus a conceptual link between intelligence and success in that acting intelligently is seen as acting in ways that typically can be expected to improve achievement.

5. For Ryle's discussion of some of these matters see *op. cit.*, chap. 9.

6. *The Measurement and Appraisal of Adult Intelligence*, 4th ed. (Baltimore: Williams & Wilkins, 1958), p. 7.

7. Related points can be made about advanced mathematical or literary skills, along lines suggested by Wechsler.

8. The link between chess and intelligence is not an a priori matter. Were there devised a simple algorithm, comparable to that for tic-tac-toe, chess playing might not be a very good sign of intelligence.

9. "Meaning and Semantics," in M. Munitz and P. Unger, eds., *Semantics and Philosophy* (New York: NYU Press, 1975), p. 11.

10. My particular concerns here are not with the more metaphysical aspects of this issue, whose substance I am skeptical about in any case.

11. *I.Q. in the Meritocracy* (Boston: Little, Brown, 1971), p. 107.

David M.
Rosenthal

REDUCTIONISM
AND KNOWLEDGE

In *Philosophical Investigations*, Wittgenstein
writes of the "feeling of an unbridgeable gulf
between consciousness and brain-process." This
feeling, he suggests, occurs "when I, for example, turn my attention in a particular way on my
own consciousness, and, astonished, say to myself: THIS is supposed to be produced by a process in the brain! - as it were clutching my
forehead" (§ 412).

The sort of puzzled cognitive disorientation
that Wittgenstein here attempts to evoke is central to an eloquent and provocative challenge to
mine-body materialism that Thomas Nagel has recently developed. In two articles, "What Is It
Like to Be a Bat?" and "Panpsychism,"[1] Nagel has
set out to articulate, in a clear and compelling
way, that sense of the mystery of consciousness
which to many seems to undercut whatever lean-
ings we otherwise have toward a materialist theory of mind. On his view, accounts of mental phenomena offered in support of such theories have
failed "to deal explicitly with [the] subjective
character" of those phenomena (167). When one
faces up to this subjectivity of experience, Nagel
believes, the reductionism central to mind-body
materialism can be clearly seen to be untenable.
In what follows, I argue that the considerations
about subjectivity which Nagel invokes do not create problems for materialism, or for any reasonable version of reductionism implied by materialism. In particular, I contest the adequacy of Nagel's account of subjectivity and argue that the
account fails exactly at that point at which it
seems to yield his antireductionist result. I then
briefly indicate an alternative way, compatible
.with materialism, of accounting for the phenomena

of consciousness and subjectivity. Finally, I consider how these competing accounts of subjectivity bear on the relation between subjective and
objective knowledge, arguing that the naturalist
alternative I develop is preferable there as well.

I

My discussion will largely skirt features of Nagel's argument that are special to his more recent article, "Panpsychism." There Nagel argues
that the denial of reductionism, combined with
three other ostensibly innocent premises, entails
that the ordinary mental states of conscious organisms are causally necessitated by nonphysical,
"proto-mental" (183) properties of the ultimate
material constituents of things. The argument for
this surprising conclusion relies, however, on a
version of antireductionism which is far from
innocuous. For it not only states that "Ordinary
mental states...are not physical properties," as
many antireductionists maintain; it also asserts
that mental states are not even causally necessitated by physical properties, or at least not
by physical properties alone (181; cf. 186).
    Nagel's argument for this unusually strong
thesis of nonreductionism hinges on his observation that we have no idea of how physical heat,
for example, or a brain process, could causally
necessitate a pain or other sensation (187). By
contrast, it may seem wholly obvious that necessary causal connections do obtain in such familiar cases as "heat causing water to boil, rocks
causing glass to break, magnets inducing electric
current, [and] the wind making waves" (186).
These observations are, by themselves, unobjec-
tionable. But Nagel seems also to think that we
can in general determine by intuition when such
necessary connections are present and, indeed,

even in what cases they might be present (186).
If so, our current lack of understanding of how
psychophysical causal necessitation could occur
might cast doubt on the view that such causal
connections actually do obtain. But without
some recourse to a suitable theory, we cannot
simply read off the necessary connections among
things from our knowledge of their intrinsic
properties. In general, we appear to intuit the
presence of necessary connections in only those
cases in which we have some theoretical account
of the relevant phenomena. Moreover, the causal
results of combining things in complex ways can
be quite unexpected, especially in the absence
of any relevant theory. In the absence of such
theory, we could imagine being no less at a loss
to say, for example, how magnets induce electric
current, to say nothing of more esoteric effects
mentioned by Nagel, such as conversion of matter
into energy and the deflection of light by gra-
vity (184). When we turn to the mental, however,
we have at present virtually no suitable theory
on which to rely. So, given that we lack any
such theory, our failure to understand how physical properties can necessitate mental states
has, by itself, no tendency to show that they do
not actually do so.

A measure of the unusual strength of Nagel's
antireductionism can be got by comparing it with
his corresponding denial of emergence. Emergent
properties are generally thought of as properties
that occur only at higher levels of organization
or are needed only to explain phenomena that occur solely at such levels.[2] But the emergence
Nagel rejects is the stronger claim that complex
systems have properties not necessitated by the
properties of their ultimate constituents and
their mode of combination (182; cf. 186). So, if
nonmental microproperties were to necessitate the

mental properties of organisms, on Nagel's account these mental properties would be reducible
but not emergent. Nagel's denials of both emergence and reductionism are keyed to his view
that physical properties cannot necessitate mental states. The result is that, though few would
contest his version of antiemergence, the corresponding thesis of antireductionism is implau-
sibly strong.

Nagel's argument for "panpsychism" relies on
his premise that the mental states of an organism must be necessitated by the properties of
its ultimate material constituents. Since the
mental states cannot derive from the physical
properties of those constituents, the ultimate
particles must have some nonphysical properties.
Those nonphysical properties will be reached by
a "chain of explanatory inference beginning from
familiar mental phenomena"(183); it is therefore
natural to count those properties as mental properties.

Such reasoning is not wholly without precedent.
Locke maintained that, if mental states do belong
to material bodies, as he thought possible, such
states must be "superadded" by God (Essay IV, iii,
6), since they cannot be produced by senseless
matter (IV, x, 5).[3] Similarly, Erwin Schrödinger
urges that, because we cannot comprehend how physical interactions could produce sensory qualities, no scientific account of natural processes
can refer to or explain such qualities.[4] These
arguments all proceed from an antecedent assumption about what physical properties and processes
can and cannot necessitate. Indeed, without some
such assumption, no basis could exist for denying Nagel's innocuous version of emergence. Post-
Galilean science has decisively discredited the
idea that one can determine natural necessitation
by appeal not to theory, but to the intrinsic

properties of things. These arguments cast the
mental as the last refuge of a pre-Galilean es-
sentialism that would now be espoused for no
other natural phenomena.

Nagel's claim that none of the current kinds
of reductionism with respect to the mental "has
any intrinsic plausibility" (194; cf. 165/7) is
convincing if what he has in mind is such reductionist programs as behaviorist analyses or the
topic-neutral translations of J. J. C. Smart and
D. M. Armstrong.[5] But these programs are meant
to show not just that mental states are causally
necessitated by physical properties, but also
that mental states actually are physical states.
So the failure of these programs cannot help
substantiate Nagel's view that even the weaker
sort of reduction is impossible. Indeed, such
failures in general show nothing whatever about
whether a physical explanation of mental phenomena is possible. We are also unable to give
successful reductionist analyses of biological
concepts, but that casts no doubt on the possibility of a physical explanation of biological
phenomena.

Nagel's principal argument that the mental
cannot have a physical basis is independent,
however, of considerations pertaining to causal
necessitation. Rather, his central argument in
both articles is that it is impossible to give a
physical explanation of the subjective features
of mental states, that is, of "what any conscious
mental state is like for its possessor" (188).
"A feature of experience is subjective," Nagel
tells us, "if it can in principle be fully understood only from one *type* of point of view:
that of being like the one having the experience,
or at least like it in the relevant modality"
(188). By contrast, "how [things] are objectively...can be apprehended from different points

of view and [does] not belong to any" (189). The
incommensurable character of subjective features
and objective properties ensures, according to
Nagel, that no physical explanation of subjective features will be possible.

Nagel's language in both articles is powerful-
ly evocative of that sense of ourselves which
seems to make it hard to see how, as conscious
selves, we could find ourselves located among
the physical furniture of the universe. Nagel
seeks to express that sense in terms of a distinction between subjective and objective. I
shall not here question whether such a distinction, suitably defended, would cause trouble for
the kind of reductionism Nagel rejects. Rather,
I shall argue that the distinction Nagel does
rely on cannot sustain the problems he believes
reductionism faces.

Pivotal to Nagel's distinction is his notion
of a point of view. It is not easy to say exactly what that notion involves. But one aspect of
the notion undermines Nagel's particular use of
it in his argument. Nagel stresses that he is
talking not about individual viewpoints, but
about types of points of view. As he puts it,
"The point of view in question is not one acces-
sible only to a single individual" (171). And,
as he observes, reference to a type of point of
view seems to be what is needed to avoid the
charge that his argument tacitly relies on "the
alleged privacy of experience to its possessor"
(171). But, in order to draw the distinction between subjective and objective as Nagel does, we
must be able to distinguish between that which
"can be understood only from one kind of viewpoint" (188) and that which can be understood
from many different kinds. And this requires
that we have some way to determine when two individual points of view are of the same type.

As noted earlier, Nagel characterizes the relevant type of point of view as "that of a being like the one having the experience, or at least like it in the relevant modality" (188). But conscious creatures are, in relevant respects, alike and unalike to varying degrees. So conscious individuals will often, if not always, share a type of point of view not totally but only to some degree. And Nagel's statement that "A feature of experience is subjective if it can in principle be fully understood only from one *type* of point of view" (188) is carefully qualified by the phrases 'in principle' and 'fully'. These qualifications seem to justify an especially narrow account of when two individual points of view are of the same type. Similarly, Nagel notes that "It is often possible to take up a point of view other than one's own" (171). And he suggests that it is this ability which lies behind our counting two individual viewpoints as being of the same type (172). But he also goes on to observe that "The more different from oneself the other experiencer is, the less success one can expect" in taking up a viewpoint other than one's own (172). So, if a human being takes up the point of view of some other sort of creature to whatever extent is possible, the human being and the other creature will to some degree have the same type of point of view. By the same token, if we stress differences in past experience and physiology that distinguish various human beings, we may wish cautiously to say that they, too, have a common point of view not fully, but only to a certain extent.

But, if the difference between types of point of view is a matter of degree, it will also be a matter of degree whether something "can be understood only from one kind of viewpoint" (188). And this will make Nagel's distinction between subjec-

tive and objective into a matter of degree as
well. This should be neither a surprising nor an
unwelcome result, for we ordinarily take things
to be objective and subjective in varying degrees.
And, as Nagel notes (173), we can legitimately
doubt whether the limiting case of absolute objectivity could ever be reached, that is, whether
anything is ever apprehended that is entirely independent of any point of view. But if the distinction between subjective and objective is a
matter of degree in this way, it will no longer
be obvious why the objective properties of things
should be unable to necessitate the subjective
properties of experiences.

This concern about Nagel's notion of a point of
view can be approached more directly. Presumably,
when I take up the viewpoint of, say, a mouse to
some degree, I have some degree of access to the
conscious experience of the mouse [Nagel's example (189)]. But my viewpoint and that of the
mouse, however similar in various modalities,
will still differ in type. It seems to follow
from this that the experiences of the mouse can
be apprehended from two distinct types of point
of view, that of the mouse and my own. But, if
the experience of the mouse can be apprehended
from different types of point of view in this
way, it is hard to see what about the experience
will be subjective, given Nagel's account of
subjectivity.

Nagel maintains, however, that even if what is
subjective and objective is a matter of degree,
this does not affect "the point that psychophysical reduction cannot be accommodated by the
subjective-to-objective model familiar from other
cases   (173, fn. 9). Thus he writes:

It is difficult to understand what could
be meant by the *objective* character of an
experience, apart from the particular point

of view from which its subject apprehends
it. After all, what would be left of what
it was like to be a bat if one removed the
viewpoint of the bat? (173)

However, the sort of relativity between objective and subjective which Nagel considers is not
the same as that described above. Since the bat
and I share to some extent a common viewpoint,
this should enable me to capture the particular
viewpoint of the bat in a way that is relatively
more objective than would be possible from just
the bat's special viewpoint. Nagel denies that
one can, in this way, fully capture the bat's
viewpoint. For he maintains that that viewpoint
involves "facts beyond the reach of human concepts" (171). But the difference between the
bat's viewpoint and my own is a matter of degree,
just as the difference between the individual
viewpoints of distinct human beings is a matter
of degree. And Nagel offers no disanalogy to explain why such reasoning would not also imply a
difficulty in our grasping the viewpoint of
other normal human beings. Nagel denies that the
inaccessibility to us of the viewpoints of other
species is a matter of "the alleged privacy of
experience to its possessor" (171). But it is
far from obvious what other sorts of consideration would justify Nagel's adaptation of such
privacy to his claim of limited access by one
species to another's mental states.

Nagel's fundamental intuition about subjectivity is the epistemic idea that viewpoints matter in our comprehension of subjective, but not
objective, features. He expresses this intuition
in his claim that subjective features can "be
fully understood only from one *type* point of
view" (188). Viewpoints can be typed with variable strictness, however; which features count
as subjective will shift accordingly, and rela-

tivity about the subjective is thus unavoidable.

Jerome Shaffer (in correspondence) has proposed a way to avoid this relativity. Let subjective features be those whose comprehension depends to some extent on how closely we resemble, in relevant respects, the conscious creature. Then, Shaffer suggests, how we type viewpoints will not matter, since we grasp objective features equally well regardless of how much we resemble the object that has them. But this seems not to be so. We find macroscopic objects far easier to understand than quarks or quasars; less dramatic comparisons also attest to the difference that familiarity and resemblance make in grasping uncontroversially objective features. Such an account of the subjective thus cannot sustain the contrast with objectivity needed to express Nagel's intuition.

II

Nagel's realism about mental states (171, 187–193) and his denial of reductionism are both geared to the assumption that ordinary mental states have subjective features. Nagel concedes that "Not all mental states are conscious," but he believes that any mental state is, as he puts it, "capable of producing" conscious states (188). So, even if we could explain how physical properties necessitate nonconscious mental states, Nagel insists that we would still have to show how nonconscious mental states can necessitate conscious states that have subjective features (188). But, since his account of subjective features relies on the problematic notion of a type of point of view, it is unclear what would satisfy this demand.

A subjective feature is "what any conscious mental state is like for its possessor" (188);

so only conscious mental states will have subjective features. Nagel's particular examples of nonconscious mental states have to do with "concepts like repression and utility function, or perhaps universal grammar" (185), which are invoked in rather specialized psychological theories. But Nagel counts as mental anything whose existence we infer only in order "to explain mental phenomena (including actions)" (185). So these examples will be far from the only cases of nonconscious mental states. For common sense and psychological theory alike infer the occurrence of nonconscious mental states that we describe by means of the very same phenomenal and intentional vocabulary we use to discriminate among types of conscious mental states. And, if conscious and nonconscious mental states have the same sorts of phenomenal and intentional properties, it is hard to see what the subjective features of conscious mental states can amount to except for the consciousness of those mental states.

Nagel's attack on reductionism does not involve denying that the intentional and phenomenal properties of nonconscious mental states can be given a physical explanation. It is rather the passage from physical properties to conscious states with subjective features which causes the difficulty. But it is possible that a satisfactory account of the consciousness of mental states can be constructed which appeals to nothing beyond the intentionality of thoughts. On such an account, a conscious mental state is simply a mental state accompanied by a thought that one is in that particular mental state. This account would explain why subjective features seem essentially to involve a mental state's phenomenal or intentional character, in addition to the mere circumstance of the state's being a conscious state. For on this account the consciousness of a mental state would imply the relevant intentional or phenomenal characteristics, because such consciousness would consist in one's having an accompanying thought that one is in a mental state with just those phenomenal or intentional properties. And, if not all mental states need be conscious, then the fact that we commonly do not notice having such second-order thoughts causes no difficulty. For there is no reason why those second-order thoughts should, in general, themselves be conscious thoughts.

Many nonlinguistic animals may well have sophisticated enough thoughts for a fair number of their mental states to be conscious mental states, on this account, and therefore to have subjective features. But we also need not suppose that, simply because a creature is conscious, its mental states are conscious mental states. A creature's being conscious often amounts to no more than that it is awake and sentient and, perhaps, exhibits purposive behavior. Such a creature can still have a rich mental life, even if many or all of its mental states are not conscious states. These considerations suggest that, *pace* Nagel (169), the idea that there is something that it is like to be such a creature can amount to no more than that theoretically inclined beings like ourselves can, to some degree, imagine what it would be like for one of us to be such a creature. If, however, the intentional and phenomenal properties of nonconscious mental states do not result in any difficulty for reductionism and if this account of the consciousness and subjective features of ordinary mental states is correct, then these phenomena, too, may turn out to have a physical explanation.[6]

Confusion is easy here because of a temptation

simply to conflate the subjective with the qualitative. The absence of a positive account of sensory qualities may lead one to assume that one
cannot comprehend such qualities except by reference to centers of consciousness, which have
points of view. In one way this is correct; we
must fix the reference of terms for qualitative
states by means of conscious subjective features.
But it is question-begging to conclude that, because we cannot know what it would be like to
have a nonconscious sensation, nonconscious sensations are impossible. Knowing what a state
would be like, in the relevant way, just is being
conscious of it. And no non-question-begging
reason exists to think we are conscious of all
our sensory states. A mystery about subjectivity
seems to emerge if one yokes together sentience
with that consciousness which constitutes subjectivity. But if many sensory states lack consciousness, there will be no basis for this un-
restricted association, and no reason to reject
an account of consciousness in terms of higher-
order thoughts.

Nagel does raise one doubt concerning his
"realism about the subjective domain in all its
forms" (171). For he notes that "When a mouse is
frightened it does not seem...that a small material object is frightened" (189). But it is far
less obvious that such discomfort exists in thinking of a small living thing as being frightened.
Indeed, much of the intuitive difficulty in thinking of physical systems as having mental states
seems to be relieved if we first think of the
physical system as a living thing. This suggests
that, if we had a clearer understanding of how
physical systems can be living things, the difficulty about their having mental states would
not seem to loom so large.

Nagel's conclusion in "Pansychism" is that

we must postulate "proto-mental" properties (183)
of fundamental physical particles, which causally necessitate mental states. It is this conclusion which distinguishes Nagel's "panpsychism"
from other, less extravagant forms of the view
that mental phenomena are somehow discontinuous
with all other natural processes. But Nagel
correctly observes that

> ...it is difficult to imagine how a chain
> of explanatory inference could ever get
> from the mental states of whole animals
> back to the proto-mental properties of
> dead matter. ... Presumably the components
> out of which a point of view is constructed
> would not themselves have to have points of
> view (194).

But this is virtually the same difficulty that
animated Nagel's argument against reductionism.
Nonmaterial souls cannot help explain subjectivity, according to Nagel, since "there is just
as much difficulty in understanding how [a soul]
could have a point of view" (190). But it is at
least as hard to see what good protomental properties could do. Indeed, the self-awareness of
Cartesian souls, by seeming to provide a way of
individuating conscious selves, contributes to
the intuitive notion of a viewpoint in a way
that protomental properties clearly cannot. The
conceptual resources of Nagel's panpsychism, no
less than those of Cartesian dualism, are
tailored to enable a full comprehension of the
subjectivity of conscious mental states. Their
inability to achieve this is therefore compelling evidence that the very demand to understand such subjectivity, at least in the way
Nagel requires, is misconceived.

III

A peculiar double standard affects Nagel's treatment of the distinction between subjective and
objective. Objectivity, on his view, not only
comes in degrees, but possibly comes only in degrees: "It may be more accurate to think of objectivity as a direction in which the understanding can travel" than as a matter of things'
having some "completely objective nature" (173).
By contrast, subjective features "can in principle be fully understood only from one *type* of
point of view" (188); such features will therefore be subjective not simply to some degree,
but without qualification. Indeed, unless subjective features do exist which wholly lack objective character, Nagel's problem about reductionism cannot be raised. For it is only the
idea that "the facts of experience...are accessi-
ble only from one point of view" that creates the
apparent "mystery [about] how the true character
of experiences could be revealed in the physical
operation of [the] organism" (172). Though one
will have less success when one "take[s] up a
point of view" (171) of a strikingly different
being, Nagel believes absolute success is possible; it consists in "understand[ing an] ascription [of experience] in the first person as
well as in the third" (172).
  Seeing objectivity as coming only in degrees
is unproblematic. Indeed, a reasonable caution
about our ability to obtain knowledge of objective reality may seem to dictate some such picture. But the idea of an unqualified realm of
subjectivity is less benign. The idea of undiluted subjectivity, and the attendant disanalogy
just noted between subjective and objective,
both result from construing the objective as deriving, in a particular way, from what is in-

trinsically subjective. The objective is ab-
stracted, on this view, from the intrinsically
subjective by stripping away whatever contributions are made by particular points of view. The
objective therefore depends on the subjective,
in that one only reaches the objective by performing suitable operations on what is in itself
subjective. The subjective not only occurs in a
pure form, therefore, unadulterated by any objectifying abstractions from particular viewpoints; it is also independent of the objective
and can stand on its own. For one's grasp of the
subjective in no way relies on or presupposes
any grasp of what is objective. On this picture,
one could readily imagine having knowledge only
of the subjective and wholly lacking even a conception of the objective.

But, rather than take the subjective to be
basic in this way, one can reverse the picture
and think instead of subjective features as
being just those features which are tied especially intimately to the particular character of
perceiving and thinking organisms. Although this
conception reflects Nagel's basic intuition that
subjective features are inherently tied to points
of view, it does so by means of a thoroughgoing
naturalism about the nature and origin of those
differences which separate creatures with distinct perceptual and cognitive apparatus. It
therefore in no way suggests that our understanding of subjective features has some special status or that our knowledge of the subjectivity of
other sorts of creatures is somehow ineluctably
impaired. Since subjective features, on this picture, are just features that depend intimately on
the character of conscious organisms, their very
subjective character will have an objective base.
And one can to some extent sustain the notion of
a variety of types of viewpoint by appealing to

whatever objective features of the organism are
relevant to the distinctive ways in which the
organism experiences things.

Nagel, however, sees objectivity as deriving
by abstraction from the intrinsically subjective.
And he insists also on an undiluted level of subjectivity, while remaining "noncommittal" about
whether anything has a "completely objective intrinsic nature" (173). This agnosticism about
absolute objectivity is a result, in his discussion, of his view of the objective as deriving
from the intrinsically subjective, as is his companion committment to undiluted subjectivity. But
these two views need not be so connected; the
existence of subjective or objective in some
pure form by itself neither implies nor precludes
seeing one of this pair as deriving from the
other.[7] And, for present purposes, the existence
of subjective or objective in pure form matters
less than simply whether one is, relative to the
other, more primary. If, as Nagel urges, the objective is a refined form of the subjective, the
kind of knowledge that is appropriate to objective reality will inevitably leave out what is
special to the subjective. The very idea of knowing the subjective in the way we know the objective will accordingly be incoherent. But if, instead, the subjective is simply a particular
form of the objective, the very attempt to say
what is special about the subjective will be
based on our knowledge of uncontroversially objective matters. (I speak henceforth of knowledge
of the subjective and of the objective as, respectively, subjective and objective knowledge,
implying nothing about the quality of either
sort.)

Seeing the subjective as basic, and the objective as the result of abstracting from particular
viewpoints, invites various familiar doctrines

that together constitute the Cartesian concept
of mind. Abstracting from particular viewpoints
implies distinguishing how things really are
from how they seem to be, from those viewpoints.
Correspondingly, no distinction can obtain prior
to such objectifying abstraction; until one dis-
regards how things seem from particular viewpoints, appearance and reality cannot help but
coincide (see 174). By contrast, if the subjective is simply that which is tied especially
closely to the particular character of conscious
creatures, we can draw an unproblematic and useful distinction between the reality of subjective features and how those features appear.
First-person reports will typically tell us how
they appear, whereas accounts in terms of the
functioning of the organism will reveal their
reality.

Similarly, the idea that the objective derives
by abstraction from what is intrinsically subjective implies that subjective knowledge, unlike
knowledge of what is objective, is immediate and
immune from error. Stripping away from subjective
representations whatever pertains to particular
viewpoints is a process fraught with risk; one
may abstract in the wrong direction or insuf-
ficiently carefully, or go wrong in countless
other ways. On this conception of objectivity,
however, some such process is required to reach
knowledge of objective reality. That process inevitably must mediate between the putative knowledge one arrives at and what that knowledge
purports to be about; the process will therefore
be an ineliminable source of error. No such medi-
ation or possible error can intrude in the case
of subjective knowledge, since, on this conception, knowledge of what is subjective is our
starting point. This conception therefore reflects the familiar Cartesian idea that, ulti-

mately, all knowledge is based on subjective knowledge. And the privilege of subjective knowledge could lead Locke to claim that nobody can "be in doubt when any *Idea* is in his Mind, that it is there, and is that *Idea* it is" (IV, vii, 4). Nagel's disclaimer, that subjectivity is not a matter of "the alleged privacy of experience to its possessor" (171), does not affect these points. For the grasp he supposes we can have of the subjective features of others will be unmediated in the relevant way, at least insofar as that grasp is distinctively subjective. By contrast, again, if the subjective is simply what is especially closely tied to the makeup of the knowing organism, subjective knowledge will have no such privileged status. For then the subjective is just a special case of the objective, and is susceptible to whatever epistemic hazards affect the enterprise of knowing, generally.

If appearance and reality coincide for subjective features and if knowledge of such features is immediate and immune from error, it is natural to see subjective knowledge as the paradigm of knowledge. The immediacy of subjective knowledge will encourage the conviction that there is nothing about the subjective that cannot be known by intuitive inspection. For example, if it seems incomprehensible that nonsubjective processes should causally necessitate subjective features, the transparency of subjective knowledge will warrant the conclusion that such necessitation is indeed impossible. Knowledge of the subjective will accordingly have the kind of transparency to intuition sometimes attributed to knowledge of abstract entities and of mathematics. It is perhaps somewhat less surprising, therefore, that the subjective is the last stronghold of reliance on pre-Galilean essences. For, on the classical picture, these essences were grasped by the immediate operation of the intellect. Moreover, if subjective knowledge is paradigmatic of knowledge, it will be tempting to extend the application of immediate intuition to other areas as well, such as determining the limits of causal necessitation.

It is sometimes urged that the recalcitrance of mental states to natural explanation forces us to treat the mental as knowable only by immediate intuition. This line of reasoning is far from convincing. The relative autonomy of the mental does not preclude naturalist explanation, and other indisputably objective areas of knowledge, such as biology, also exhibit substantial autonomy. Taking subjective knowledge to be paradigmatic of knowledge generally does, however, explain the tendency to insist that only immediate introspective knowledge can do justice to mental states. For, if subjective knowledge is paradigmatic knowledge, our grasp of mental states, at least of our own, is automatically superior to any understanding of such states that represents them as objective. By contrast, if the subjective is just a special case of the objective, subjective knowledge will lack privileged status and there will be no reason to rule out knowledge of subjective features that represents them in nonsubjective terms. It is not recalcitrance to natural laws that accords special status to introspection; rather, the idea that introspection is privileged leads to doubts about the possibility of objective knowledge of the mental.

The presumed perfections of subjective knowledge make it inviting to see such knowledge as the paradigm of knowing. Its immediacy and infallibility guarantee its excellence as a kind of knowledge. Equally well known are the adverse consequences this view has with respect to the

possibility of knowing objective reality. The
immediacy of subjective knowledge suggests that
objective knowledge, too, must somehow make direct contact with its object. This measure of objectivity suggests that a tactile model of knowing underlies Cartesian views about knowledge,
rather than the optical model so often described.
The frustrations attendant on modern efforts to
articulate standards of justification that can
certify direct contact with objective reality
are familiar, and their lesson discouraging.

Less often noticed is the way this dramatic
disparity between subjective and objective knowledge depends on one's prior conceptions of the
objective and subjective, and the relation between them. On the Cartesian conception, the
subjective has independent status, and the objective derives from it by abstracting away from
particular viewpoints. And, if subjective knowledge is paradigmatic, it stands on its own,
needing no external validation. One obtains objective knowledge, however, by taking subjective
representations, such as beliefs or sense impressions, and screening them by reference to suitable conditions of justification. Just as a process of abstraction from what is special to particular viewpoints takes one from what is subjective to what is objective, so the process of justification is intended to take one from subjective to objective knowledge.

This dual primacy of subjective over objective
does justice to neither side. Not only does the
presumed purity of subjective knowledge impose
the unattainable goal of a parallel purity in
knowing the objective; taking subjective knowledge as a model leads to needless and perhaps
unresolvable problems about knowledge in general.
For example, it seems impossible to have subjective knowledge of which one is unaware; this

suggests that, unless one knows that one knows, one's knowledge will fail to satisfy the standards set by subjective knowing. On a common-sense view, knowledge can be explicit or tacit, conscious or not. So the problem about knowing that one knows is, in a way, idle. For knowing that one knows is ordinarily thought to mean that one is conscious that one knows. But, unless one adopts the model of subjective knowledge and assumes from the outset that all knowledge implies consciousness, there will be no reason to assume that second-order knowing will succeed in introducing consciousness. And, if one adopts that model, consciousness will come with all knowledge, whether or not knowing implies knowing that one knows.

One may well doubt whether abstracting from what is special to particular points of view can help achieve actual objectivity, as opposed to merely minimizing the vagaries of our apprehension of the subjective. Refined subjective knowledge is still simply refined knowledge of the subjective; such refinement cannot reach beyond the subjective to make contact with objective reality. On the other hand, without some independent idea of knowledge of objective reality, it is far from obvious that knowledge of the subjective realm can be made intelligible. Wittgenstein suggests that it may be impossible "to imagine someone else's pain on the model of one's own...: for I have to imagine pain which I *do not feel* on the model of the pain I *do feel*" (§ 302). Once I have crossed the boundary between myself and another, even another of the same type, I cannot help but have some sort of objective knowledge. But, as Wittgenstein urged, there may be nothing to knowing my own pain unless I tie that knowledge to my knowledge about the pains of others. If so, pure subjective knowledge, so

called, may be no more than merely being in particular conscious mental states, and not actually a form of knowledge at all. Nagel is right
that knowing bat physiology will not make one be
in the mental states of a bat. But, if subjective features are just those features which are
intimately tied to the specific constitution of
the organism, insofar as the organism has mental
capacities, being in the mental states of a bat
is just part of being a bat. That being in such
states is beyond our powers is no more a mystery
than that we cannot perform the bodily feats
bats can. Nor do these considerations suggest
the existence of subjective features inacces-
sible to objective understanding.

Footnotes:

    I have greatly benefited from numerous con-
versations with Sidney Morgenbesser, always as
enjoyable as they have been rewarding, on subjectivity, mind, knowledge, and related topics;
hence this paper.

    1. "What Is It Like to Be a Bat?", *Philosophi-
cal Review*, LXXXIII, 4, (October 1974): 435–50;
reprinted in *Mortal Questions* (New York: Cambridge, 1979): 165–180. "Panpsychism," first
published in *Mortal Questions*: 181–195. Unless
otherwise indicated, page references in the text
are to *Mortal Questions*; all quoted emphasis is
original. Also original in *Mortal Questions* is
"Subjective and Objective," which discusses the
issues of concern here in relation to other ins-

tances of the contrast between subjective and objective. See also Nagel's "The Limits of Objectivity," in Sterling M. McMurrin, ed., *The Tanner Lectures on Human Values,* vol. I (University of Utah Press and Cambridge University Press, 1980): 77-139, esp. 77-96.

2. See P. E. Meehl and Wilfrid Sellars, "The Concept of Emergence," in Herbert Feigl and Michael Scriven, eds., *Minnesota Studies in the Philosophy of Science,* vol. I (Minneapolis: Univ. of Minnesota Press, 1956): 239-252, esp. 249-251.

3. For a helpful discussion of Locke's views on this issue, see Margaret D. Wilson, "Superadded Properties: The Limits of Mechanism in Locke," *American Philosophical Quarterly,* XVI, 2 (April 1979): 143-150, esp. 145-147.

4. *Mind and Matter* (New York: Cambridge, 1959), ch. 6. Sellars' argument that categorial transformations of sensory qualities must occur, at the level of microstructure, in an adequate scientific account of things relies on considerations pertaining to conceptual frameworks in ways not reflected in the discussions of Nagel, Locke, and Schrödinger. See esp. "Scientific Realism and Irenic Instrumentalism," in R. S. Cohen and M. W. Wartofsky, eds., *Boston Studies in the Philosophy of Science,* vol. II (New York: Humanities, 1965): 171-204, sec. V and esp. § 57; and his Carus Lectures, "Foundations for a Metaphysics of Pure Process," *Monist,* LXIV, 1 (January 1981): 3-90.

5. E.g., in Smart, "Sensations and Brain Processes," in V.C. Chappell, ed., *The Philosophy of Mind* (Englewood Cliffs: Prentice-Hall, 1962): 160-172, pp. 167/8; and Armstrong, *A Materialist Theory of Mind* (New York: Humanities, 1968), pp. 76-85.

6. In "Two Concepts of Consciousness," type-

script, I defend a naturalist account of the consciousness of mental states along these lines; in "Thinking that One Thinks," typescript, I argue that no other sort of account can be made coherent. In "Mentality and Neutrality," *Journal of Philosophy*, LXXIII, 13 (July 15, 1976): 386-415, sec. I, I argue that, by themselves, intentional and qualitative properties cause no difficulty for even the strong reduction implied by mind-body materialism.

7. Zeno Vendler, e.g., articulates an account in *Res Cogitans* [(Ithaca: Cornell, 1972), chs. IV and V, esp. 85-88 and 114-119] which accords pride of place to subjectivity, but also recognizes an undiluted realm of objectivity. According to Vendler, objective facts and possibilities derive by abstraction from subjective representations (87), but the resultant objectivity is pure, in that it relies on reference uncontaminated by sense (87, 115). Subjectivity, by contrast, admits of degrees (114). Vendler refines this account in "Escaping from the Cave: A Reply to Dunn and Suter," *Canadian Journal of Philosophy*, VIII, 1 (March 1978): 79-87.

Bernard Berofsky

AUTONOMY

Discussions of free will typically proceed in two stages. The first is addressed to the conditions of freedom of action and concerns factors, such as desires and beliefs, that enter into the explanation of action. Debates emerging on this level are initially engaged on the tacit assumption that issues that arise concerning the genesis of the pertinent psychological states can be dealt with separately. To be sure, there is a traditional distinction between freedom of action and freedom of will which facilitates this bifurcation - my freedom to do what I will is surely a different matter from my freedom to have a will different from the will I have.

If, however, some philosophers, e.g., C.A. Campbell, are somewhat more reluctant to dissociate will from action where moral responsibility is involved, it may be due to the feeling that more is at stake here. If I am going to say not just that a person acted freely, but that he is, as well, now liable to certain possibly unpleasant responses and onerous demands, I had better be sure that he has indeed merited this status, and it may (justifiably) be felt that responsibility for his will is required in this connection.

The term 'autonomy' is traditionally used to characterize the state required, in addition to freedom of action, for full freedom (or freedom of will) and moral responsibility. Our concern in this paper is the relation between autonomy and moral responsibility.

The view of Harry Frankfurt, that concern about
the genesis of a person's motivational structure
is misplaced as long as he has a stable character of some sort, is based upon his belief in
the all-importance of identification with one's
volitional nature. "To the extent that a person
identifies himself with the springs of his actions, he takes responsibility for those actions
and acquires moral responsibility for them; moreover, the questions of how the actions and his
identifications with their springs are caused
is irrelevant to the questions of whether he performs the actions freely or is morally responsible for performing them."[1]
   Identification is puzzling in its nature and
its object. If identification is an act of some
sort, it cannot be characterized entirely in
terms of the state of desire. Yet Frankfurt sometimes talks as if a person's *having* second-order
volitions is constitutive of identification. This
may not sound problematic because the term 'volition' conveys the idea of "act of will"; but, on
Frankfurt's account, a volition is not an act
at all, but rather a desire that is distinguished
from other desires by its content. Specifically,
a second-order volition is a desire that a certain first-order desire be effective; but it does
not necessarily involve even a bare attempt to
bring this state of affairs about. At other times,
he talks about the person's forming a second-order
volition; but, although formation would presumably
be an act, he does not seem to preclude the case
of a person who just *finds* that he has   second-
order volitions - perhaps having been provided by
the philosopher's omnipotent demon (henceforth
"OD") - and, on that basis alone, may be said to
have identified with certain first-order desires.
   Yet, in a discussion specifically devoted to
the concept of identification, Frankfurt does

come around to the position that identification
is a species of action, namely, decision or something decision-like (in spite of his implausible
insistence that identification with *desire* requires
no act).[2] If so, what is its content? Frankfurt
appears to identify identification, for reasons
I do not find compelling, with appropriation or
the assumption of ownership. Hence one may have
a desire that can be rendered external to oneself by a contrary act, expulsion. He criticizes
Terence Penelhum for a failure to be sensitive
to the possibility of a sense of externality
other than the mundane one according to which
each desire that arises in my psychic history is
of necessity internal to me and for his exag-
gerated fears that the freedom to perform such
banishments is tantamount to a license to engage
in moral evasion and self-deception.[3]

No doubt, feelings that passions and desires
we experience are alien occur; but these feelings
are neither necessary nor sufficient for externality on Frankfurt's account. The description
he ultimately adopts is given in terms of an
example of an ambivalent response to another's
achievement. "By deciding that what he wants
after all is to compliment his acquaintance, and
that his desire to injure the man is finally to
be excluded from the order of candidates for
satisfaction, the person renders the second external to himself and identifies himself with
the first."[4]

Identification, it would appear, is constituted by a commitment to reinforce or to attempt
to do what one can to ensure that a certain desire will be one's will. In fact it is the very
feature missing from Frankfurt's concept of a
second-order volition which would allow us to
call it a volition in the traditional sense,
i.e., an act of will.

Moreover, it is almost exactly the sort of action selected as crucial for freedom of will by libertarians, viz., the reinforcement of certain desires by an effort of will emanating from the self. The libertarian's metaphysical description is, however, different from Frankfurt's. Whereas Campbell and Roderick Chisholm would refuse to identify the self with either desire, the rejected or the endorsed one, Frankfurt is not motivated to retain a conception of the self or person that totally excludes components of empirical or introspective psychology. The central reason is Frankfurt's rejection of libertarian incompatibilism, i.e., his benign attitude, in the context of concern about free will and moral responsibility.

Although, for the libertarian, desires, as natural elements in the causal nexus, are excluded from the self, it is not clear why the rejected desire is described by Frankfurt in these terms. The act of rejection is not extrusion from self, but simply the refusal to act on the desire, if possible. I see no philosophical need and find no introspective basis for reporting the experience in these metaphysical terms. If I refuse to support my son's excesses, I do not ipso facto conceive of him as ostracized from the family. Penelhum was basically right. Alcoholics are reminded that they continue to be alcoholics and must continue to so regard themselves even if they succeed in resisting temptation forever more.

Also, it might be difficult to explain why a person *regrets* the fact that the rejected impulses continue to arise if they are not arising in *him*. To be sure, he may regret the unpleasant effort he must each time expend to prevent the unwanted action from ensuing. But why should he feel - and he may no doubt have this feeling - that he has fallen short of his ideal to the extent that these feelings recur?

This sense of *personal* disappointment, moreover,
precludes the attempt to explain away the phenomenon of regret as regret about the existence in
the world of yet another undesirable impulse. Also, the fact that he may feel no guilt if he is
rational and has done all that can reasonably be
expected of him to thwart or remove these impulses
does not preclude the presence of this distinct
feeling of disappointment or regret.

If you threaten me with harm in the event I
fail to cooperate with you to further your evil
ends and if, on each occasion, I thwart you in
one way or another, I will feel neither personal
regret nor guilt. But if I must periodically
thwart my own evil desires - I should say evil
desires I happen to experience - success in this
case is not incompatible with a self-appraisal
that results in or sustains a diminished self-
image. I would be much happier with *myself* if
these desires never cropped up at all in my consciousness.

Frankfurt's attempt to assimilate nonidentification with desires to nonidentification with a
bodily movement that is not an instance of agency
is similarly unsuccessful. To see this, we need
only modify the above case by supposing that you,
realizing that I will not participate in your
evil venture, physically coerce me by moving my
limbs in an appropriate way. I can obviously divorce myself from the movements of my body in the
same way I can divorce myself from a bodily movement of mine that constitutes a bumping into you
on a lurching bus. Though I regret the fact that
you were jostled and though politeness requires
that *I* say "Excuse me," my self-image is unaffected.
My self-image may be affected, however, if I experience a desire to hurt you, whether or not I
succumb.

Frankfurt's position may sound more plausible

for the case of a unique and quickly passing whim.
I may be simply amused that I once had a brief
urge to pull a chair from under that heavy person
about to sit upon it. I neither acted on nor ever
again entertained such impulses. But if, like an
alcoholic, I experience such desires regularly,
if they are very powerful, and if I join Chair
Pullers Anonymous and am there taught to avoid
dinner parties, card games, and business meetings, then my never having succumbed to temptation may help my self-image in respect to my
strength of will, but it certainly does not en-
title me to omit reference to these strange impulses in an (honest) autobiography. There is,
in Frankfurt's account, an inordinate emphasis
upon action as the central element in personhood,
an emphasis which appears paradoxical in light
of his conception of a person as one capable of
second-order volitions. The reason is that Frankfurt conceives of the second-order process not
just as determining which of *my* desires will be
supported in their quest for satisfaction, but
rather as determining which of my desires will
continue to be mine in virtue of my continued
support in various possible situations. Acts of
identification, that is, are acts of self-crea-
tion. For example, some conflicts among desires
are resolved not by expulsion, but rather by cal-
culation (once preference is known) or introspection (to determine preference). In these cases
I need not identify with the strongest desire,
if known, and must only determine whether it is
prudent to act on it. Wantons, who have no second-order volitions, resolve such conflicts all
the time. Consequently, they *own* all the desires
they *experience* even if they never act on some
types.
   In spite of the difficulties attending the attempt to link acts of identification with appro-

priations to self, there would appear to be a
conceptual relationship between autonomy and pro-
prietorship, a relationship conceded by libertarians, for whom, however, considerations of genesis are crucial. On Frankfurt's account, since
the agent's identification with a desire renders
the desire his and his will free, it matters not
that the desire was induced by an omnipotent demon. His will is free because it conforms to his
higher-order volition; i.e., he experiences no
volitional dissonance. Frankfurt concedes that
there is a sense of freedom according to which a
person lacks freedom if he lacks the power to
have a different will; but he regards his notion
of freedom of will as relatively unimportant and
certainly inessential to moral responsibility.[5]

Moral responsibility, not freedom, is our primary
concern. To judge a person morally responsible
for an action A is, I believe, to regard it as
proper to include certain of A's features as relevant in drawing up a moral estimation of the
agent.[7] I think that both Frankfurt and the libertarian can agree on this. The libertarian tells
us that, under determinism, it would be unfair to
lower our estimate of a person's worth in virtue
of his faulty actions. Insofar as Frankfurt insists that the key question in the determination
of moral responsibility concerns the features of
the explanation of the action, his view can at
least be illumined by the above definition of
moral responsibility in the following way.
     Suppose we are told that a person is selfish,
mean, inconsiderate, niggardly, and sadistic,
and accordingly, draw up a very low appraisal of
him. Our initial estimate, however, can be affected by information pertaining to the way in
which these traits were manifested in action.
Learning that he led a saintly life by continual

interventions of an unqualifiedly good and inde-
fatigable will, capable of heroic bursts of energy, we will dramatically raise our estimate now
that we know why he acted in the way he did.[7] If,
on the other hand, he behaved as his character
indicated he would, we *might* grade him even lower. Here again we must be careful regarding the
details of the explanation. We will not grade him
lower if, as in the first case, he set out to
overcome his unfortunate natural and, possibly,
acquired moral endowments by will energy, but
fails because he suffers as well from significant
nonmoral failings such as low intelligence, various physical infirmities, poor judgment, etc.

Frankfurt sees, then, the importance of genesis in ascertaining moral responsibility for actions, but shifts his position when he considers
moral responsibility for wills. The libertarian
may rightly be puzzled. If action *A* may be charged
against Smith's account because he did it out of
a desire to do that sort of thing, why do we not
ask why he had that desire in order to determine
his moral responsibility for that psychological
state?

The agent, on Frankfurt's account, becomes
morally responsible for a desire not necessarily
by creating it, but simply by identifying with
it, regardless of source. This position has a
ring of plausibility, I think, because Frankfurt is really invoking a different conception
of responsibility on the higher level. He is
telling us that, on the level of springs of action, an agent may *take* responsibility for his
character. But, on any level, that is different
from and compatible with the absence of moral responsibility. One can take responsibility for
many things one is not morally responsible for,
e.g., the actions of a child or employee, though
one then becomes morally responsible for possi-

ble failures to discharge the assumed liabili-
ties.

If Frankfurt denies that he intends to shift
to this different concept, the libertarian may
reiterate his puzzlement. Why does explanation
matter on the level of action, but not on the
level of springs?

A partial answer Frankfurt provides is that OD's
creation of a desire does not preclude full responsibility on the part of its possessor. Just
as two persons can each be fully responsible for
turning on a light (each simultaneously flips
a switch at opposite ends of a room), so Harry
and OD can each be fully responsible for Harry's
desire. But the example of the switch flipping
is one in which two persons are responsible because each is causally responsible. Again, though,
Frankfurt is considering not a case in which
Harry and OD each create, through an independent causal series, Harry's desire, but rather
one in which OD creates it and Harry identifies
with it. Here it is no longer clear that Harry
is in any way morally responsible.

In siding with the libertarian and, thereby,
endorsing our intuitions that, at least in *some*
cases, identification does not totally nullify
the relevance to moral responsibility of the
genetic story, I am not endorsing a central
tenet of the libertarian which often motivates
the acceptance of anti-libertarian accounts
like Frankfurt's. The tenet in question, call it
"MRE," is: The class of entities an agent is
morally responsible for is closed under the relation of explanation. That is, if Jones is responsible for an act, he is responsible for the
desire that explains the act, and whatever explains the desire, and so on. So, under determinism, since this chain will break at some point,
we can be responsible for nothing, whereas, under

libertarianism, we are responsible for those desires - and, therefore, the actions they explain
- which are not explained by any prior states.

I reject MRE. If a desire D is induced to arise
in me by OD, I am not responsible for its presence whether I identify with it or not. But unless
D is compulsive, I can choose not to act on it
and be responsible for whatever I do, even if,
in fact, I choose to satisfy D. To rebut this,
a libertarian would have to suppose both that an
action that satisfies D is determined (in part
by D) and that its being so precludes the agent's
being morally responsible for it (incompatibilism).
These are grand assumptions which, preferring
not to engage them here, I will simply and arbitrarily disallow.

Thus, some resistance to libertarian skepticism regarding the responsibility of an agent
for his volitional nature in case certain conditions pertaining to genesis are met is undermined once we reject the implications the libertarian draws from his skepticism. We may agree
that an agent does not bear (full) responsibility
for his nature without necessarily having to deny
that he is morally responsible for his actions.

Our position on moral responsibility is also
closer to Frankfurt's now insofar as he is primarily concerned with moral responsibility for
actions. That is, we do concede that facts concerning the genesis of our wills are inherently
limited in their power to affect, by themselves,
moral responsibility for actions.

In order to see more clearly the relevance
of genetic considerations, we will suppose that
OD implants in Jones a desire that Jones eventually acts upon, but will not suppose, therefore, that Jones performs this action, A, unin-
tentionally or that the desire in question is
compulsive or that he in any way minds being in

the situation and acting as he does. To find out what bothers us about certain genetic stories, we render the immediate context of action as ideal as possible, in fact satisfying several distinct accounts of free action.

(1) The fact that OD completes a sufficient condition of A is not disturbing. If I borrow a hammer from Smith, his providing me with it does not absolve me from responsibility for putting in the nail.

(2) OD's knowledge that Jones will do A is as harmless as Smith's knowledge that I will put in the nail.

(3) The fact that OD creates a desire need not be disturbing. For example, I might create a desire for X in Jones by pointing out features of X that Jones would find appealing.

Of course, OD creates desires in a very different way, and an exploration of this difference looks promising. At one extreme, exemplified in (3), the influence works entirely through Jones's rational and appetitive nature. His autonomy is respected insofar as his desiring nature as given is accommodated and the method of influence is restricted to the techniques of rational persuasion.

(Although nonrational methods, e.g., coercion and bribery, also appeal to the present desires of Jones, they do not respect Jones's desire not to be moved in these ways. Moreover, our concern in such cases may be due to factors we are supposing not to be present here, i.e., the irresistible or compulsive character of the desire. And should Jones desire to be moved by coercion or bribery, his autonomy is intact.[8] He may, for example in his quest for fortune, seek opportunities to submit to bribes. Or he may prowl dangerous neighborhoods because of a wish to acquire a desire to surrender his wallet in a holdup just in order to display his bravery by subduing the robber instead of succumbing to that desire. Or consider the case of the utterly content slave or disciple. Here, the slave lacks autonomy, though the master apparently accommodates entirely the slave's desiring nature. The solution I would but sketch here appeals to distinct senses of 'system of desires'. There is evidently a difference between a bona fide system of desires that can (at least logically) be frustrated and one that is really a kind of metasystem: "I want whatever you want (for me).")

Manipulation, therefore, can take two forms. Either we may employ nonrational methods to create desires, where a knowledge of the actual desires of the person are taken into account, e.g., we appeal to a person's vanity, ego, or fears, or we create desires without regard to the present desires of the person. We either do not demand his rational assent to the course of behavior we are inducing him to perform or coherence with his desiring nature. In essence, we by pass the self or crucial elements thereof.

We may be inclined to argue that, since OD is a manipulator, that is, he does not work through Jones as constituted, then Jones's moral responsibility is diminished because the act does not really represent him.

I would again express suspicion concerning extrusion from self. We must, first of all, see that manipulation is not the issue, since the process initiated by OD and terminating in the creation of a desire can be imagined to have come about naturally. I am no less morally responsible for a murderous impulse that arises in virtue of mysterious processes that begin with the appearance of a full moon than I am for that same sort of impulse as transmitted by OD.[9]

For that matter, nature provides us with desires,
e.g., to drink, that do not depend on our rational
faculty and, in a sense, do not have to mesh
with our other desires. Surely we own the desire to drink as well as the murderous impulse,
as initiated by the appearance of the full moon,
especially since we have no other agent to whom
to assign these desires.

In an attempt to formulate the conditions of
moral responsibility or autonomy for our wills
or desiring natures, the concept of ownership
appears again to be unhelpful, and the issue of
ownership, I suspect, is bogus. We earlier
found the notion of identification equally unacceptable, and have just rejected as well the
idea of manipulation (but not yet the idea that
genesis has *some* role to play here).

Suppose we can isolate facets of character and
personality which can be charged to the agent
in virtue of past acts and omissions of his that
had a causal bearing on genesis. For the libertarian, we have isolated all that can rightfully
be attributed to the agent (as well as a great
deal - in particular those desires whose ancestry is traceable through a past act to elements
outside the self - that the agent is not responsible for).

I do not wish to take issue with the libertarian here, partly becuase his position does
not have two unattractive consequences one may
erroneously infer from it. We have already
pointed out that the rejection of MRE permits
us to regard agents sometimes as morally responsible for actions explained by natures the agent
is not responsible for. Secondly, we shall come
to grips with the problem before us by separating two notions we have hitherto taken as identical, moral responsibility and autonomy, and

the libertarian view may then be more plausibly
cast in such a way as not to deny autonomy even
in a deterministic world.

We can see the necessity for this divorce most
clearly in the case of a person who finds himself attracted to an activity or vocation, organ-
izes his life in order to pursue it, and proceeds
willingly and steadfastly in this direction,
never regretting his decision, and continually
finding that his pursuit is deeply satisfying.

The only ground we can have for holding this
person morally responsible for this trait, if
the libertarian is right, would be based upon
(tacit) decisions he may have made at various
stages to continue this pursuit or not to in-
hibit its development. Even if he is a Frank-
furt-wanton and never considered a course contrary to his desires, it may be reasonable to
hold him responsible for failures to question
the direction in which his life is going when
circumstances suggest that a reappraisal is in
order. Under a liberal interpretation, then,
the libertarian will always be able to find
people morally responsible for their character
and personality traits.

But even if we decide that this person is not
morally responsible for having this interest,
either because we are impressed with the influence of the attractiveness of the pursuit -
perhaps he cannot be held responsible for that -
or because we agree with the libertarian that
those causally relevant reinforcing decisions
whose causal ancestry can themselves be traced
to heredity or environment do not confer moral
responsibility upon the agent, we cannot deny
that this agent is autonomous. The concept of
autonomy involves the idea of self-generation,
and we cannot deny that this agent is autonomous.

The concept of autonomy involves the idea of self-generation, and we cannot deny that occurrences of the impulse to pursue this activity, by a certain stage in his life, are generated from within.

The libertarian may part ways here since he will concede autonomy only on his own metaphysical terms, i.e., only if an efficacious decision to support this activity can be found *and* if it emanates from the agent as an absolute source outside the causal scheme of things.

Although the metaphysics of libertarianism may not be viable, I am not familiar with serious attempts in the compatibilist literature to provide an alternative.

The idea that an agent is autonomous with respect to a certain desire involves the indecently vague idea that the external stimuli that are partly responsible for the appearance of desire-tokens must work through a complex psychological structure, especially the rational or deliberative components together with the interests and desires that are already a part of that structure. Thus, whether it be the moon or a hypnotist that explains my impulse to murder, that impulse arises heteronomously because its source does not filter through either my deliberations or my interests. The daily urge to pursue my philosophical project, on the other hand, is clearly dependent upon various intellectual desires and, perhaps, decisions regarding the best way to satisfy my philosophical interests.

On this account, a paranoid schizophrenic may be quite autonomous when he forms a desire to avoid the man he takes to be a serious threat, since that man's behavior is unimportant relative to the role played by the schizophrenic's complex delusion and associated pattern of cognitive processes. A normal person, however, is

not autonomous with respect to his appetites.
This may be clear enough in those cases in which
a person is aroused by an external stimulus. But
even in a case in which the principal cause is
deprivation - a man is deprived of water for a
long period of time - the explanation of the
thirst refers primarily to features of his body,
not his psyche. On the other hand, a painter who
forms a strong desire to paint because he has
been deprived of the opportunity to do so is
satisfying deeper longings by his activity and
is, to that extent, autonomous with respect to
that desire. (We must not forget that none of
these people may be *morally responsible* for the
appearance of these desires.)

In light of this account, we can understand
the appeal of Frankfurt's ideas about identification. Insofar as an agent identifies with a
second-order desire, he has taken a step toward
the integration of this element into his psyche,
so that, eventually, future token-desires of this
type will arise autonomously. A decision to support certain desires can obviously contribute to
their subsequent internalization. But this achievement is the result of an integrative process and
is not independent of genesis. Consider again
our mischievous chair puller Charlie. On the
first occasion this impulse arises, he may experience mild regret even if it never recurs.
This, I contend, is due to the suspicion that
the desire is linked to other facets of his self.
Though vague, the idea has a meaningful opposite
insofar as personal regret will disappear once
Charlie discovers that his suspicion is ill-
founded. He finds out, let us suppose, that OD
has produced this impulse in an utterly capri-
cious manner. Moreover, should OD continue to
induce these desires in Charlie in ways that
have no other pervasive effects on his person-

ality, Charlie may continue to be disappointed;
but the object of his disappointment will be not
himself, but rather his fortune. He may legitimately be asked to be absolved from moral responsibility, of course; but *further*, he lacks autonomy, not because he refuses to identify with
these desires, but rather because they arise independently of his personality structure.

Have we not, however, depicted an agent as
possessing a far greater degree of unity than
obtains in fact? If autonomy requires coherence
of all our propensities, desires, and attractions,
we would lack autonomy in relation to many psychological episodes, including not just passing
whims, but recurrent, yet apparently isolated
episodes. What are we to say, for example, of
the strange and incongruous hobbies of some people? First of all, we know obviously that psychological structures need not be easily acces-
sible, either to the person himself or, for that
matter, to a professional psychologist. But why
should it be supposed that a structure must exhibit a level of integration requiring that each
desire be linked with every other desire? A person can have distinct and genuinely unrelated
interests.

If unrelated interests are permitted, it is
not a large step to the admissibility of conflicting interests. Disharmony, in other words,
can be internal in spite of the hierarchical
theorist's view that freedom of will is constituted by a lack of dissonance across levels of
desire. If freedom is denied us when we lack the
will we want, the explanation may be that two
impulses, embedded deep in our personalities,
have surfaced in a context that displays their
incompatible natures. And I am not talking just
of inabilities, due to circumstances, to satisfy
two desires that are, in themselves, perfectly

acceptable to the agent, but also of those deeper conflicts in which one part of us wants to condemn another, although the latter has, perhaps, the upper hand in terms of control over action. The woman who has suppressed powerful desires in order to devote her energies to the rearing of her children *may* be dishonest if she identifies herself with those suppressed desires to the exclusion of her maternal desires. The satisfaction of her maternal desires may be deeply satisfying and may become "self-generated," so that dissonance persists indefinitely as an internal phenomenon. Her attraction to an ideal represented by a woman who satisfies desires she has suppressed incorporates elements of self-deception, so that the resultant identification is not entirely honest. Frankfurt's "either-or" picture of identification fails to take these crucial dimensions into account. Identifications can be thoughtful or rash; honest or inauthentic; firm or wavering.[10]

If freedom is the absence of dissonance across volitional levels, as the hierarchical theorist says, then autonomy is different from freedom because autonomy permits reservations about first-order volitional structures. How arbitrary it can sometimes be to cast out a level for the sake of a harmony that "is not meant to be." And if our earlier conclusion is sound, an agent may be autonomous without moral responsibility for his will. From the point of view of freedom and moral responsibility, therefore, our failure to characterize autonomy carefully may not be a serious deficiency. There is a difference between a man who develops murderous impulses as the result of the appearance of the full moon (where the moon's efficacy is contingent only on physiological features, say the shape of the man's head) and one whose impulses develop out of the paranoid structure of his own personality; but it matters little to his moral responsibility.

Footnotes:

1. "Three Concepts of Free Action: II." *Proceedings of the Aristotelian Society*, suppl. vol. XLIX (1975): 113-125, pp. 121/2.

2. "Identification and Externality," in Amelie O. Rorty, ed., *The Identities of Persons* (Berkeley: University of California Press, 1976), pp. 239-251.

3. See Penelhum, "The Importance of Self-Identity," *Journal of Philosophy*, LXVIII, 20 (Oct. 21, 1971): 667-678.

4. Identification and Externality," p. 250.

5. Freedom of the Will and the Concept of a Person," *Journal of Philosophy*, LXVIII, 1 (Jan. 14, 1971): 5-20, p. 19.

6. I fully acknowledge that this position requires elaboration and defense which cannot be provided here.

7. I take no stand on the merit of this person in comparison to one who leads the same life because of his natural dispositions.

8. Frankfurt would, in general, agree. See his "Coercion and Moral Responsibility," in Ted Honderich, ed., *Essays on Freedom of Action* (London: Routledge & Kegan Paul, 1973), pp. 80-82.

9. Here, too, Frankfurt would agree, *ibid.*, p. 83.

10. For a more detailed critique, see my "The Irrelevance of Morality to Freedom," in

Faculty of the Department of Philosophy, Bowling Green State University, eds., *Action and Responsibility* (Bowling Green: Department of Philosophy, Bowling Green State University, 1980), pp. 42-45.

WHAT WE ARE MORALLY RESPONSIBLE FOR

Harry
G. Frankfurt

It might have been expected that the freedom of
a person's *will* would most naturally be construed
as a matter of whether it is up to him what he
wills. In fact, it is generally understood as
having to do with whether it is up to the person
what he *does*. Someone's will is regarded as being
free at a given time, in other words, only if at
that time it is up to him whether he does one
thing or does another instead. When this conception of free will is joined to the supposition
that free will is a necessary condition for
moral responsibility, the result is the Principle
of Alternate Possibilities (PAP): a person is
morally responsible for what he has done only if
he could have done otherwise.

For those who accept PAP, it is an important
question whether people ever *can* do anything
other than what they actually do. Incompatibi-
lists maintain that if determinism is true, this
is not possible. On the other hand, compatibi-
lists insist that even in a deterministic world
a person may have genuine alternatives in the
sense PAP requires. In my view, PAP is false.[1]
The fact that a person lacks alternatives does
preclude his being morally responsible when it
alone accounts for his behavior. But a lack of
alternatives is not inconsistent with moral
responsibility when someone acts as he does for
reasons of his own, rather than simply because
no other alternative is open to him. It is therefore of no particular significance, so far as
ascriptions of moral responsibility are concerned,
whether determinism is true or false, or whether
it is compatible or incompatible with free will
as PAP construes it.

I

The appeal of PAP may owe something to a presumption that it is a corollary of the Kantian thesis that "ought" implies "can".[2] In fact, however, the relation between Kant's doctrine and PAP is not as close as it may seem to be. With respect to any action, Kant's doctrine has to do with the agent's ability to perform *that action*. PAP, on the other hand, concerns his ability to do *something else*. Moreover, the Kantian view leaves open the possibility that a person for whom only one course of action is available fulfills an obligation when he pursues that course of action and is morally praiseworthy for doing so. On the other hand, PAP implies that such a person cannot earn any moral credit for what he does. This makes it clear that renouncing PAP does not require denying that "ought" implies "can" and that PAP is not entailed by the Kantian view.

Constructing counterexamples to PAP is not difficult. It is necessary only to conceive circumstances which make it inevitable that a person will perform some action but which do not bring it about that he performs it. Thus let us say that a person decides to take and does take a certain drug, just in order to enjoy the euphoria he expects it to induce. Now suppose further that his taking the drug would have been made to happen in any case, by forces which were in fact inactive but which would have come into play if he had not on his own decided and acted as he did. Let us say that, unknown to himself, the person is addicted to the drug and would therefore have been driven irresistibly to take it if he had not freely gone about doing so. His dormant addiction guarantees that he could have avoided neither deciding to take nor taking the drug, but it plays no role in bringing about his decision or his act. As the actual sequence of events develops, everything happens as if he were not addicted at all. The addiction is clearly irrelevant in this case to the question of whether the person is morally responsible for taking the drug.

The distinctively potent element in this sort of counterexample to PAP is a certain kind of overdetermination, which involves a sequential fail-safe arrangement such that one causally sufficient factor functions exclusively as back-up for another. The arrangement ensures that a certain effect will be brought about by one or the other of the two causal factors, but not by both together. Thus the backup factor may contribute nothing whatever to bringing about the effect whose occurrence it guarantees.

II

Peter van Inwagen has argued forcefully that even if counterexamples of this kind - adapting his usage I shall refer to them as "F-style counter-examples" - do require that PAP be abandoned, the compatibilism-incompatibilism dispute retains its significance.[3] In his view the supposition that PAP is false does not, as I have claimed, entail the irrelevance to questions concerning moral responsibility of the relationship between determinism and free will. "Even if PAP is false" he says,

...it is *nonetheless* true that unless free will and determinism are compatible, determinism and moral responsibility are incompatible. Thus, Frankfurt's arguments do not, even if they are sound, rob the compatibilist-incompatibilist debate of its central place in the old controversy about determinism and moral responsibility (223).

To support this position van Inwagen formulates

three principles, which he regards as "very similar to PAP" but which he believes are unlike it
in being immune to objections of the sort by
which PAP is undermined (203). He contends that
demonstrating this immunity serves to reestab-
lish the relevance of alternate possibilities
and, hence, of the compatibilism issue, to the
theory of moral responsibility.

Van Inwagen calls his first principle "the Principle of Possible Action":

PPA: A person is morally responsible for failing to perform a given act only if he could
have performed that act (204).

This principle concerns "unperformed acts (things
we have left undone)" (203). The second and third
principles, which van Inwagen calls "Principles
of Possible Prevention," have to do with "the
consequences of what we have done (or left undone)
(203):

PPP1: A person is morally responsible for a
certain event (particular) only if he could
have prevented it (206).

and

PPP2: A person is morally responsible for a
state of affairs only if (that state of
affairs obtains and) he could have prevented
it from obtaining (210).

PAP is concerned only with a person's moral responsibility for *what he has done*. Thus the supposition that PAP is false leaves it open that
there may be things *other* than items of his own
behavior - viz., unperformed acts, or events or
states of affairs that are consequences of what
he has done or left undone - for which a person
cannot be morally responsible unless his will
is or was free.

Corresponding to each of his three principles
van Inwagen provides a version of incompatibilism. According to the first of these, determinism entails that anyone who has failed to perform a given act could not have performed it.
The second and third add up to the claim that
determinism entails that there are no events or
states of affairs - and hence no consequences
of what someone has done - such that anyone
could have prevented them from occurring or
from obtaining. Now van Inwagen is convinced
that PPA, PPP1, and PPP2 are true. So his position is that if the versions of incompatibilism
that correspond to those principles are also
true, then "determinism entails that no one has
ever been or could be responsible for any event,
state of affairs, or unperformed act" (222).
   I believe that, despite van Inwagen's denial,
his first principle actually is vulnerable to
F-style counterexamples. On the other hand, it
may well be that the same strategy does not also
work against his other two principles. But if
this is so, it is only because PPP1 and PPP2 are
irrelevant to the relation between free will and
determinism. Their immunity to F-style counterexamples therefore provides no support for the
conclusions van Inwagen proposes to draw concerning how the theory of moral responsibility is
affected by considerations pertaining to determinism and to free will.

                        III

In his discussion of PPA van Inwagen does not
consider the rather natural suspicion that the
principle is simply equivalent to PAP. Instead
he proceeds directly to examine a putative
counterexample. Since he regards the construction of the example as adapting to the case of

unperformed acts the general strategy that makes
trouble for PAP, he supposes that the example
provides a critical test of whether this strategy is effective against PPA.

In the example, van Inwagen witnesses a crime
and considers telephoning the police to report
it. Because he does not want to get involved, he
decides against calling the police and does nothing. However, unknown to him, the telephone
system has in fact collapsed, and every relevant
telephone is out of order. Concerning this situation, he poses the following question: "Am I responsible for failing to call the police?" His
response is unequivocal and emphatic: "Of course
not. I couldn't have called them." Given the circumstances, he says,

> I may be responsible for failing to *try* to
> call the police (that much I *could* have
> done), or for refraining from calling the
> police, or for...being selfish and cowardly.
> But I am simply not responsible for failing
> to call the police (205).

In van Inwagen's opinion, then, the example leaves
PPA altogether unscathed. His conclusion is that
"Frankfurt's style of argument cannot be used to
refute PPA" (205).

Now being responsible for something may mean, in
a certain strong sense of the notion, being *fully*
responsible for it, i.e., providing for it *both* a
sufficient *and* a necessary condition. A person is
fully responsible, then, for all and only those
events or states of affairs which come about because of what he does and which would not come
about if he did otherwise. The person in van Inwagen's example (hereafter, "*P*") is not in this
sense responsible for his failure to call the
police. The fact that he behaved as he did was a

sufficient condition for his having failed, but
it was not a necessary condition: given the collapse of the telephone system, he would have
failed no matter what he had done. Perhaps the
reason van Inwagen finds it so obvious that *P*'s
inability to do what he failed to do entails that
P is not morally responsible for his failure is
that he construes moral responsibility as presupposing responsibility in this strong sense.

In my opinion, full responsibility is not a
necessary condition for moral responsibility.
Thus I believe that *P* may be morally responsible
for failing to call the police even though he
could not have avoided the failure. But I do not
propose to defend this position here. Instead I
shall attempt to establish two other points,
which I think are more germane to van Inwagen's
ultimate conclusions. The first is that the question of whether moral responsibility presupposes
full responsibility has no *moral* interest.   The
second is that even if moral responsibility does
presuppose full responsibility, van Inwagen's
putative counterexample to PPA cannot serve his
purpose.

IV

Suppose that, as it happens, we do not know whether the telephones were working when *P* made
and acted upon his decision against calling the
police. The fact that we lack this information
would not stand in the way of our making a competent moral appraisal of *P* for what he did. At
the very most it would make us uncertain just
how to *describe* *P*'s failure to act - i.e., just
how to *identify* what it is that we are evaluating him *for*. If the telephones were working, it
might be more appropriate to refer to his failure *to call* the police; if they were out of

order, it might be more appropriate to refer to
his failure *to try to call the police*. But both
the quality of the moral judgment and its degree
– whether P is blameworthy or praiseworthy, and
to what extent – will be exactly the same in
both cases.

Which of the two failures his moral responsibility is construed as being *for* depends entirely, after all, upon the condition of the telephone system. In no way does it depend upon any
act or omission or psychological state or property, whether faulty or meritorious, of his own.
The difference between evaluating P for failing
to call and evaluating him for failing to try to
call can therefore have no *moral* significance.
It is pertinent only to a decision concerning
whether it would be more suitable to couch in
one set of terms or in another what, in either
case, remains the same moral estimate.

The point is not that a person's behavior is
relevant to moral judgments concerning him only
as evidence of his character or of his mental
state. To be sure, P's intentions and his other
psychological characteristics do remain identical regardless of whether circumstances dictate
that he be judged for failing to call the police
or for failing to try to call them. But the
reason why the moral evaluation of P will be the
same in either case is not that he is subject to
moral praise or blame exclusively for his psychological characteristics. What a person does is
not relevant to moral evaluations of him merely
because it is an indicator of his mental state.
People merit praise and blame *for* what they do,
and not just *on the basis of* what they do.

Notice that P's intentions and the like are
not the only things that remain the same whether
the telephones are working or out of order. It
is also clear that, whatever the condition of

the telephone system, P makes or does not make
the same bodily movements. Now *this* is what P is
morally responsible for: it is for making these
movements. He is morally responsible for making
them, of course, only under certain conditions –
only, for instance, when he makes them with certain intentions or expectations. But if those
conditions are satisfied, then what he is morally responsible for is just making the movements
themselves.

There are various ways in which a person's
movements can be identified or described. Whether
it will be more appropriate to describe what P
does as calling the police or only as trying to
call them will depend heavily upon what consequences his movements have. And the consequences
of his movements will in turn depend upon whether
the telephones are working. But it is precisely
because P is judged simply for the making of his
movements that the quality and the degree of his
moral responsibility for what he does remain the
same in either case. It goes without saying that
his movements are unaffected by the consequences
to which they lead, however decisively those consequences may affect the terms in which it is
appropriate for the movements to be described.[4]

V

Since P would have failed to call the police no
matter what he had done, he is not *fully* responsible for failing to call them. This provides
van Inwagen with a reason for his claim that P
is not *morally* responsible for the failure. But
even if we suppose that moral responsibility requires responsibility in the strong sense, the
judgment that PPA is immune to counterexamples
would still be unwarranted. This is because the
ineffectiveness of van Inwagen's counterexample

is due to the particular characteristics of P's
failure rather than to the charcteristics of all
failures as such. Therefore the counterexample
does not provide a decisive test of PPA.

Why is P not fully responsible for his failure
to call the police? It is because it is not within his power to bring it about that the police
telephone rings: regardless of what bodily movements he makes, his movements will not have consequences of the kind that must occur if P is to
be correctly describable as having called the
police. But there are also failures which, unlike
P's, do not depend at all upon the consequences
of what a person does. They are failures for
which the person's movements themselves, considered wholly apart from their consequences,
are both a sufficient and a necessary condition.
For example, suppose that as Q is driving he
fails to keep his eyes straight ahead because
he prefers to examine the interesting scenery to
his left; and suppose further that if the scenery
had not distracted him something else would have
brought it about that he was looking to his left
at that time. In these circumstances, Q cannot
keep his eyes straight ahead. Is he morally responsible for failing to do so? Of course he is!
The fact that he cannot avoid failing has no
bearing upon his moral responsibility for the
failure, since it plays no role in leading him
to fail.

Notice that Q is *fully* responsible for his
failure. Failing to keep one's eyes straight
ahead is exclusively a matter of what movements
a person makes; it is *constituted* by what the
person himself does, and what the person does
is therefore both a sufficient and a necessary
condition for it. It cannot be said, then, that
Q's failure would have occurred no matter what
he had done - i.e., regardless of what bodily

movements he made. If he had not moved his eyes
to the left at all he would not have failed.
Thus there is not the same reason for denying
that Q is morally responsible for his failure as
there is for denying that P is morally responsible for having failed to call the police. Even
if the assumption that moral responsibility presupposes full responsibility is granted, accordingly, it is possible to find counterexamples
that are effective against PPA.

Evaluating PAP and the three principles van
Inwagen adduces is a matter of deciding whether
a person may be morally responsible for performing or failing to perform an action, or for consequences of what he has done, despite the fact
that the action or the failure or the consequences could not have been avoided. Now there are
two ways in which a person's action, or his failure to act, or a consequence of what he has done,
may be unavoidable. It may be unavoidable in virtue of certain movements which the person makes
and which he cannot avoid making; or it may be
unavoidable because of events or states of affairs
that are bound to occur or to obtain no matter
what the person himself does. For want of better
terminology, I shall refer to the first type of
unavoidability as "personal" and to the second
as "impersonal".

Apparently van Inwagen supposes that a person
cannot be fully responsible for a failure which
he is unable to avoid. This supposition would
be correct if unavoidable failures were all like
P's failure - i.e., if their unavoidability were
always *impersonal*. In fact, however, the unavoidability of some failures is *personal*. Of these
it is not true that they will occur no matter
what the person in question does. They are unavoidable just because the person, like Q, cannot avoid making the bodily movements by which

they are constituted.

VI

It seems to me that there is no inherent difference between performances and failures, in virtue of which PPA might be true even though PAP
is false. Nor is PPA immune to counterexamples
of the sort to which PAP succumbs. On the other
hand there is a variant of PPA which *does* enjoy
immunity to F-style counterexamples. This restricted version of PPA, which I shall call
"PPA'", refers exclusively to failures whose
unavoidability is impersonal. It concerns a
person's moral responsibility for failing to
bring about some event or state of affairs, when
the fact that he does not bring it about is independent of what he himself does - i.e., of the
movements he makes. Thus PPA' closely resembles
PPP1 and PPP2, since these also concern a person's moral responsibility for events or states
of affairs that can occur or obtain regardless
of what movements the person himself makes.[5]

Now it is true by definition that a person
cannot be *fully* responsible for something that
happens or comes about regardless of his own
bodily movements. Whether he can be *morally* responsible for such things depends upon the relationship between moral and full responsibility.
Let us suppose that the former presupposes the
latter. In that case PPA', PPP1, and PPP2 are
immune to F-style counterexamples. But this does
not imply, as van Inwagen evidently believes,
that there are things for which a person can be
morally responsible only if his will is free.
Unlike PAP and PPA, the three principles in question have nothing at all to do with free will.

The fact that there are events or states of
affairs which a person cannot bring about plain-

ly does not in itself mean that the person lacks
free will. Given that the freedom of a person's
will is essentially a matter of whether it is up
to him what he does, it is more a matter of
whether it is up to him what bodily movements he
makes than of what consequences he can bring
about by his movements. Imagine that the equipment malfunction that makes it impossible for P
to call the police, despite his freedom to move
his body in any way he likes, is due to negligence on the part of the telephone company; and
imagine that because of this negligence large
numbers of people are unable to do various things.
These people may quite properly be resentful. But
they will be carrying their resentment too far,
and attributing too portentous a role in their
lives to the telephone company, if they complain
that the company has through its negligence
diminished the freedom of their wills.

Just as PPA', PPP1, and PPP2 have nothing to do
with the relationship between moral responsibility and free will, neither have they anything to
do with the relationship between free will and
determinism. Suppose that it is causally undetermined whether the telephones are working. Then
it is also undetermined whether P can call the
police. But this implies nothing whatever concerning the freedom of P's will.

It has a significant bearing, of course, on the
extent of his *power* - i.e., on the effectiveness
of what he does. However, in no way does it
affect his freedom to move as he likes; nor is
it pertinent to the question of whether his movements themselves are undetermined. It is altogether irrelevant, in other words, to the sorts
of interests and anxieties by which people have
been driven to resist the doctrine that human
life is wholly and ineluctably subject to causal
determination.

Footnotes:

1. I have argued for this in "Alternate Possibilities and Moral Responsibility," *Journal of Philosophy*, LXVI, 23 (Dec. 4, 1969): 829–839.

2. Cf. Robert Cummins, "Could Have Done Otherwise," *The Personalist*, LX, 4 (October 1979): 411–414.

3. Peter van Inwagen, "Ability and Responsibility," *Philosophical Review*, LXXXVII, 2 (April 1978): 201–224. Hereafter in my text, numbers within parentheses refer to this essay.

4. I am here invoking Donald Davidson's well-known view – developed with compelling lucidity in his essay entitled "Agency" [in Brinkley, Bronaugh, and Marras, eds., *Agent, Action and Reason* (New York: Oxford, 1971), pp. 3–25] – according to which "we never do more than move our bodies; the rest is up to nature" (23). Adapting and paraphrasing his account (cf. 21) to the case of *P*, it might be said that after *P* has moved his hands in the ways one must move them in order to make a telephone call, he has done his work; it only remains for the telephone company to do its.

5. As I have already pointed out, van Inwagen says that PPP1 and PPP2 have to do with "the consequences of what we have done (or left undone)" (203). This is not explicit in his formulations of the principles. On a rather natural reading of them, in fact, they are vulnerable to any counterexample that is effective against PAP. For, assuming that doing something entails the occurrence of an event and the obtaining of a state of affairs, anything that shows that

a person may be morally responsible for what he
has done even though he could not have done
otherwise also shows that he may be morally responsible for an event or a state of affairs
which he could not have prevented. However, in
view of van Inwagen's assurances that PPP1 and
PPP2 concern the *consequences* of what people do,
I shall construe them as *not* referring to the
bodily movements people make or to what those
movements necessarily entail.

FICTION FOR FIVE FINGERS

Nelson Goodman

This article sets forth the following theses:
(1) All fiction is literal, literary falsehood.
(2) Yet some fiction is true. (3) Truth of
fiction has nothing to do with realism.
(4) There are no fictive worlds. (5) Not all
literal, literary falsehood is fiction.

1. All fiction is literal, literary falsehood

Literal falsity distinguishes fiction from true
report; but falsity alone does not make fiction.
"Plain lies, damn lies, and statistics" are not
fiction; neither are mistakes, whether computer
or human, whether misprints, miscalculations,
or misconceptions. Only literary falsehood is
fiction. That no more implies that all fiction
has literary merit than to say that the pictures
in an exhibition are works of art implies that
all are good. What consittutes art, literary
or otherwise, is not a question to be settled
here. I have suggested elsewhere[1] certain
features that are symptomatic of art; and perhaps the most prominent of these for literature
are the use of exemplification and expression,
and of multiple and complex reference. With the
scientific text or book of instructions, what
matters most is what is said; for the literary
work, forms and feelings and other features
exemplified or expressed or signified through
varied short or long referential chains usually
count for more.

2. Yet some fiction is true

Although all fiction is literally false, some is metaphorically true. And while metaphorical truth is compatible with literal falsity, metaphorical truth contrasts with metaphorical falsity quite as cleanly as does literal truth with literal falsity.[2] In other words, a term with a literal range of application - that is, a literal extension - often has another, metaphorical extension. The two extensions may, but need not, be quite separate. Most terms, indeed, are ambiguous both literally and metaphorically, having several different literal and several different metaphorical extensions; but that does not obscure the distinction between literal and metaphorical truth. The sound of thunder is not literally, but is metaphorically, a lion's roar.

3. Truth of fiction has nothing to do with realism

What constitutes truth of a work, fiction or not, is a notoriously difficult question. But we need not answer it to see that truth of description, literal or metaphorical, like correctness of depiction, is independent of realism. For while truth or correctness depends upon what is told or depicted, be it factual or fictive, realism in both cases depends upon the telling rather than the told.[3] A realistic novel or painting may be full of mistakes while a fantastic painting or novel may be, metaphorically, true or right. *Gulliver's Travels* is unrealistic no matter how true in the way fiction can be true; and a painting by an academic novice will be realistic no matter how wrong. Realism is a matter of the familiarity of symbols used in the telling; truth is a matter of what is told, literally or meta-

phorically, by means of symbols familiar or fantastic.

"Realism" may of course be used in other ways;
but under none of the well-grounded interpretations does realism either imply or follow from
rightness.

4. There are no fictive worlds

Although some fiction consists of statements,
literally false but perhaps metaphorically true,
about actual persons, things, and events, most
fiction seems to be about fictive persons,
things, and events or about imaginary and even
impossible beings and entities. Works of fiction,
we often hear, are about fictive worlds. But
strictly speaking, fiction cannot be about anything nonactual, since there is nothing nonactual,
no merely possible or impossible worlds; for saying that there is something fictive but not actual amounts to saying *that there is something such
that there is no such thing*. Thus there are no
pictures *of* unicorns or stories *about* ghosts but
only unicorn-pictures and ghost-stories.[4]

Fiction, then, no matter how false or how far-
out, is about what is actual when about anything
at all. There are no fictive worlds. The littera-
teur pained by that deprivation may or may not
be comforted when I add that neither is there
any such thing as the actual world. Since there
are conflicting truths, there are many worlds
if any, but no such thing as *the* world.[5]

Fiction must be and nonfiction may be literally
false; both may be metaphorically true or false.
Nonfiction and fiction do not differ in that the
one but not the other is about actual things.
Both are about actual things if anything; and
different works of either kind may be about the

same or different actual worlds.

5. Not all literal, literary falsehood is fiction

Although all fiction is literal, literary falsehood, the converse does not hold. Literature
includes not only fiction but some biographies
and histories, and among these some are partly
or wholly false. And while literal falsity,
requisite for fiction, is a literary defect in
history, falsity does not disqualify a history
as a literary work; for as noted earlier, a work
of art need not be a good work of art.

But does the false, purported history qualify
as nonfiction? If we bear in mind the frequency
of human error and remember that a conjunction
is false if any component of it is, so that a
history with one false statement is itself false,
we may well suspect that most literary works,
histories as well as novels, are literal falsehoods. The difference among literary works
between fiction and nonfiction thus seems to
become less a matter of over-all literal truth
or falsity than of percentage of true and false
component sentences. The novel containing a high
percentage of literally true statements (Doctor-
ow's *Ragtime* perhaps?) approaches nonfiction;
the history with a high percentage of false
statements (Carlyle's *French Revolution* perhaps?)
approaches fiction. Pure fiction and pure nonfiction are rare.

These five simple theses may seem obvious or
shocking. Neglect of them, I think, has often
hindered understanding of what fiction is and
does.

Footnotes:

1. *Ways of Worldmaking* (Indianapolis: Hackett, 1978), pp. 57–70, esp. 67–68.
2. See my *Languages of Art*, 2nd ed. (Indianapolis: Hackett, 1965), pp. 68–71.
3. See my "The Telling and the Told," *Critical Inquiry*, VII (1981): 799–801, and "Realism, Relativity, and Reality," forthcoming in *New Literary History*.
4. See *Ways of Worldmaking*, pp. 102–105.
5. *Ibid.*, pp. 1–7.

PLEASURE IN THE PAINFUL

Richard Kuhns

> One must not seek any and every kind of
> pleasure from tragedy, but only the one
> proper to it.   ` Poetics 53b11

A variety of explanations have been given down
through the centuries to account for the delight
we mortals take in depictions of our sufferings.
Plato constructed a model of the psyche not very
different from models advertised today. He put
the issue baldly: the eyes lust to see, though
the higher faculties of thought may wish to deny
them. Dead bodies beside the city walls draw our
vision to them magnetically, though we would turn
away. And, letting that serve as a witness to an
inner depravity, Plato went on to liken stage
shows to scenes of carnage. That comparison, Aristotle found, called for a refutation, which he
supplied in the *Poetics*, separating out the peculiar pleasure of the response to the dramatically
serious: the pleasure appropriate to the dramatic
representation. But the whole justification was
attacked once again by Augustine, who saw the
theatre as a violation of all that tends to good
in our sinful selves, and from that Christian
assault upon our innate proclivity to pleasure in
suffering a whole set of critiques depend.
  In our time we tend to be more psychological,
referring to innate propensities, to masochism
and sadism; I have always found such accounts sim-
plistic, and would prefer an Augustinian harangue
to a Sadean diagnosis. But perhaps there is a more
interesting way to examine the curious ambivalences of response to dramatic representations if
we seek the constant, recurring elements in the
dramas we have found most attractive and persuasive.

I shall argue that the ambivalences, the pain-
pleasure co-extensiveness of a complex response
to dramatic representation, is generated by, and
can be counted an effect of, three causal conditions that appear again and again in serious
scenes of suffering. They are, briefly: a riddle;
a sexual conflict; "splitting." Each of these
presences has been the subject of extended examination in a clinical-psychological tradition that
Freud named "psychoanalysis," and although I do
not intend to comply with the directives of psychoanalytic inquiry as it is traditionally carried
out, I shall draw from psychoanalytic theory in an
effort to account for the peculiar pleasure we
take in representations of suffering.

I.   A Riddle and Its Strangeness

The most famous riddle in the West is that put to
Oedipus by the Sphinx, a riddle, Oedipus believed,
he had solved satisfactorily. And indeed he seemed
to have, if the evidence of the Sphinx's annihila-
tion as a consequence of solution is honestly reported. Yet, once we reconsider the riddle and its
solution as it appears in the most eloquent examination, by Sophocles, we are forced to question
Oedipus' belief that he succeeded; for had he truly
solved it, would he not have seen more deeply into
his own predicament? We shall never know; evidence
that the riddle has been solved is scarce, harder
to verify than most conditions revolving around
human self-understanding.

One aspect of the Sphinx's riddle that we often
fail to note is the strangeness of it. There is a
quality in the riddle itself that we might think
of as "spooky"; here is the rare bird-woman-beast
who propounds riddles that are about us. Why? And
what business is it of hers that we toddle, stride,
and hobble in our lives? Just fortifying ourselves

to face the frightening presence draws upon all
our resources; and once we answer right (if we
do) we must witness the horrifying destruction
of the Sphinx; and if we fail, we satisfy her
dire wants.

Yet, let us compose ourselves with as much
distance as possible to consider the question
and what might be a truly satisfying answer. It
seems to me that the given answer, "human-kind",
hardly meets the propounded riddle, for when we
ask of ourselves what we are, we can hardly rest
satisfied with "we are What We Are," which is
the answer if we were to answer deeply, correctly, with some self-satisfaction.

An attempt to answer with some degree of insight is elicited by riddles in many narrative
representations, for the riddle is not peculiar
to the Sphinx story; rather, riddles appear over
and over again in folk tales, fairy stories,
plays, novels, and so on, and they always have
about them the aura of the spooky that I associate with the Sphinx's riddle, as well as an
answer that never really does satisfy us; we go
along with the answer in the narrative because
that is all we are given, but we long for something deeper, more satisfying.

I shall consider the riddle as a *topos*, a recurrent event, in tragic drama.

A riddle may provide a model for the larger
story of which it is a part; and if we can rightly read the riddle, we may find our way through
to the deeper understanding of the larger plot.
However, getting the riddle right still leaves
us with a sense of incompleteness because of the
disproportionate parts of statement and answer.
Oedipus, we know, was asked, "What goes on four
in the morning, two at noon, and three in the
evening;" and possessing that question as a preliminary to the Sophoclean plot, we can test the

belief, so forcefully boasted by Oedipus, that
he indeed answered the riddle satisfactorily. We
are set a companion riddle in the plot of the
drama, for it poses a puzzle that is as difficult for us to solve as the original. The very
life of Oedipus is an example of the riddle put
by the Sphinx, and the audience joins the protagonist in undertaking to find an answer. Indeed, the distinguishing characteristic of the
tragic riddle is the protagonist-audience joint
venture in solving the riddle. Seeking an answer,
itself a force moving to action in the drama,
presents its own progression through the events
of the plot. It has always seemed to me that the
riddle of the Sphinx, propounded by the feline-
woman to the desperate youth who has, unknowing-
ly, just killed his father, possesses an element
of the comic, for wit has, in this case at least,
such a desparate penalty attached.

Freud pointed out, in *Jokes and Their Relation
to the Unconscious*, that there is a close, inverse relationship between jokes and riddles, the
first exhibiting, the second concealing. In a
riddle we must solve a problem, as indeed we must
when we witness a tragic drama. In a joke, a problem is solved for us. Jokes make us laugh; riddles leave us with bemusement and sometimes a
sense of mystery.

One of the peculiar, and indeed touching aspects
of riddles is that though the answer will be short
and trivial, the question is elaborate and profound.
This is true of the Oedipean riddle, but it is more
evident in the Anglo-Saxon tradition in which riddles tell little stories, the answer to which is a
seeming simple answer; but the story itself touches
on deep matters. Thus, no. 9 in the Exeter Book
goes like this:

Me in those days my father and my mother
Gave up as dead; I had as yet no life,
No spirit. Then a loyal kinswoman
Wrapped me in clothes and kept me and cherished me,
Enfolded me in a protective cloak,
As kindly as she did for her own children,
Until, as was my nature, in her care
I became mighty-hearted among those
Who were no kin of mine. Yet my protectress
Still nourished me till I grew up and might
More widely travel. She by doing that
Had less dear sons and daughters of her own.

(Trans. Richard Hamer)

The answer, Cuckoo, seems a simple conclusion
to such a rich description; but riddles are like
that: it is in the posing that we find the deepest thought; and the very saying of the riddle is
itself a little story.

Freud's examples, interestingly taken from philosophers (G.T. Fechner and Schliermacher), also
present mysterious collocations that call for a
solution, that is, finding the syllables that give
an "answer," though the answer is very simple when
compared to the statement. Philosophers, like poets,
entertain the riddles of the deepest and darkest in
an effort to clarify the forms and functions of experience. Fechner posed the following, which is quoted in *Jokes and Their Relation to the Unconscious*:

Die beiden ersten finden ihre Ruhstätte
Im Paar der andern, und das Ganze macht ihr Bette.

The solution: My first two (*Toten*, the dead) find
their resting place in my last two (*Gräber*, graves),
and my whole (Totengräber) makes their bed.[1]

Even in these modern riddles, with their philosophical play on words, we sense the mystery of
such posings; to hear a riddle is to feel strange-

ness, and the strangeness is central to the dramatic consequences I am calling to our attention.
We burn with eagerness to have the answer when
we hear a riddle; for the strangeness arouses
not only curiosity but a bit of unease.

The complex feelings thus generated are especially keen when frustrated, as they are in a not-
able modern fable that reverses all the values of
tragedy. When the Gypsy in the Kleist story,
Michael Kohlhaas, gives the good Staatsberger the
answer to a riddle concerning the Elector's future,
we seek the opportunity, we burn with curiosity,
to possess the knowledge Kohlhaas has been given.
But, like the poor Elector, we shall never know
the answer, for it dies with the hero. But *he knew*
the answer, because he read what was written on
the slip of paper before he swallowed it, and then
went to his death. Kleist reverses all the values
of tragedy and the force of riddles in the mystery
of justice by ending his tale with a modern re-
working of ancient *topoi*, an unanswered riddle
that must forever remain unanswered. The riddles
of tragedy remain, in a deeper sense, forever unanswered, for though they presumably are "solved"
through native wit, the "answer" never leads to a
diminution of strangeness. Rather, the anxiety
provoked by strangeness is counterbalanced by the
test the riddle imposes upon us, the audience, as
it tests the protagonist.

We are put to the test by the plot, to see if
we are wanting, or if we come up to the mark. But
what is the mark? It is the level at which we can
see through to truths, we can generate affects
that carry us beyond the immediacies of the plot
itself, presuming, as I do, that a well-construc-
ted tragedy says something on that order. For example, (taking a modern narrative perspective,
which like Kleist's throws into relief a complexity of tragedy) when in Melville's *The Confidence*

Man the man in cream-colors comes aboard the
Fidèle in St. Louis, to begin the journey down
the Mississippi, we are confronted with a riddle.
Who is he? His appearence suggests he is either
or both St. Paul and Christ, but he cannot be
that, for this is an American quai-side scene.
Who is he? -- we puzzle and puzzle, then realize
that the story poses a version of the liar's
paradox, that the utterances we read are true if
false, false if true. So we shall never, never,
however hard we probe, and probe, discover the
identity of the man in cream-colors. But in the
effort to identify him, we move beyond the story
in its superficial presence to a narration of
magnificent complexity and comprehensiveness.
Within the brief tale, *The Confidence Man*, lie
compacted all the books of the tradition, or
nearly all, depending upon how much we give ourselves over to the ever deepening puzzle of the
book. A riddle, then, is also a transporting
medium that pushes us beyond the immediate story,
just as the *Fidèle* is a transporting medium
(*faith*, indeed!) for all the bedeviled passen-
gers who must cope with the many masquerades of
the Confidence Man. *Who is he?* Through him the
characters, as we the reader, pass through the
mere incidences, the mere meetings on the ship,
to visions and visions, yet in the end the
visions are extinguished in the guttering lamp
that finally falls into darkness. Riddles leave
us both the glimpses and the dark.

   Riddles suffuse narrative alternatives to
reality with the strangeness that permits us to
join our fantasies to theirs. If we were pure
sorts, imagined by Augustine, we would reject
stage-plays as interferences to our this-wordly-
suffering, and our other-worldly dedications.
Yet even Augustine found a secret narrative substitute for the sufferings of this world in, of

all places, story: for Augustine imagined that
he relived the adventures of Aeneas. I hesitate
to reveal in such an abrupt manner the worldly
strangeness Augustine found to fuel his quest;
but bestow, dear reader, your thought with the
possibility. If my discovery is sound, Augustine
had no need in his own life for tragic representations; he had meat his theater-loving friends
knew not of.

And so do we, common readers and witnesses
that we are. Our actions in the world are accompanied by representations, both conscious and
unconscious, of our deepest internal conflicts
whose pain we may or may not - depending upon
the degree of our honesty and insight - acknowledge as we attempt to subdue them. Our simultaneous participations in external action and
internal representations find *their* externaliza-
tions and shared publicities in dramatic narratives of the serious, and sometimes tragic,
kind. We follow them avidly in the belief that
their conclusions will yield resolutions, yet
the results we grasp are both banal and mysterious. The riddle, whose posing frequently initi-
ates action, gives us both the pleasure of recognition to which Aristotle pointed, as well as
the pain of our impotence before the unanswerable.

II. Political-Sexual Conflict

The second source of our delight in the terrible
comes through a condition most frequently met
with in tragedy: it is the sexual conflict which
has its source in an ignoble, although inevitable,
conflict of private need and public obligation.
The most obvious example is, again, Oedipus; but
we see it in Lear, Hamlet, Othello, and indeed all
the great tragic heroes. Simply stated, story gains
inextinguishable energy and force from a conflict

that is unresolvable, unresolvable because each
side of the need cannot be satisfied without
violation of the other. Lear cannot both divide
the Kingdom (a canny political move as he has
arranged it) and possess Cordelia. When the incongruity is forced upon him, he blows up the
whole scheme, turning to the worst solution.
Oedipus cannot both rule as king and possess his
mother as his wife. No resolution is possible;
tragic suffering, as Aristotle pointed out, then
follows with *inevitability*. We might call the
well-made plot a syllogism of suffering. Grasping such a structure gives pleasure, but more
than that, the inevitable and unresolvable conflict arouses a deeper pleasure in us, for we
respond to it with our own sense of godlike
power. We survey the tragic plot as if it were
ours to dominate and control; we achieve immor-
tal prescience, and that encourages the celebration of sufferings as evidence of our now-trans-
cendent (although woefully transitory) powers.
We seek to resolve an inevitable conflict with a
fantasy of omnipotence. What could give more
pleasure than that?

And thus we are brought to the affective state
Aristotle referred to as "katharsis," the con-
cluding set of feelings that mark the end of the
well-wrought plot. We are forced to accord the
protagonist an accommodation in our own awareness of the political goal pursued, as we at the
same time accept the doom he suffers. We can be
the truly magnanimous observer, according justice where justice cannot be realized, to be
sure a godlike dispensation, even beyond what
the gods can bestow. For the irresolvable conflict that led to moral incongruities of the
most unacceptable kind resides in us as well,
however Lilliputian our strivings and our ter-
rors. And we shall then accept into ourselves

the unacceptable sufferer; a generous act that
can only ennoble us in our own eyes.

III. Splitting

I come now to the mysterious underlying force
that tragedy makes use of in leading an audience
to enjoy painful affects as they are generated
by the representations of tragic plots. The
force manifests itself in the maturational project of the human being as the child moves from
early family relationships to full cultural functioning. I shall draw upon the thought of D.W.
Winnicott, as well as more traditional psychoanalytic theory, to account for this force.

Dramatic representations, I maintain, function
for us as culturally developed "transitional objects." The phrase 'transitional object' I take
from Winnicott and extend its application beyond
his own, for he argued that transitional objects,
after an early phase as the first "not me" objects, functioned for the young child as the
first cultural objects. I go further - beyond
teddy bears and blankets - to sophisticated
stories whose function is continuous with the
first objects, but far more complex.

For Winnicott, the 'transitional object' referred to the things children play with which help
them to leave the mother, to move out to the
world beyond, carrying, as it were, a bit of maternal protection as a safeguard. That the transitional object should be considered the first cultural
object and a means into the realm of cultural tradition is easily understood, for early transitional
objects become participants in play-acting, story-
telling and a variety of other exchanges between
child and parent which build a cultural presence.
That presence grows and intensifies throughout a
life, determining some of the defining character-

istics of those objects which constitute a cultural tradition. My elaboration of Winnicott's views suggests that the possession of common cultural objects enables individuals to move out from the immediacy of everyday life to realities that are recognized in stories told and retold.

If we consider repetition and continuity as making a tradition, the earliest transitional objects stand in a sequence in which the objects we think of as *art* relate developmentally to the childhood manipulation of stories and objects in play with the parent. There, frightening accounts produce real terror which can be modified as the representational nature of narration becomes understood. As the transitional object becomes a work of art, shared by the community as a whole, it retains in some respects the properties of the earlier objects and relies upon psychological conditions laid down in early years, conditions that function in later years when the transitional object has been succeeded by things like tragic plots.

The earlier condition, however, remains in some respects present and operative, for tragic plots are surrounded by much the same risks as early transitional tales: the hearer feels anxiety, and suffers the painful affects that Aristotle referred to as "pity" and "fear." Yet, the over all experience possesses deep and abiding satisfactions that make taking the risks worth while.

In two late papers Freud speculated on the psychological process by which the ambivalences of our experiences with tragedy may be understood and our willingness to take the risk of tragedy accounted for. Introducing the terms 'split' and 'splitting', Freud suggested in the uncompleted "An Outline of Psychoanalysis," and in the fragment, "Splitting of the Ego in the Process of Defense,"[3] that we possess and use "splitting" as a means to cope with fearful and threatening situations. "Two psychical attitudes," he writes, "have been formed instead of a single one - one, the normal one, which takes account of reality, and another which under the influences of the instincts detaches the ego from reality. The two exist alongside of each other." Splitting of the ego, Freud goes on to say, characterizes many psychological processes, and we often find, especially in psychosis and neurosis, that "two different attitudes, contrary to each other and independent of each other" are to be found in many interactions between the ego and external reality.[4]

Developing these views in a posthumously published fragment, Freud points out that in children we see the capacity to tolerate "a conflict between the demand by the instinct and the prohibition by reality," by taking two positions simultaneously and therefore splitting the ego. The child both turns away from reality and turns toward reality, thus resolving what appears to be a contradiction with simultaneous affirmations: experience countenances and finds room for both *A* and *not A*, or for the contraries *A* and *B*, through maintaining a fantasy construal alongside of a realistic construal of the world.[5]

Transitional objects, in the limited sense explored by Winnicott, and in the broader sense introduced in this essay, become the first cultural objects through splitting. The participants assume two positions simultaneously: they recognize the terror and the suffering of the action, as they also deny the reality of the presentation because it is a representation. Story telling, whether in the simple mode of familial play or in the sophisticated mode of serious drama, relies upon the process of splitting for the special pleasure it engenders.

One way in which that pleasure is encouraged
and allowed to manifest itself is through the
very content and structure of the dramatic plots
themselves, for they too employ the process of
splitting. In tragic drama splitting of objects
and of selves occurs in many fascinating ways;
but those I have noted above contribute in a
fundamental way to the tragic. The riddle, in
posing the question, what is it to be human,
both gives and withholds answers; the conflict
between private sexual need and public political
obligation splits persons and actions into seemingly irreconcilable dualities that yet must
find a possible coexistence in the plot, and in
so doing call upon the audience to participate
in the splitting and the reconciliation.
    Splitting occurs in the riddle through reveal-
ing and concealing in such a way that the manifest "solution," what is revealed through an
"answer," is split off from the deeper latent
and contrary implications that the riddle points
to. The "solver" of the riddle represses the
deeper answer, as does the plot, only to allow
it to surface at the scene of suffering. In the
scene of suffering the audience is vouchsafed a
moment of perspicuous awareness that, in rendering both sides of the split manifest, permits
the pleasure appropriate to tragedy to occur.
The two previously separated and contrary or
contradictory objects and actions are beheld in
a single vision.
    The conflict of private and public in its
tragic representation also relies upon the process of splitting. I offer an example that somewhat simplifies the dramatic mode of representation. In the brief, beautiful tale, "The Boy and
the Deer," recorded by Denis Tedlock in his translation of Zuni stories, *Finding the Center*,[6] we
possess a plot in which splitting occurs in both

persons and actions.

Like many folk-stories, "The Boy and the Deer" relates the remarkable adventures of an abandoned child. Left by his high-born mother (a daughter of a priest, impregnated by the sun) the child is reared by deer; his deer mother who nurtures him and his biological mother who abandoned him are closely described, and a confrontation between the natural deer-child and the cultural mother brings the story to its scene of suffering; for, in following the request by the mother for Yucca leaves to weave basket plaits, the child stabs himself to death in pulling the sword-shaped leaves for an essentially cultural making which will use the products of nature.

The story emphasizes the splitting of the mother between the biological-wicked and the nurturing-good parent, as it depicts the nature-culture conflict in the communities of animals and humans. Upon hearing the story, we are ourselves brought into the various bifurcations which enable us to maintain a dual set of responses, holding at once the painful and the pleasurable in an unresolved tension which is also a coordination. The affective life of the hearer now must arrange these dualities into an acceptable response. Just how is that brought about?

'Acceptable response' refers to the pleasure peculiar to scenes of suffering that conclude tragic narratives. This is a pleasure unlike the pleasure of revenge, unlike the pleasure of simple excitement, unlike the pleasure we take in the beautiful. For in all these respects, in terms of these values - values of seeing an enemy fall, of entertainment, of the aesthetic - the pleasure Aristotle referred to is distinct, it is the pleasure *appropriate to* tragedy: we seek not any and every kind of pleasure from tragedy, but only the kind it demands.

Since tragic drama both elicits and directs powerful feelings that are in other contexts painful, to experience the pleasure appropriate to tragedy suggests that the feelings are manipulated in a special way peculiar to this kind of representation; and it is not satisfactory to say that the pleasure we experience derives from the representational as such, for there are many representational effects that are revolting and thoroughly unacceptable. There must be a way that the tragic representations work for us and in us which will help to explain the pleasure we take in scenes of suffering.

I propose that the process of splitting, as sketched out in the above discussion, accounts for the pleasure appropriate to tragedy, and in the brief space for a conclusion I shall attempt to give some support to my contention.

Splitting occurs, I have argued, as a content of tragic action, and that is necessitated by two fundamental, and recurring presences in tragedy: riddles and sexual-political conflict. The audience must participate in splitting because (a) the plot requires it as a response; (b) the individual imposes it as a means of resolving what would otherwise be unacceptably painful into the acceptably pleasurable.

Tragic drama, and some novels, provide evidence that they represent splitting, both in the ego and in the objects and events that occur as parts of plots. We learn, as participants in a cultural tradition, to take a position in regard to the transitional objects that provide representations of ourselves and the world around us, and to come to terms with the splitting they make manifest as a part of our development from early childhood into the communal action of "being-an-audience." We learn to participate in a whole

varied, complex realm of the transitional which
I have glanced into in my account of how we
achieve some of our most gratifying experiences
in witnessing events that are in themselves painful. Through the splitting of the ego as a response to the splitting of objects and events in
tragic plots, we learn to make an essential orientation in the process of growing up: we become,
as social beings, cultural beings; that is, we
enter into a cultural tradition. And that, I believe, requires the toleration of conflicting ambivalences to which we have, in our tradition, a
complex response: we discover the pleasure appropriate to tragedy.

To be sure, we discover the pleasure appropriate to tragedy at a late stage in our cultural
maturation; it succeeds a much more simplified
and simplifying view of ourselves which begins
to take shape in our commerce with transitional
objects. Each of the events embodied in tragic
plots occurs over and over again in the stories
we hear as we grow up. Riddles appear early in
life, and appear again with fascinating complexity in tragedy. The strangeness they generate
may still arouse confusion, but they can be
mastered now in a larger setting that reveals a
deeper, previously hidden relationship to our
quest for political understanding.

The central cultural conflict that energizes
tragic plots, the irresolvability of private
sexual need and public political obligation,
drives the action forward to a disclosure of the
full incongruity humans must forever struggle to
resolve. In that lifelong, and indeed historically constant, effort, an internal bifurcation expresses itself in the splitting of persons and
objects. In taking up splitting as a part of its
own representational concerns, tragedy separates
out the painful and the pleasurable in plots so

that we witnesses are led to perform the same kathartic clarification in ourselves.

'Katharsis' assumes a broader application as we endeavor to establish the implications of that seemingly simple phrase, 'the pleasure appropriate to tragedy,' that Aristotle formulated as partial answer to Plato. The developmental trajectory of our quest to achieve wholeness in ourselves as part of our participation in both historical tradition and present political life finds support in many different kinds of cultural undertakings. One of the most interesting, though by no means the most successful, is the capacity humans have to find pleasure in depictions of suffering.[7]

Footnotes:

1. Std. Ed., vol. VIII, p. 67.
2. The philosopher, Karl Popper, has elaborated a theory similar to Winnicott's, though it lacks a developmental profile. See Popper, *The Unended Quest* (his autobiography), and his answer to E. Gombrich in *The Philosophy of Karl Popper* (LaSalle, Ill.: 1974). For Winnicott's views, see *Collected Papers: Through Pediatrics to Psychoanalysis* (New York: Basic Books, 1958).
3. Std. Ed., vol. VIII, p. 67.
4. "An Outline of Psychoanalysis," p. 202-204.
5. "Splitting of the Ego in Defense," pp. 275-277.
6. New York: Dial Press, 1972.
7. I am grateful to Helen Bacon, Bernard Beckerman, and Eric Marcus for their comments and criticisms.

FOUR QUESTIONS OF FICTION

Israel
Scheffler

I. How Can Null Singular Terms Be Meaningful?

Russell's theory of descriptions[1] and Quine's
theory of proper names[2] free us from bondage to
fictional reference by null singular terms – at
least, on the score of meaning. For, together,
they show that meaninglessness does not follow
upon failure to name. Russell paraphrases

    (1) The minotaur lives in a labyrinth
as: (2) Something is a minotaur and lives in a
       labyrinth and nothing else is a minotaur

thus eliminating the null singular descriptive
phrase of the original and providing no naming
unit as a counterpart, though retaining (through
deployment of the quantifiers 'something', 'nothing') all the content of the original. (2) is
clearly false, hence meaningful, and, since its
equivalent (1) must be equally false and likewise
meaningful, the connection between meaningfulness
and reference is here effectively severed:
(1) has meaning, though its singular description
fails to refer; the denial of (1) is, moreover,
true under the very same condition.
   Quine extends the Russellian treatment to
proper names by construing each such name as a
predicate entering into a singular description.
Thus

    (3) Zeus dwells on a mountaintop
becomes:
    (4) The thing that is–Zeus dwells on a moun-
       taintop
which in turn is transformed into:

(5) Something is-Zeus and dwells on a moun-
    taintop and nothing else is-Zeus

Again, since no singular referential unit remains in (5) although it is clearly false and
therefore meaningful, the same must hold for its
original equivalent, (3): It has meaning despite
the referential failure of its proper name, and
the same holds for its true denial.

The severance of meaning from reference frees
us from having to affirm, under threat of loss
of meaning, that our names or singular descriptions are invariably satisfied by actual things.
Fictional discourses do not collapse into meaninglessness upon referential failure of their
descriptions. Whether we talk about something -
or about nothing - we may make perfectly good
sense.

II. How Can Null Terms Differ in Meaning?

An assumption of both Russell's and Quine's devices is that general terms, certainly, may fail
to refer without failure of meaning. (2) and (5)
are meaningful even though nothing satisfies
either the general term 'is a minotaur' or the
general term 'is-Zeus'. But how account for the
patent *difference* in meaning of these terms?
Bare significance needs no reference, but *variation* in significance seems to require appeal to
reference if we are to avoid invoking either
Platonic entities (e.g., forms, concepts, attributes, intensions) or psychological entities
(e.g., thoughts, ideas, conceptions, images)
underlying general terms.

Here the direction of our interest has changed.
Our earlier concern to rid ourselves of unwanted
references of fictional terms has given way to
the finding of references explaining the meaning

differences among these very terms. The strategy
of Nelson Goodman[3] is to look to the references
of suitable compounds. Though nothing is-Zeus and
there are no minotaurs, there are Zeus-pictures
and minotaur-pictures, Zeus-descriptions and
minotaur-descriptions. Moreover, the compound 'is
a Zeus-description' differs referentially from
its parallel compound 'is a minotaur-description'. There is, in fact, some Zeus-description
that is not a minotaur-description and some
minotaur-description that is not a Zeus-description. Similarly, there are Zeus-pictures that are
not minotaur-pictures, and minotaur-pictures that
are not Zeus-pictures. Taking the likeness of
meaning of two terms to consist, then, not only
in the sameness of their own references (their
primary extensions, in Goodman's terminology) but
also in the sameness of reference of their parallel compounds (their secondary extensions), we
can hope to explain how null terms (such as 'is-
Zeus' and 'is a minotaur') may differ in meaning
though uniformly referring to nothing.[4]

III. How Can Null Replica-Inscriptions
Differ in Meaning?

Extensionalism is not yet inscriptionalism. The
parallel compounds that differentiate meaning
through their own varying extensions serve thus
only for syntactically different terms, i.e.,
for terms construed as word-types spelled differently, as are 'is-Zeus' and 'is a minotaur'. For
the compounds of the one are easily separable (by
spelling) from the compounds of the other. Such
appeal to compounding fails, however, when we
seek meaning differentiation for null concrete
inscriptions with identical spelling. For, being
replicas of one another, such identically spelled
inscriptions share all their compounds, and the

notion of distinguishable "parallel compounds"
collapses.[5] Thus, in

    (6) A green centaur is a more naive consumer
        than an experienced centaur
and (7) A green centaur is harder to spot in the
        forest than a red or yellow centaur

there are two 'green centaur' inscriptions,
different in meaning, but incapable of having
separate groups of parallel compounds assigned
to them on the basis of syntax, since themselves
syntactically indifferent.

An answer that suffices here is one that
appeals not to compounds but rather to constituents. For the two 'green' inscriptions compris-
ing, respectively, the first word-constituents
of our 'green centaur' inscriptions in (6) and
(7) are themselves different in extension, the
first referring to inexperienced things, the
second to things of a certain color. Thus we can
again understand meaning differences among null
terms without reversion to Platonism or psychologism - even taking such terms nominalistically,
i.e., as inscriptions rather than repeatable
word-types. We need, for this purpose, to take
into account the references not only of the inscriptions themselves and of their compounds,
but also of their constituents.

This plan fails, however, where no word-
constituents are available. "The child Linus of
Argos must be distinguished from Linus, the son
of Ismenius, whom Heracles killed with a lyre."[6]
This distinction has to be made in the face of
the fact that neither Linus-inscription refers,
that they have, moreover, no separable groups of
compounds nor word-constituents. To this end, I
have suggested use of a relation of *mention-
selection*,[7] whereby a term is employed to caption

mentions, or representations, rather than to denote objects. Thus a given Linus-inscription may
mention-select, i.e., serve as a suitable caption for, a certain range of pictures or descriptions different from those mention-selected by a
replica Linus-inscription. Analogously, a student producing a Jones-inscription purportedly
to discuss a fictional character in a certain
novel may be considered thereby to have mention-
selected certain Jones-inscriptions in that
novel (or elsewhere) and thus to have produced
something differentiable in its meaning from a
replica applied in discussing another novel.[8]
It is worth noting, incidentally, that although
mention-selection was proposed originally for
the case of inscriptions lacking word-constituents, it has considerably wider range, capable
of yielding also the differentiations earlier
effected by recourse to parallel compounds and
to constituent extensions.

IV. What Truth Is There in Fiction?

Fictional, or null, terms, though literally referring to nothing, may metaphorically refer to
actual things of any sort. As Goodman has said,
"Whether a person is a Don Quixote ... or a Don
Juan is as genuine a question as whether a person is paranoid or schizophrenic and rather
easier to decide."[9] Literally fictional works
may thus express metaphorical truths, or contain
literally fictional terms metaphorically applicable to things. Thus, not only is the threat of
meaninglessness eliminated from the literally
fictional, but also the general threat of falsehood - a point beyond the reach of the Russell-
Quine strategy applied to literal expressions.
(Recall that (2), and therefore (1), are meaningful but, alas, false.)

To say this much is, however, not sufficient,
for we need still to account for the differential
metaphorical behavior of terms that are uniformly
null taken literally. If we analyze

(8) Hamlet is neurotic
taken literally, in accordance with the Russell-
Quine treatment discussed above, we get:
   (9) Something is-Hamlet and is neurotic and
       nothing else is-Hamlet

which is literally false. Moreover, if we try to
interpret (8) metaphorically, as applying to
Hamlet-like persons, we face this difficulty: How
can we liken anyone to Hamlet if there is no
Hamlet? The clues to a metaphorical interpretation
cannot lie in a null literal reference shared with
every other null term.

Goodman suggests recourse to compounds here
again: "In sum, 'Don Quixote' and 'Don Juan' are
denoted by different terms (e.g., 'Don-Quixote-
term' and 'Don-Juan-term') that also denote other
different terms (e.g., 'zany jouster' and 'invet-
erate seducer') that in turn denote different
people" (p. 104, fn. 97).

Put in terms rather of mention-selection, "a
person metaphorically described as Don Quixote is
not literally likened to Don Quixote nor does he
share the satisfaction of important predicates
with the literal Don Quixote; rather he satisfies
certain important predicates constituting
[mention-selected] Don-Quixote descriptions"
(*Beyond the Letter,* p. 142, fn. 97). Where, as in
(8), a null term is the grammatical subject of an
attribution with a non-null predicate, some important description mention-selected by the null
term literally refers to actual things to which
the predicate is ascribed. Thus, 'vacillating
person' is mention-selected by 'Hamlet' and

literally refers to actual individuals to whom
'is neurotic' is applied.

In a somewhat related way, when, during the
course of a performance, a member of the audience
says, "There's Hamlet, coming on stage now!", he
is not to be understood as merely uttering a literal falsehood; he is saying something accurate.
I take his "Hamlet" utterance to be mention-
selecting a Hamlet-representation, that is, the
actor playing Hamlet. Though there is in such
cases no fusion of literal reference with mention-
selection, I have suggested that such fusion may
play a role in so-called "mimetic identification"
in certain religious contexts.[10] Perhaps it has a
more general role also in play.

Footnotes:

1. Bertrand Russell, *Introduction to Mathematical Philosophy*, 2nd ed. (London: Allen & Unwin,
1920), Chap. XVI.
2. W.V. Quine, "On What There Is", in his *From
a Logical Point of View* (Cambridge, Mass.:
Harvard, 1953).
3. *Problems and Projects* (Indianapolis:
Hackett, 1972), pp. 221-230.
4. My special concern in this paper is with
fiction, hence with null terms. But all the
meaning-differentiating devices referred to
throughout the paper are of course applicable
also to non-null coextensive pairs, e.g., the
singular terms 'Morning star' and 'Evening star',
and the general terms 'rational animal' and
'featherless biped'.

5. This section is based on Part I of my *Beyond the Letter* (London: Routledge & Kegan Paul, 1979). Details of the argument here may be found especially in secs. 7 and 8 of Part I. The compounding of an inscription is not its literal embeddedness in a larger inscription but rather the embeddedness of any of its replicas therein. Since the replica relation is transitive, it follows that replicas share the same compounds.

6. Robert Graves, *The Greek Myths* (New York: Braziller, 1957), vol. II, p. 212, sec. 147.

7. See secs. 9 and 10 of Part I, *Beyond the Letter, ibid*.

8. Catherine Z. Elgin has called to my attention that non-null terms in fiction also function mention-selectively in an important way, the name of an actual historical figure appearing in a novel serving to select relevant portrayals in the novel - to which, indeed (and whether true in fact or not), primary interest may attach, rather than to the denotation. I am grateful to Dr. Elgin for her helpful comments on the initial version of this paper.

9. *Ways of Worldmaking* (Indianapolis: Hackett, 1978), p. 103.

10. See my "Ritual and Reference", *Synthese*, XLVI, 3 (March 1981): 421-437, esp. 429-431.

Richard
Wollheim

OURSELVES AND
OUR FUTURE

The story is told of the famous Viennese wit and
actor, Johann Nestroy, that someone once remon-
strated with him for being so prodigal with his
gifts. Instead of frittering them away in anec-
dote and improvisation, he should sit down and
produce proper texts. He should do this for the
sake of posterity. "And what", said Nestroy,
"has posterity done for me?"

I

If we take Nestroy's remark as he did not intend
it - seriously, and not as one more example of
the irony against which he was being warned - we
can see it as expressing a principle we might
call that of living in the present. Living in the
present is a principle of the vulgar, and we can
contrast it with a philosophical principle which
goes behond it and which might be called living
exclusively in the present. The two principles
differ in this way: the vulgar principle is one
of indifference to future persons, the philosophical principle one of indifference to persons
in the future. The vulgar principle exempts
from indifference present persons or persons now
leading their lives, or at least those now leading adult lives: the philosophical principle does
not; it extends indifference from all future persons to all future states of persons. Specifically - and this is the crux of the matter - the
philosophical principle requires a person who
adopts it to be indifferent to future states of
himself. Nestroy indicates no indifference to
himself, for, after all, no man is part of his
own posterity. Nestroy, it is true, shows him-

366

self indifferent to his fame, but this is because he thinks of it as something in which he
cannot be harmed. It is because the philosophical principle does require a person to be indifferent to his own future states that it cannot
be put forward in the spirit of Nestroy. It exemplifies not irony, but insanity. The vulgar
principle conjoins with detachment, the philosophical principle with dementia.

But why is this so, if it is? Why should a
person be thought out of his mind if he projects the principle that Nestroy professed in
such a way as to apply it to himself: if he becomes indifferent in his own case? Why should
each person be so special to himself when after
all he *isn't* so special?

To answer this question we need to have some
idea of that relationship which a man does have
to himself in the future and of which, if I am
so far right, we know two things: that it excludes indifference, and that a person would be
insane to abandon it. I shall call this relationship *self-concern*.

II

I am fully prepared to believe that the philosophical principle of indifference, or that of
living exclusively in the present, is objectionable on more charges than one. I find, for instance, highly plausible the charge that living
exclusively in the present violates rationality.
If a future state of mine will warrant concern
on my part when the time comes round for it to
be a present state of mine, then, though it may
not follow (as some philosophers would maintain)
that this constitutes reason enough for it to be
a matter of present concern to me, there will
surely be certain circumstances in which it must

concern me here and now: and the must is that of
rationality. Given that the future state has a
certain character - say, it is perilous - or
that it stands in a certain relation to me - say,
it is imminent - I would be deficient in rationality to be indifferent to it now or to post-
pone concern until it was actually upon me. However, though this may well be so, though it may
be a violation of rationality to live exclusively in the present, all I claim is that this is
not the only objection to living exclusively in
the present. Another objection is that the principle offends against self-concern, and it is
this objection that I want to pursue, and I do
so without prejudice to the existence or force
of any other charge that might be made out.

III

I am told that something good, something bad,
will happen to someone I know.

In this connection 'something' means either a
mental state or else a state of affairs or event
that includes a mental state - what I call a
partly mental state. Examples of partly mental
states would be an action, an illness, or a be-
reavement. For the something to happen to a
given person, the mental state that it is or includes must be that person's. Of course good
things and bad things can befall persons which
neither are nor include mental states, but I
shall omit these from consideration.

So I am told something like the following:
Someone whom I know will tonight meet a friend
whom he loves and misses. Someone whom I know
will tomorrow wake up blind.

Than I learn that this someone, the someone
whom I know and to whom this will happen, is
me.

There is a characteristic - characteristic, I
insist, not invariable - way in which I shall
respond to such a lesson. This response I call
the tremor.

The tremor is not an invariable response to
such a piece of news, and it is not a response
that is even to be anticipated unless a further
condition is assumed satisfied. This is an epistemic condition, and it is a condition which,
for all its importance within self-knowledge, is
neglected in conventional epistomology. It is a
condition upon beliefs, and I shall call it *acceptance*.

So, I am told that someone whom I know will
tomorrow morning wake up blind: then I am told
that the someone is me. Now I shall tend not to
believe this: told it, I shan't learn it. Suppose however I do believe what I have been told.
Then I shall tend not to accept it. I shall reject it, and, if I do, it is not to be anticipated that I shall respond with the tremor. However if I do believe the terrible news and accept it, then a characteristic response would be
the tremor. (Another pattern of response might
be that I initially believe what I am told, I
also accept it, I respond with the tremor, and,
then, just because I have, or in revulsion to
the tremor, I reject or cease to accept the
news: and a step beyond this might be that I
cease to believe the news.)

The tremor is a part of our natural sensibility, and we may think of it as a sensible index
of self-concern. Self-concern we may now define
as the concern that a person has for his future
mental and partly mental states.

IV

I am told that something good, something bad,

will happen to someone whom I know. Then I learn
who the someone is. It isn't me this time, it's
an acquaintance. The news is likely to affect me,
and this response, which I shall call *the impact*,
is to be distinguished, and nonarbitrarily, from
the tremor.

What do I mean by 'nonarbitrarily'?

It would be an arbitrary way of making the distinction if there was a response that I had when,
having been told that something good, alternatively something bad, would happen to someone I know,
I then learned who it was to whom it would happen,
and I simply called this response "the tremor"
when the person turned out to be me and called it
"the impact" when it wasn't me, and the identity
of the person - that is, me in the one case, someone other than me in the other case - was the only
difference on which the distinction was made: so
that, shuffling the characters around, I might
equally have called this very same response 'the
memor' when the person to whom the something good,
something bad, would happen turned out to be Sidney Morgenbesser and 'the impact' when it wasn't
Sidney Morgenbesser - when it was anyone other
than him including me. In other words, the distinction between the tremor and the impact would
be arbitrary so long as it corresponded to no difference within the response itself: that is to say,
within the response viewed as part of our natural
sensibility.

But there is a prior point to be made. The impact - and here the tremor and the impact differ
- comes in two forms. It comes in a generalized
form, and it comes in a particularized form.

When the impact comes in its generalized form,
it simply registers the fact that *an* answer has
been given to the question, To whom will this happen? The generalized impact records, or is a sensible index of, the passage, the effected passage,

from ignorance to belief. It is a response to
the fact that curiosity has been satisfied, not
to the way in which it has been. By contrast,
the impact in its particularized form registers,
but does not simply register, the fact that an
answer has been given to the question, And to
whom will this happen?, for it also acknowledges
the particular answer that has been given. The
impact in its particularized form, though not in
its generalized form, is sensitive to the identity of the person to whom the something good,
the something bad, will happen.

The impact in its particularized form comes
more sharply into focus when we suppose this:
that, having been told, say, that someone whom
I know will tomorrow wake up blind, I ask who
this will be, I am told that it will be Charles
a friend, and then this is corrected, it will
not be Charles but it will be George an enemy.
Now if it seems reasonable to think that on each
occasion when I am given news who it is, I respond in a way that simply registers the fact
that I have been told something, or in a uniform
way, it surely also seems reasonable to think
that, when I am given the first piece of news,
which turns out to be incorrect, and again, when
I am given the second piece of news, which is
correct, I shall on each occasion respond in a
way that registers what I have been told, or in
a differential way.

With the impact thus anatomized, I return to
the question whether, and, if so, how, the impact and the tremor differ.

The impact in its generalized form clearly
differs from the tremor, just because the impact in its generalized form is a mere response
to a cognitive increment as such. By contrast
when I learn that it is I who will today meet
a friend loved and missed, that it is I who will

tomorrow wake up blind, then, though the tremor
that I experience is a response to a cognitive
increment, it is certainly not a response to a
cognitive increment as such. It is not simply
the index of curiosity satisfied.

But does what distinguishes the tremor from
the impact in its generalized form assimilate it
to the impact in its particularized form? There
is a temptation to think so, but it is one to be
resisted.

Both the tremor and the impact in its particularized form are sensitive to the identity of
the person, news of whom provokes the response.
But the identity of the person enters into the
two responses in very different ways, We can begin to see this by supposing a slight extension
to the situation I last imagined. So, having been
told that someone I know will tomorrow wake up
blind, and asking who it will be, I am, succes-
sively, told that it will be Charles my friend,
that it will be George my enemy, that it will be
me. In each case I respond to the news in a way
that reflects the identity of the person. But in
the first two cases the identity of the person -
first, of Charles, then of George - is reflected
in the response in a way that involves my attitude to the person. My attitude to the person
modifies the response. By an attitude to a person I mean at once my conception of that person
or my picture of what he is like, and the favor,
disfavor, or indifference with which I consequently regard him. However in the third case in
order for the identity of the person - that is,
of me - to be reflected in my response, there is
normally no involvement of an attitude. Characteristically no attitude of mine to myself modifies the tremor. In pathological cases the tremor may be mediated by the way I conceive myself and the favor, disfavor, or indifference in

which I hold myself: so, I am holy, and therefore this misfortune is a welcome trial, or I am
evil, and therefore this misfortune is a just
punishment. But in cases this side of the pathological self-concern suffices, and self-concern
neither is nor includes an attitude toward myself.

I shall go on to pursue this last point, but
first I must guard against a misunderstanding of
what I have just said. In saying that in the case
of others my response to news of good or bad
things that will befall them, or the particularized impact, is mediated by my attitude toward
them, I am not suggesting that, having been told
that someone I know will tomorrow wake up blind,
then, if I learn that it is a friend to whom this
will happen, I shall be appalled by the news,
whereas, if I learn that it is an enemy, I shall
be delighted. All I am saying is that how I take
the news will depend on the nature of the news
and my attitude toward the person, and that my
attitude toward a person will include such things
as whether I regard him as a friend or an enemy.
But just how I take, say, bad news about an enemy is a further question: whether the news about
him saddens me, or whether I find it sweet, or
whether (as the Old Testament counsels) I seek
to alleviate his misfortune so as to make it
even worse for him, to heap coals of fire upon
his head, is a matter of how far the civilizing
process has gone.

V

I have so far been trying to illuminate the tremor, or the response that I characteristically
have to learning that certain news I have been
told is true of me, by contrasting it with the
impact, or the response that I characteristical-

ly have to learning that the news is true of
someone I know but who is other than me. But
light can also be thrown on the tremor by contrasting it with other responses that I can have
to learning of some news that it is true of me,
where these responses, unlike the tremor, involve
or presuppose an attitude on my part. I now want
to turn and consider these attitudes themselves.
These attitudes are optional, which is one reason why they are not presupposed by self-concern.

The first such attitude is egoism. Egoism requires me to believe that my future states are
more valuable or more important - at least within certain broad limits - than the future states
of others, so that I always have a reason, at
any rate within those limits, for trying to regulate the future states of others so as to get for
myself the states that I desire. Probably I would
be crazy if I tried to bring about the destruction of the world so as to avoid the discomfort
of a pricked finger, but within the bounds of day-
to-day pleasure and pain egoism would justify me
in seeking out my pleasure at the expense of another's pleasure.

It is worth making the familiar point that egoism does not involve selfishness, nor for that
matter does selfishness involve egoism. Selfishness is a property of my desires, and derivative-
ly of me in virtue of my desires: it accrues to
my desires because of what they are directed upon. Egoism, by contrast, is an attitude that I
may adopt toward my desires and their satisfaction, and it does not require that my desires
have any specific character. My desires are selfish in so far as they are directed toward *my*
well being, *my* good name, *my* mental or bodily
health, not necessarily at the expense, but certainly to the neglect, of someone else's well-
being, someone else's good name, someone else's

mental or bodily health: and I am selfish insofar as I am motivated by such desires. Selfishness determines, roughly, how I get my pleasures.
(Only roughly, because satisfied desire does not
always bring pleasure in train.) Egosim is indifferent how I get my pleasure but leads me to
place a special value or importance upon my doing
so. It is one of life's ironies that there are
few people who are quite so egotistical, or so
insistent on the satisfaction of their desires,
as the unselfish, or those who desire the well-
being of others as they see it.

Self-concern does not involve egoism. Self-
concern involves the thought that, for instance,
my future states are valuable or important to me
in a way that yours aren't or couldn't be: but
not the thought that my future states are more
important or more valuable to me than yours are
or could be. Furthermore self-concern implies the
thought that your future states are valuable or
important to you in the very way in which my future states are valuable or important to me. And
to someone who thinks that there is a residual
question whether the value or importance to me
of my future states is or isn't more valuable
or more important - not to me, but absolutely -
than the value or importance to you of your future states, self-concern, properly understood,
is likely to retort that there is not necessarily, perhaps that there is not usually, an answer
to this question. If I am very old and frail and
you are very young and healthy, or if I am a poet
of genius and you are a cretin, then, maybe, but
only maybe, there is an answer. But if ever there
is an answer, it is certainly not provided by
self-concern.

To think that self-concern presupposes egoism
seems to me on a par with thinking that because
I insure my property and not yours against fire,

this shows that, if there were a fire, I should
prefer your property to burn down to mine doing
so. Self-concern does not presuppose egoism: nor
does it eliminate it.

The second attitude that I want to consider is
that of finding life worth living. For me, say,
to find life worth living is for me to think that
my life, as it stretches ahead of me, offers a
tolerable balance of pleasure and pain. How pleasure and pain are to be gauged, and what counts
as a tolerable balance between them, are further
questions and do not need to have a Benthamite
interpretation placed on them.

Self-concern does not involve finding life
worth living. It does not do so in either of two
ways that might suggest themselves. My concern
for some particular future state of mine is not
concern whether that state will or will not make,
or contribute to making, my life worth living.
Nor is my concern for any such state dependent
upon my already finding my life worth living.

One and the same consideration can be employed
to show that both these ways of connecting self-
concern and finding life worth living fail. The
consideration is that of the rational suicide,
and to appreciate it we do not have to believe
that anyone ever actually kills himself on rational grounds. Now if we think of the rational
suicide as someone who kills himself just because
he finds his life in prospect not worth living,
we may then ask how, if at all, self-concern enters into the deliberative process by which he
arrives at such an estimate. And the answer seems
to be this: that the person, in surveying his individual states and coming to find them good, bad,
or terrible, as the case may be, has in each case
not only to believe that this is how they will be,
he has also to accept it; in other words, if he
had first had the states described to him, then

been told that they would be his he would,
characteristically, have experienced the tremor.
They must be for him the objects of self-concern.
So it would much alter the character of Sade's
novel if we were to read that one of the young
prisoners in the Chateau de Silling who were
awaiting, with ribbons in their hair, first the
pillage, then the destruction of their bodies
had decided to anticipate the somber events that
were to unfold in the banquet room and the tor-
ture chamber of the castle, and had attempted
suicide. The reason is that the pliance of the
victims to the phantasies of their masters is
presented as so absolute that it would be a
surprise to learn that there is room left in
their psychology for self-concern. But if the
rational suicide is required to feel concern
for his future states before he can decide on
the basis of them that life is no longer worth
living, nevertheless it is true that the concern
he feels, or his acceptance of his future states
as what they are, cannot by itself settle the
question whether his life is worth living. To
answer that question values must be consulted
that go beyond self-concern. Such values are
required, on the one hand, for the determination
of what is pleasurable and what is painful, and,
on the other hand, for the assessment of what is
a tolerable balance between them. Now, if this
is so, it follows that self-concern is not involved in finding life worth living in either
of the two ways proposed. It cannot be that a
person experiences self-concern only when he
finds life worth living: since his future states
have to be the object of his concern for them to
lead him to find life not worth living. Nor can
it be that a person's concern for his future
states is concern whether they do or don't make
life worth living: since he can feel such

concern and still be undecided whether life is
worth living.

The third attitude that I want to consider is
that of finding life worth while. I distinguish
between finding life worth living and finding
life worth while. As we have seen, my finding my
life worth living is a matter of the balance it
appears to offer of pleasure and pain. By contrast my finding my life worth while is a matter
of the opportunities it seems to provide for the
satisfaction of those desires or plans of mine
which I think are important. And my life becomes
more worth while for me if my future states turn
out to be not only sufficient conditions, or
parts of sufficient conditions, for the realization of what I value, but also necessary conditions. I might find life worth living but not
worth while: this was presumably the fate of Na-
poleon on St Helena. And I might find life worth
while but not worth living: such was the fate
sought out by some of the early Saints, or is
that endured by someone who spies for a foreign
power and lives in constant danger of detection.

Self-concern does not involve finding life
worth while: it does not involve it in either of
the two ways that propose themselves. My concern
for some particular future state of mine is not
concern whether that state will or will not make,
or contribute to making, my life worth while. Nor
is my concern for any such states dependent upon
my already finding my life worth while. And once
again a single argument suffices to show that the
connection does not hold either way round.

The crucial consideration is this: that self-
concern does not require that I should already -
that is, before self-concern develops - have the
capacity to form desires or plans, whereas such
a capacity is presupposed both by my trying to
find out whether, and by my believing that life

is, alternatively is not, worth while. I am ready
to concede that in the absence of desire self-
concern would not exist. But this is not to assert the priority of desire over self-concern.
Indeed it seems to me that in the absence of
self-concern desire would be, at most, a highly
attenuated phenomenon. In the absence of self-
concern desire would degenerate into a purely
behavioral phenomenon: it would become a behavioral disposition, like a skill, and the link
between desire and action would cease to be mediated, as it characteristically is, by the person's imagining the object of his desire satisfied and going on to anticipate the pleasure
that satisfied desire promises. Such a sequence
of mental events, such an imaginative project,
has within the psychology of the person the psychic function of getting him to fulfill his desires, and it is for this reason that desires
are motives behind, and not just patterns of,
a person's behavior. But remove self-concern,
and things would no longer be like this. If persons were without concern for their future states,
the anticipation of pleasure, now something purely cognitive, would cease to have motivational
force. (Indeed if we seek the real link between
self-concern and the capacity to form desires and
plans - and so ultimately the attitude of finding
life worth while or not - it is to be found, I
believe, in a common source on which both depend:
that is, the susceptibility to pleasure and pain.)
   I have contended, then, that both the proposed
ways of connecting self-concern with finding life
worth while fail, and they do so because they
both assert the priority of a person's capacity
to form desires and plans over his concern for
his future states. Additionally the proposal that
a person's concern for his future states is just
concern whether that state will or will not make,

or contribute to making, life worth while is implausible because it makes self-concern derivative in a way which cannot be right. It converts
the importance or value to me of my future states
into an instrumental importance or value: I set
store by them as means to the end of getting my
desires satisfied and my plans implemented, and,
when they cease to hold out earnest of this, I as
a rational creature should lose interest in them.

VI

In point of fact I think that self-concern *is*
derivative: though I don't think that the importance or value to us of our future states - that
is to say, the importance or value that they
have for us in virtue of being our future states
- is instrumental.

In holding that self-concern is derivative, I
derive it from the process of living - the process, that is, of living as a person.

I have three things in mind by this derivation.

In the first place, self-concern, or our concern with our future mental and partly mental
states is correlative with appropriately modified relationships to our present and to our past
mental and partly mental states. Just how much
can be said about the relationship to our present states, which is in effect that of entering
into or having them or the very relationship that
makes them our states, is a dark issue, but the
relationship to our past states that is the co-
relative to self-concern is that of lying under
their influence.

This might seem surprising, and to some the
obvious correlative to self-concern directed on
to our past states would be regret, or remorse,
or pride, or, rather, some determinable of which
these would be determinates. But I do not think

that this is right, because regret, remorse,
pride, and the determinable of which these are
determinates are unlike self-concern in that they
involve particular attitudes toward oneself. These
attitudes draw upon independent values in a way
that is, I have maintained, alien to self-concern.
   Secondly, of the three correlative relationships the one in which we stand to our present
states - that of which, I have suggested, least
can be said - is primary. The others can be understood (though not analyzed) in terms of it and our
experience of the passage of time. But only, of
course, if it itself is properly understood: which
it often isn't. The way in which we enter into our
mental states requires that we conceive of ourselves as persisting persons or as things with a
past and a future, and it is because this is so
that this relationship generates both that in which
we stand to past states of ours that we believe in
and accept and that in which we stand to future
states of ours that we believe in and accept. It is
something of an absurdity in contemporary philosophy that the very philosophers who deny that we enter into our present states as persisting persons
then, trying to find a way of attaching to these
present states a posterity of future states, look
to self-concern to achieve this for us: this is an
absurdity because if our relationship to our present states were as they wish it to be - that is
to say, such that each state, taken singly, could
be conceived of as without a person entering into
it - then self-concern, or our relationship to our
future present states, would be a mystery.
   Thirdly, once a person believes and accepts that
a certain future state will be his, he does not
need, nor indeed could he use, any further reason
for being concerned about it. That the state will
be his is, disbelief and rejection overcome, reason enough. Specifically the intervention of pru-

dence is not called for.

In point of fact prudence often occupies an
ambiguous place in philosophical discussion of
how a person stands to his future. If the role
of prudence is merely to activate concern for
the future states of a person, then it is otiose
– if, that is, those states are believed in and
accepted. If, however, prudence is understood
differently, and its role is to pattern this
concern in a specific way, in a way, that is,
that cultivates the advantageous and abhors
risk or danger, then there is no reason to
think that prudence codifies intuitive, or indeed acceptable, attitudes that a person might
have toward his future.

VII

An issue that remains, and will remain after
this paper is concluded, is what acceptance is.
Earlier I introduced the tremor as the index,
the sensible index, of self-concern, and now I
want to introduce as the sensible index of acceptance a mental phenomenon that I shall call
"previsagement".

Previsagement is a mode of imagination directed onto the future. In previsaging a future
event I imagine that event: I imagine it, not
just that it will occur. If the future event
that I previsage is a mental or partly mental
state of mine, I imagine that state from the
inside. Imagining a mental or partly mental
state of mine from the inside means, among other
things, that, if there is something that I imagine myself doing, then I shall tend, even as
I imagine it, to imagine myself feeling what I
would at the time: furthermore, that, if I do
imagine myself feeling what I would at the time,
I shall tend, even as I imagine it, to feel that

very thing.

Previsagement, as I have sketched it, is phenomenologically the counterpart of experiential memory, or that mode of memory which we characteristically have of past events that we have lived through.

Nor does the similarity end there. For in virtue of being phenomenological counterparts the two faculties are also functional counterparts within the psychology of the person. Just as, and in the same way as, experiential memory serves to bring the person under the influence of the past, so previsagement serves to sharpen his concern for the future - *his* past in the one case, *his* future in the other. But if experiential memory and previsagement make it easier for us to live, ironically they also make it harder for us to die. Nature has set certain limits upon these faculties. We cannot experientially remember birth - not, that is, the process of being born, but the beginning of life; nor can we previsage death - not, that is, the process of dying but the cessation of life. And from these two limitations much encouragement is given to the cruellest illusion under which we try to live - the illusion that death is unreal.

ON THREE ARGUMENTS FOR NATURAL LAW

Ernest
Nagel

If the word 'law' is taken to signify *positive
law* - that is, some system of socially authorized
rules for regulating human conduct by using certain distinctive techniques - the assertion that
laws are not always just and are not exempt from
moral criticism, is hardly a controversial thesis, and it is rarely challenged except perhaps
by apologists for absolute despotisms. What is
undoubtedly controversial, and has been the subject of debate since ancient times, is the question whether there are objective grounds, and if
so what they are, for distinguishing rationally
defended from arbitrary moral evaluations of individual laws or even entire legal systems. It
is no less controversial whether there are minimal moral requirements, and if so what these are,
that a legal system must satisfy as a condition
for its effective operation. These issues occupy
a prominent place in the political and jurisprudential discussions of earlier centuries. Interest
in them has become markedly acute in our own day,
in good measure because of concern over the bru-
talities committed by modern governments in many
parts of the world, as well as over the increasing regulation of human activities that has been
generated in many societies because of the growth
of populations and technological developments.
The need for firm principles of social criticism
which would provide among other things a sound
basis for moral assessments of legal rules and
their administration is certainly genuine and
widespread. What continues to be disputed is
whether, and if so in what manner, this need
can be satisfied.

Contemporary legal philosophers who deal with

these issues agree in the main that moral criticism of the law can be supported by what appear
to be rational arguments. However, they differ
considerably in their views concerning the logical character and cognitive status of their premises. Many of them believe that none of the
moral assumptions explicit or implicit in them
is binding on all men, universally valid irres-
pective of the historical period or the social
and economic class to which a person belongs;
and some writers on the subject even maintain
that fundamental moral assumptions are neither
true nor false, but are just expressions of personal preference. These and analogous types of
so-called "moral relativism" and "ethical skepticism" have been characterized by Roscoe Pound –
in my opinion rather indiscriminately and unfair-
ly – as "The Give-It-Up-Philosophies" that see
nothing else in "jurisprudence than force and
threats" and are therefore the seeds of political absolutism.[1]

On the other hand, much recent jurisprudential
literature is an attempt to establish more secure
foundations for the moral guidance of legal development than are provided by any species of moral
relativism, foundations which, it is hoped, will
preclude the possibility of "contraverting the
jural postulates of civilization" (36). The
foundations that have been proposed, and the arguments used on their behalf, differ widely. But
perhaps no proposals have been urged with greater
energy and confidence than those which represent
some form of that "brooding omnipresence in the
sky" of Justice Holmes: the doctrine of natural
law (or of natural rights) which, though often
declared to have been conclusively refuted, has
nevertheless been repeatedly revived, and is
widely professed currently in several of its protean versions.

Unavoidable limitations of space make it impossible in this paper to examine the numerous arguments that proponents of the doctrine have advanced in support of their claim that there are indeed natural laws or natural rights which can serve as the objective basis for the moral evaluation of the law. The aim of this brief essay is much less ambitious: it is to assess just three influential arguments that have been recently presented in support of that claim.

I

The central idea underlying the arguments for a currently professed version of natural law doctrine - a version that does not assume the universal natural teleology basic in the views of the subject of such classical thinkers as Aristotle and Aquinas - is that if a legal system is to achieve the objectives for the sake of which it was instituted (in general, the social regulation of human conduct), the system as a whole and the individual legal rules that it comprises must take into account a number of common traits of human beings. For example, John Dewey maintained that although there is much diversity among men, there is also a uniformity with respect to their uneliminable needs. Thus, all men are alike in requiring food, companions, sex mates, protection from aggressors, and so on; and if any form of human association is to endure, a number of conditions must be satisfied, such as some degree of peace and order.[2] Accordingly, if a society is to have an effective legal system, the contents of its legal rules must reflect in some fashion these imperatives of human existence; and those contents are the "natural law" components in systems of law.

But perhaps the fullest and most cogent recent

presentation of this view is given by H.L.A.
Hart. He calls attention to five well-known and
well-established general facts about mankind,
labeled by him as "truisms." They are: the
physical vulnerability of human beings; the ap-
proximate equality of men in physical strength
and intellectual capacity; their limited willingness to devote themselves to the welfare of
others; their possessing only limited resources;
and their finite understanding and strength of
will. Hart then argued that *if* the minimal objective of men in associating with one another
is *survival*, these truisms "afford a *reason* why
...laws and morals should include a specific
content" (187). Put more concretely, on the assumption that survival is an aim which human beings have in common, those truisms are also *reasons* why there are legal rules that, for example,
prohibit battery and homicide, prescribe ways
for effecting a compromise when men's interests
are in conflict, provide public aid to the indi-
gent, institute property rights, and establish
sanctions to enforce legal rules.

Hart referred to these principles of conduct
which form the specific content of many legal
rules, and for which the truisms are the reason,
as "the minimum content of natural law." But he
also thinks it is important to recognize that
the connection between this minimum content and
the generalized natural facts about human beings
is "rational" rather than *causal*. For according
to him the connection presupposes the existence
of deliberate aims (such as survival), and is
mediated by reasons; on the other hand, a causal
relation does not in general depend on the existence of conscious purposes, and can be established only with the aid of inductive procedures.

It would of course be absurd to deny Hart's
central contention that, in the sense he ex-

plains, there is a minimum "natural law content"
in the legal rules of all societies sufficiently
developed to have legal institutions. However,
it is also important to note that Hart's truisms
do not - indeed, cannot - determine the *specific*
rules of conduct that may be adopted (or ought
to be adopted) in order to cope with those general facts. The fact that, for example, men are
vulnerable physically, does not settle the question what, if anything, is to be done about homicide: whether the prevention of homicidal behavior is to be a public or private responsibility; whether different kinds of homicides should
be recognized; and whether those found guilty of
such behavior are to be punished, and if so whether they are to be executed, imprisoned, or
fined. An analogous indefiniteness attaches to
the ways of meeting the problems raised by the
other truisms: knowing those truisms and given
that the primary aim of men is survival, it is
impossible to predict what principles of conduct
a society will adopt in order to realize that
objective. In short, even when those truisms are
supplemented by an assumed fundamental objective
of human activity, they offer little if any guidance to ascertaining the minimum natural law
content of an existing legal system. Moreover,
and what is surely more important, neither the
truisms nor the rules of conduct adopted for
dealing with the facts the truisms formulate,
provide a basis for the moral evaluation of
those rules or unambiguous directives for replacing unjust legal rules by morally sound ones.
A commonly urged *raison d'être* of natural law is
therefore not satisfied by Hart's minimum content
of natural law.
Furthermore, although it is obvious that no one
can pursue any goal unless he remains alive, it
is an oversimplified view of human life to hold

that "the proper end of human activity is survival." It is not easy to forget the multitude of men who, throughout the ages, willingly sacrificed their lives for some cause other than their own survival. But persons wanting to survive not for its own sake, but in order to continue in some undertaking (e.g., raising a family, improving the human condition, or finding an answer to some problem) are likely to adopt principles of conduct for dealing with the contingencies covered by Hart's truisms which are in general markedly different from the rules adopted by those seeking only personal survival. It is only fair to add that Hart recognizes that according to classical natural law doctrine survival is "merely the lowest stratum in a much more complex... concept of the human end or good for man." He nevertheless thinks that survival has a special status in the economy of human life, since the desire to live is reflected in the structure of the language in terms of which the world and its human inhabitants are described. And he agrees with Hobbes and Hume in seeing "in the modest aim of survival the central indisputable elements which give empirical good sense to the terminology of Natural Law."[3] Hart may be right in believing all this. But the price he pays for these beliefs is a distorted presentation of human life, and the exclusion from his account of the minimum content of natural law of any consideration of the latter's traditionally assumed normative function.

II

Hart also addressed himself directly to the question whether there are any natural rights.[4] And he believed he had established the conditional thesis that *if* there are any *moral* rights at all, there is at least one general *natural* right: the right which all men possess equally to be free from interference by others. As he explained, this means that all human adults capable of making choices have the natural right to be free from restraint by anyone, except when the restraint is undertaken to prevent coercion - it is a natural right, for it has not been created by human beings (176). However, Hart does not explain just what is the overt force of a natural right (if it has any), as distinguished from a *legal* right; and it therefore remains quite obscure what he believes is the effective value of a supposed natural right.

Hart's argument for his thesis is essentially as follows. He first postulates that having a natural right entails (or "presupposes", as he sometimes says) having a *moral* right (or moral justification of a special sort) for limiting the freedom of other persons. This special sort of moral justification is said to derive either from the fact that the claimant of the right stands in a special relation to some other person or persons (e.g., from the fact that a promise had been given) or from the fact that the claimant is an adult who is resisting interference by another person as unjustified (183,187).

However, Hart pointed out that the postulate as stated does not suffice to establish the thesis concerning natural rights as these are usually understood. For unless some restrictions are placed on the kinds of justification that may be offered for interfering with people's freedom, the postulate can be trivially satisfied; but the "natural rights" so established would then usually violate customary conceptions of what is a natural right. For example, without a suitable qualification of the postulate, *any* differentiating trait of human beings (such as belonging to a certain ethnic group, having red hair, or being unemployed) could then be offered as a "moral" justification for interfering with the freedom of those possessing it. Hart confessed, however, that he was unable to specify the appropriate qualifications for the postulate; and he also admitted that when we justify interference with other people's freedom "we are in fact indirectly invoking as our justification the principle that all men have an equal right to be free"(190). In the light of that confession and that admission, it is evident that Hart offers no general rule for identifying genuine instances of natural right, and also that he employs a question-begging argument to establish his main thesis about there being at least one natural right.

Moreover, Hart's argument rests squarely on a tacit and undefended decision concerning which actions require moral justification and which do not. In point of fact he assumes that what needs justification is interference with the freedom of others. But there surely are other decisions that one could make - one could assume, for example, that what needs moral justification is *noninterference* with the pursuit of knowledge or with religious worship, so that on this assumption it would be a natural right to obstruct research or to place obstacles to church attendance. However, Hart does not discuss assumptions alternative to his own, nor does he give reasons for the one he does adopt.

It is instructive to note the similarity between his argument for the natural right to freedom from coercion and the argument once widely accepted for the principle of the lever: if two equal weights are placed on the arms of a uniformly dense lever at equal distances from the fulcrum, the lever will be in equilibrium. Ac-

cording to the latter argument, the equilibrium
is obtained because the arms are in symmetrical
states, so that there is "no reason" why they
should not be in a horizontal position when they
finally come to rest. However, though the lever
arms may be symmetrical in respect to the features mentioned, they will be asymmetrical in
other respects - e.g., they may be differently
colored, their distances from the earth's poles
may be different, and so on - without affecting
the equilibrium of the lever. Clearly, experimental evidence is needed for deciding whether
or not a particular asymmetry of the arms is relevant to their behavior. Similarly, Hart's argument for the natural right of every man to be
free from coercion tacitly invokes the symmetry
that obtains when all men are equally free from
interference by others. But the assumption that
men have a natural right to be free because of
this particular symmetry, overlooks the fact
that even when this symmetry obtains men are a-
symmetrical in other respects (such as in respect to age, sex, or education). Although Hart
does not do so, cogent reasons must be supplied
- it is not clear what sort they must be - for
the assumption that a given symmetry is relevant
to the existence of an alleged natural right,
although the various asymmetries also present
are not.

In view of these difficulties in Hart's argument, his thesis concerning natural rights must
receive the Scotch verdict of "Not Proven."

                          III

A different sort of argument for natural rights
doctrine is based on some version of social
contract theory. According to such theories it
is possible to determine "rationally" the mini-

mum conditions under which men would be willing
to discontinue living in a "state of nature" and
accept the obligations entailed by membership in
a social order, in which the terms of such a hypothetical "contract" would then determine the
inalienable "natural" or "human rights" of that
society's members. It must be added that according to social contract theory those minimum conditions are in general ascertained not by empirical inquiry into the probable consequences of
instituting those conditions, but rather by a
"rational" analysis of (or "insight" into) the
structure of a just society.

This is the line of reasoning followed by John
Rawls in his carefully argued presentation of a
contract theory of society, whose members then
necessarily possess a number of human rights.[5]
Rawls maintains that if persons seeking to further their own best interests were given the opportunity to choose the principles giverning the
social order in which they would then live, and
if they were to select those principles "behind
a veil of ignorance" (i.e., no person knows how
he would fare in the distribution of natural
assets and abilities, the position he would occupy in the society, or the society's economic,
political and cultural character), they would
adopt two fundamental principles (137). According to the first, which has priority over the
second, the inviolable basic civel rights, lib-
erties, and duties of the society's members must
be distributed equally; according to the second,
social and economic inequalities (e.g., in authority and income) are permissible only if they result in corresponding benefits for the least ad-
vantaged members of the society (250, 14/5, 302).

According to Rawls, these principles are not
self-evident; on the contrary, they are the objects of an "original agreement" between persons

"in the original position" - i.e., in the hypothetical situation in which the persons are "rational", have equal freedoms, and make their
choices behind the veil of ignorance. He explains
that a "rational" person is one who has a coherent set of preferences between the options open
to him, ranking them according to how well they
further his purposes and assigning a higher ranking to an option that is likely to satisfy more
of his desires to one that satisfies fewer of
them (28/9, 44). He then concludes that since
in the original position the relations of persons to each other are symmetrical, it is not
possible for anyone to obtain special advantages for himself when he is contracting for the
principles that will govern the structure of
society. He therefore believes that "since it
is not reasonable for [such a person] to expect more than an equal share in the division
of equal goods, and since it is not rational
for him to agree to less, the sensible thing
for him to do is to acknowledge as the first
principle of justice one requiring an equal distribution. Indeed, this principle is so obvious
that we would expect it to occur to anyone immediately" (12, 150/1, 176).

Rawls' assumption that it would not be rational for a person to agree to accept less than an
equal share of the goods to be distributed is
certainly debatable, but the question will not
be pursued further in this paper. In the present
context it will suffice to examine his claim
that adoption of his first principle of justice
rather than anything contrary to it is alone consistent with the original position (121). Now it
is permissible, according to Rawls, for a person
in the original position to know "general facts
about human society" (137); and such a person
might know that there are fewer greatly gifted

people than there are people with only modest
or inferior abilities. Such persons might therefore also believe as generally true that members
of societies in which power and authority are
vested in those with superior intellectual and
administrative abilities are better off than
members of societies in which this is not the
case. In consequence, persons with such a conviction might conclude, as Plato argued in the
Republic, that rule by the elite is more likely
to result in a satisfacotry society than rule
by men with inferior endowments, so that it is
not rational to distribute civil rights and li-
berties equally. But if these suppositions are
well taken, they undermine Rawls's claim that
his first principle is the only rational choice
that can be made in the original position.

Accordingly, the present argument in support
of the doctrine of natural or human rights must
be judged to be inconclusive.

Footnotes:

1. *Contemporary Juristic Theory* (Claremont,
Calif.: University Press, 1940), pp. 37/8.
2. "Anthropology and Ethics", in W.F. Ogburn
and A. Goldenweiser, eds., *The Social Sciences*
(Boston: Houghton Mifflin, 1927), p. 25.
3. *The Concept of Law* (New York: Oxford University Press, 1961), p. 189.
4. "Are There Any Natural Rights?", *Philosophical Review*, LXIV (1955): 175-191.
5. *A Theory of Justice* (Cambridge, Mass.:
Harvard University Press, 1971).

JUSTICE AND THE VIRTUES: A MEDIEVAL PROBLEM

James J. Walsh

The treatment of the later middle ages by the few historians to discuss the period is dominated by the theological writings of William of Ockham at the expense of the more narrowly philosophical literature.[1] Ockham is found basing an ethics of obligation directly on divine prescriptions, and this may strike historians as truer to the legalistic Judeo-Christian tradition than the exotic Aristotelian ethics of teleology and the virtues propounded by the philosophers. And perhaps Ockham's restrictions on the role of reason fit the widespread image of a collapse of reason preparing for the fideistic strain in the succeeding era. Of course, that image ignores the growth of universities, and these very philosophers. Perhaps historians also assume that since the medium for those philosophers was commentary on the text of Aristotle, little of interest is to be found in such derivative work. But some recent explorations of this literature suggest it is of considerable historical and intellectual importance.[2] I propose here to further this exploration a bit by investigating a set of Questions in which three of these commentators dealt with what they called legal justice and what we might call the prescriptive dimension of ethics. It so happens that all three were involved with the career of Ockham, but if his theological positions had any philosophical impact on this subject, it is found in certain views cited by these figures only to be refuted - and these views seem to owe as much to Thomas Aquinas as to anyone. Further speculation on the significance of the Questions can wait until the exposition is completed.

I

In the opening section of Book V of the *Nicomachean Ethics*, Aristotle offers a perfunctory acknowledgement of legal justice as distinct from particular justice, the justice of fairness in distribution and rectification:

> We may then set aside that Justice which is coextensive with virtue in general, being the practice of virtue in general towards someone else, and that Injustice which is the practice of vice in general towards someone else. It is also clear how we should define what is just and unjust in the corresponding senses. For the actions that spring from virtue in general are in the main identical with the actions that are according to the law, since the law enjoins conduct displaying the various particular virtues and forbids conduct displaying the various particular vices (1130b19-25, Rackham translation).

When he discriminates between this justice and that total virtue with which it is coextensive, he says that, as *hexis*, developed habit, they are the same, but they differ in being, in that justice is with respect to another (1130a10-15). This leaves without special comment the fact that these virtuous habits are enjoined by law.[3] The medievals saw three features in this type of justice: it is practiced in relation to others, it pursues the common good of the civil community, and it is prescribed by law. Some exploited one or another of these features to minimize the distinction between justice and the virtues, and others, to give justice greater independence.

We shall consider five figures, the first three rather briefly. We shall use Albert the Great and

Thomas Aquinas from the thirteenth century to
set the stage. They served as standard references
for later commentators, including the fourteenth-
century figures we shall consider.[4] The first is
Walter Burleigh (or Burley), an Englishman with
an international career, once chiefly known as a
philosophical opponent of Ockham, but now appreciated as an important thinker in his own right.
His commentary has been shown to draw heavily
from Aquinas, but his treatment of this topic is
independent.[5] The second is Gerald of Odo, known
as the *doctor moralis*. He also was an opponent of
Ockham, but a political one; he became minister-
general of the Franciscans under John XXII, and
carried on a bitter controversy with Ockham. He
is seen by some as having tried to allay Franciscan suspicion of Aristotle.[6] I have suggested
that his Aristotelianism has a Platonic cast and
that within the framework of Aristotelian teleology he makes much of law, obligation, and obedience.[7] The third figure is John Buridan, until
recently regarded as the leading Parisian follower
of Ockham, and now famous not only for the legend-
ary ass, but also for his work in physical theory
and logic. His ethical work was very popular for
a long time. His Aristotelianism is anything but
Platonic, and I have tried to show it is strongly
teleological in a distinctive way. In this it
differs sharply from the ethical thought of Ockham.[8]
Buridan shows extensive dependence on Odo, which
suggests that his omission of striking positions
taken by Odo is deliberate.[9] These three are
characteristic and influential masters; they have
good credentials in logic and physical theory;
one may presume their ethical writings will be no
less representative.[10] I should add that it is
not only their conclusions that are of interest,
but the positions they report and reject as well.
After all, Buridan decided against the rotation

of the earth; what is interesting is the fact
that he discusses it at all (and says it is a
difficult question).[11]

II

According to Gauthier (*op. cit.* 122-124) the best
medieval commentary on the *Ethics* is by Albert,
and appropriately influential. We can look to it,
then, for an introduction to the problems the
medievals found in Aristotle's text. Albert wants
to know whether law prescribes (concerning) everything, whether legal justice is a specifically
distinct virtue, whether it is the most perfect
virtue, whether it is concerned for the good of
another, whether it is the same to be a good man
and a good citizen.[12] Much of his discussion is
not reflected in our later figures, and I shall
cite only a few of the more pertinent remarks.
One argument would separate law from virtue on
the grounds that law is concerned only for what
is common and not for what is personal (*propria*),
for what is overt and not for the interior acts
of will that constitute virtue. Albert's reply
is that the *use* of interior virtue is common or
public and that interior acts cause exterior
ones.[13]   An objection to the claim that justice
is a specifically distinct virtue is that recti-
tude is attributed to justice just as due measure
(*modus*) is to temperance. But measure is a feature
of all the virtues, and yet no *further* general
temperance is posited. Why then a further virtue
of legal justice? His reply claims a special
abstractness and rational generality for justice
beyond the other virtues.[14] Regarding the distinction of the personal and the common, it is argued
that one is no more obligated to another than to
oneself, so that justice should order one to one's
own good rather than to another's. The reply is

that the good of the community cannot be neglected without the loss of one's own, through shame
and dishonor.[15]

Albert may be the best commentator for the
medievals, but the treatment by Thomas in the
Second Part of the *Summa Theologiae*, which amounts
to a commentary in Question form, is clearer for
the modern. The story is that when Thomas was Albert's student he edited Albert's commentary, so
we may consider some of his remarks to be revisions of those of Albert. Where Albert says that
justice orders man to himself and also to another
as disposed to civil good, Thomas amplifies by
saying that justice orders man with respect to
another in two ways, as a single person and as a
part of a community. The good of any virtue, then,
whether ordered to oneself or to some other, can
be referred to the common good, which justice
orders. Thomas also revises Albert's remarks about
the abstractness of justice: temperance, courage,
and the other moral virtues are found in the sensory appetite, ordered to particular goods; justice is ordered to a universal good and is thus
in the will, the intellectual appetite.[16]

The crucial article for our purposes asks
whether justice, as it is general, is the same
in essence with all virtue. He follows Albert in
deploying the distinction between predicative and
causal generality. In the latter, cause and effect
need not be of the same essence; the sun, for
instance, need not share the essence of the bodies
it illuminates. The application to justice goes as
follows:

> But it is in this way...that legal justice is
> said to be general virtue, that is, insofar
> as it orders the acts of the other virtues to
> its end, which is to move all the other virtues
> through command (*imperium*). For just as charity

can be called general virtue insofar as
it orders the acts of all the virtues to
the divine good, so also legal justice,
insofar as it orders the acts of all the
virtues to the common good. Thus just as
charity, which looks to the divine good as
its proper object, so justice is a certain
specific (*specialis*) virtue according to
its essence, as it looks to the common
good as its proper object. And thus it is
chiefly and as it were architectonically
in the ruler, but secondarily and as it
were administratively in subjects. Yet
any virtue can be called legal justice
according as it is ordered to the common
good by the foresaid virtue, specific indeed in essence but general in power (*virtutem*). And it is in speaking this way that
legal justice is the same in essence with
all virtue but differs in reason. And the
Philosopher speaks in this way.[17]

By bringing forward the political setting of the
problem, Thomas has clarified the generality of
justice. This is causal generality, and it is
exercised primarily through the command of a
ruler and secondarily through the obedience of
his subjects. (The question whether a virtue, as
distinct from a person, can be politically com-
manded, is not asked here.) Despite the remark
that any obedient virtue can be called legal justice, this treatment works toward the separation
of justice from the other virtues. It will be of
interest to see how this emphasis on the political setting of the problem fares with our
fourteenth-century figures.

The first of these is Burleigh. His usual
dependence on Aquinas can be seen in his adoption
of the view that justice is in the will, whereas

the other moral virtues are in the sensory appetite.[18] But his treatment of this subject differs
significantly. He asks whether legal justice is
specifically distinct from the other virtues.[19]
Thomas's ruler and subjects play no role in Burleigh's treatment. The causal-political separation of justice is not so available, then, and
Burleigh concludes that justice is indeed predi-
catively common to every moral virtue. His central passage follows:

> Hence it seems to me according to the inten-
> tion of the Philosopher and the Commentator
> here that justice is common through predica-
> tion to every moral virtue. For virtue whose
> act the law prescribes is legal justice, ac-
> cording to the Philosopher. But the law pre-
> scribes the acts of all the virtues; hence
> every virtue is legal justice. It should be
> known, therefore, that legal justice is the
> virtue by which man is well disposed as
> ordered to the common good, and particular
> justice, through which he is disposed to
> acting well as ordered to a single person.
> And virtue taken unqualifiedly is the habit
> through which man is well disposed as order-
> ed to himself. But now it is through the
> same habit through which man is well disposed
> as ordered to himself that he is well dis-
> posed as ordered to the common good. For
> through temperance a man is well disposed in
> himself, and through temperance he is well
> disposed as ordered to the common good. For
> a temperate person lives well in a community
> by means of the habit of temperance, in not
> committing injury to another in carrying out
> his concupiscent desires; and a gentle person
> lives well according to himself and without
> turmoil, and also lives well in a community,
> without violent abuse and anger and con-

> tention.   Hence I say that virtue and
> legal justice belong to the same class
> as to the things which are indicated,
> nor is legal justice a virtue specific-
> ally distinct from the other virtues,
> just as this common virtue is not a
> distinct virtue. Hence the Philosopher
> says that legal justice is whole virtue,
> since it is a whole universally contain-
> ing under it every virtue as ordered to
> the common good.[20]

Against the background of the passage from
Aquinas, this seems to intend a closer relation
of justice to the virtues, to reduce justice to
a mere feature of them. And one should note that
even though it is through moral virtue that one
is well-ordered regarding oneself, it is also
through just such virtue that one lives well
regarding a community. The role of relation to
others as distinctive of justice seems on the
verge of disappearance.

I turn now to Gerald of Odo. Although he was
close to the pope who canonized Aquinas, Odo does
not mention Aquinas and occasionally dismisses
his doctrines (e.g., he says the view that the
moral virtues are in the sensory appetites is
"false and iniquitous").[21] There is no evidence
that he knew Burleigh's work, but he carries forward reservations about the social dimension of
virtue as distinctive of legal justice. A moral
virtue, says Odo, can be related to one other
than its bearer in three ways: (a) the generic
operation of every virtue involves another, (b)
every virtue redounds to the benefit of others,
and (c) every virtue requires the perfection of
some feature referable to another. He argues for
(a) by an inductive survey of virtues - only
temperance is troublesome, but he takes temper-

ance to be aimed at the virtuous generation of
offspring, which certainly involves others. As
for (b) he argues that a virtue can hardly be
injurious or otiose: even the death of a criminal
redounds to the public good. Induction is again
used for (c): temperance requires a temperate
wife, courage a brave foe, liberality the worthi-
ly needful, and so on. Where, then, is the dis-
tinctiveness of justice in its relation to
another? Odo claims that these conclusions show
that legal justice does not differ in species
from the other virtues, but does differ from
them in genus. The basis for this seems to be
that however much each virtue calls for an appropriate partner in its operation, only justice
calls for the mention of such a partner in its
definition.[22]

Perhaps I miss something in this resolution,
but at least one can see that with such strong
emphasis on the social dimension of virtue, Odo
does not find it easy to spell out the distinc-
tiveness of justice along that line. It would be
natural to turn to the most obvious feature of
legal justice, obedience to law. This would seem
especially tempting for the author of the following passage, which certainly gives to law and
obedience primary ethical importance:

> There are three rules for a virtuous act.
> The first is the law of nature; the second
> is what is owed by human nature; the third
> is the dictate of human reason. For natural
> law commands one to do what ought to be
> done and forbids what ought not be done. And
> this is the divine law and also the original
> reason of things which imposes manner and
> order and end to each thing. What is owed by
> human nature is the obligation by which it
> is bound to obey the law of nature. And the

dictate of human reason is the disclosure
of a precept on the part of natural law
and of an obligation on the part of our
nature.[23]

Odo's central text is Book V, Question 5. The
central point is that merely obeying the law may
yield the *works* of virtue, but those works will
not be done *virtuously*. Odo claims that legal
justice is not a habit distinct from the other
virtues, on the strength of a division of the
ways an act can be attributed to a virtue. The
standard way he calls "directive" (we might call
it "direct"). An act thus directed by a virtue
is done virtuously. The second way he calls "imperative" or "prescriptive". Thus the virtue of
magnificence may prescribe a skillful act, but
not direct it nor hence make it skillful. The
third way he calls "obedient", as when a bodily
movement obediently carries out the act or a subject obeys the law. (Perhaps we may think of a
wealthy biship magnificently commissioning a
master-builder to construct a cathedral, and a
mason obediently following the builder's skillful instructions.) So if justice does virtuous
things directively, it will not be a distinct
habit, since any disposition by which one
performs, e.g., temperately, is simply temperance. Nor can a distinct justice do things merely prescriptively, for then, not being directive
of the acts of other virtues and having no
proper act of its own, it would do nothing virtuously, and so not be a virtue at all. As for
the third, the argument is as follows:

> But if you say that (it is related) neither
> directively nor prescriptively, but obedient-
> ly, so that such justice is the habit obedient
> to the law with love for the common good, this
> is again less than reasonable. For then it

would follow that legal justice would not
unqualifiedly be moral virtue, neither
excellent nor perfect. For such a habit of
obedience to the law is unqualifiedly the
virtue of a subject, to whom belongs neither
virtue nor prudence, but true opinion, as is
maintained in Book III of the *Politics*, at
the end of chapter 2. But with true opinion
without prudence nothing can be perfect and
outstandingly moral virtue, as below through
the whole of Book VI. Wherefore that obedience or habit of obedience to the law is not
legal justice, however much it is a good
habit, as is maintained above on Book I, concerning one who does not himself understand
what is to be done, but obeys one who does
understand.[24]

Despite the insistence on law and obedience in
the three rules for a virtuous act, then, Odo
refuses to countenance a virtue distinct as prescriptive or as commanding obedience. In his
solution of Question 5 he pursues the political
dimension ignored by Burleigh, but to a conclusion quite different from that of Aquinas. In
perfecting a citizen as citizen, justice does
differ from the virtues, which perfect man as
man. And it differs from the virtues in its end,
as the happiness of the community differs from
that of the person. But how great are these differences? It is the same person who is man and
citizen; they do not differ as two men. And what
aims for the happiness of the community must include that of the person, for no habit can more
directly attain the happiness of someone other
than that of the one who has it. Further, Odo's
politics seem to differ significantly from
Aquinas'. Merely obedient citizens are not unqualifiedly good even as citizens. For the vir-

tue of a zealous citizen is not merely to be
able to obey well, but also to rule well, should
the ruler be absent. Otherwise the citizen would
merely be following the prudence of another,
like a being without its own reason. But having
prudence and being disposed to follow it is just
the situation of the good man. Justice and the
virtues, then, differ only in ways that do not
call for a difference in underlying habit.[25] And
in his reply to the argument that at least their
respective *objects* differ as differentially characterized, he insists that the moral virtues,
"with nothing added to them, with no intention or
choice added to them" make man happy and good
both as man and as citizen.[26] The virtues remain
primary.

So Odo has encountered the proposal to distinguish justice from the virtues through an
emphasis on obedience to law, and even the suggestion that obedience to law can do everything
the virtues can, and he resists both even though
he must be under strong doctrinal temptation to
adopt them. Buridan is under no such temptation.
I have made much elsewhere of his point-by-point
rejection of Odo's three rules for a virtuous
act, and his substitution of teleology for Odo's
law and obligation.[27] It is disconcerting that,
though his debt to Odo is heavy in Book V, there
is no mention of the directive, prescriptive,
and obedience modes of attribution.[28] Indeed, I
have the impression that Buridan simply does not
see what all the fuss is about. But though his
criticisms may be perfunctory, he faithfully
reports what he takes to be leading views. I
shall skip over his recapitulation of material
we have already covered, and concentrate upon a
view that he introduces as going one step beyond
the three ways a virtue is related to others set
out by Odo.

This position he says is different from all
the others. By it, if one acts only because the
act is honorable for the agent, e.g., in giving
money, only one of the other virtues is at work,
in this case, liberality. But if one acts to fulfill an obligation, as in the repayment of a
debt, then the virtue is justice. This basic
position is then set in the political context.
Subjects are obligated to their lords, both to
obey their ordinances and not to disturb other
subjects in what has been granted by lords. The
former is legal justice and the latter, particular justice. He summarizes the position thus:

> These ones therefore say, first, that
> justice, taken together for legal and par-
> ticular, is distinguished in species from
> the other virtues, first on account of ends,
> since justice is done for the sake of what
> the doer is obligated to another to do. But
> the other virtues are done for the sake of
> the honorableness of such an act for the
> doer. Second, on account of the objects,
> since the objects of justice are human
> actions under the characteristic of being
> owed, but the objects of the other virtues
> are human acts under the characteristic of
> the honorable alone. Third, on account of
> the subjects, since many place justice in
> the will, but other virtues in the sensory
> appetite.
> Second, these ones say that legal justice
> differs in species from particular justice,
> or equal justice, since while justice taken
> together differs from the other virtues
> through the characteristic of the owed or of
> obligation, it is required if the characteris-
> tics of obligation are diverse in species that
> justice also be divided in species. But one

act of courage, it is liberality itself which
will withhold.[32]
   In the end, Buridan follows Eustratius and
opts for an unadventurous reading of Aristotle.
Moral virtue can be simple orcomposite, the composite merely aggregated through the operation
of prudence. The composite is not a distinct
species of virtue, any more than the world, the
ordered aggregate of all things, is a distinct
species of being.[33] Finally, this justice characteristic is not a substantive differentia of
virtues, but rather a perfective property of all
virtues when they operate for another's good.

III

This has been a long and perhaps confusing exposition. Limitations of space forbid sorting out
loose ends, but some effort should be made to
gain a sense for what it adds up to. But first I
should like to enter two *caveats*. As we have
noted, medieval thinkers could borrow and even
plagiarize without thinking much of it, and without attention to sectarian loyalties such as
realism, nominalism, or whatnot. Second, in these
sprawling commentaries (they may run for a thousand pages), they do not seem to make a fetish of
consistency.[34] We cannot expect to put too fine
a point on things. But this much is clear: a
topic which hardly gave Aristotle pause stopped
these thinkers in their tracks. It may be hard
for us to grasp just what their problem was. The
points of detail do not seem so problematic;
perhaps I may be forgiven a brief review. To
specify what is distinctive about legal justice,
one line they pursue is the relation to others.
They discover problems: Is the other singular or
communal? Is personal virtue not just a part of
the common good? Is the common good not a personal good for the virtuous? Are not others required

characteristic of obligation is of a subject to a lord, and another is of subjects
to one another. For the first is assumed
according to the disposition of inequality,
but the second according to the disposition
of equality.[29]

Despite his care in presenting this historically
prophetic position, Buridan seems unaware of any
serious implications it may have. He dismisses
it with a brief reminder of the need to take all
circumstances into account, including whatever
obligations may obtain, in the operations of any
moral virtue.[30] He can even add that the just
man acts for the common utility but intends
primarily to gain the decoration of virtue for
his soul and the honor the community is obligated to render to him.[31] Obligation, then, is not
a criterion for justice as a specifically distinct virtue.

Buridan presents another opinion almost as prophetic, but one whose impact belongs with the
topic of the unity of the virtues. I hope to take
this up elsewhere, but a brief review is in order
here. He sets out what we might call a trade-off
situation: enemies are at the gate, the wronged
cry redress, the poor clamor for aid. No single
moral virtue, it is claimed, can carry through
the balancing of accounts and tell us what to do.
Some master common prudence will have to put it
all together, and a common moral virtue will have
to back that up. Such a virtue is legal justice.
But even if there were such a virtue, Buridan cannot see what it would have to do with the law nor
why it should be called justice. Even in such complex situations, the normal repertoire of virtues
will suffice without any special supervening one.
A virtue is not always inclined merely to its
positive act, e.g., giving money in the case of
liberality. Where reason judges that giving
should be withheld, e.g., to permit a required

as participants in virtuous action and as
recipients of the benefits of such action? Mere
relation to others will not mark out justice, it
seems. A further suggestion links this line with
the other one we have followed. This is the obli-
gatoriness of those relations to others which
are covered by the relation of subject to ruler
and hence by the ruler's ordinances. But if obedience to these ordinances is not informed by the
same kind of understanding which the ruler employs
in issuing them, it is not fully virtuous. And
if it is so informed, how is the situation different from that of a primary virtue? Justice has no
act of its own apart from those of the primary
virtues; so with the bankruptcy of both relation
to others and obedience to law, its status as a
virtue is in doubt. But what of the deeper issue
to which all these details are relevant? Aquinas
and the unnamed legalists and obligationists seem
to want legal justice to be a distinct yet en-
compassing species of virtue; Burleigh, Odo, and
Buridan want to reduce it to a mere feature of
the other, more primary virtues. Is this merely a
dispute hinging on the notion of a species of
virtue?

One of Odo's Questions asks whether justice can
do the works of all the virtues.[35] Perhaps that
is what so-called "Ockhamism" looked like to
these philosophers - an ethics with legal justice
replacing the virtues. That speculation may call
to mind the recent large historical interpretation
of Alasdair MacIntyre, in which the transition
from Aristotle's ethics to much modern moral
philosophy hinges on the role of *rules*. MacIntyre
claims that, for Aristotle, rules play at best a
marginal role flanking the virtues. But for the
moderns, rules become primary, with the virtues
reduced to dispositions to obey them; indeed the
several virtues are reduced in the post-medieval

era simply to "virtue".[36] A conception of legal justice in which it is distinct from the other virtues and hence is not merely a feature of them, in which it is capable of doing all their works, in which its concern is for obligations resting on obedience to the ordinances of a ruler looks very much like a way station between the old world stemming from Aristotle and the new world culminating in Kant. If such is the case, it is interesting that this conception is resisted by those very fourteenth-century figures who provide such a transition in the history of natural science. And it is also interesting that the materials for both the transitional conception and the resistance to it are drawn from the resources of the Aristotelian corpus (which may suggest that MacIntyre's contrast is somewhat overdrawn).[37]

None of this is definitive. But I hope that the interest of the problem, the wealth of argumentation (which I have only skimmed here), and this indication of possible historical importance have shown that new chapters in the history of moral philosophy remain to be gleaned from this formidable and fascinating medieval literature.

Footnotes:

I wish to thank Deborah Goldberg, Bonnie Kent, Paul Kristeller, and Charles Larmore for comment on a previous version of this study. Space forbids responding to all their numerous remarks, but I assure them they all have been carefully considered.

1. See H. Sidgwick, *Outlines of the History of Ethics*, London, 1946, 147-148; V. Bourke, *History of Ethics*, Garden City, N.Y., 1970, vol. I, 153-155; A. MacIntyre, *A Short History of Ethics*, New York, 1966, 119. Bourke's treatment is much fuller than the others: he spends some time on Duns Scotus, and, on p. 128 even mentions the commentaries we shall discuss. His conclusions on Ockham convey the tenor of his treatment: "The consequences of this Ockhamist doctrine are tremendous: moral law is reduced to positive divine law, obligation is contingent, and it is doubtful that a valid ethics can be constructed apart from theology" (*op. cit.*, 155).

2. See R.-A. Gauthier's Introduction to *L'Éthique à Nicomaque*, introduction, traduction et commentaire par R.-A. Gauthier et J.Y. Jolif, T. 1, première partie, deuxième édition, Louvain/Paris, 1970, 134-138; J. Korolec, *Filozofia Moralna Jana Burydana*, Warsaw, 1973; J. Korolec, "Les principes de la philosophie morale de Jean Buridan," *Mediaevalia Philosophiia Polonorum*, XXI (1975): 53-71; N. Kretzmann, A. Kenny, J. Pinborg, eds., *The Cambridge History of Later Medieval Philosophy*, Cambridge, 1982; my "Nominalism and the *Ethics*: Some Remarks about Buridan's Commentary," *Journal of the History of Philosophy*, IV (1966), 1-12; and, "Teleology in the Ethics of Buridan," *ibid.*, XVIII (1980): 265-286. Above all, see O. Langholm, *Price and Value in the Aristotelian Tradition*, Bergen, 1979. I consider this a minor masterpiece.

3. Since he says at 1129b20 ff. that the law he has in mind, that which prescribes the conduct of a brave or a temperate man and so on for the rest of the virtues does so rightly if the law has been rightly enacted and not so well otherwise, this law of legal justice looks to be the enacted law of a civil community. This conclusion hardly fits nicely with the distinction presented

at 1134b18-1135a15 between natural and political
or conventional justice. It hardly seems that a
rule which settles a matter that is indifferent
in the first instance is of the proper authority
and, as it were, dignity, to command all the
acts of virtue. Surely Aristotle must intend the
law of legal justice to include natural law, but
he does not seem to say so. Oddly, this problem
is not taken up by our medieval figures, though
they discuss the relations between the varieties
of law at some length.

4. A convenient and authoritative discussion
of the various treatments of Aristotle's ethics
by Thomas and Albert can be found in Gauthier,
op. cit., 120-132. We shall use the first of
Albert's commentaries. Agreeing with Gauthier
that not much of wider interest on our topic is
to be found in the commentary by Thomas, we shall
utilize the treatment in the Second Part of the
Summa Theologiae.

5. I use the Venice, 1500 edition of *Expositio
Gualteri Burlei super Decem Libros Ethicorum
Aristotelis*. For the relation to Aquinas, see G.
Gomes, "Foundations of Ethics in Walter Burleigh's
Commentary on Aristotle's Nicomachean Ethics,"
Columbia University dissertation, 1973.

6. I use the Venice, 1500 edition of the *Expositio in Aristotelis Ethicam*. Gauthier calls
attention to the effort to show the concord between Christian and Aristotelian ethics at *op.
cit.*, 135. See Odo's Question 31 of Book I. There
is some difficulty with the transliteration of
his name. The Latin is 'Geraldus Odonis'. Gauthier
has objected in correspondence to 'Gerald Odo'.
Perhaps 'Gerald of Odo' will do.

7. See "Some Relationships between Gerald Odo's
and John Buridan's Commentaries on Aristotle's
'Ethics'," *Franciscan Studies*, XXXV (1975): 237-
275.

8. I use the Oxford, 1637 edition of *Questiones in Decem Libros Ethicorum Aristotelis ad Nicomachum*, which closely follows the 1513 edition and differs rarely from *Ms. Bib. nat. lat. 16128*. For the characteristics of Buridan's moral teleology, see my "Teleology in the Ethics of Buridan;" for differences from Ockham see the same, and "Nominalism and the Ethics: Some Remarks about Buridan's Commentary."

9. See "Some Relationships...".

10. The writings of Burleigh and Buridan on these subjects are too well known to be catalogued here. Those of Odo may come as a surprise to those who have seen Langlois' humorous disparagement of his devotional works. See footnote 21 of "Some Relationships...". Much natural philosophy has been found in his *Sentences* commentary. See E. Sylla, "Autonomous and Handmaiden Science ..." in J. Murdoch and E. Sylla, eds., *The Cultural Context of Medieval Learning*, Dordrecht/Boston, 1975, 349-396, footnote 21. V. Zoubov has discussed his work on the continuum and shown its influence in "Walter Catton, Gerard Odon et Nicolas Bonet," *Physis*, I (1959): 261-278. S. Brown has edited and published his treatise on the logic of supposition in "Gerard Odon's 'De Suppositionibus'," *Franciscan Studies*, XXXV (1975): 5-44. His importance, along with that of Buridan, in the history of economic theory is brought out in detail by O. Langholm, *op. cit*. It may also be worth noting here that the ethical commentaries of Burleigh, Odo, and Buridan are cited by Gauthier, *op. cit.*, 134-138, and by Bourke, *History of Ethics*, 128.

11. See his *Quaestiones super libris quattuor De Caelo et Mundo*, ed. E. Moody, Cambridge, Mass., 1942, Book II, Question 22, 226-233.

12. S. Alberti Magni, *Operum Omnium*, T. XIV, Pars I, Fasc. I. *Super Ethica Commentum et Quaes-*

tiones, ed. W. Kübel, Aschendorff, no date, 315-326.

13. *Ibid.*, para. 372m 315 Col. B-316 Col. A.

14. *Ibid.*, para. 376, 320 Col. A.

15. *Ibid.*, para. 380, 322 Col. A-B.

16. *Summa Theologiae*, Second Part, Question 58, Article 5.

17. *"Hoc autem modo...justitia legalis dicitur esse virtus generalis, in quantum scilicet ordinat actus aliarum virtutum ad suum finem; quod est movere per imperium omnes alias virtutes. Sicut enim charitas potest dici virtus generalis, in quantum ordinat actus omnium virtutum ad bonum divinum: ita etiam justitia legalis, in quantum ordinat actus omnium virtutum ad bonum commune. Sicut ergo charitas, quae respicit bonum divinum ut proprium objectum, justitia est quaedam specialis virtus secundum suam essentiam, secundum quod respicit commune bonum ut proprium objectum. Et sic est in principe principaliter et quasi architectonice in subditis autem secundario, et quasi administrative. Potest tamen quaelibet virtus secundum quod a praedicta virtute, speciali quidem in essentia, generali autem secundum virtutem, ordinatur ad bonum commune, dici justitia legalis. Et hoc modo loquendi justitia legalis est idem in essentia cum omni virtute, differt autem ratione. Et hoc modo loquitur Philosophus."* Summa Theologiae, Secunda Secundae, Q. 58, a.6. There are many editions of the *Summa Theologiae*. I use the Vives edition, Paris 1868, vol. IV, 800-801. One should distinguish in this passage between *virtus* as moral virtue and *virtus* as causal power.

18. See the discussion of the "second doubt", concerning the superiority of justice, *op. cit.*, Fol. 78ro, Col. B.

19. *Ibid.*, Fol. 77vo, Col. B.

20. *"Ideo videtur mihi secundum intentionem*

Philosophi et commentatoris hic quod iustitia
est communis per predicationem de omni virtute
morali: quia omnis virtus cuius actum lex preci-
pit est iustitia legalis secundum Philosophum.
Sed actus omnium virtutum precipit lex: ideo
omnis virtus est iustitia legalis. Sciendum est
igitur quod iustitia legalis est virtus qua homo
bene disponitur in ordine ad bonum commune. et
iustitia particularis per quam homo bene disponi-
tur ad bene operandum in ordine ad personam singu-
larem. et virtus simpliciter accepta est habitus
per quem homo bene disponitur in ordine ad seip-
sum. nunc autem per eundem habitum per quem homo
bene disponitur in ordine ad seipsum bene disponi-
tur in ordine ad bonum commune. nam per temperan-
tiam homo bene disponitur in seipso: et per tem-
perantiam homo bene disponitur in ordine ad
bonum commune. Temperatus enim mediante habitu
temperantie bene vivit in communitate non facien-
do injuriam alteri propter concupiscentiam suam
adimplemendam: et mansuetus bene vivit secundum
se et sine perturbatione: et etiam bene vivit in
communitate absque contumelia et ira et rixa.
ideo dico quod virtus et iustitia legalis sunt
eiusdem communitatis quantum ad supposita, nec
est iustitia legalis virtus specialis distincta
ab aliis virtutibus: sicut nec hoc commune vir-
tus est virtus distincta. et ideo dicit philoso-
phus quod iustitia legalis est tota virtus:
quia est totum universale continens sub se om-
nem virtutem in ordine ad bonum commune." (*ibid.,*
Fol. 78ro Col. A-B). I do not know what commentator Burleigh has in mind here, Grosseteste,
Averroes, or a Byzantine.

21. See the treatment of objection 7, Question
5 of Book V, which refers as well to the last
Question of Book I. *Op. cit.*, Fol. 97ro, Col. A.
See also "Some Relationships...," 260-262.

22. *Op. cit.*, Book V, Question 8, Fol. 99vo,

Col. A-B. Bonnie Kent, who is at work on Odo's commentary, suggests that since justice is *essentially* related to another, one cannot choose to act justly without acting for the sake of the good of another or the common good. This in turn suggests that the role of the other for the primary moral virtues may be difficult to assimilate to the Aristotelian four causes – it can hardly be that of the material cause, which presumably is the relevant passion. The issues thus raised cannot be pursued here; the medieval topic of the "subject" of the virtues is perhaps the place to start.

23. "...*operis virtuose tres sunt regule: Prima est lex nature, 2^a debitum humane nature, 3^e est dictamen rationis humane. Lex enim nature precipit facere facienda et prohibet non facienda. Et hec enim est lex divina et primeva rerum ratio que singulis rebus modum et ordinem et finem imponit. Debitum autem humane nature est obligatio qua tenetur obedire legi nature. Dictamen vero rationis humane est ostensio precepti ex parte legis nature et debiti ex parte nature nostre.*" Book II, Question 12, Fol. 33vo. I suppose I should apologize for citing this striking passage now for the third time. See "Some Relationships...," 270, and "Teleology...," 267.

Bonnie Kent has pointed out a cross-reference to these rules at Book V, Question 2, at Fol. 93vo, Col. C. She also suggests that rules for a virtuous act may not suffice for performing an act *virtuously*. This anticipates what will be said below about attributing an act to a virtue directively. Space forbids pursuing here the large topic of natural law in Odo's work. The present Question is relevant, as is Book V, Question 16, and an interesting passage in the opening exposition of Book VII at Fol. 138vo, Col. B-Fol. 139ro, Col. A, which claims that moral goodness requires the observance of the natural law of an individual, species, and genus.

24. "*Si vero dixeris quod non tantum nec directive tantum preceptive sed obeditive. sic quod huius iustitia sit habitus obeditivus legi: amore communis boni. hoc est iterum minus rationabile: quia tunc sequitur quod iustitia legalis non esset simpliciter virtus moralis. nec preclara nec perfecta. pro eo quod talis habitus obeditivus legi est simpliciter virtus subditi: cuius non est virtus nec prudentia. sed opinio vera ut habetur tertio politice capitulo 2^0 in fine. sed cum opinione vera sine prudentia nulla potest esse moralis virtus perfecta et maxime tam preclara: ut infra per totum libro 6^0. quare illa obedientia vel ille habitus obeditivus legi non est legalis iustitia quamvis sit bonus habitus: ut habetur supra libro primo de illo qui per se facienda non intelligit: sed intelligenti obedit*" (*Ibid.*, Fol. 96vo, Col. B-Fol. 97ro, Col. A). The foundations for this threefold distinction can be found in the analysis of virtuous action in Book II, Question 8.

25. The main reply is Fol. 96ro, Col. B-Fol. 96vo, Col. B. The reply to the fourth objection is on Fol. 97ro, Col. A-B. Odo also says that in the best civil community one is ruled by free men like oneself. See. Fol. 96vo, Col. A. This emphasis on civil freedom may have something to do with a general emphasis on freedom and free will reported by Bonnie Kent.

26. "*Item nullo eis addito nulla quidem intentione vel electione eis addita ipsemet simul sumpte sunt nate reddere simpliciter bonum*" (Fol. 97ro, Col. B).

27. See "Teleology...," 267-268.

28. See "Some Relationships..., 249, 251.

29. "*Dicunt igitur isti primo, quod justitia, communiter accepta ad legalem et particularem,*

*distinguitur specie ab aliis virtutibus: primo
propter fines, quia justitia operatur ejus gratia
quod operans ad hoc operandum alteri obligatur:
aliae autem virtutes ejus gratia operantur, quod
tale opus est honestum ipsi operanti. Secundo,
propter objecta quia justitiae objecta sunt agibilia humana sub ratione debiti, objecta autem
aliarum virtutum sunt agibilia humana sub ratione
honesti solum. Tertio, propter subjecta, quia
multi ponunt justitiam in voluntate, alias autem
virtutes in appetitu sensibili.*

*Secundo dicunt isti, quod justitia legalis
differt specie a justitia particulari, sive aequa-
li, quoniam cum justitia communiter accepta dif-
ferat ab aliis virtutibus per rationem debiti vel
obligationis, oportet si rationes obligationis
sint diversae specie, quod etiam justitia specie
dividatur. Sed alia est ratio obligationis sub-
jecti ad Dominum, et alia subditorum ad invicem.
Prima namque sumitur secundum habitudinem in-
aequalitatis, secunda autem secundum habitudinem
aequalitatis"* (*op. cit.*, 381-2).

30. The criticisms are on *ibid.* 382.

31. See *ibid.*, Book V, Question 6, 393, 396.

32. The position and Buridan's criticism are
found at 383-4. I should add that he adopts what
looks to be just such a common supervening moral
virtue in Book VI, Question 21.

33. See *ibid.*, 384-5. This is reminiscent of a
remark by Odo that a whole can be connumerated
with its parts, as in the case of the greatest
quantity of water being the quantity of all
waters at once. See *op. cit.*, Fol. 97ro, Col. A.

34. See fn 32, above. In view of his rejection
of the obligation criterion, it is surprising to
find Buridan saying that justice is according to
the type of some obligation or other: "*dicamus
quod iustitia, ius, et iustum ad alterum sunt
secundum modum cuiusdam obligationis:...*" (*ibid.*,

Book V, Question 20, 443). He goes on to elaborate
Cicero's division of natural *jus* into six sub-
species. Odo also refers to this division in
Book V. Question 16, Fol. 109vo, Col. B. These
obligations seem to be derived from various specific relationships: bestowal, consanguinity, friend-
ship, citizenship, and so on. This whole topic of
obligation and its basis is worthy of detailed
pursuit, but not now.

35. *Op. cit.*, Book V. Question 4. Odo notes that
it is not only justice that can do the works of
the virtues; so can charity and *philautia*, virtuous self-love. See Fol. 95ro, Col. B–Fol. 95vo,
Col. A.

36. See A. MacIntyre, *After Virtue*, Notre Dame,
1981, especially 50, 141–144.

37. Whatever one is to make of the notion of
rules in Aristotle's ethics, one certainly should
not minimize the *prescriptive* role of reason. See
Gauthier, *La morale d'Aristote*, Paris, 1958, 88–
91, for a discussion and collection of cases and
terminology. Although Odo rejects the mode of
mere obedience, he certainly includes in his
notion of virtue the *dictamen rationis* and what
reason *dici faciendum*. See, for example. Fol. 33vo,
Col. A, *op. cit.* Another topic too large to pursue
is thus opened up: the *varieties* of prescription
within the Aristotelian tradition. It would be a
nice question just how they fit into Kant's
scheme of hypothetical and categorical imperatives.

Frederic Schick   AN INDIFFERENT ASS

In their paper, "Picking and Choosing," Sidney
Morgenbesser and Edna Ullmann-Margalit take up
the problem of Buridan's ass and present a
rationale for an optimistic view of the ass's
situation.[1] The story is that the ass stood mid-
way between two bales of hay, equally attracted
to each. Being indifferent between them, he
could not choose which one to eat and wound up
starving in the midst of plenty.

The authors of "Picking and Choosing" doubt
that he was such an ass as that. They agree that
he could not choose, that no one can choose where
he is indifferent. This they find implicit in the
concept of choosing itself: to *choose* is to
select an item because we prefer it to each of
the others. But they also note a more general
concept of selection that does not imply a
preference for what is chosen. That is, not all
selections are choices. The nonchoice selections
they call pickings: a *picking* is a selection in
which the agent is indifferent between his
options. The ass could not choose, but he could
pick, which no doubt is what he did. So he went
home full-bellied.

The authors are right in thinking that the ass
was in no trouble. They may also be correct in
their opinion of the contrary view. They hold
that "at the root of this...position lies a
biased and misleading form of expression" (767),
that the question is begged from the start. Still,
their language is prejudicial too, and this is
hardly a fault. Every philosophical analysis is
designed to stack some cards. I will lay out a
set of concepts from which it follows that the
ass *can* choose. It will moreover follow that all

choosers, both asses and people, are in a situation of his sort. Not only can agents choose
where they are indifferent between the options
they have, but where they are not indifferent
they cannot make any choices.

I

Must the ass remain in the middle? Can he select
between A and B where he prefers neither alternative to the other? Morgenbesser and Ullmann-
Margalit hold that the question derives from
thinking of a selection in terms such as this:
"The agent selected (grabbed, did) A rather than
B" (767), the "rather than" being meant to imply
a preference for A over B. On this construal,
all selections are choices. The authors remark
that the quoted expression does not cover all
cases. Sometimes a selection should be reported
in this way instead: "The agent selected
(grabbed, did) A to the exclusion of B" (767),
this meaning only that he selected A and did not
select B. Here no preference is implied. This
second formula covers choosing (where the exclusion is based on preference) and also picking
(where it is not).
   On their proposed way of thinking, the authors'
conclusion follows - that is, the ass can't
choose but he might yet pick. Their basic concept
here is however not very promising, a selection
being identified by them (parenthetically) as a
grabbing or doing. This fails to distinguish
selecting an option from the agent's acting it
out. It does not allow us to say of some action
that it was in no way selected, and it does not
allow for selectings that don't get expressed in
action. The derivative ideas of choosing and
picking are flawed in the same respects.
   The central concept needs rethinking, which

means we might as well start over. The ass stands
indifferent between the two bales. If he wanted
either of them, he would simply walk over. But
he does not yet want either - where the alternatives exclude each other, indifference implies
nonwanting. Neither, however, does he want to
stay put. He wants to come to want one of the
bales. This suggests a simple idea: that the ass
would be choosing (selecting) in coming to want
just *this* bale or *that* one, that choosing is
coming-to-want.

Here we must certainly qualify, for not all
comings-to-want are choices. Suppose I hear you
speak of some movie and come to want to see it.
Or suppose I read about Paris and come to want
to go there. In neither case have I made a choice,
no more so than the ass would have chosen had he
seen a single bale only and come right off to want
it. What made the scene a choice context for the
ass was that he had options, that he faced an
issue. I will say that we have a *choice problem*
where we face an issue and that we *choose* in
coming-to-want in such a situation. Or we might
put it this way: to choose is to come-to-want
something that is an option for us.

II

A person debating what to do sometimes has his
alternatives fixed. In such a case he faces an
issue. I will refer to all his alternatives
collectively as the *issue* he faces. What I am
calling his *options* are these same alternatives
singly.

A person's options are the possibilities he
considers. They are the projects he puts to himself, those he has neither yet ruled out nor
chosen. An option isn't just any course open but
one of a set of possibilities that, in conjunc-

tion, raise a problem for the agent. More fully,
a person's set of options is some set of possible
actions of which all the following holds. The
person thinks that he will take one and only one
of these actions, but does not yet know which he
will take and which not. He expects to take whichever one of them he will want to take. And he
wants to take one of these actions, though not
yet to take or not to take any particular one.
(For some purposes, it is better to say that the
agent's set of options is the finest partition
of possibilities of which all this is true.)

I am defining options in a way that rules out
a person's wanting some option and also rules
out his already excluding any. If a person wants
A, he does not have A as an option. He faces no
issue on that matter and has no occasion for
choice. So also where he wants not-A.[2] This will
of course be obvious - a person can choose only
where he is undecided. What is less obvious is
the related point, that a person must be indifferent regarding all his options, that where he
has preferences he has no choice to make.

We need a concept of preference that connects
a person's preferences to what he wants and what
he doesn't, or better, to what in various situations he would and wouldn't want. First, the
concept of an alternative's being holistic for
someone. I will say that an alternative is
holistic for some person where it is not a disjunction of other items some of which he wants.[3]
A person *prefers* A to B where, if he believed
that not both A and B, and B were holistic for
him, he would not want B, and if he believed that
either A or B, and B were holistic, he would want
A.

(To see why we need the holism clauses, suppose
that you are indifferent between X and Y and prefer each to Z, believe that either X or Y or Z

but that not any two together, and prefer X to Y-or-Z and also Y to X-or-Z. There should be nothing wrong with this. But our analysis minus the holism clauses would have you wanting both X and Y though you see that each rules out the other. And it would have you *not* wanting X-or-Z even where you want X.)

Let O be among a person's options and let A be the disjunction of those of his options each of which he prefers to O. Let B be the disjunction of the options not in A - one of these options is O. This person prefers A to B.[4] He can't yet want any specific option (this by our definition of options), which makes B holistic for him. Since each of his options is in one or the other, he believes that either A or B (by the same definition). His preferring A to B thus implies that he wants A (by our concept of preference). It follows that he wants not-B and so also not-not-O.[5] But then (by definition) O is no option, which pulls out the rug on which all this stands. This simple reductio argument shows that the agent cannot prefer any option to any other. He must be indifferent pairwise regarding all his options.

Let us be careful not to read this as a constraint on the agent's interests. A person can lay out his preferences in any way whatever. But if he prefers some A to some B, both of these are not options he has. The constraint is not on a person's interests but on what counts as an issue that he faces, on what counts as an option-set for him. He may be indifferent or not, as he pleases. But where he is not indifferent he faces no issue and has no choice to make.

III

This only gives the ass company. It says that his

case is not unique, that all people facing options are indifferent regarding them. It shows that, unless an agent is indifferent, there can be no talk of his choosing. It doesn't show that an indifferent agent can ever make a choice. So our initial question remains; indeed it now is much wider. We no longer have to do only with a hypothetical stupid beast but with all agents facing issues. Can there be any choices at all? Or rather, perhaps, how are choices possible?

Why is there a problem here? If we think of choices as Morgenbesser and Ullmann-Margalit say people often do - as grabbings or doings of A in preference to B - then a preference is presupposed in choice. A chooser can't be indifferent. But this isn't the concept of choosing that has raised our new question for us. If we think in terms of that concept, the chooser *must* be indifferent. Again then, where is the problem? The fact that a person now is indifferent does not mean that he can't form a preference. His not yet wanting any option does not mean that he can't come to want any.

The problem may lie deeper. Back once again to the ass. He is indifferent, but this may yet change. He wants to *make* it change. And wanting to do this rationally, he considers the likely effects of taking this bale or that one. So he lists the relevant points: the bale on the right is bigger, the one on the left is in the shade, etc. Suppose that in the end all these considerations balance. Here the ass may seem to be in a predicament of a second sort. (Some authors find no distinction; on their view, a rational agent's indifference implies a balance of considerations, and vice versa.)

We can here make a courtesy reference to Buridan himself. The story of the ass never comes up in his writings. But A.N. Prior notes a Buri-

danian thesis that bears indirectly on it.[6]
Buridan proposed what Prior labels a 'principle
of equity' for the logic of belief. The principle
says (I am editing slightly) that where our
evidence in support of some propositions is
equal, we must believe either all or none, and
in this form it has been used as part of an argument for skepticism. An analogue for the logic
of choice would say that, where the considerations
supporting some options balance, either all must
be chosen or none. Since only one option can be
chosen - the agent thinks that each rules out all
others - this boils down to directing the agent
in such a situation to make no choice. The principle of equity is offered as a principle of
rationality. On our first report of his case, it
seemed that the ass will starve. If we adopt the
principle of equity, it turns out he will starve
if he is rational.

Can a rational agent choose between options
that have equal backing? In the language of
"Picking and Choosing," can he choose where he
"has no reason to prefer one alternative to the
other(s)" (768)? The choice that he made would
not be *deliberate* - let this say that it would
violate equity. The agent would not have chosen
on grounds that marked the option he chose as
better than each of the others. He would have
chosen an option where he had an equal warrant
for choosing some other. But does rationality
exclude all such choices? Must a rational agent's
choices be deliberate in our special sense?

How we answer this question depends on how we
understand rationality. I cannot offer a proper
treatment of that concept here.[7] Let me just say
that my view of it does not require the agent to
be deliberate. On my view, a rational person
chooses so as to do as well as he can. He will
not choose *A* where he thinks that *B* has the

better prospects. Where the two look equally good (and no third option looks better), rationality rules out neither for him. The agent may, if there is time, defer a choice and think some more. But if the time for action has come, he cannot be faulted for choosing. Where he thinks he would do as well taking A as taking B, he might choose either option.

The Buridanian reader may be unpersuaded. He may hold that rationality demands that people have reasons for their choices. And he may say that anyone who is not deliberate goes beyond his reasons. We may be at the heart of it here: the ass had no reason for choosing either way, so he could not choose rationally. Whether or not we agree depends on how we conceive of reasons.

We need not agree if we think of reasons as belief-and-desire causes.[8] This allows an undeliberate agent to have a reason for whatever choice he makes. By assumption, his considerations balance, but very likely the physical factors do not. In the ass's case, it may be that the bale on the right had the greater mass and so the greater gravitational pull. Or that this bale was further east and that the sun was rising. The ass thought he could not do better than to take the bale on the right, and he wanted to choose some option than which none looked better. Suppose that, in the full physical context, this belief and desire of his caused him to take that bale. The physical factors alone would not have moved him in this direction, but in their context this belief and desire brought him over to it. Then this belief-and-desire pair was his reason for this choice.

Sometimes the agent himself contrives a physical imbalance. The ass might have seen he was getting nowhere and tossed a coin, having first decided to

choose A if it fell heads and B if it fell tails.
Suppose he then noted it had fallen heads. This
plus the disposition established by his decision
to let heads mean A would have tipped the scales
A-ward - that is, tipped them physically, not
logically. His reason would again have been his
believing that he could not do better than A and
his wanting to choose some option than which he
could not do better. He could have said the same
about B. But the result of the coin toss plus
his prior toss-outcome decision would have made
it his reason for choosing A and not B.

   What if the physical forces too were evenly
balanced in his case, or were so distributed that
they made for no causes? What if he had no coin
and could think of no other way of tipping the
scales? The ass would then have been in a fix: he
would have had to stay put. But this only singles
out a very exceptional situation. The impossibility
thesis we are debating is meant to be fully general.
It holds that indifference regarding the options
must always keep an agent undecided and also that,
if he is rational, a balance of considerations
always keeps him hanging. It is the 'always' part
of this that has to be established. So the ass is
best imagined in an everyday physical setting, its
only special aspects being his balance of interests
- his indifference between the options - and the
balance of his reflections in support of this or
that.

   I conclude that the ass had no problem. Though
he preferred neither bale to the other, he could
still choose between them. And he could do this
rationally, even if all he saw in favor of this
one and that one balanced. If the ass were *not*
indifferent, he could not have made a choice. But
no problem there either. Suppose he preferred the
bale on the right. He would have simply gone and
eaten it and that would have been the end of the
story.

If the story has a moral, it isn't that people can't always choose, that certain issues can't be resolved. Nor is the moral that there are issues that can't be resolved in a rational manner. The only likely moral is that being deliberate does not always pay. We cannot always afford to wait until one option looks clearly best. A person who is too deliberate may be making an ass of himself.

Footnotes:

1. "Picking and Choosing," *Social Research*, XLIV, 4 (Winter, 1977): 757-785.
2. I am taking the objects of preference and wanting to be propositions, so the usual connectives can be used in speaking of them. (The ass's being indifferent regarding the bales means that he was indifferent between *his having this one* and *his having that one*.)
3. Again, the 'alternatives' and 'items' here are all propositions.
4. This is because of dominance.
5. These steps by the deductive closure of the agent's desires.
6. In "Some Exercises in Epistemic Logic," in *Knowledge and Experience*, ed. by C.D. Rollins (Pittsburgh: University Press, 1963).
7. I present an analysis of rationality in my *Having Reasons: An Essay on Rationality and Sociality*, forthcoming in 1983 from Princeton University Press.
8. For this concept, see Donald Davidson, "Actions, Reasons, and Causes," *Journal of Philosophy*, LX, 23 (Nov. 7, 1963): 685-700.

REASON, EQUALITY, AND THE DILEMMA OF PRACTICE

David
Sidorsky

In developing an affirmative answer to the question "Does Political Theory Still Exist?" Isaiah Berlin focused upon the inevitability of plural and competing models of political society. These models are the coherent intellectual structures in reference to which data are perceived, facts are grouped, and values are defended determining, in Berlin's phrase "the form of beliefs and behaviour".[1] The idea of a model is a broad one, however, and there is a wide range of interpretations of its significance and use in political philosophy.

At one extreme of that range, the model of society is a systematically elaborated metaphor or fiction. This is what Yeats suggests in his account of the political thought of Burke:

And haughty-headed Burke that proved the State
   a tree,
That this unconquerable labyrinth of the birds,
   century after century,
Cast but dead leaves to mathematical equality;

At the other extreme, the political paradigm is compared to the formal models of logic and mathematics. The terms used in an axiom set of the language are assigned definitions that coordinate them with real properties. The application of the transformation rules of the language then allow the deduction of the properties of the constructed coordinate model. Some conception of model in this sense is suggested when self-evident truths or intuitions of the universal properties of all men in a system of nature permit the rational derivation of civil or legal rights in a new political society.

The authors of the classical texts of political philosophy locate their models between these two extremes. The descriptive features of their social landscape are bound by empirical claims in a way that differentiates them from works of social fiction; their moral prescriptions are provided with rational justification which distinguishes them from the moral and political claims urged in the novels and theater of utopianism or of social criticism. At the same time, even those books of political philosophy which are most expressive of "l'esprit de la géometrie" resist explicit formulation as formal systems, with axioms of history, morals, or politics from which specific policies can be derived by a technique of particularization to circumstances of time and place.

Although the examples that exhibit the argument are familiar, the very familiarity of their use in philosophy may obscure their ambiguous function. It is recognized as a matter of course, for example, that although Hobbes's *Leviathan* involves a dramatic explication of a mythic, literary metaphor, the development of the scenario of *The Leviathan* does not place Hobbes's work alongside *The Tempest*, *Robinson Crusoe*, *Lord of the Flies*, *As You Like It*, or the various quasi-historical forbears of *Paradise Lost*, as another more emphatically dystopian parable of human political behavior in hypothetically plotted natural environments. So the political wisdom that is to be learned by imagining human beings disrempted from social context in the *Leviathan* must be of a different kind than that gleaned from the drama, the novel, or the religious myth. Yet the difference of kind between model and fiction in political philosophy remains unexplicated.

In parallel fashion it would also be consider-

ed an inappropriate *reductio* to argue that the
principles of the *Leviathan* should be universally applicable to a system of sovereign states
functioning as power-maximizing individuals in an
international system lacking world government or
effective rule of law. The Hobbesist conclusion
that a perpetual striving for power is inevitable
would then exclude such possibilities as a stable
balance of power, coalitions with effective deter-
rent capabilities, treaties of arms limitation
or reduction, conventions of tacit reciprocal
restraint, or actions of unilateral appeasement.
Such derivations improperly assume that the open-
textured language and the vagueness of metaphor
of the *Leviathan* can be related with unequivocal
correspondence to individuals in particular historical circumstances. Yet the significance of the
rejection of that assumption for the use of
models goes unexamined.

Even with much skepticism about social derivations from models of Nature or Reason, the aspiration to connect preferred social institutions to
models of rationality continues. Thus, Kant, even
after his Humean awakening, could argue that the
nature of rationality must lead all men to choose
to spend their lives developing their intellectual capacities in places like Königsberg rather
than decide to become beachcombers in the recently discovered and attractively publicized islands
of the South Pacific in the 1770's.

The demand that a model in political philosophy
should have consequences or operational significance for moral and political decision making,
however, has always been considered legitimate.
In contemporary philosophy the most dramatic re-
currence of this aspiration to ground social
policy judgments in a rational philosophical
basis has been in the area of distributive justice.
There are striking illustrations of the effort to

relate policy on the distribution of goods to
the meaning of equality (notably by Bernard
Williams), to the concept of human rights (by
Gregory Vlastos, among others), and to the nature
of social contract among rational persons (for
example, by John Rawls). The dilemma confronted
by the earlier rationalist mode recurs, particularly in recent efforts to trace social patterns
of distributive justice to moral imperatives
associated with models of Nature, Reason, or
Contract.

I

There is a gap between the idea of distributive
justice and the many factors that are morally
relevant for decision making on economic issues.
Only to a degree can this gap be attributed to
the distance between ideal "reach" and practical
"grasp," to the legitimate difference in detail
between an abstractly delineated economic scenario and a concrete set of circumstances, and to
the disparate idioms and metaphors of theoretical
and practical discourse. Rather, the gap indicates a fundamental problem with the concept of
distributive justice. The problem is that, even
if distributive justice in abstract formulation
is accepted as a value, its application in economic decision making is indeterminate. That statement asserts an inapplicability thesis for distributive justice.

This thesis rests on two related lines of argument: "contextualist" and "pluralist." The contextualist argument is that the proposals of distributive justice are formulated in "noncontextual"
partial models of economic discourse which cannot
be appropriately transposed to decisions embedded
in institutional contexts. The pluralist argument
is that demands for distributive justice are de-

veloped with an assumed small set of moral values
but are applied in frameworks where a much larger
number of values are operative, including tacit
and emerging values.

The contextualist and pluralist arguments are
intended to support the inapplicability of distributive justice. Before turning to them, a
preliminary methodological analogy can show the
pattern of the arguments.

Demonstrations of impossibility are familiar
in contemporary philosophy. There is an analogy
to the arguments made by Michael Oakeshott,
Isaiah Berlin, Karl Popper, and others about the
impossibility of a science of history. Those arguments rest on the significance of the difference
between the ways scientists seek to isolate crucial causal variables and discover correlations
among them in a theoretically isolated domain,
and the ways in which historians must describe
and interpret the historical process without any
insulation from temporal context. There is an
element of formal analogy with an incompleteness
theorem, in the sense that the concept of distributive justice postulated in simple social and
economic models involves so many other moral
factors in application to complex economic decisions as to render its use indeterminate.

The development of the contextualist argument
for contemporary accounts of distributive justice
requires, accordingly, the specific demonstration
of the significance of the differences between
the ways in which crucial terms are used in con-
text-transcendent paradigms and the ways these
terms are used in historical and realistic situations. The argument applied to Rawl's theory, for
example, would focus upon his equivocal use of
terms like 'distribution', 'lottery', 'contract',
'improper influence', 'equality of opportunity',
where there are important elements of analogy and

of disanalogy to the function of these terms
when placed in their economic contexts. For the
present purpose, only one illustration of the
contextualist argument can be sketched.[2] The
point of departure is Bernard Williams's defense
of the idea of equality and the opportunity it
provides to indicate, not necessarily in contradiction of Williams's thesis, the gap between
such a defense in a limited context and the justification of egalitarianism in social practice.

II

In "The Idea of Equality" Williams[3] states the
general moral rule that "for every difference in
the way men are treated, some general reason or
principle of differentiation must be given," but
points out that, since there are no agreed restrictions on what constitutes a "reason" or a
"principle of differentiation," this rule is
compatible with many conflicting kinds of moral
behavior. Williams pursues ways of strengthening
the rule in its application to concrete moral
circumstances. One particularly appropriate
demonstration involves the reasonableness of the
grounds for medical care. Williams writes:

> Leaving aside preventive medicine, the
> proper ground of distribution of medical
> care is ill health: this is a necessary
> truth. Now in very many societies, while
> ill health may work as a necessary condi-
> tion of receiving treatment, it does not
> work as a sufficient condition, since such
> treatment costs money and not all who are
> ill have the money; hence the possession
> of sufficient money becomes in fact an
> additional necessary condition of actually
> receiving treatment (121).

Thus, in the case of medical care, the formal
rule is strengthened with the substantive criteria that "the reasons should be relevant" and
that these reasons "should be socially operative."
Ill health is the relevant reason for treatment,
and, if this replaces ability to pay, the relevant reason is becoming socially operative as well.

In an inegalitarian medical system, according to
Williams, discrimination is not based on a relevant reason. This is a state of affairs which is
not only deplorable in terms of social consequences
or as an expression of humanitarian solidarity,
but also irrational. Williams writes:

> When we have a situation in which, for
> instance, wealth is a further necessary
> condition of the receipt of medical treat-
> ment...in connexion with the inequality
> between the rich ill and the poor ill, we
> have straightforwardly the situation of
> those whose needs are the same not receiv-
> ing the same treatment, though the needs
> are the grounds of the treatment. This is
> an irrational state of affairs (122).

There are contexts of medical care in which discrimination only for the relevant reason of illness would seem to be the rational procedure.
Military doctors treating their own wounded
troops in battlefield hospitals present one such
context. Here the severity of wounds and the
patient's responsiveness to treatment are the
relevant and the determining criteria. Yet even
in the restricted context of medical care in military operations where concerns about competing
budgetary costs, freedom of decision for patients
and doctors, and many other relevant features are
bracketed, there are questions as to the rationality of distribution of medical care exclusively on
the basis of need.

In setting up the medical corps for the distribution of medical resources, most planners would
consider it irrational not to allocate human and
material resources disproportionately in favor
of commanders and scarce or valued leadership
groups. Even more clearly, most soldiers would
view it as the height of irrationality to treat
wounded soldiers on the basis of need, without
discriminating as to whether the wounded person
in the queue is an enemy prisoner or a member of
one's own forces. There are plausible reasons
that can be advanced for or against any policy
decision, but they require reference to factors
of history, morale, conventions of reciprocity,
in addition to any necessary relationship between
illness and treatment. The standard contexts of
health care systems for diverse civilian populations result in an even broader list of relevant
reasons for decisions.

As previously indicated, neither the preceding
argument nor the following discussion of the
rationality of equality necessarily involves disagreement with Williams's views. The relevance of
illness for treatment in the specified context is
granted, and Williams could concede or even insist
that its application to the complex context of
the health-care system would generate other relevant reasons for discrimination. Again, Williams's
exclusion of "preventive medicine" signals his
recognition that in the ongoing contexts of medical practice considerations other than the fact
of illness condition the allocation of the
resource of medical treatment. Further, in pointing out that a system of medical care not concerned with treating the ill would be irrational,
Williams need not deny the significance of context
for rationality nor claim that there is one uniquely rational approach to planning systems of health-
care services; that is, the egalitarian.

There is particular historical philosophical
interest in Williams's justification of his position in terms of rationality. As a rough historical generalization, the empiricist and pluralist
counterclaim has characteristically been that
what is rational is partly relative to context.
In the familiar analogy used in the *Republic*, it
is true that a rational shepherd qua shepherd is
concerned with the welfare of the sheep, but qua
rational wool manufacturer his concern is with
their fleece and qua rational sheep raiser his
concern is with their slaughter. Thus, a system
of medical care, embodying the point of view of
doctor qua doctor or medical-instrument manufacturer qua medical-instrument maker is not the
uniquely rational system. From the point of view
of doctor or instrument maker regarded as entre-
preneur, as scarce resource, as depreciating
asset, or as funded instrument of society's
savings, other norms of rationality, with other
kinds of relevant reasons, may emerge to determine distribution.

The recognition of various contexts does not
obscure the clear moral judgment that ill persons,
even when they are poor, should receive medical
treatment. It can show, however, that a number
of reasons other than illness may be relevant
grounds for discrimination in the development of
health-care services. To evaluate the egalitarian approach, it is important to sketch how the
neglect of these other reasons may also be viewed
as irrational.

Thus consider the rational egalitarian model
from the point of view of the patient as client.
The context is a society in which persons exercise freedom of choice in purchasing goods.
People choose safer or better cars; rarer, older,
or better furniture; or better seats in the
theatre. They believe, perhaps even on the basis

of reliable information, that some surgeons or
diagnosticians are better than others. It would
seem to them intuitively irrational that a society that permits people to pay for better choices
in so many areas of life would not permit them
to exercise that choice where their health or
the health of their children is or even may be
believed to be at stake. Obviously they would
search for a remedy for this "irrationality."
The most direct remedies would be to travel abroad
for better medical treatment or to import better
doctors. If such remedies are permitted, certain
systemic changes follow, under which ill health
is not the sole determinant for treatment in the
society. If such remedies are denied, a number
of important values which may have serious social
consequences will be frustrated for the sake of
equality. Either option may turn out to be optimal, yet neither is more rational than the other.
   A similar conclusion can be generated by considering Williams's model from the point of view
of the social need to recruit a superior medical
profession or to develop a better research pharma-
ceutical industry. If the fact of illness were
the sole operative ground for treatment, then
profitability could be affected negatively. Yet
doctors and research biologists know that lawyers
and accountants, like farmers and manufacturers,
receive differentially higher incomes related to
performance. The idea that those entering the
health-services field would be involved in a non-
market determination of reward could limit entry
into these fields or lead to emigration to other
countries. Policies that lead to medical "brain
drain" or to disinvestment in drug research
would be considered irrational, from the point
of view of those concerned with furthering health
care. Williams's approach need not have these
empirical consequences, and there are institution-

al ways of safeguarding against them while providing health care for the poor. But without empirical experience in differing social contexts it is not clear which of several possibilities is better, and none may be irrational. For, just as there is a pattern of rationality in the relationship between illness and treatment, to which Williams has appealed, so there is a pattern of rationality in the area of freedom of choice to be exercised by patients and a pattern of rationality in the differential recruitment of talent of doctors or research scientists.

There is also a pattern of economic rationality. Any economic activity, particularly one with the growth potential of health-care services, would seem to require that the prices paid for the products be related to the escalating costs, lest their subsidization overwhelm other sectors of the economy. (Analogously, the rationality of farming as an economic activity cannot be determined solely by reference to the feeding of the hungry, for example, without some reference to the control imposed by return on investment.) A system of health services that introduces severe constraints on treatment based on pricing may be a reasonable way in which some economies can cover the costs of medical treatment or provide incentives and controls for the growth of the medical sector. This may be particularly true where other critical welfare resources - food, shelter, or education - are scarce. A policy that would permit need to be the only relevant reason could then have negative consequences on the development of the medical capacities of the society. An egalitarian solution, a system of rationing with priorities based on need, or other welfare subsidy options could be pursued as a matter of moral choice, or even as better choices; yet they are not uniquely rational, and they may even be empirically counterproductive.

The contextualist thesis emerges from the recognition of the different sets of reasons that are applied for decision making in practice on the distribution of medical care. In this field, as in the other activities of human welfare, there will be relevant reasons for discrimination embedded in the social arrangements that relate to the distribution of these goods. Moral claims for equal distribution or wider access may be significant claims in these contexts, but they will not uniquely determine outcome in the complex context of a historical society with a developed and developing set of values.

III

The pluralist argument, like the contextualist argument, takes its point of departure from the gap between the theoretical account of distributive justice and the institutional framework in which it is applied. Any significant social decision in such a framework involves the weighing and adjudication of a large number of values, some of which have been explicitly affirmed whereas others are tacitly present or potentially emergent. The values associated with ideals of egalitarianism and distributive justice are factors in the making of decisions. To the degree to which plural values are recognized in decision making, the unique position given to egalitarianism as a primary social virtue or as a Kantian deontic priority in morality is either lessened or denied.

The relationships between the contextualist and the pluralist arguments - their independence, overlap, or reducibility - are not examined here. Both arguments form part of an empirical and historical, rather than a rational and deductive, approach to social values, and both are sources for converging lines of criticism on the applicability of distributive justice.

Among the ways of demonstrating value pluralism, two are of particular interest for this discussion. One of these is a dialectical approach that recognizes that social virtues function within a spectrum of balancing or countervailing values. Thus the demand for equality would be asserted only within a framework of complementing and modifying values.

A historical exemplification of this is that equality arose in modern republican societies as part of a short list of social virtues which included liberty and fraternity. Thus, the justification of each of these republican virtues assumes the context of confrontation relevant for identifying its historic function.

Although liberty was intended to exclude slavery or serfdom, or the "old order, " it was not intended to deny the virtue of order as rule of law. For many political philosophers, including philosophers of the eighteenth century, order or rule of law was seen as a condition for liberty. A justification of liberty is that it makes possible the realization or order without repression or violent excess. In any event, the establishment of a structure of liberty usually involves the recognition of the virtue of order, since the problem of liberty is defined as the correct drawing of the line between liberty and order.

Similarly, the value of fraternity as universal equality of legal rights was intended to exclude arbitrary discrimination against the alien, the stranger, the unrecognized "other." It did not deny the virtues of otherness, that is, of family, ethnic, or religious differences. Universality of citizenship was not intended to transform the multiplicity of human relationships into political comradeship, with fathers and sons, masters of

crafts and apprentices, acquaintances and second
cousins, all equally related as the objects of
fraternal affection.

The value that is particularly related to distributive justice is equality. The egalitarian
principle that discrimination must be for relevant reasons only, recognizes that there are con-
textually appropriate reasons for discrimination.
Thus, discrimination has been justified on the
basis of such functional differences as skill or
talent, such market differences as supply, incen-
tive, or demand, and such other claims as need,
history, utility, or legitimate personal associations, preferences, or tastes. The pluralist
point is that, even in the development of the
standards of equality, there is awareness of the
virtue of some aspects of hierarchy.

The affirmation of slogan values like liberty,
equality, and fraternity require, on pain of
their caricature as chaos, indiscriminateness,
and sameness, an appreciation of the values of
order, hierarchy, and difference. Social problems
are often described as requiring a balance between liberty and order, between universalist
fraternity and particularist affiliation, or between equality and hierarchy, where both polar-
ities are recognized as sources of value.

The preceding "dialectical" argument may also
serve to point to the more general empirical
claim that a very large number of values require
consideration, adjudication, or compromise in any
social decision.

Thus, a second way to exhibit plurality of
values is through examination of the processes of
disagreement on moral issues. Even when the dispu-
tants share a short list of ultimate moral ideals,
their dispute does not easily reduce to a technical debate about alternative ways of realizing
those ideals. In the course of disagreement values

not initially recognized as relevant emerge at
critical junctures and impinge upon the conflict.
There seems to be no general antecedent formula
that determines how values that are not initially seen as determining or decisive become crucial
in the course of decision making. An example will
illustrate. In this case an initial decision was
made based - roughly at least - on the egalitarian notion that illness can be the sole operative
relevant reason for medical treatment.

The Board of Trustees and the medical administration of a major Brooklyn hospital decided
that the hospital would not refuse treatment for
sick illegal aliens. The income of the hospital
is dependent upon governmental reimbursement for
patient care. Since illegal aliens are not eligible for such reimbursement, the hospital was soon
faced with involuntary bankruptcy proceedings.

The governmental health agencies refused to
intervene to bail out the hospital, citing
several moral reasons. They would not act in violation of the law or to condone illegal immigration. Nor could they distribute funds collected
from employers and employees in a participatory
system to beneficiaries who worked illegally and
had not made any financial contribution to these
funds. Several governmental welfare agencies
supported this denial, while seeing the crisis
as an opportunity to press the moral argument
for retroactive amnesty for illegal aliens. Other
governmental agencies, especially those related
to immigration services, supported ad hoc financial relief to the hospital on humanitarian
grounds, while preserving the moral view that
retroactive amnesty would involve a breach of
trust with the many potential immigrants who
had opted for legal entry procedures at personal
or family sacrifice.

The hospital board sought aid from the federa-

tion of philanthropies with which it was affilia-
ted for fundraising purposes. Among the issues
cited by the trustees of the federation were the
fiduciary irresponsibility of the hospital board,
which had embarked on a course leading to bankruptcy. This had jeopardized moral commitments
given to persons who had endowed this and other
hospitals. Also cited was the moral responsibility of the hospital board to inform and consult
with the federation before deciding to provide
treatment for illegal aliens. One emergent
question was the good faith of the hospital
board in explicitly rejecting such consultative
procedures since it feared that these would lead
to a compromise course of action. A decision
that was clearly morally praiseworthy within one
framework of perception became in another framework an abdication of responsibility to continue
a viable hospital providing medical services to
the legal residents of the community.

As the dispute progressed to include other
constituencies, other moral principles were invoked. These included community control of the
hospital board, racial discrimination in the immigration laws, the conflict of interest between
illegal aliens and historically deprived minority
groups, and many others. Appeal to a single antecedent moral principle would prevent consideration of the plural values that emerge in the
process of adjudication.

IV

In order to avoid inundation in the historical
reality that James Joyce once likened to an "alma-
ziful" river of "plurabilities," we can formulate
the issue posed by value pluralism and contextualism in the form of a dilemma which confronts any
rationalist appeal to distributive justice.

On the one hand, if the principle of distributive justice is viewed as the determinative criterion of policy on issues that critically affect the distribution of income, then it involves neglect of values that have emerged as relevant considerations for decision making. Thus if distributive justice were a kind of *condition precedent* to the adjudication of these issues, the result would be a distortion of moral or practical reasoning on complex issues of policy.

On the other hand, if the set of relevant moral factors that derive from empirical institutional experience are taken into account, then the values of equality and the claims of the most disadvantaged will have been included. It will then be possible to argue that the moral claims appealed to by distributive justice have been considered, along with other related values like legality and liberty as well as many other specific moral concerns that emerge in the cause of the inquiry. Distributive justice is then satisfied trivially as a *condition subsequent* to a process of moral reasoning and adjudication.

The dilemma restates the inapplicability thesis. Even when the theoretical elaboration of the demands of distributive justice are granted in contexts of practice with their necessary plurality of values, the theory provides no policy determination.

The formulation of the argument as a dilemma carries with it the suggestion that there is a generic counterstrategy of slipping between its horns. One way to do that is to chart how principles of distributive justice need not be trivial even if they are not determinative of policy. There is an analogy to the old problem of revisionist Marxists who wished to show how the social relations of production could condition (*bedingung*) but not determine (*bestimmung*) the

cultural superstructure. Thus, one exponent of
Rawls has argued that the Rawlsian principle of
difference can "inform but not determine" social
policy.

A second way of slipping between the horns
would be to delineate the intermediate entities
that are derived from rational moral principles
of distributive justice, even though such principles do not directly apply to social policies
or empirical institutions. This Plotinian strategy is exemplified in the Rawlsian claim that the
"basic structure" of society is constituted by
the difference principle, even though major
social policies from taxation to immigration
need not directly reflect or embody this principle.

These counterclaims are an assertion of the
more general view that models of Reason can com-
prise the means to become operative in historical circumstances and are not to be interpreted
as literary fictions with general moral implications. In a sense, therefore, the inapplicability thesis advanced here returns to the opening
comments on the forms of application of models
of the rationalist type to the contexts of
value complexity. The result may be seen as a
via negativa, a necessary preliminary to establishing an alternative view that social "models"
should be more closely linked to sentiments,
interests, histories, and preferences.

From that perspective, the issue discussed here
is part of a perennial philosophical division.
The criticism is directed against those who
champion an antecedent vision of Reason, by chal-
lenging them to show the implications of that
vision for contemporary social action. The contrary position would be to take as a starting
point diverse social sentiments, interests, and
preferences and to demonstrate that there are

possibilities of convergence toward objective moral values. Those values provide justification for particular social institutions and practices, even though they are not derivable from a rationalist model.

Footnotes:

1. "Does Political Theory Still Exist?" in *Concepts and Categories: Philosophical Essays by Isaiah Berlin*, Henry Hardy, ed. (New York: Viking Press, 1978), p. 154.

2. For a fuller discussion, with application of the argument to the works of Rawls and Vlastos, see my "Contextualism, Pluralism, and Distributive Justice," *Social Policy*, I, 1 (Spring 1983).

3. In Peter Laslett and W.G. Runciman, eds., *Philosophy, Politics and Society*, second series (Oxford: Basil Blackwell, 1962).

SOME PRESUMPTIONS

Edna
Ullman-Margalit

This paper is a companion piece to "On Presumption" (*Journal of Philosophy*, 3, 1983). It is meant to provide some flesh to cover, partially, the rather bony explication of the notion of presumption offered there. It is concerned, that is, to illustrate the explication: to take up a few examples and case studies and carry them somewhat further than could be done in the expository paper. It is, accordingly, somewhat fragmented. After an initial section introducing the notion of presumption by way of a brief summary of the main points of the explication, it falls into four parts, each dealing with its own presumption-related topic.

Since I regard this contribution to the Festschrift as a *gift*, I have allowed myself to devote two of its sections (the last two) to areas which I believe to be personally significant to Sidney Morgenbesser: the first focuses on an article ("On Tenure") he himself co-authored, and the second on the Talmud which I know to be a source of lifelong fascination to him.

1. The Explication of Presumption: An Outline

The *presumption formula* is 'pres(P,Q)', to be read as "P raises the presumption that Q." (For example, a person's unexplained absence for seven years or more raises the presumption that this person is dead.) P is said to be the presumption-raising (generic) fact, Q the (generic) presumed fact. (Lower-case letters will stand for *particular* descriptions of states of affairs.) The presumption formula is said to *apply* in a certain concrete instance when the generic presumption-raising fact is instantiated in that instance.

The presumption formula is interpreted as expressing a *presumption rule*, directed at the *rule subjects*. A rule subject is any person who is engaged
in a process of practical deliberation whose resolution materially depends, among other things, on
an answer to the factual question of whether *q* is
or is not the case. The rule is this:

> Given that *p* is the case, you (= the rule
> subject) shall proceed as if *q* were the case,
> unless or until you have (sufficient) reason
> to believe that *q* is not the case.

Even though the presumption formula is propositional in nature ("---the presumption *that Q*") and thus
ostensibly about facts, it is concerned not so much
with *ascertaining* facts as with *proceeding* on them.
This praxis orientation (as opposed to theory orientation) is brought out by the rule interpretation.
The presumption rule is not to be construed as involving an inference from the presumption-raising
fact *P* to the presumed fact *Q*. Rather, it is construed as sanctioning, for its subjects, the practical passage from *p* to *q*: it enables the subject
whose practical deliberation process is stranded on
the factual question '*q* or not *q*?' to get on and
take action on the assumption that *q*, given that *p*.
Thus, it functions as a means of extrication from
unresolved deliberation processes; it supplies a
procedure for decision by default.

The presumption-that-*q* is rebuttable, however.
The unless-or-until clause in the presumption rule
is the *rebuttal clause*. The presumption that *q* and
the proceed-as-if-*q* injunction corresponding to it
are taken to be triggered *in the absence of* certain
reasons for belief (i.e., reasons to believe that
not-*q*). But once the deliberator is *in possession
of* reasons for belief (that not-*q*), the presumption
(that *q*) is rebutted and the injunction (to proceed
as if *q*) is annulled. The weight of the reasons

required for the rebuttal of a presumption varies
with *the degree of strength* of the presumption.

   If a presumption rule applies in a certain instance, it is there prior to the deliberation
process and may at times preempt that process altogether. The situation may be pictured as involving scales which, owing to the presumption rule
and the bias inherent in it, are tilted (toward
the *q* side) *to begin with* - hence the 'pre-' of
'presumption' - and where the balance can be
reversed only when a certain weight is put on the
other side.

So much for the explication. Now many interesting
questions relate to the context of the *justification* of presumptions. This is taken to involve
two distinct justificatory tasks. The first concerns the justification of there being a presumption rule - some presumption rule - in situations
of a certain type, rather than there being no
presumption rule in those situations at all. It
is here that the role of presumption rules as a
method of extrication is expounded. The second
concerns the justification of the specific presumption espoused by the presumption rule: why
this presumption rather than some alternative?
It is here that the peculiar blend of considerations justifying a specific presumption is spelled out. This consists primarily, on the one hand,
of inductive-probabilistic considerations (having
to do with the likelihood of *q*, given *p*) and, on
the other, of two-tiered normative considerations
[having to do (a) with the question of which sort
of error is morally or socially more acceptable:
acting on *q* when not-*q* is in fact the case, or
vice-versa; and (b) with the moral or social
evaluation of the regulative effect on people's
behavior of the presumption rule's being instituted and operative].

2. Grice's Cooperative Principle[1]

In this section I propose to recast H.P. Grice's Cooperative Principle[2] as a presumption governing the interpretations of utterances rather than as a principle governing the production of utterances. My purpose in so doing is two-fold: first, I believe that the reconstruction in presumptive terms is truer to the facts of the conversational situation, and, second, I believe it may offer a solution to a problem Grice himself poses, referring to it as "fundamental" (68) and confessing to be unhappy with his own answers to it.

The Cooperative Principle (CP) - "a rough general principle which participants will be expected (ceteris paribus) to observe" - is this:

> Make your conversational contribution such as is required, at the stage at which it occurs, by the accepted purpose or direction of the talk exchange in which you are engaged (67).

Given that talk exchanges characteristically have some goal, or at least a mutually accepted direction, Grice contends that they will be profitable only on the assumption that their participants in general observe the CP and its attendant maxims, which he proceeds to list and discuss.

The rendition of this principle as an Interpretative Presumption of Cooperation (IPC) will be this:

> Your interlocutor's having uttered a sentence in a talk exchange in which you are both engaged raises the presumption that the sentence is an appropriate contribution to the accepted purpose or direction of the talk exchange.

This is the presumption formula. The way it is spelled out as a rule is this:

> Given that your interlocutor has uttered
> u in a talk exchange in which you are both
> engaged, you shall proceed (i.e., inter-
> pret u) as if u is an appropriate contri-
> bution to the accepted purpose or direct-
> ion of the talk exchange, unless or until
> you have (sufficient) reason to believe
> that it is an *in*appropriate contribution
> thereto.

The presumption may of course be rebutted. This
will happen once one has what one judges in the
circumstances to be sufficient reasons to believe
that one's interlocutor has violated one of the
maxims of appropriateness, or opted out, either
explicitly or implicitly, of the conversational
goal altogether. This is not at all uncommon. (To
the extent that one believes one's interlocutor
to have "flouted" a maxim, this will not rebut
the presumption but will lead one instead, in
Grice's spirit, to impute to one's partner a conversational implicature.)

The way I view the matter, this rule of IPC is
a member, perhaps an honorific member, of a class
of interpretative presumptions that come to our
aid in resolving practical deliberations involving a bit of human behavior, either verbal or
nonverbal. Given, on the one hand, the pressing
and continuous need for us to get on in situations
of transaction with people, where we necessarily
have to base our actions (or reactions) on an
ascription to them of certain intentions and
motivations, and, on the other hand, the fact
that people's intentions and motivations are to
us always a matter shrouded in some degree of
doubt or uncertainty, the call for some interpretative presumptions as a useful extrication method
is apparent.

We are dealing, then, not with situations in
which a prescription - concerning the production

of utterances – is being imposed upon the speaker, but rather in which a way out – from a potential interpretation problem – is being offered to the hearer. Incidentally, the main use to which Grice himself puts his CP, namely, that of characteriz-ing the notion of conversational implicature, turns on the interpretation of utterances, not on their issuance: "the hearer is faced with a minor problem: how can [the speaker's] saying what he did say be reconciled with the supposi-tion that he is observing the overall CP? This situation is one which characteristically gives rise to a conversational implicature" (69).

As for the justification of this specific IPC, as distinct from the justification of there being a presumption rule in this area to begin with, I take it to be grounded in the following considera-tions. First, there is the inductive–probabilis-tic consideration spelled out by Grice himself[3]:

> ...it is just a well–recognized empirical
> fact that people *do* behave in these ways;
> they have learned to do so in childhood,
> and have not lost the habit of doing so;
> and indeed it would involve a good deal of
> effort to make a radical departure from
> the habit. It is much easier, for example,
> to tell the truth than to invent lies" (68).

That is, according to Grice, when a person contri-butes to a conversation usually his contribution is indeed appropriate to its purpose or direction. But the last sentence in this quotation already touches on another justifying consideration, the determinateness consideration: once the need for a presumption rule in this area of interpreting one's interlocutors' utterances is recognized, there is little real choice in the matter of *which* presumption it should espouse. The presump-tion that the converser's contribution is appro-

priate is determinate and useful (*both* where its
application in a concrete instance is straightforward *and* where it seems "flouted" and leads
to the postulation of a conversational implicature). The presumption that it is *in*appropriate
is so indeterminate (e.g., is it a lie? is it
underinformative? is it irrelevant? and, if any
of these, how? etc.) as to be quite useless as a
guide for action (reaction, response).

And then there is also the two-tiered evaluative consideration. To begin with, to presume one's
conversers' contribution appropriate is to take
them as compeers, to reflect an attitude of
respect for and trust in one's fellowmen and
-women. These attitudes are judged in our society
desirable and laudable: it is after all no accident that people "have learned to do so in childhood" rather than to adopt the attitudes of dis-
respect, suspicion, or haughtiness that go with
any contrary presumption. In addition there is
the way the very fact that the IPC is known to
be operative and prevalent itself serves to
regulate behavior. If you know how your utterances are likely to be interpreted and if you
care about the goals that are central to the
conversation in which you are engaged and hence
can be expected to have an interest in its being
profitable, you will surely issue your utterance
in such a way as to ensure that its interpretation turns out correct. Hence, you will comply
with the CP and its attendant maxims. (Grice's
own remark is very fitting here: "In any case one
feels that the talker who is irrelevant or obscure
has primarily let down not his audience by himself"; p. 69.) And to the extent that this effect
which the IPC has on the production of utterances is judged to be a good thing, a socially
valuable practice greatly facilitating - indeed
perhaps even enabling - smooth verbal transact-

actions among people, this constitutes the
second tier of the evaluative justification of
our presumption.

This leads me, finally, to Grice's Problem.
It is put thus:

> ...a fundamental question about the CP and
> its attendant maxims [is] what the basis is
> for the assumption which we seem to make...
> that talkers will in general (ceteris pari-
> bus and in the absence of indications to the
> contrary) proceed in the manner which these
> principles prescribe (68).

Grice then expresses his dissatisfaction with the
"dull but no doubt at a certain level adequate"
answer (quoted earlier) that it is an empirical
fact that people do behave in these ways, and
proceeds to say this:

> I am, however, enough of a rationalist to
> want to find a basis which underlies these
> facts, undeniable though they may be; I
> would like to be able to think of the
> standard type of conversational practice
> not merely as something which all or most
> do *in fact* follow, but as something which
> it is *reasonable* for us to follow, which
> we *should not* abandon (*ibid.* 68).

It seems to me that within the framework of the
reconstruction offered here the "basis" Grice
searches for is readily available. I shall sum
it up in the form of two chains.

Grice's chain:

The Outset: we are often involved in talk ex-
    changes; they are typically to some degree
    cooperative efforts; they typically have
    some purpose or direction that is recognized
    by the participants. (Let us agree to refer

to the participant, who has an interest in
pursuing the purpose or direction of the
conversation and does not "opt out", as an
interested participant.)

At this point the focus of attention is on the
prospective interested *speaker*: a certain
principle, the CP, is introduced, and the
claim is put forth that, given the Outset,
the speaker is expected to observe it.

The additional (allegedly empirical) observation:
the CP is in fact generally observed.

The question: what is the basis of our assumption
that people will go on observing the CP? Or
more incisively: what is the reason - the
rational reason - for observance of the CP?

Here Grice professes to be stuck with unsatisfac-
tory answers. [He expresses (a) dissatisfaction
with the idea that the observance of the CP and
the maxims is "a quasi-contractual matter"; and
(b) a belief that an answer will be forthcoming
only once he is "a good deal clearer about the
nature of relevance" (69).]

My chain:

The Outset: the same as Grice's.

At this point the focus of attention is on the
(interested) hearer: it is recognized that
he might typically be faced with an interpretation problem, and a certain prescription, the IPC, is introduced as offering a
way out.

The IPC is then shown to be *justified*, i.e., to
be well grounded in the appropriate variety of
justifying considerations.

The additional (allegedly empirical) observation:
the IPC is in fact operative and prevalent.

From here the attention shifts to the prospective
interested *speaker*, and the chain continues as
follows:

Given that the speaker recognizes that the IPC is operative and prevalent, he recognizes that his utterance is likely to be interpreted according to the IPC. We assume that he is an *interested* speaker, hence he has a reason to issue utterances whose IPC-governed interpretation will be correct. An interpretation of an utterance according to the Interpretative Presumption of Cooperation will be correct if and only if the utterance was issued in observance of the Cooperative Principle. From this it follows that the interested speaker has a good reason for observing the CP and its maxims. Or, if you will, it follows that it is reasonable for the speaker to observe the CP and its maxims.

As for its being *rational* too, I shall venture the following comment. It seems to me that any speaker who gears his utterances to the method likely to govern their interpretation is being reasonable. The question of rationality, I believe, concerns the interpretation method itself: I can easily think of downright crazy interpretative principles, which may nevertheless be imagined to work provided that both speaker and hearer cooperate with respect to them. What makes for rationality in our case, however, is, I contend, the nature of the considerations in which the IPC is grounded. The fact that our interpretative presumption is justified, as it was shown to be, on the basis of both inductive-probabilistic and normative considerations, as well as the determinateness consideration, makes it, in my view, rational.

I conclude, then, that the conversational practice of interpreting utterances in accordance with the IPC and hence of issuing utterances in observance of the CP has been shown to be, indeed, "something which it is *reasonable* for us to follow, which we *should not* abandon."

3. The Presumption of Normality

In the philosophical literature one occasionally comes across arguments involving presumptions (or: *the* presumption) of normality. I shall refer to a few of them presently. The use of this notion, however, is not sufficiently critical, and, consequently, several issues tend to be lumped together which ought in my view to be separated. I shall proceed then to introduce a distinction among three areas where normality may bear upon the notion of presumption.

(i) *Normality as the presumed fact*. Given the rendering of the presumption formula 'pres(P,Q)' as 'P raises the presumption that Q', the presumed fact Q may be that a certain (generically described) state of affairs (object, person, utterance, etc.) is normal. Normality here then is that which the presumption is about; the presumption-*raising* fact (P) consisting of some background assumptions or some "frame"[4] description.

It should be noted that 'normal' is ambiguous between the statistical sense of "the usual, the average, the most frequent" on the one hand, and the normative (so to speak) sense of "conforming to some standard or norm" on the other. Often these two senses mesh - after all it is the average, or that which is not extraordinary, which usually serves to fix the norm - but not always. (Thus, take a backward region where most of the population still suffers from glaucoma: is "the normal person" there glaucomatous or healthy?) This ambiguity may afflict the presumption of normality, and this may or may not be detrimental to its uses.

It is my suspicion that most cases where a

presumption of normality is alluded to are *not*
cases where the normality of something or someone is the presumed fact. I suspect, that is,
that even where it appears as if normality is
that which the presumption is about, this appearance is misleading, or the use of the notion is
misguided, and that the role normality plays in
those cases is actually one of the two discussed
next. One case that does seem to me to fall
under the present category occurs in James W.
Lamb's proposed analysis of knowledge in terms
of justified presumption.[5] He puts forward a
principle which he refers to as *the principle
of the presumption of normality*, according to
which "if subject *S* knows proposition *P* and has
no reason for believing *P* abnormal, then *S* would
be justified in presuming *P* normal" (125). I
find this principle problematic on various counts
(for one thing, it is surely not the *proposition*,
as distinct from either the utterance expressing
it or - what seems closer to Lamb's intention -
the circumstances of the state of affairs depicted by it, which can be believed normal or abnormal;
besides, can one *know* an abnormal proposition?)[6].
But this is beside the point, which is merely
illustrative: it does seem that Lamb intends the
normality of *P* as the presumed fact[7].

(ii) *Normality as a justifying consideration* . In
her paper "Contextual Implication"[8] Isabel Hungerland talks about the presumption that in a situation of communication acts of stating are normal.
Now this formulation is misleading if it is construed as follows: "*x*'s being an act of stating
in a situation of communication raises the presumption that *x* is normal." I submit that it is
not the normality of certain acts of stating
that is here presumed. The construal, rather,
should be something like this: "an indicative

sentence x's being uttered in a situation of
communication raises the presumption that the
utterance of x is an act of stating." Where
normality plays a role here is in the justification of this presumption.

It is because utterances of indicative sentences in situations of communication are (allegedly) normally acts of stating that there is a presumption from an indicative sentence being
uttered in a situation of communication to the
utterance being an act of stating. Generally
speaking, then, the presumption that Q espoused
by a presumption rule expressed by the formula
'pres(P,Q)' is often (partially) justified by the
consideration that cases of P are *normally* (i.e.,
commonly, most frequently, on average) cases of
Q. Broadly speaking, this fits into the inductive-probabilistic realm of justifying considerations in which the justification of presumptions
is grounded.

(iii) *Normality as a premise in the presumption
inference*. Consider the following question: what
role does the fact that there is no reason to
believe some thing abnormal play with regard to
presumptions about that thing? I contend that
this fact is indeed a factor in presumptions
about the thing in question, but that it does
not play the role of a presumption-raising fact
with respect to the presumption that that thing
is normal. In order to see the way this factor
comes in let us consider the following rule of
inference:

(1)   pres(P,Q)
(2) p
       Therefore, pres q

The conclusion that q is presumed here follows
from two premises, the first stating the presump-

tion formula and the second asserting that the presumption-raising generic fact is instantiated in the concrete case in hand. The point now is that it may be argued that, if the inference is to go through, a third premise has to be added:

(3) p is not abnormal.

Premise (3) may be interpreted to mean that there actually is evidence that p is normal or else that there is *bona fide* absence of evidence that p is relevantly abnormal. Also, (3) may arguably be construed as a tacit rather than as an explicit premise. But in any case with regard to many presumption rules this may well be considered a necessary component of the total evidence required for the presumption rule to apply in the particular instance.

Thus, Mats Furberg[9] speaks of two kinds of conditions that have to be satisfied for a term T to be flawlessly applied, the first being that a sufficient number of T's criteria be satisfied, and the second consisting of what he refers to as certain *presumptions of normality* associated with T (73-74, 178-179). The way I take this to be rendered is this: even where the presumption-raising fact is instantiated in a given concrete instance, i.e., a sufficient number of the criterial conditions associated with a given term T are satisfied with respect to a certain object, the presumption that T applies to this object will not go through if the object manifests freakish, extraordinary, miraculous, or otherwise abnormal behavior.[10]

4.   Tenure

In their paper "On Tenure"[11] Margaret Atherton, Sidney Morgenbesser, and Robert Schwartz (henceforth AMS) consider two competing claims with

respect to newly appointed faculty members of a
university: the desirability, on the one hand,
for them to be afforded job stability and security so as to be able to practice their profession fully and freely, and, on the other hand,
the desirability for the university to achieve
its goals unhampered by incompetent staff. They
suggest that some sort of probationary period
"would seem to be in order" as a governance
procedure ensuring as much protection as possible
while still allowing hiring mistakes to be corrected. They then make the following statement:

> We believe, however, there is one general
> overarching commitment that would provide
> a structure or basis for such governance
> procedures. The commitment requires treat-
> ing each job as belonging to the person
> who holds it from the moment she or he is
> hired, so long as within a given time they
> do not show themselves incapable of meet-
> ing the professional standards of the uni-
> versity (344/5).

Furthermore, they point out that adherence to the
commitment they recommend would demand a reversal
of attitudes currently prevailing at most universities toward junior faculty, according to
which they are often treated "as if they had to
prove themselves worthy, prove that they are not
hiring mistakes".

Now all I shall be here concerned to show is
that AMS's "general overarching commitment" can
be construed as a presumption. More specifically,
AMS's claims would be recast thus:

(a) The situation where the future employment
of a person is to be decided at the end of a
certain probationary period is of the type that
calls for the institution of a presumption rule.
If the persons either excel or flunk, there is

obviously no deliberation problem; but, if
neither, should they be kept for lack of proof
that they are failures or should they be fired
for lack of proof that they are hits?

(b) Current policies of academic institutions
toward junior faculty often indeed tacitly employ a presumption rule, but the presumption it
espouses is the wrong one: they proceed as if
all untenured persons are hiring mistakes, unless they prove themselves "worthy".

(c) This presumption ought to be replaced by
its counterpresumption. To wit: given that a
person has gone through the institution's hiring
process, whatever its degree of stringency, and
was hired as qualified for the job, the presumption ought to be that the job belongs to this
person; he or she is not to be fired at the end
of the probationary period "so long as within
[the] given time they do *not* show themselves *in*-
capable of meeting the professional standards of
the university" (345, my emphasis). Again: "From
the start [note: the 'pre-' of 'presumption'],
junior people would be seen as fully entitled
to keep their jobs unless the unexpected occurs
and a particular individual fails to meet the
academic standards publicly specified by the
university" (*ibid*.). In order for the reconstruction of AMS's "general overarching commitment" as a presumption to be clinched, the arguments they offer in support of their view have
to be examined. And indeed one finds that they
do not justify the "commitment" they propose
along anything like statistical lines (e.g.,
that most people hired to do an academic job in
fact perform it adequately; that hiring mistakes
are rare; that a sophisticated hiring process
all but guarantees success; etc.). Rather, the
justificatory grounds they cite are mainly, and
passionately, ones of value. They make it plain

that they are arguing "for a more *just* system"
(346), that their suggestion "calls for changes
in *moral attitudes* toward our jobs and security"
(352), and that "if it is *a good thing*...to
provide [academics] with job stability, to pro-
tect them against unfair labor practices, it
would seem good for all academics" (344, my em-
phases).

5. Presumptions in the Talmud

The entry 'presumption' ('Chazaka') in the Talmudic Encyclopedia (Jerusalem, 1977, vols. XIII-XIV)
comprises some 365 pages, apart from additional
pages devoted to certain specific presumptions.
I can claim no more than having glimpsed at this
vast ocean, and even of that I can hope to convey not more than a mere droplet.

The cases dealt with, in extensive detail, are
numerous; many of them fascinating, the upshot
of most of them controversial among the various
interpreters, early and late, of the Halakha.
Providing a cursory enumeration of examples
would be pointless, and a serious examination
of principles and arguments is beyond my capacity, not to mention beyond the confines of this
paper. What I am interested in reporting here
is my understanding of the Talmudic classification of presumptions. In addition to being, in
my view, of intrinsic interest, this can then be
related to certain aspects of the explication I
have offered of the notion of presumption.

Apart from a variety of substantive presumptions in areas such as proprietary (life) entitle-
ment to office, and more, there are to be found
these categories of presumptions in the Talmud:

(a) From "the previous state". When there is
doubt or uncertainty as to whether something that
was once known to be in a certain state has now

changed or ceased to be in that state, the
presumption is that it is in its previous state
so long as it is not known by us to have changed.
   Examples. (i) Where there is uncertainty as to
whether the slaughter of a certain animal was
done in accordance with the Halakhic rules or
not, its flesh is presumed forbidden food, since
in its life the flesh of the animal *is* forbidden,
and, hence, until you know that it was properly
slaughtered the presumption-from-the-previous-
state holds. (ii) One may go out on the Sabbath
with a (kosher) fringed *talith* (prayer shawl)
without constantly worrying lest without one's
knowledge it has ceased to be kosher through its
fringes having come into defect, since from the
previous state it is presumed kosher until known
(i.e., seen) to be damaged.
   (b) *From human nature.* A large number of presumptions are based on human characteristics,
either mental or physical. In distinction from
the presumptions of the first kind, where a
certain previous state is clearly known to have
obtained and the question concerns the present
state, here no state - or trait - is clearly
known to have obtained, but certain things are
presumed to be so because this is human nature.
Such presumptions have to do mostly with cases
of doubt whether a certain act was performed,
cases of doubt concerning people's intentions in
what they said or did, and cases of doubt regarding the reliability of witnesses.
   Examples. (i) There is a presumption that a
man does not repay his debt before settling day.
(ii) There is a presumption that a man does not
drink from a glass unless he's examined it first
(i.e., does not enter into an engagement with a
woman without examining her first for possible
blemishes and defects). (iii) There is a presumption that a man's coition is not for whoredom

(but with the intention of betrothal). (iv) There is a presumption that a woman's menstrual period comes on time.

(c) From repetition. When certain types of (usually adverse) events recur two or three times, there is a presumption that it was no accident and that they will recur again.

Examples. (i) When two (or, according to some, three) of a woman's sons die following their circumcision, there is a presumption that the blood of the family is "weak", and hence the next son born is not to be circumcised. (ii) After goring thrice, an ox is presumed *mu'ad* (bound-to-gore), hence its owner is liable to full indemnity upon the next goring instance.

(d) From common knowledge. What is common knowledge among people about people's being in a certain state is presumed to be so.

Examples. (i) Persons commonly known to be (blood) relatives are presumed to be so related (for purposes of marriage, inheritance, etc.) even without clear evidence that they are. (ii) When a person is known in a town by a certain name for thirty days there is a presumption that it is his real name.

What sort of a classification is this? What are we to draw from it? It does not, quite obviously, correspond to the common, contemporary Western treatment and classification of legal presumptions.[12] Equally obviously, it is wholly practical in orientation. The concern is not with theoretical problems such as the principle of the uniformity of nature or induction from instances, or with psychological and biological truths about human nature as such. The concern is rather with resolving pressing, practical, and - to the people involved - vital decision problems. It must be appreciated that the world

these presumptions relate to is regulated in
accordance with numerous distinctions between
categories, such as kosher vs. nonkosher, pure
vs. impure, holy (e.g., days) vs. common, sacred
vs. profane, eligible vs. disqualified, banned
vs. permitted, and so on. These distinctions,
determining as they do every aspect of everyone's
daily life, are categorical and absolute, allowing of no borderline cases and no vagueness.
Their applications to concrete instances, however,
are often highly problematic, for they turn in
many cases upon people's intentions, or in general
upon facts which are not of a public nature and
hence may not be known at the relevant time. It
is, I suggest, in order to facilitate the application of these distinctions that a large part of
this wealth of presumptions is instituted: they
help determine what category each specific case
is to *count as* falling under. "The reason why we
go by the presumptions", says Maimonides, "is
that if we do not go by the presumptions we shall
not be able to resolve any matter".

As for the classification of the Talmudic presumptions itself, I tend to regard it as belonging under the heading of the justification of
presumptions. More specifically, to the extent
that the remarks in the previous paragraph may
be viewed as having to do with the justification-
of-being, or the *raison d'être*, of a large number
of Talmudic presumption rules, the categories
classified relate to the second justificatory
task involved in justifying presumptions - that
of justifying the specific presumptions espoused
by the presumption rules vis-à-vis their possible
alternatives. In fact, all four categories
enumerated are concerned to elaborate the justifying considerations from what I have referred
to as the inductive-probabilistic realm. They
are concerned, in their own way, to elaborate

on, as well as to make distinctions among, what
is to be considered common, ordinary, normal,
plausible, likely. Some thing (state, act, intention) is presumed to be so because it was so, or
because it has shown a disposition to be so, or
because it's human nature to be so, or because
it's generally assumed to be so.

But of course this is double-edged: once these
presumptions - whatever their justifying considerations - are laid down and codified and are known
to hold, they *ipso facto* serve to regulate behavior: given that you know that a person is presumed not to have repaid his debt before settle-
ment day, when you yourself for some reason
decide to pay your debt earlier, you realize
that you'd better have witnesses or keep the
receipt; given that you know that in your new
town of residence the children you raise will be
presumed brother and sister, if they in fact are
not and you do not want to preclude their marry-
ing each other in due course, you'd make sure to
produce and register the necessary evidence in
time, and so on.

So, the presumptions needed to facilitate daily
transactions and decisions in face of the variety
of Halakhic rules and distinctions imposed upon
life are instituted on the basis of the common
run of things. At the same time the very existence of these presumptions contributes to the
fashioning and regulating of individual behavior
as well as of social institutions. It must, I
believe, be assumed that, at least with some of
these presumptions, some judgment concerning
the value, both moral and social, of the resulting patterns of behavior and institutions forms
part of the justification of presumptions. This
constitutes, then, the (second-tier) normative
consideration justifying the pertinent presumptions, augmenting the considerations that have
to do merely with that which is probable.

Footnotes:

1. I am grateful to Avishai Margalit for having pointed out to me the relevance of the notion of presumption to Grice's discussion in the first place, and also for valuable discussions on the matter, as on most other matters dealt with in this paper, since. He himself offers an extended treatment of related topics in his forthcoming *Meaning and Metaphor*.

2. William James Lectures, Harvard University, 1968, 2nd lecture. Reprinted as "Logic and Conversation" in D. Davidson and G. Harman, eds. *The Logic of Grammar* (Berkeley: Univ. of California Press, 1975), pp. 64-75. All page references will be to the latter.

3. Grice refers to it as "dull" (68). The reason is that he is considering it as a candidate answer to his question of what makes people issue their utterances in observance of the CP, and as *such* he finds it wanting. Within the present framework, however, this consideration serves as one among several justificatory considerations of the IPC, and, as such, even though possibly obvious, it is not dull.

4. For a useful statement of the notion of "frame" see Marvin Minsky, "Frame-System Theory" (1975), reprinted in P.N. Johnson-Laird and P.C. Wason, eds., *Thinking* (New York: Cambridge, 1977), pp. 355-376.

5. "Knowledge and Justified Presumption," *Journal of Philosophy*, LXIX, 5 (March 9, 1972): 123-127.

6. For further criticism of this principle, as well as of Lamb's central argument, see William Edward Morris, "Knowledge as Justified Presumption", *Journal of Philosophy*, LXX, 6 (March 22, 1973): 161-165 (esp. p. 164).

7. It is possible, I think, to regard the legal presumption of sanity as a special case of the presumption of normality: a person brought to trial is presumed sane, i.e., normal (in which sense?).

8. Isabel C. Hungerland, "Contextual Implication", *Inquiry*, IV (1960): 211-258.

9. Mats Furberg, *Saying and Meaning* (Oxford: Basil Blackwell, 1963).

10. On the issue of presumptions of reference, see Edna Ullmann-Margalit and Avishai Margalit, "Analyticity by Way of Presumption", *Canadian Journal of Philosophy*, XII, 3 (September 1982): 435-452.

11. Margaret Atherton, Sidney Morgenbesser, and Robert Schwartz, "On Tenure", *Philosophical Forum*, X, 2-4 (Winter/Summer 1978-79): 341-352.

12. Some points of comparison are of interest, but cannot be taken up here. Among them: There is some Halakhic distinction between "ceasing" presumptions (e.g., those from the previous state) and "non-ceasing" ones (e.g., those from human nature), but this distinction does *not* correspond to the rebuttable/conclusive distinction: it has, I believe, more to do with the possible ambiguity between the generic presumption rule on the one hand and the particular presumption when the rule is being applied to a concrete instance on the other. Also, there are various discussions of the different degrees of strength of different presumptions: whether and under what circumstances they count as weaker than, equal to, or stronger than evidence-by-majority. Interestingly, the matter of rebuttal does not, as far as I can ascertain, occupy a central role in the Talmudic discussion of presumptions (it is partially covered under the recurring heading of "When it is possible to investigate").

GIAMBATTISTA VICO
Isaiah
Berlin AND CULTURAL HISTORY

I

The study of their own past has long been one of
the major preoccupations of men. There have been
many motives for this, some of them discussed by
Nietzsche in a famous essay: pride, the desire
to glorify the achievements of tribe, nation,
church, race, class, party; the wish to promote
the bonds of solidarity in a given society -"We
are all sons of Cadmus"; faith in the sacred
traditions of the tribe - to our ancestors alone
has been vouchsafed the revelation of the true
ends of life, of good and evil, right and wrong,
how one should live, what to live by; and, associated with this, a sense of collective worth,
the need to know and teach others to understand
the kind of society that we are and have been,
the texture of relationships through which our
collective genius has expressed itself, and by
which alone it can function. There is the ethical
approach: history provides us with authentic examples - and exemplars - of virtue and vice -
with vivid illustrations of what to do and what
to avoid - a gallery of portraits of heroes and
villains, the wise and the foolish, the successful and the failures - history as being in the
first place a school of morals as, for example,
Leibniz declared, or of experimental politics,
as Joseph de Maistre (and perhaps Machiavelli)
believed. Then, again, there are those who look
for a pattern in history, the gradual realization of a cosmic plan, the work of the Divine
Artificer who has created us, and all there is, to
serve a universal purpose, hidden from us, perhaps, because we are too weak or sinful or fool-

ish, but real and unalterable, with lineaments
which can be discerned, however imperfectly, by
those who have eyes to see. One of the forms of
this vision is the conception of history as a
cosmic drama, which, according to some doctrines
must culminate in a final *dénoument* beyond the
frontiers of history and time, in a total spiritual transfiguration not to be fully grasped by
the finite human intellect. According to others
history is a cyclical process which leads to a
peak of human achievement, then to decadence and
collapse, after which the entire process begins
afresh. It is held that such patterns alone give
meaning to the historical process, else what can
it be - the mere play of chance combinations and
divisions, a mechanical succession of causes and
effects? Then, again, there are those who believe
in the possibility of a sociological science for
which historical facts are the data, which, once
we have discovered the laws that govern social
change, will enable us to predict the future and
retrodict the past - this is the conception of
history as a systematic collection of observations that stands to a developed scientific sociology much as the observations of the heavens by
Tycho Brahe stood to the laws discovered by Kep-
ler or Galileo, a new and powerful instrument
which makes return to the mere accumulation of
such data unnecessary save to verify specific hypotheses. That was the hope of such nineteenth-
century positivists as Comte and Buckle, who believed in the possibility of, and need for, a
natural science of history created by methods in
essence analogous to those of, if not physics, at
any rate the biological sciences. Again, there
are those who own to no better motive for studying history than simple curiosity about the past,
the quest of knowledge for its own sake, the
wish to know what happened, and when and why,

without necessarily drawing general conclusions
or formulating laws. Last but not least is the
ambition of those who wish to know how we, the
present generation, came to be what we are, who
our ancestors have been, what they have done,
what were the consequences of their activities,
what was the nature of the interplay between
these activities, what were their hopes and fears
and goals, and the natural forces with which they
had to contend; for it seems obvious that only
barbarians feel no curiosity about the sources
of their own forms of life and civilization,
their place in the world order as determined by
the antecedent experiences of their ancestors,
as well as the very identity of these ancestors,
which alone can give a sense of identity to
their successors.

This last motive for the study of history
springs from a desire for self-knowledge - something which, however implicit in earlier writers,
came to the surface only in the eighteenth century, principally among thinkers in the West who
reacted against a central doctrine of the French
Enlightenment, then the dominant influence on
the majority of European intellectuals. This was
the belief that a universally valid method had
finally been found for the solution of the fundamental questions that had exercised men at all
times - how to establish what was true and what
was false in every province of knowledge; and,
above all, what was the right life that men
should lead if they were to attain those goals
which men had always pursued - life, liberty,
justice, happiness, virtue, the fullest development of human faculties in a harmonious and
creative way. This method consisted in the application of those rational (that is, scientific)
rules, which had in the previous century produced
such magnificent results in the fields of mathema-

tics and the natural sciences, to the moral,
social, political, economic problems of mankind,
so long bedeviled by ignorance and error, super-
stition and prejudice, much of it deliberately
spread by priests, princes, ruling classes,
bureaucrats, and ambitious adventurers who dis-
seminated falsehoods as a means of keeping men
obedient to their will. The greatest publicist
of the Enlightenment, Voltaire, even while he
advocated the widening of historical inquiry to
embrace social and economic activities and their
effects, strongly believed that the only objects
worthy of historical study were the peaks, not
the valleys, of the achievements of mankind; he
had no doubt about what they were: Periclean
Athens, Rome of the late republic and early
principate, Renaissance Florence, and France
during the reign of Louis XIV. These were the
finest hours of mankind, when the true, the only
true, ends that all wise men sought at all times
- in art, in thought, in morals and manners -
determined the lives of states and individuals
alike. These ends were timeless and universal,
known to all reasonable men - those who had eyes
to see - not touched by change or any kind of
historical evolution. Just as answers to the
problems of the natural sciences could be solved
once and for all, just as the theorems of geometry, the laws of physics and astronomy were unaffected by changes in human opinion or ways of
life, so, at any rate in principle, equally
clear and final answers could be found to human
problems also. Even Montesquieu, who believed in
the unavoidable variety of customs and outlooks
due largely to the influence both of physical
factors and human institutions determined by
them, nevertheless assumed that the fundamental
goals of mankind were identical at all times,
everywhere, even if the particular forms they

took in various climates and societies necessarily differed, so that no uniform legislation
for all human societies could be sucessfully
devised. The very conception of progress among
the *philosophes* in the eighteenth century,
whether its champions were optimistic, like Con-
dorcet or Helvétius, or assailed by doubts about
its prospects, like Voltaire and Rousseau, entailed the view that the light of the truth, *lumen
naturale*, is everywhere and always the same, even
if men were often too wicked or stupid or weak to
discover it, or, if they did, to live their lives
by its radiance. The dark periods of human history were, for Voltaire, simply not worthy of the
attention of intelligent men. The purpose of history is to impart instructive truths, not to
satisfy idle curiosity, and this can only be done
by studying the triumphs of reason and imagination, not the failures. "If you have no more to
tell us," Voltaire declared "than that one barbarian succeeded another on the banks of the Oxus
or the Ixartes, what use are you to the public?"
Who wants to know that "Quancum succeeded Kincum
and Kincum succeeded Quancum"? Who wants to know
about Shalmaneser or Mardokempad? Historians must
not clutter the minds of their readers with the
absurdities of religion, the ravings of idiots
and savages, or the inventions of knaves, unless
it be as cautionary tales to warn mankind of the
horrors of barbarism and tyranny. This deeply unhistorical approach to the nature of men and societies is common enough in the eighteenth century, and derives in part from the phenomenal
success of the exact sciences in the previous
century, which led Descartes, for example, to
look on the study of history as unworthy of intelligent men interested in the advancement of
objective knowledge, which in such muddy waters
could scarcely be hoped for. The view that the

truth is one and undivided, and the same for all
men everywhere at all times, whether one found
it in the pronouncements of sacred books, traditional wisdom, the authority of churches, democratic majorities, observation and experiment
conducted by qualified experts or the convictions
of simple folk uncorrupted by civilization - this
view, in one form or another, is central to Western thought, which stems from Plato and his dis-
ciples.

It did not go entirely unchallenged. Apart
from the Skeptics in ancient Greece and Rome,
the revolt against Papal authority led some of
the Reformers in the sixteenth century (particularly the Protestant jurists among them) to
claim that the differences of various cultural
traditions were as important, if not more so, as
that which was common to them. Jurists like Hot-
man in France and Coke and Matthew Hale in Eng-
land, who rejected the universal authority of
Rome, developed the beginnings of the view that,
as customs, ways of life, outlooks differed, so,
necessarily, did the laws and rules by which
various societies lived, and that this expressed
deep and basic differences in their growth as
distinct and at times widely dissimilar social
entities. Thereby these lawyers contributed to
the notion of cultural diversity. The very
notion of cultures - of the interconnection of
diverse activities on the part of members of a
given community - of the links that exist between
legal systems, religions, arts, sciences, customs,
and above all, languages, as well as myths and
legends and ritual forms of behavior, and bind
them into identifiable ways of life with differing ideals and values - this entire notion, in
its fully conscious, explicit form, is not very
old. It owes a great deal to the rise of interest
in the classical world of Greece and Rome during

the Italian Renaissance, when the obvious and
profound differences between their own societies
and those of the classical period drew the attention of scholars and those influenced by them to
the possibility of more than one true human
civilization. Paradoxically, the very idea of a
restoration, the wish to revive the splendors of
Greece and Rome after the dark night of the Middle
Ages, to reorganize life on the eternally valid
principles that were held to govern classical
civilization, gave way gradually, as knowledge of
the past increased, to its very opposite, the
perception of the irreconcilable differences of
outlook and behavior - and rules and principles -
between ancient and modern societies. A number of
historical writers in France in the sixteenth
century, men like Vignier, La Popelinère, Le
Caron, Bodin, maintained that the study of antiquities - customs, myths, religious rites,
languages, as well as inscriptions, coins, works
of art, and, of course, literary monuments - provided the evidence on which reconstruction of
entire cultures could be based. Nevertheless, the
view according to which all high cultures were
so many branches of the same great tree of enlightenment - that human progress was basically
a single forward movement, broken by periods of
retrogression and collapse, but never destroyed,
constantly renewed, drawing ever nearer to the
final victory of reason, continued in general to
dominate Western thought. Historians and jurists,
mainly Protestant, who stressed the all but unbridgeable differences between the old and the
new, Romans and Franks, continued to question
this assumption. The remote, the exotic, began
to be studied seriously and sympathetically. The
differences, e.g., between East and West, or
Europe and the Americas, were noted, but little
was done by way of producing actual histories or

analyses of these dissimilar societies, which
fascinated scholars and travelers by their very
unlikeness to their own. A major advance in this
direction was made by the early opponents of the
literary mandarins of Paris in the eighteenth
century, critical of those who took it for granted that the past was to be judged by the degree
of the proximity of its theory and practice to
the canons of taste of our own enlightened day.
Thus we find British and Swiss scholars in the
early years of the century who began to investigate legends, sagas, early poetry historically,
as the vehicles of the self-expression of
particular peoples. Such critics held that the
Homeric poems, the songs of the Niebelungs, the
Norse sagas, owed their power and beauty to the
peculiar traits of the societies by which, in
their own times and places, they were generated.
The Regius Professor of Hebrew at Oxford University, Bishop Lowth, spoke of the Old Testament
as the national epic of the inhabitants of ancient Judea, not to be judged by the criteria
derived from the study of Sophocles or Virgil,
Racine or Boileau.

The most famous proponent of this approach is
the German poet and critic, Johann Gottfried Herder, who insisted upon and celebrated the uniqueness of national cultures, above all, their in-
commensurability, the differences in the criteria
by which they could be understood and judged. He
was, all his life, fascinated by the very variety
of the paths of development of civilization, past
and present, European and Asian, of which the new
interest in oriental scholarship, the languages
of India and Persia, provided much convincing
concrete evidence. This, in its turn, animated
the German Historical school of jurisprudence,
itself directed against the claims to timeless
rationality, the assertion of universal validity,

whether of Roman law, or the *Code Napoléon*, or
the principles proclaimed by the ideologues of
the French Revolution and their allies in other
lands. At times opposition to the authority of a
single immutable Natural Law, whether as formulated by the Roman Church or the French *lumières*,
tended to take highly reactionary forms, justifying oppression, arbitrary rule, and inequalities
and injustices of various kinds. Nevertheless,
the obverse side of this coin was the attention
it attracted to the rich diversity of human institutions and the deep differences of outlook
and experience which informed and divided them,
and, above all, the impossibility of reducing
them to a single pattern, or, indeed, even to
deviations from such a pattern of a systematic
kind.

It is worth remarking, in this connection,
that the history of ideas offers few examples of
so dramatic a change of outlook as the birth of
the new belief not so much in the inevitability,
as in the value and importance, of the singular
and the unique, of variety as such; and the corresponding conviction that there is something
repressive and deeply unattractive in uniformity;
that whereas variety is a symptom of vitality,
the opposite is a dreary and dead monotony. This
notion, indeed, this feeling which seems so
natural to us now, is not compatible with a view
of the world according to which truth is everywhere one, while error is multiple; that the
ideal state is one of total harmony, while apparently irreconcilable differences of outlook or
opinion are a symptom of imperfection - of incoherence due to error or ignorance or weakness
or vice. Yet that kind of worship of oneness is
the basis of Platonism and of much subsequent
thought, in both Judaism and Christianity, and
no less so in the Renaissance and the Enlighten-

ment, deeply influenced as it was by the triumph-
ant progress of the natural sciences. Even Leibniz, who believed in plenitude, in the value of
the greatest possible variety of species, supposed
that they must be compatible with one another;
even Pericles, who in Thucydides' version of his
funeral oration, compares the rigid discipline of
the militarized state of Sparta unfavorably with
the looser texture of Athenian life, nevertheless
wanted a harmonious city, to the preservation and
enhancement of which all its members should consciously bend their energies. Aristotle conceded
that some differences in outlook and character
were unavoidable, but did not celebrate this as
a virtue and merely recognized it as a part of
unalterable human nature. As for the greatest
champion in the eighteenth century of variety,
Herder, who passionately believed that every
culture has its own irreplaceable contribution
to make to the progress of the human race, even
he believed that there need be - indeed, there
should be - no conflict between these dissimilar
contributions, that their function is to enrich
the universal harmony between nations and institutions, for which men have been created by God
or nature. No doctrine that has at its heart a
monistic conception of the true and the good and
the beautiful, or a teleology according to which
everything conspires toward a final harmonious
resolution - an ultimate order in which all the
apparent confusions and imperfections of the life
of the world will be resolved - no doctrine of
this kind can allow variety as an independent
value to be pursued for its own sake; for variety
entails the possibility of the conflict of values,
of some irreducible incompatibility between the
ideals, or, indeed, the immediate aims, of fully
realized, equally virtuous men.
    Yet it is this worship of rich variety which

484   VICO AND CULTURAL HISTORY

was at the center of the Romantic movement, both
in the arts and in philosophy. This seems to me
to have led to something like the melting away
of the very notion of objective truth, at least
in the normative sphere. However it might be in
the natural sciences, in the realm of ethics,
politics, aesthetics, it was the authenticity
and sincerity of the pursuit of inner goals that
mattered; this applied equally to individuals
and groups - states, nations, movements. This is
most evident in the aesthetics of Romanticism,
where the notion of eternal models, a Platonic
vision of ideal beauty, which the artist seeks
to convey, however imperfectly, on canvas or in
sound, is replaced by a passionate belief in
spiritual freedom, individual creativity. The
painter, the poet, the composer, do not hold up
a mirror to nature, however ideal, but invent;
they do not imitate (the doctrine of Mimesis),
but create not merely the means but the goals
that they pursue; these goals represent the self-
expression of the artist's own unique, inner
vision, to set aside which in response to the
demands of some "external" voice - church, state,
public opinion, family, friends, arbiters of
taste - is an act of betrayal of what alone justifies their existence for those who are in any
sense creative. This voluntarism and subjectivism, of which the most passionate prophet is the
true father of romanticism, Johann Gottlob Fichte,
did, of course, in the end lead to wild anarchy
and irrationality, Byronic self-intoxication,
the worship of the gloomy outcast, sinister and
fascinating, the enemy of settled society, the
satanic hero, Cain, Manfred, the Giaour, Melmoth,
whose proud independence is purchased at the
cost of no matter how much human happiness or
how many human lives. In the case of nations,
this rejection of the very notion of universally

valid values tended at times to inspire national-
ism and aggressive chauvinism, the glorification
of uncompromising individual or collective self-
assertion. In its extreme forms it took criminal
and violently pathological forms and culminated
in the abandonment of reason and all sense of
reality, with often monstrous moral and political consequences.

Yet in its earlier phase this very movement
marked the birth of a great extension of historical understanding, whereby the development of
human civilization was conceived not as a single
linear movement, now rising, now declining, nor
as a dialectical movement of clashing opposites
always resolved in a higher synthesis, but as
the realization that cultures are many and various, each embodying scales of value different
from those of other cultures and sometimes incompatible with them, yet capable of being understood, that is, seen by observers endowed with
sufficiently acute and sympathetic historical
insight, as ways of living which human beings
could pursue and remain fully human. The principal, officially recognized, exponent of this
view was Herder; but it may be that the man who
first gave it flesh and substance was Walter Scott.
The best of Scott's historical novels for the
first time presented individuals, classes, and
indeed entire societies, in the round, as fully
realized characters, not as figures on a stage,
the two-dimensional, generalized types of Livy
or Tacitus and even Gibbon and Hume. Scott's
characters are, as a rule, men and women into
whose outlook and feelings and motives the reader
can enter; Scott is the first writer to achieve
what Herder preached: the conveying of a world
that the reader apprehends as being as full as
his own, equally real yet profoundly different,
but not so remote as not to be understood as we

understand contemporaries whose characters and
lives differ greatly from our own. The influence
of Scott on the writing of history has not been
sufficiently investigated.   To see the past
through the eyes of those who lived through it,
from the inside, as it were, and not merely as a
succession of distant facts and events and
figures in a procession to be described from
some external vantage point as so much material
for narrative or statistical treatment - to be
able to achieve this kind of understanding, even
though with considerable effort, is a claim to a
capacity that could scarcely have been made before the modern age by historians concerned with
the truth.

  Herder may have been the effective discoverer
of the nature of this kind of imaginative insight, but the man who first conceived, in concrete terms, the possibility of it, and provided
examples of how such a method could be employed,
was the early eighteenth-century Italian thinker
Giambattista Vico. Vico's principal work remained unread save by a handful of Italians and those
few Frenchmen to whom, years later, the Italians
spoke of him, until, at the beginning of the last
century, Jules Michelet came upon him, caught
fire, and celebrated his achievements across
Europe.

II

Vico is the true father both of the modern concept of culture and of what one might call cultural pluralism, according to which each authentic culture has its own unique vision, its own
scale of values, which, in the course of development, is superseded by other visions and
values, but never wholly so: that is, earlier
value systems do not become totally unintelli-

gible to succeeding generations. Unlike such
relativists as Spengler or Westermarck, Vico did
not suppose that men are encapsulated within
their own epoch or culture, insulated in a box
without windows and consequently incapable of
understanding other societies and periods the
values of which may be widely different from
theirs and which they may find strange or repellent. His deepest belief was that what men have
made, other men can understand - it may take an
immense amount of painful effort to decipher the
meaning of conduct or language different from
our own. Nevertheless, according to Vico, if anything is meant by the term 'human', there must
be enough that is common to all such beings for
it to be possible, by a sufficient effort of
imagination, to grasp what the world must have
looked like to creatures, remote in time or
space, who practised such rites, and used such
words, and created such works of art as the
natural means of self-expression involved in
the attempt to understand and interpret their
worlds to themselves. Fundamentally, Vico's is
the same sort of method as that used by most
modern social anthropologists in seeking to
understand the behavior and imagery of primitive
tribes (or what there is left of them), whose myths
and tales and metaphors and similes and allegor-
ies they do not dismiss as so much nonsense,
confusion in the heads of irrational, childlike
barbarians (as the eighteenth century was apt
to do): rather they seek for a key to enable
them to enter into their worlds, to see through
their eyes, remembering that men (as a later
philosopher has said) are at once subjects and
objects to themselves. They look upon the primi-
tives, therefore, not as so many creatures who
can only be described, but whose motives cannot
be fathomed - plants or animals, with only the

laws of physics or biology to account for their
behavior - but as beings akin to ourselves, inhabitants of a world in which such behavior and
such words can be interpreted as intelligible
responses to the natural conditions in which
they find themselves and which they seek to understand. In a sense, the mere existence of an extraordinary variety of very dissimilar languages -
sometimes among neighboring societies (as, for
example, in the Caucasus or in Pacific islands)
is itself an index, or, one might say, a model of
the irreducible variety of human self-expression,
such that even in the case of cognate languages,
complete translation of one into any other is in
principle impossible; and the gap - indicative
of differences in ways of perceiving and acting -
is at times very wide indeed.

In a sense this approach is not so very different from what is involved in any act of understanding others, their words, their looks, their
gestures, which convey to us their intentions
and aspirations. We have recourse to purely
scientific methods of decipherment only when communication breaks down; we formulate hypotheses
and seek to verify them, to establish the authenticity of documents, the dates of antiquities,
the analysis of the materials of which they are
made, the degree of reliability of testimony,
sources of information, and the like. For all
of this we have recourse to normal scientific
methods, and not to the kind of inspired guesswork that must inevitably enter to some extent
into any attempt to understand what it must have
been like to have lived in a given situation at
a particular time, to have to cope with the
forces of nature or other men, to grasp what
things must have seemed like to those who believed
in the efficacy of witchcraft, incantations,
sacrifices to placate the gods or to make nature

more amenable to human will. Because our ancestors were men, Vico supposes that they knew, as
we know, what it is to love and hate, hope and
fear, to want, to pray, to fight, to betray, to
oppress, to be oppressed, to revolt. Roman law
and Roman history is what Vico knew best; consequently many of his examples come from the history and legislation of early Rome. His etymolo-
gies are often fanciful, but his account of the
economic circumstances which, in his view, led
to this or that type of legislation in what he
regards as continuing class warfare between ple-
beians and patricians is a great advance on
earlier theories. The historical details may be
wrong, even absurd, the knowledge may be defect-
ive, the critical methods insufficient - but the
approach is bold, original, and fruitful. Vico
never tells us what he means by what he calls
"entering into" or "descending to" the minds of
primitive men, but from his practice in the
Scienza Nuova it is plain that it is imaginative insight that he demands, a gift which he
calls *fantasia*. Later German thinkers spoke of
verstehen - to understand - as opposed to *wissen*,
the kind of knowledge we have in the natural
sciences, where "entering" is not in question,
since one cannot enter into the hopes and fears
of bees and beavers. Vico's *fantasia* is indispensable to his conception of historical knowledge; it is unlike the knowledge that Julius
Caesar is dead, or that Rome was not built in a
day, or that thirteen is a prime number, or that
a week has seven days, nor yet knowledge of how
to ride a bicycle or engage in statistical
research or win a battle. It is more like knowing what it is to be poor, to belong to a nation,
to be a revolutionary, to be converted to a religion, to fall in love, to be seized by nameless
terror, to be delighted by a work of art. I give

these examples only as analogies, for Vico is interested not in the experience of individuals
but in that of entire societies. It is this kind
of collective self-awareness - what men thought,
imagined, felt, wanted, strove for, in the face
of physical nature at a particular stage of
social development, expressed by institutions,
monuments, symbols, ways of writing and speech,
generated by their efforts to represent and explain their condition to themselves - that he
wished to analyze, and he thought he had found a
path to it not trodden by others. The door that
he opened to the understanding of cultural history by the "decoding" of myths, ceremonies, laws,
artistic images, he regarded as his major achievement. No wonder that Karl Marx, in a well-known
letter to Lassalle, said that Vico had moments of
genius as a writer on social evolution.

No one has stronger claims than Vico to be considered as the begetter of historical anthropology. Jules Michelet, who regarded himself as his
disciple, was right: Vico was indeed the forgotten anticipator of the German Historical School,
the first and, in some ways the most formidable
opponent of unhistorical doctrines of natural
law, of timeless authority, of the assumption
made by, e.g., Spinoza, that any truth could have
been discovered by anyone, at any time, and that
it is just bad luck that men have stumbled for
so long in darkness because they did not or
could not employ their reason correctly. The
idea of historical development in this large
sense, as a succession of cultures, each of which
stems from its predecessor in the course of men's
constant struggle against the forces of nature,
which at a certain stage of social development
generates the war between economic classes, themselves formed by the very process of production,
is a major event in the history of the growth of

human self-understanding. This conception of the nature of historic change (whatever adumbrations of it are to be found in social thought from Hesiod to Harrington) had never before been so fully stated.

Vico's critics in modern times have pointed out that his doctrine that man can understand only what he makes is insufficient for the discovery and analysis of cultures - are there not unconscious drives, irrational factors, of which we are not aware, even retrospectively? Do acts not often lead to unintended consequences, unforseen accidental results not "made" by the actors? Is not Vico's view of Providence - his form of Hegel's "Cunning of Reason" - that uses our very vices to create forms of life which are to mankind's benefit (a somewhat similar idea was advanced by Vico's contemporary Bernard Mandeville), something that cannot be "understood" by men, since, according to Vico, it springs from the will of God, a Spirit to whose workings we are not privy? Moreover, are we not unavoidably committed to importing some of our own concepts and categories in understanding the past? Did not the great classical scholar, Ulrich von Wilamowitz-Moellendorff, tell us (alluding to Homer's account of Achilles, whose ghost was summoned from the nether regions by Odysseus) that the dead cannot speak until they have drunk blood - but since it is our blood that we offer them it is with our own voices that they talk to us, and in our words, not theirs; and, if this is so, is not our claim to understand them and their worlds to some degree always illusory? All these considerations are doubtless valid, and an obstacle to the idea that, since human history is made by men, it can therefore, even in principle, be wholly understood by "entering" into the minds of our ancestors. Yet even though human

history is more than an account of men's hopes
or ideas and the actions that embody them, and
not solely an account of human experience or
stages of consciousness (as, at times, both
Hegel and Collingwood seemed to believe), and
even though Marx is right in saying that it is
men, indeed, who make human history, but not out
of whole cloth, but in conditions provided by
nature and by earlier human institutions, which
may lead to situations not necessarily related
to the purpose of the actors - even though Vico's
claims now seem overambitious, yet something of
importance survives despite these qualifications.
Everyone is today aware of the fundamental difference between, on the one hand, those historians who paint portraits of entire societies or
groups within them that are rounded and three-
dimensional, so that we believe, whether rightly
or mistakenly, that we are able to tell what it
would have been like to have lived in such conditions, and, on the other, antiquaries, chroni-
clers, accumulators of facts or statistics on
which large generalizations can be founded,
learned compilers, or theorists who look on the
use of imagination as opening the door to the
horrors of guesswork, subjectivism, journalism,
or worse. This all-important distinction rests
precisely on the attitude to the faculty that
Vico called *fantasia*, without which the past cannot, in his view, be resurrected. The crucial
role he assigns to the imagination must not blind
us - and did not blind him - to the necessity for
verification; he allows that critical methods of
examining evidence are indispensable. Yet without
fantasia the past remains dead; to bring it to
life we need, at least ideally, to hear men's
voices, to conjecture (on the basis of such evidence as we can gather) what may have been their
experience, their forms of expression, their

values, outlook, aims, ways of living; without
this we cannot grasp whence we came, how we come
to be as we are now, not merely physically or
biologically and, in a narrow sense, politically
and institutionally, but socially, psychologically, morally; without this there can be no genuine
self-understanding. We call only those men great
historians who not only are in full control of
the factual evidence obtained by the use of the
best critical methods available to them, but
also possess the depth of imaginative insight
that characterizes gifted novelists. Clio, as the
English historian G.M. Trevelyan pointed out long
ago, is, after all, a muse.

III

One of the most interesting corollaries of the
application of Vico's method of reconstructing
the past, is what I have called cultural pluralism - a panorama of a variety of cultures, the
pursuit of different, and sometimes incompatible,
ways of life, ideals, standards of value. This,
in its turn, entails that the perennial idea of
the perfect society, in which truth, justice,
freedom, happiness, virtue, coalesce in their
most perfect forms, is not merely utopian (which
few deny), but intrinsically incoherent; for if
some of these values prove to be incompatible,
they cannot - conceptually cannot - coalesce.
Every culture expresses itself in works of art,
of thought, in ways of living and action, each
of which possesses its own character which can
neither be combined nor necessarily form stages
of a single progress toward a single universal
goal.
    The conception of different visions of life
and their values, which cannot be represented
as capable of fitting into one great harmonious

structure, is illustrated vividly in that part
of Vico's *Scienza Nuova* which deals with Homer.
His views stand in sharp contrast with the prevalent aesthetic doctrines of his time, according
to which, despite some deviations toward relativism, standards of excellence are objective, universal, and timeless, *quod semper, quod ubique,
quod ab omnibus.* Thus, to give a well-known example, while some held that the ancients were
better poets than the moderns, others maintained
the opposite - it was over this that the famous
Battle of Ancients and Moderns was fought in
Vico's younger days. The relevant point is that
the opponents in this conflict defended their
positions in terms of identical values which
both sides considered to be eternally applicable
to all times and all forms of art. Not so Vico.
He tells us that "in the world's childhood men
were by nature sublime poets." For imagination
is strong in primitive peoples, thinking power
feeble. Homer, Vico believed, lived toward the
end of the civilization that he described with
a degree of genius that no later writer had been
able to approach, let alone equal. Homeric men
are "crude, boorish, savage, proud, stubborn."
Achilles is cruel, violent, vindictive, concerned only with his own feelings; yet he is depicted as a blameless warrior, the ideal hero of
the Homeric world. The values of that world
have passed away; Vico was living in a more
humane age. But this does not mean, so he maintained, that the art of this later day is necessarily superior to that of the most sublime of
all poets. Homer clearly admired the values of
these frightful men; his marvelous celebration of
savage and truculent warriors engaged in cruel
butchery, his account of the Olympian gods which
had so shocked Plato and caused Aristotle to wish
to "correct" him, could not have been composed by
the cultivated poets of the Renaissance or of

Vico's own times. Vico is clear that this is an irremediable loss. So, too, he speaks of Roman writers who hold up men like Brutus, Mucius Scaevola, Manlius, the Decii, for our admiration - men who, as he points out, ruined, robbed, crushed the poor unhappy Roman plebs. He reminds us that when, in an even earlier age, King Agis of Sparta tried to help the oppressed, he was executed as a traitor. Yet it is grim, ferocious men of this kind by and for whom unsurpassed masterpieces were written - works that we cannot rival. We may be superior to these barbarians (Vico believes) in rational thought, knowledge, humanity, but we do not, for that very reason, possess the marvelous, elemental power of imagination or language of the magnificent epics and sagas which only a brutal and primitive culture can produce. For Vico there is no true progress in the arts; the genius of one age cannot be compared with that of another. He would have thought it idle to ask whether Sophocles is not a better poet than Virgil or Virgil than Racine. Each culture creates masterpieces that belong to it and it alone, and when it is over one can admire its triumphs or deplore its vices: but they are no more; nothing can restore them to us. If this is so, it follows that the very notion of a perfect society, in which all the excellences of all cultures will harmoniously coalesce, does not make sense. One virtue may turn out to be incompatible with another. The uncombinable remains uncombinable. The virtues of the Homeric heroes are not the virtues of the age of Plato and Aristotle in the name of which they attacked the morality of the Homeric poems; nor are the virtues of fifth-century Athens, for all that Voltaire thought otherwise, similar to those of Renaissance Florence or the Court of Versailles. There is both loss and gain in the passing from one stage of civilization to another, but, what-

ever the gain, what is lost is lost forever and
will not be restored in some earthly paradise.

There is something boldly original about a
thinker who, in so self-satisfied a civilization
as that into which Vico was born, one which saw
itself as a vast improvement on the brutality,
absurdity, ignorance of earlier times, dared
maintain that an unapproachably sublime poem
could have been produced only by a cruel, savage,
and, to later generations, morally repellent age.
This amounts to a denial of the very possibility
of a harmony of all excellences in an ideal
world. From this it follows that to judge the
attainments of any one age by applying to them
a single absolute criterion - that of the critics
and theorists of a later period - not only is
unhistorical and anachronistic, but rests on a
fallacy, the assumption of the existence of
timeless standards - the ideal values of an ideal
world, when, in fact, some of the most greatly
admired works of men are organically bound up
with a culture some aspects of which we may -
perhaps cannot help but - condemn, even while
claiming to understand why it is that men
situated as these were must have felt, thought,
and acted as they did.

The notion of a perfect society in which all
that men have striven for finds total fulfill-
ment, is consequently perceived to be incoherent,
at any rate in terrestrial terms: Homer cannot
coexist with Dante; nor Dante with Galileo. This
is a truism now. But the anti-utopian implications of the section on Homer in the *Scienza
Nuova*, largely neglected as they were in the
author's time, have lessons for our own day. The
unparalleled services of the Enlightenment in
its battle against obscurantism, oppression, in-
justice, and irrationality of every kind are not
in question. But it may be that all great libera-
ting movements, if they are to break through the

resistance of accepted dogma and custom, are
bound to exaggerate, and be blind to the virtues
of that which they attack. The proposition that
man is at once subject and object to himself,
does not lie easily with the views of the *philosophes* of Paris, for whom mankind is, in the
first place, an object of scientific investigation. The underlying assumption that human nature
is basically the same at all times, everywhere,
and obeys eternal laws beyond human control, is
a conception that only a handful of bold thinkers
have dared to question. Yet to accept it in the
name of science is, in effect, to ignore and
downgrade man's role as creator and destroyer of
values, of entire forms of life, of man as a subject, a creature with an inner life denied to
other inhabitants of the universe. The most celebrated utopians of modern times, from Thomas More
to Mably, Saint-Simon, Fourier, Owen, and their
followers, provided a somewhat static picture of
men's basic attributes, and, in consequence, an
equally static description of an attainable
perfect society. Thereby they ignored the character of men as self-transforming beings, able to
choose freely, within the limits imposed by
nature and history, between rival, mutually
incompatible ends.

The conception of man as an actor, a purposive
being, moved by his own conscious aims as well
as causal laws, capable of unpredictable flights
of thought and imagination, and of his culture
as created by his effort to achieve self-knowledge and control of his environment in the face
of material and psychic forces which he may use
but cannot evade - this conception lies at the
heart of all truly historical study. To exercise
their proper function, historians require capacity for imaginative insight without which the
bones of the past remain dry and lifeless. To do
so, is, and always has been, a risky business.

There is always the possibility of substituting
a plausible fiction for reality. But this is a
risk that cannot be avoided; our intuitions may
betray us - we can never be sure of the truth of
our accounts; but unless we are able to conceive
a human society as a single organized whole, in
its many aspects, whether it is real or imaginary, and only then seek to verify our conjectures
by reference to the available evidence, we shall
succeed in conveying not what the past of mankind
has been, but only isolated aspects of it - political, economic, demographic - only the trees,
not the wood; we shall remain historical scholars
and researchers, but not historians in the full
sense. Mere narrative is a great deal, but not
enough. Without our being able to integrate our
knowledge of detail into the pattern of a living
whole, the very idea of culture - and still more,
of history - could not have arisen. The fate of
Vico, like that of the Hellenistic Greek who, we
are told, discovered the steam engine to no
purpose in a society incapable of realizing its
possibilities, was the fate of those who are too
far in advance of their time. By the time their
genius is recognized, their ideas have occurred
independently to others, sometimes in more developed forms, and in due course become commonplace.
Vico's ideas found little response in his own
time. They are better known today. Yet some of
their more disquieting implications, not only
for the study of history, but for ethical, political, and social thought, have not been fully
realized even in our own time.

SIDNEY MORGENBESSER:
A Bibliography

1944

Review of *Science, Philosophy and Religion*, Third Symposium: Conference on Science, Philosophy and Religion, New York: 1943, *The Reconstructionist*, IX 20 (Feb. 4, 1944): 19-25.

1945

Review of Brand Blanshard and Herbert Schneider, eds., *In Commemoration of William James*, *The Reconstructionist*, XI, 7 (May 18, 1945): 21-23.

1946

Review of R.M. MacIver, ed., *Civilization and Group Relations*, and F. Ernest Johnson, ed., *World Order: Its Intellectual and Cultural Foundations*, *The Reconstructionist*, XII, 9 (June 14, 1946): 29-32.

Review of Sidney Hook, *Education for Modern Man*, and Benjamin Fine, *Democratic Education*, *Commentary*, 2 (October 1946): 397-398.

1947

Review of F.S.C. Northrop, *Meeting of East and West*, *The Reconstructionist*, XIII, 10 (June 27, 1947): 36-39.

Review of Philipp Frank, *Einstein: His Life and Times*, *Commentary*, 4 (July 1947): 92-94.

1953

"The Decline of Religious Liberalism," *The Reconstructionist*, XIX, 7 (May 15, 1953): 17-24.

"Types of Concept Formation," Columbia University Planning Project for Advanced Training in Social Research.

1954

Review of James Conant, *Modern Man and Modern Science*, *The Reconstructionist*, XIX, 17 (Jan. 1, 1954): 26-29.

"Virtue or the Cult of Self-Expression," *The Reconstructionist*, XIX, 20 (February 12, 1954): 14-21.

"A Faulty Prescription for the Maladies of the Rabbinate: A Reply to Dr. Shudofsky," *The Reconstructionist*, XX, 6 (May 7, 1954): 16-19.

"On the Justification of Beliefs and Attitudes," *The Journal of Philosophy*, LI, 20 (Sept. 30, 1954): 565-576.

Review of Viktor Kraft, *The Vienna Circle*, *Social Research*, XXI, 1 (Spring 1954): 118-120.

1955

"Reconstructionism and the Naturalistic Tradition in America" (with David Sidorsky), *The Reconstructionist*, XXI, 1 (February 18, 1955): 33-42.

Review of William Elton, ed., *Aesthetics and Language*, *The Journal of Philosophy*, LII, 11 (May 26, 1955): 296-300.

"Infinite and Infinity," *Encyclopedia Americana* (1955 edition).

1956

Theories and Schemata in the Social Sciences (Doctoral Dissertation), Department of Philosophy, The University of Pennsylvania.

Sidney Morgenbesser: A Bibliography   501

Review of P.F. Lazarsfeld and Morris Rosenberg, eds., *The Language of Social Research*, *The Journal of Philosophy*, LIII, 7 (Mar. 29, 1956): 248–255.

"The Queen of the Sciences," Review of James R. Newman, *The World of Mathematics*, *The New Republic* (Nov. 19, 1956): 22–25.

"Peirce e il pragmatismo americano," G. Tagliacozzo, trans., *Voice of America* lecture (Rome: U.S. Information Service, 1956). Delivered on April 6, 1956, as "Peirce and American Pragmatism."

1957

"Approaches to Ethical Objectivity," *Educational Theory*, VII, 3 (July 1957): 180–186. Reprinted in Barry I. Chazan and Jonas F. Soltis, eds., *Moral Education* (New York: Teachers College Press, 1973): 72–79.

Review of James Brown, *Subject and Object in Modern Theology*, *The Reconstructionist*, XXIII, 12 (Oct. 20, 1957): 24–27.

"Character and Free Will," (with A.C. Danto), *The Journal of Philosophy*, LIV, 16 (Aug. 1, 1957): 493–505.

1958

"Role and Status of Anthropological Theories," *Science*, CXXVIII (1958): 285–288.

Review of Sidney Hook, ed., *American Philosophers at Work*, *The Reconstructionist*, XXIV, 3 (March 21, 1958): 23–26.

Review of Gustav Bergmann, *Philosophy of Science*, *The Journal of Philosophy*, LV, 4 (Feb. 13, 1958): 169–176.

"Social Inquiry and Moral Judgment," in Israel Scheffler, ed., *Philosophy and Education* (Boston: Allyn and Bacon, 1958): 180-200.

Review of John Ladd, *The Structure of a Moral Code: A Philosophical Analysis of Ethical Discourse Applied to the Ethics of the Navaho Indians*, *The Journal of Philosophy*, LV, 18 (Aug. 28, 1958): 785-790.

1959

"Contemporary Philosophy," *Teachers College Record*, LX, 5 (February 1959): 255-261.

Rejoinder, "Role and Status of Anthopológical Theories," *Science*, CXXIX (1959): 298, continued on pp. 347-348.

1960

Philosophy of Science, edited with A.C. Danto (New York: Meridian Books, 1960).

"A Comment on Toulmin," in Sidney Hook, ed., *Dimensions of Mind* (New York: Collier Books, 1960): 214-221.

1961

"A Note on Justification," *The Journal of Philosophy*, LVIII, 23 (Nov. 9, 1961): 748-749.

Review of Mario Bunge, *Causality*, *Scientific American* (February 1961): 175-178.

1962

"Goodman on the Ravens," *The Journal of Philosophy*, LIX, 18 (Aug. 30, 1962): 493-495.

Free Will, edited with James Walsh (Englewood Cliffs, N.J.: Prentice Hall, 1962).

1963

Editor's Introduction: Symposium on Human Action, *The Journal of Philosophy*, LX, 14 (July 4, 1963): 365-367.

"Perception: Cause and Achievement," in Marx Wartofsky, ed., *Boston Studies in the Philosophy of Science*, Proceedings of the Boston Colloquium for the Philosophy of Science, 1961-1962 (Dordrecht: D. Reidel, 1963): 206-212.

"The Deductive Model and Its Qualification," in Henry E. Kyburg and Ernest Nagel, eds., *Induction: Some Current Issues* (Middletown, Conn.: Wesleyan University Press, 1963): 169-180.

"The Explanatory Predictive Approach to Science," in Bernard Baumrin, ed., *Philosophy of Science: The Delaware Seminar*, vol. I, Delaware Studies in the Philosophy of Science (New York: John Wiley, 1963): 41-55.

1964

"Belief and Disposition" (with Isaac Levi), *American Philosophical Quarterly*, I, 3 (July 1964): 221-233. Reprinted in Raimo Tuomela, ed., *Dispositions* (Dordrecht: D. Reidel, 1978): 389-410.

"Psychologism and Methodological Individualism," *Voice of America Forum Lectures*: Philosophy of Science Series, No. 3.

1966

"Is It a Science?" *Social Research*, XXXIII, 2 (Summer 1966): 255-271. Reprinted in Dorothy Emmet and Alasdair Macintyre, eds., *Sociological Theory and Philosophical Analysis* (New York: Macmillan, 1970): 20-35.

1967

Philosophy of Science Today, editor, "Introduction"; "Psychologism and Methodological Individualism" (New York: Basic Books, 1967): xi-xiv; 160-175.

1968

"Scientific Explanation," in David Sills, ed., *International Encyclopedia of the Social Sciences*, vol. XIV (New York: Macmillan, 1968): 117-122.

1969

Philosophy, Science and Method: Essays in Honor of Ernest Nagel, edited with Morton White and Patrick Suppes (New York: St. Martin's, 1968).

"The Realist-Instrumentalist Controversy," in *Philosophy, Science and Method*, *op. cit.*: 200-218.

"Fodor on Ryle on Rules," *The Journal of Philosophy*, LXVI, 14 (July 24, 1969): 458-472.

1971

Comments, in Alexander Klein, ed., *Dissent, Power and Confrontation* (New York: McGraw-Hill, 1971): 250-253; 263; 273-277.

1973

"Imperialism: Some Preliminary Distinctions," *Philosophy and Public Affairs*, III, 1 (Fall 1973): 3-44. Reprinted in Virginia Held, Sidney Morgenbesser and Thomas Nagel, eds., *Philosophy, Morality, and International Affairs* (New York: Oxford University Press, 1974): 201-245.

1974

Philosophy, Morality and International Affairs, edited with Virginia Held and Thomas Nagel (New York: Oxford University Press, 1974).

"Mordecai Kaplan: Thirty Some Years Ago," *Sh'ma*, IV, 79 (October 18, 1974): 148-149.

1976

"Homage to Yehoshua Bar-Hillel," in Asa Kasher, ed., *Language in Focus* (Dordrecht: D. Reidel, 1976): xv-xvii.

1977

"Picking and Choosing" (with Edna Ullmann-Margalit), *Social Research*, XLIV, 4 (Winter 1977): 757-785.

Dewey and His Critics: Essays from The Journal of Philosophy, editor; "Introduction," (New York: The Journal of Philosophy, and Indianapolis: Hackett, 1977): ix-xlv.

"Experimentation and Consent: A Note," in S.F. Spicker and H.T. Engelhardt Jr., eds., *Philosophical Medical Ethics: Its Nature and Significance*, (Dordrecht: D. Reidel, 1977): 97-110.

1978

"A Note on Bioethics," in Elsie L. Bandman and Bertram Bandman, eds., *Bioethics and Human Rights: A Reader for Health Professionals* (Boston: Little, Brown, 1978): 360-362.

"On Tenure" (with Margaret Atherton and Robert Schwartz), *The Philosophical Forum*, X, 2-4 (Winter-Summer 1978-1979): 341-352.

1979

"Surplus Value: The Oft-neglected Argument" (with Roger Alcaly), *Social Research*, XLVI, 2 (Summer 1979): 282-291.

1980

"The Questions of Isaiah Berlin" (with Jonathan Lieberson), *The New York Review of Books*, XXVII, 3 (March 6, 1980): 38-42.

"The Choices of Isaiah Berlin" (with Jonathan Lieberson), *The New York Review of Books*, XVII, 4 (March 20, 1980): 31-36.

Review of Bryan Magee, ed., *Men of Ideas*, *The Nation*, CCXXX, 10 (March 15, 1980): 312-315.

Comments on William Appleman Williams, "Empire as a Way of Life," *The Nation*, CCXXXI, 4 (August 2-9, 1980): 125-126.

List of Contributors and Editors

Margaret Atherton is Assistant Professor of Philosophy at the University of Wisconsin at Milwaukee.

Isaiah Berlin is former President of Wolfson College and Fellow of All Souls College, University of Oxford

Bernard Berofsky is Professor of Philosophy, Columbia University.

Leigh S. Cauman is Managing Editor of the Journal of Philosophy and Adjunct Associate Professor of Philosophy at Columbia University.

Noam Chomsky is Institute Professor, Massachusetts Institute of Technology.

Arthur C. Danto is Johnsonian Professor of Philosophy, Columbia University.

Gary Feinberg is Professor of Physics, Columbia University.

Harry G. Frankfurt is Professor of Philosophy, Yale University.

Nelson Goodman is Professor Emeritus of Philosophy, Harvard University.

James Higginbotham is Associate Professor of Philosophy Massachusetts Institute of Technology.

Arnold Koslow is Professor of Philosophy, Brooklyn College and the Graduate Center, City University of New York.

Richard Kuhns is Professor of Philosophy, Columbia University.

Henry E. Kyburg, Jr. is Professor of Philosophy, University of Rochester.

Isaac Levi is Professor of Philosophy, Columbia University.

Jonathan Lieberson is Assistant Professor of Philosophy Barnard College, Columbia University.

Avishai Margalit is Associate Professor of Philosophy, Hebrew University, Jerusalem.

Edna Ullmann-Margalit is Senior Lecturer in Philosophy, Hebrew University, Jerusalem.

Mary Mothersill is Professor of Philosophy, Barnard College, Columbia University.

Ernest Nagel is University Professor Emeritus, Columbia University.

Robert Nozick is Professor of Philosophy, Harvard University.

Charles Parsons is Professor of Philosophy, Columbia University.

Hilary Putnam is W.B. Pearson Professor of Mathematic and Mathematical Logic, Harvard University.

David M. Rosenthal is Professor of Philosophy, Lehman College and the Graduate Center, City University of New York.

Israel Scheffler is Professor of Philosophy, Harvard University.

Frederic Schick is Professor of Philosophy, Rutgers University.

Robert Schwartz is Professor of Philosophy, Universit of Wisconsin at Milwaukee.

David Sidorsky is Professor of Philosophy, Columbia University.

Fred Sommers is Harry A. Wolfson Professor of Philosophy at Brandeis University.

Mark Steiner is Associate Professor of Philosophy, Hebrew University, Jerusalem.

James J. Walsh is Professor of Philosophy, Columbia University.

Richard Wollheim is Professor of Philosophy, University College, London, and Columbia University.